SOVIET URBAN MANAGEMENT:

WITH COMPARISONS TO THE UNITED STATES

SOVIET URBAN MANAGEMENT:

WITH COMPARISONS TO THE UNITED STATES

Carol W. Lewis

Stephen Sternheimer

PRAEGER PUBLISHERS
Praeger Special Studies

New York • London • Sydney • Toronto

Library of Congress Cataloging in Publication Data

Lewis, Carol Weiss, 1946-
   Soviet urban management, with comparisons to the
United States.

   Bibliography: p.
   Includes index.
   1. Municipal government--Russia. 2. Municipal
finance--Russia. 3. Municipal government--United
States. 4. Municipal finance--United States.
I. Sternheimer, Stephen, joint author. II. Title.
JS6064.A1L48   352'.008'0947   78-19748

ISBN 0-03-046136-7

PRAEGER PUBLISHERS
PRAEGER SPECIAL STUDIES
383 Madison Avenue, New York, N.Y. 10017, U.S.A.

Published in the United States of America in 1979
by Praeger Publishers,
A Division of Holt, Rinehart and Winston, CBS, Inc.

9   038   987654321

© 1979 by Praeger Publishers

Printed in the United States of America

To our families who managed . . .
with endurance, love, and encouragement.

FOREWORD

William John Hanna

Cities throughout the world are in crisis. In the United States, we have become familiar with the near bankruptcies of New York City and Yonkers and the inner city decay of Cleveland and Detroit. Over a period of two decades, four large American cities have lost more than a fifth of their populations. But urban crisis is not confined to the United States. Manchester and Liverpool in England have also lost more than a fifth of their populations, and many of their neighborhoods are in advanced states of decay. Many Italian cities are suffering from enormous gaps between revenues and expenditures as they struggle to provide services for their vast number of in-migrants. Interest charges in Rome absorb about one-third of the city's spending. London has 30,000 squatters, Istanbul must somehow accommodate 200,000 new in-migrants each year, and in Karachi 200,000 people sleep on the streets each night. Similar portraits of crisis could be drawn of cities from all the world's regions.

What has caused this worldwide urban crisis? For developing countries still rapidly industrializing, massive urbanization is a key factor. The population of cities over 100,000 has, over a 20-year period, more than doubled in countries such as France, Yugoslavia, New Zealand, and the USSR. Yet, countries that are entering the postindustrial age are selectively deurbanizing ("creaming"), often leaving their cities with large dependent populations while middle-class families escape to suburbs and nonmetropolitan areas. In the latter countries, there is unfolding "a newly emerging order whose signal qualities are complexity and diversity. These changes may well be compatible with, and perhaps call forth, metropolitan forms that are neither concentrated nor concentric nor contained."[1]

The processes of urbanization and deurbanization are the result of two great—in some countries contemporaneous—revolutions. The massive movement to cities, which began around 1700, stemmed from the use of inanimate energy, the development of large-scale industry, the emergence of nation-states, and, more generally, the revolution of values. Deurbanization, a process responsive to a decline in the cost of transportation and communication, began with residential suburbanization facilitated by the streetcar, railroad, and then auto. (In the United States over the past three decades, the number of automobiles has increased much more rapidly than the population of the people!) The availability of electric power outside urban centers has also been a factor.

It has only been in the past decade, however, that deurbanization has come to characterize business and industrial, as well as residential, choice. Additional factors responsible for this process include a shift away from labor-intensive manufacturing, a relative drop in the costs of moving information, and a correlate improvement of information storage, processing, and retrieval due to developments in computer software and hardware.

We have now reached the stage in the United States where there need no longer be a specific stock exchange on Wall Street. Rather, it can be a computer center in New York City or Omaha. Furthermore, we can watch the New York City Ballet in our homes, without the costs of tickets or transportation (I still prefer to see ballet at Lincoln Center!). So the scale economies of production and consumption have changed enormously in recent decades. The evidence is dramatic: in the United States, for instance, population statistics reveal that, prior to the 1950-60 period, no major metropolitan area had experienced a decline of population; only one did so between 1960 and 1970. But since 1970, many large metropolitan areas have lost population.

New sociodemographic patterns are also a factor in the current crisis. For one, there has been a sharp drop in the birthrate of many postindustrial societies. This has revealed a fairly long-term trend of out-migration from cities, masked until recently by population replacement through natural increases. Second, there has been an increase within the middle class of prolonged singles status and childless couples, that is, the type of people inclined to choose city living when a noncity alternative is available. Thus, the population composition of many cities is shifting from a socioeconomic and age balance to a disproportion of dependent families and middle-class young adults. Systems of revenue and expenditure, and of institutions and services, have not been designed with the new population composition in mind.

Some observers see population changes, the development of a postindustrial economy, and the overload of complexity as intermediate explanations that should direct attention to a larger historical process involving political-economic trends. If this is correct, then significant improvement of the urban condition clearly awaits larger political-economic change. However, within structural limits one may still see the possibility of a better quality of life. This involves improved urban management.

Contemporary changes have placed severe stress upon the institutions and processes of urban governance. The situation is of course particularly acute when budgets decline. Thus, an observer of the New York scene writes:

> The fiscal crisis which has plagued New York is also a symptom of its endemic managerial crisis. As the city faces the prospect of having to further reduce its expenditures, it is becoming increasingly imperative that those responsible for the delivery of local services perform their duties in a more efficient and effective manner.
>
> As the functions of government have become more diverse and complex, the nature of public affairs has become increasingly administrative. Therefore, the key to responsible government in a bureaucratic age is effective management.[2]

And from two Soviet writers: "Urban forms of settlement have now brought to the forefront a complex of serious problems whose solution is possible only within the framework of better city management and through a strengthening of the regulatory role played by management functions."[3]

The response to crisis can be national and local, political and administrative. National urban planning in some countries is concerned with resource allocation to stem or moderate the consequences of deurbanization. The readjustment of city boundaries constitutes a political attempt to solve current problems; cities as diverse as Houston and Leningrad are trying to contain within their boundaries the enlarging urban agglomerations.

At any level, contemporary problems should be managed, not administered. With urbanization/concentration, the manager must deal with one set of problems of space-management, coordination, complexity, and so forth. With deurbanization/deconcentration, there is an entirely new set of management problems. For societies undergoing both processes simultaneously, the management problems are greatly multiplied. And if these changes are accompanied by a fiscal crisis and class conflicts stemming from gentrification, the need for management becomes even more apparent.

"Post-crisis managers are operating in a fundamentally different environment than in the recent past," an urbanist has recently observed. He continues: "Strategies developed for dealing with incremental changes, whether increases or decreases, are unlikely to be applicable."[4] The greatest challenge to traditional managers operating in today's world may be cultural: the manager of urban decline must realize that growth and development do not necessarily go together. That is, a city increasing in population may be economically and socially decaying; whereas absolute population decline may be accompanied by improvements in the quality of life for those who remain.

Clearly, there is an enormous difference between administration and management, not unlike the dictionary distinction between dispense/apply and take charge/accomplish. The urban manager must have the ability to generate and allocate resources; to coordinate agency operations and integrate activities around problem areas; and to organize the information dimension of needs assessment, implementation, and evaluation.

This is not a mandate for regional governance, for the manager presumably seeks only those scale solutions appropriate to the problems or functions involved. Some services, such as police, are usually better delivered through a decentralized structure; others, such as air quality control, are more effectively handled at a regional level. Here, then, is another challenge for contemporary management: structuring different services according to the needs of the particular service, and then coordinating across services that are not isomorphically related.

Thus, the manager is a very special person with special personal and technical abilities. He or she must understand the high technology of information storage, processing, and retrieval. At the same time, the manager must be sensitive to citizen needs and the diversity of cultures within the domain of responsibility. He or she must also be committed to equity, which probably involves differential service delivery to meet the special needs of a diverse population. Thus, the person involved must be carefully recruited and trained. Political systems in which prospective managers are selected on the basis of proper family or political connections, for example, are not likely to benefit from the kind of managerial leadership that is called for in the contemporary world.

In the twentieth century, governance increasingly involves management. What conditions facilitate the development of a management approach to government? Is the governance of Soviet cities increasingly dominated by the managerial approach? What governance future can we expect in the Soviet Union given its managerial and other developments? These are among the key questions addressed by Carol Lewis and Stephen Sternheimer, using a comparative approach.

The efforts to place Soviet municipal management within a larger perspective is particularly welcome. This is done in four ways. First, the authors use their knowledge of U.S. urban management as an informal comparative foil for their examination of the USSR. This is enormously helpful in attempting to highlight what is cross-nationally unique or ordinary. Furthermore, as most readers of this English-language work will be familiar with the U.S. scene, the comparison provides a series of bench marks for understanding. (Some commentators insist that different systems cannot be compared. A subway in Boston is different than a subway in Moscow, it is argued, because of the different class composition of the ridership, and the like. But, of course, the different composition is in itself important; by means of broad comparison, important differences become clearly visible.)

Second, as data permit, the authors engage in intranational comparisons within the USSR. This is an application of the "most similar systems" approach to comparison, that is, controlling large contrasts by delimiting a study's scope so that it becomes possible to explore relationships within a common political-economic (and, to some extent, sociocultural) setting. This approach permits the authors to draw contrasts between large and small cities, Russian and non-Russian cities, and along other dimensions.

Third, the authors draw upon the discourse community of urbanists (Soviet specialists and others) for theories, methods, and orientations. Thus, a discussion of interregional migrations is linked with Charles Tiebout's work on local expenditures, and a discussion of citizen access is linked with the organizational theoretic work of Amatai Etzioni. As a result, the findings are of more than parochial interest; rather, they are relevant to public managers and comparative urbanists in the Soviet Union and elsewhere.

It may well be that major changes in the quality of urban life depend on revolutionary changes in the political economies of nations. Redistribution of power, wealth, and other values does not come voluntarily; and the evolutionary path of change is long. However, management does make a difference. Innovation, coordination, and other attributes of good management can moderate crises. For this reason, we must know more about the qualities of good management and the situational possibilities for their emergence. This book contributes to the needed knowledge.

NOTES

1. Melvin M. Webber, "Order in Diversity: Community without Propinquity," in *Cities and Space: The Future Use of Urban Land*, ed. Lowdon Wingo, Jr. (Baltimore: The Johns Hopkins Press for Resources for the Future, 1963), p. 25.

2. Joseph P. Viteritti, "New York's Management Plan and Reporting System: A Descriptive Analysis," *Public Administration Review* 38 (July-August 1978), pp. 376, 381.

3. A. S. Gruzinov and V. P. Riumin, *Gorod: Upravlenie, Problemy* (Leningrad Lenizdat, 1977).

4. Andrew Glassberg, "Organizational Responses to Municipal Budget Decreases," *Public Administration Review* 38 (July-August 1978), p. 327, emphasis removed.

ACKNOWLEDGEMENTS

The authors express their appreciation to the following institutions and individuals for their generous support and assistance in the preparation of this study: Boston University; Graduate Research Foundation of the University of Connecticut; Russian Research Center of Harvard University; International Research and Exchanges Board, New York; New Communities Administration of the U.S. Department of Housing and Urban Development; and the National Association of Counties, Washington, D.C. Special thanks are in order to Marilyn Parks for her graphic designs and to Mary Towle, Mary Christopher, and Rose di Benedetto of the staff of the Russian Research Center whose perseverance made the preparation of the manuscript possible. Finally, we wish to express our appreciation to our Soviet colleagues and the Soviet officials who gave generously of their time and assistance in many interviews and discussions.

We alone are fully responsible for the views and interpretations, inaccuracies and omissions. We appreciate the opportunity to reinforce our conviction that collaboration offers a great deal. Fully outweighing the long hours of intense criticism, multiple rewrites, and reconciliation of competing interpretations are the intellectual stimulation and provocative challenges that collaboration entails.

CONTENTS

LIST OF TABLES AND FIGURES

INTRODUCTION

WHY CITIES?

Four propositions provide the intellectual foundations for this study. First, urban life is susceptible to both human understanding and human manipulation. Therefore, as a mode of human organization, cities are an inherently interesting and significant focus for investigation. Second, we need to organize the (dominant) human habitat in forms that foster the pursuit of individual and social aspirations. The third proposition asserts that an investigation into urban life and its organization sheds new light on problems related to the scope and direction of social and political change. Urban research thus constitutes an intellectually legitimate and important part of more general forms of social inquiry. From this follows a final proposition: only the cross-national, comparative study of cities can generate the kinds of insights that will enable the study of urban organization to make sound theoretical contributions to social inquiry. The answer to the query "why cities" requires further examination of the propositions just described.

Urbanization and urban growth represent contemporary upheavals in patterns of human organization. They produce such profound effects that only the geological metaphor of the earth's development captures their scale and importance.[1] The pace of such change, however, calls to mind a vehicle hurtling along an expressway rather than the progress of stones in a glacier. Forecasts indicate that by the end of this century a fundamental relationship of recorded history will have been reversed: urban populations will outnumber rural populations. Such developments suggest that cities will remain the dominant form of human organization for some time to come.

Even apparently contradictory perspectives on the value of urban life reinforce our view that cities are an interesting and significant focus for study. For those who view urban life as a negative (and perhaps even pathological) phenomenon, the study of cities can provide clues to a radical transformation and perfection of human organization. Like knowing one's enemy, the study of cities becomes a sine qua non for dealing with what has been labeled a "global urban crisis." For those who adhere to more positive outlooks on the urban present, there are equally compelling arguments for urban studies. As Robert E. Parks wrote in 1936,

> Cities, and particularly the great metropolitan cities of modern times . . . are, with all their complexities and artificialities, man's most imposing creation, the most prodigious of human artifacts. We

must conceive of our cities . . . as the workshops of civilization, and, at the same time, as the natural habitat of civilized man.[2]

In the same vein, a contemporary Soviet architect has labeled the city "the sum of nearly all the constructive, creative actions performed by man," both an embodiment and reflection of the highest achievements of the society that "organizes all forms of man's activity."[3]

Whether the city is praised as among the most sophisticated or damned as among the most pernicious modes of human organization, ways to improve the organization of urban life (according to the second proposition) form a core element in urban studies. Urban studies per se lack a discipline rather than constitute one, and, frequently, by virtue of their very Balkanization, they suggest that there may be, in fact, nothing distinctively "urban" to be studied or explained.[4] Such a position ignores the fact that cities represent a unique pattern of human organization that daily challenges our capacity to sustain the human habitat. "Organization" refers to informal rules and patterns of associative behavior whereby the social structures and physical artifacts of urban life take on meaning in terms of human interactions.[5] The term also refers to structures geared to delivering goods and services as well as the arrangements usually associated with the governance and administration of urban life.

The city is defined by a conjunction of features that together make an investigation into patterns of social interaction critical. At a minimum, it is clear that the large population size associated with cities relates to questions of government performance, the cost of service delivery, and the introduction of an irreducible level of complexity into human relations. More than sheer numbers are involved, however. Structural imperatives emerge from a range of other characteristics associated with urban life: density, complexity, interdependency, and uncertainty.[6] The picture of the city that emerges is one of a politically, socially, and ecologically fragile organization, subject to breakdown and disruption from the very factors that define it as a unique pattern of human settlement.[7] Underscoring this vulnerability is the fact that cities continue to play the part of political hostages to events and individuals beyond the control of those responsible for sustaining the urban organization: devastating strikes by public workers, urban terrorism, the dissatisfactions of marginal groups expressed in civil violence, and the missiles of hostile powers deployed in countervalue strategies.[8] This combination of vulnerability, large size, high density, complexity, interdependency, and uncertainty moves organization to the forefront among the large number of issues upon which urban studies potentially could focus.

According to our third proposition, the study of cities can provide a basis upon which to analyze more general social and political phenomena. Much of the scholarly literature in this field has demonstrated a relationship between the shape of urban phenomena in a particular setting and the larger pattern to which the political development of the whole system conforms. Several studies indicate that urbanization induces changes in the quantity and distribution of political power on a national scale.[9] More specifically, over time cities become the focal point and, indeed, the locus of national politics.[10] The redistribution of the population into cities, the relocation of major social problems to the urban locale, the cultural dominance of urban modes of life—all these developments have important and direct implications for the changing shape of national policies and politics. To be effective, political power at the national level must be exerted within cities. Cooperation by city leaders becomes an important ingredient in the capacity of national leaders to carry out development programs. Conversely, cities function as bases from which individuals and groups can capture and wield political power in the national political arena.[11]

Owing to the high level of interdependency that characterizes the urban-national linkage, the study of cities can serve as "a vantage point from which to capture some salient features in the social processes operating in the society as a whole, . . . a mirror in which other aspects of society [are] reflected."[12] Marxist analyses stress the centrality of the interaction between subnational (in this case, urban) and national levels with respect to political as well as economic dependencies.[13] Non-Marxist approaches as well suggest that it is in and through cities that much of what a society possesses is distributed, wasted, fought over, and produced. This leads to a situation in which the problems and functions of cities become national in scope, even as urban leaders, drawing upon national resources, come to exercise increasing control over their populations, certain problems, and certain issue areas. "Interdependency" highlights the fact that cities are not closed systems, for much that goes on within a city lies beyond the control of urban leaders. Thus, intergovernmental relations are a fundamental aspect of any perspective on urban phenomena. But such a perspective ought not to obscure the fact that autonomy and power within the city do not always vary directly. Reduced autonomy enhances the problem-solving capabilities of local leaders when it is accompanied by increased resources, greater direction, and improved coordination. By the same token, reduced autonomy also increases the level of complexity in the environment of urban decision makers, particularly with reference to the intricacies of cooperation and coordination in an already complex jurisdictional network.

Questions of interdependency aside, the study of cities (microlevel investigations) also sheds light on macrolevel questions simply because the urban sector has come to dominate many societies. In the USSR, for example, the city provides the territorial, political, and administrative framework within which the majority of the population is housed, fed, educated, and employed.[14] And, as Henry Morton, among others, has observed, the way in which urban policies take shape in the USSR in turn determines the meaning of modern development for the society as a whole.[15] The potency of such observation is reinforced when we note that the building and maintaining of cities, the provision of services to a predominantly urban labor force, and the costs of urban administration consume a substantial portion of the national wealth in the USSR as elsewhere. From a slightly different perspective, it is the sum of urban labor policies, urban educational policies, urban welfare policies, and urban transportation policies that in large part defines policy directions along national lines. Such observations lead us back to the initial proposition, namely, that the study of urban organization in its policy, process, or administrative aspects tells us much about the nation as a whole. The claim acquires added credibility when we remember that even in the absence of a primate city (as in the Soviet case) a few cities can and often do play special roles in national development. Insofar as a nation's wealth, population, and problems are concentrated in these cities, the capacity of their leaders to cope with challenges helps shape the development of the larger society.

The fourth proposition, stating the importance of cross-national, comparative urban research, assumes that the study of cities contributes to the building of empirical social theory. Comparative research takes account of variation in sociocultural factors and thereby encourages recognition of relationships often overlooked in single-nation studies.[16] It has been argued that much contemporary urban research is parochial and that such ethnocentrism too frequently results in theoretically barren findings. For example, studies focusing on U.S. cities as yet have not been able to provide satisfactory explanations for some key urban phenomena (for example, urban violence) of the last two decades.[17] U.S. scholarship does not stand alone in its "sin of omission." A Soviet sociologist also confesses that "as the situation stands today, our literature has either ignored or given no adequate evaluation of even those fundamental theoretical conclusions about and conceptions of the city which dominate foreign scholarship."[18]

Recognition of the inadequacies generated by parochial studies encourages the comprehensive investigation of urban phenomena from a comparative perspective. Several international conferences, including the 1976 United Nations Conference on Human Settlements (Habitat) have focused comparatively on a wide range of urban issues and urban problems. Others have stressed the comparative importance of specific obstacles to improved urban problem solving, for example, inadequate information and poor training of public officials.[19] More recently, a U.S. congressional committee took testimony on the urban experiences of other nations, presumably in order to better grapple with domestic challenges.[20]

From a theoretical perspective, narrow conclusions can be avoided only by considering propositions the utility of which has already been demonstrated in other societies. Similarly, urban policies can be formulated by incorporating in a regular fashion experiences from a variety of settings; policy makers thereby avoid unnecessary repetition of tactical and strategic errors. Unthinking projections of culturally limited interpretations must also be resisted. For example, community power findings derived from the U.S. experience explain very little of interest or consequence about urban issues in Kiev or Calcutta.[21]

For a better understanding of U.S. urban issues, Soviet experiences can be particularly instructive. These societies share key structural similarities, including territory and population size. In both cases, a majority of the population is urban and highly educated (relative to a global standard). Both societies enjoy relatively high levels of industrialization with highly differentiated economies and labor forces. Each possesses a large number of cities and a wide range of city types, while neither has a primate city. As a Soviet commentary points out, in each case the problems of cities are urgent and spill over city boundaries.[22]

At the same time, the two societies differ with regard to several important factors. Soviet urbanization has occurred relatively recently and very rapidly. Moreover, the organizational environment in which city government operates appears quite different in each case. The two settings also differ with regard to social and cultural factors, not the least of which is the valuation attached to urban life in general and big city life in particular; it is high on the Soviet side and low on the U.S. side.[23] Physical and spatial contrasts in U.S. and Soviet urban arrangements give concrete expression to these differences. In U.S. cities, a central business district dominates the skyline, while Soviet cities center around a basically concave area consisting of large squares and public facilities.[24] Soviet and U.S. urban development strategies also can be opposed as two logical extremes: high density and concentration at the one end and sprawl and dispersal at the other.[25] Thus, an exploration with urban organization at its center is not meant to imply that there is an identity. Nor does this represent an argument for convergence. It does represent, however, a recognition that on both theoretical and applied planes a search is under way for a common core in urban organization, common problems in urban management, and uncommon solutions to urban problems. The search is important insofar as the Soviet Union is important to both our futures.

While providing an explanation for the initial query, "why cities?" the evidence also points to the usefulness of a comparative study of aspects of the U.S. and Soviet urban experiences. In many respects, responses to the two questions "why cities?" and "why Soviet cities?" overlap. The similarities and differences between U.S. and Soviet cities described above suggest that empirical investigations along these lines can combine the advantages of both a similar-systems and a dissimilar-systems approach in comparative analysis.[26] Such a study appears particularly appropriate in light of the observation that the U.S. and Soviet urban scene displays a single overriding flaw: a failure to build or govern cities satisfactorily.[27] In sum, they share "urban mismanagement."[28]

WHY URBAN MANAGEMENT?

The preceding arguments for the study of cities imply that issues related to urban implementation, outputs, and outcomes must quickly be brought to bear in a discussion of urban dynamics. The reasoning is simple: urban outcomes cannot be understood or explained fully as long as they are treated as political by-products. Too frequently the study of cities has ignored the effect of urban management on policy outputs and outcomes, treating them only as a residue of the political process (patterned conflict) or political structure (institutional operations). But if, as has already been suggested, urban studies ought to address themselves to such questions as "how can urban life be better organized?" and "how can urban problems be better managed?" then three lines of inquiry must necessarily be pursued. First, how are cities managed at present? Second, in what ways does the method of management (or administration) concretely affect urban outputs and outcomes? Third, how might urban administration be changed so as to make it more managerial?

These questions point to the fact that the management dimension is a key element shaping what Leonard Reissman some time ago described as "the genius of the urban achievement."[29] When applied to the study of U.S. cities such a focus on urban management calls attention to the fact that civil service rigidity, public employee unionization, and antiquated budgeting techniques, when combined with mandated expenditures, intergovernmental dependency, and fragmented authority, place a special kind of burden on those officials responsible for service delivery. To develop a cogent answer to the perennial query of urbanists, "how can cities be better governed?" it is no longer sufficient to seek refuge in the assertion that better government depends upon a different kind of politics.[30] The assumption that urban governance and urban politics are synonymous ignores the impact of an intervening variable—organization and management—on policy outcomes.

Much as the growth of the large-scale industrial corporation brought in its wake an appreciation of the benefits of modern management techniques within the business community, so a steady increase in the size of municipal units worldwide has provided a major catalyst for the adoption of a managerial approach to urban problem solving. Urban political leaders and bureaucrats, like the denizens of Plato's cave, have become almost totally dependent on indirect representations of reality. The situation is much the same whether the location is New York, Tokyo, Moscow, or Calcutta. Everywhere it is the tools of modern management—statistics, plans, reporting processes, role orientations, the dynamics of organizational structures—that reproduce images of the problems demanding policy solutions.[31] And, as one of the United States' leading management consultants, Peter Drucker, has added, the management of public service institutions at all levels will represent the "new frontier" of public administration, in large part, because management problems in the public sector have been ignored for so long.[32]

A management perspective applied to the study of cities includes a number of quite specific concerns and issues that traditional research either minimizes or ignores.[33] Following in the political science mainstream of the 1950s and 1960s, urban research quickly discarded its institutional-structural focus to take up certain select aspects of Lasswell's famous aphorism that "politics is who gets what, when, where, how and why."[34] Community power studies of the 1960s focused largely on the "who" and "where" of the equation, while the related issues dealt with by decisional analysis provided exhaustive answers to questions dealing with "how" urban policies take shape.[35] But scholars on the whole displayed little interest in "what" was gotten, and then only with respect to the size (relative outputs levels) of the policy pie on which different constituencies fed. Only very recently has urban research interested itself in the allocative and distributional aspects of policy performances.[36]

Cross-national and comparative studies displayed the same preoccupation with process over outcomes.[37] Neither U.S. urban research nor its cousin, comparative urban studies, has stepped back at any point to assess realistically the administrative and organizational variables shaping the problem-solving capacity of urban units.[38] Nor has implementation (and its effect on capacity) received sufficient attention. In short, urban research of any stripe has yet to display a sustained interest in the way in which the operations of a city bureaucracy shape what city government can do, does, or fails to do. Such questions form a critical ingredient of the "how" and "why" components of the Lasswellian equation. For these reasons a focus on the organizational dimensions of implementation, together with reference to the administrative factors shaping policy outcomes, defines the parameters for a study of urban management.[39]

The availability of resources as inputs into the management process plays a central role in shaping administrative outputs. From an urban management perspective, it is the quality of resources (the credentials, role orientations, authority, and autonomy of administrators) as well as the sheer quantity (vis-a-vis personnel and budgets) that ultimately dictate what municipal authorities can and cannot do. *Resource management*, defined as the ability to generate, coordinate, and properly allocate resources to solve problems at hand, performs important functions as one aspect of the urban management syndrome.[40]

While money and people define basic management capacities, these resources will be squandered purposelessly without a work environment in which their potential can be realized. For this reason, we postulate that the organization of work roles and administrative units—with particular reference to flows of authority and power between them—operates as a second factor in urban management. The ability of administrators to coordinate agency operations, to integrate activities around problem areas, and to plan for social as well as economic factors in an integrated fashion provides the basis for what can be labeled the *program management* component of the urban management syndrome.[41] In the context of this second set of criteria, planning and organization interact to define the goals toward which members of urban bureaucracies strive.

Policy management factors describe the third kind of input into the urban management process.[42] These factors emerge chiefly as a function of the application of various tools to problem solving: information gathering and processing as applied to implementation and programming; the organization of network structures for project control; the use of program scheduling (for example, PERT, critical path analysis) and evaluation methods; and the use of service delivery measurements and consideration of cost effectiveness (for example, PPBS). The information dimension of policy management requires application of new technology (computers, automated control systems), methods for needs assessment and client analysis, and the development of in-house capacity to understand and apply the new information.

As one component of urban management, policy management also concerns itself with the question "implementation to what effect?" To do so, it requires distributional analysis at either the micro- (subcommunity) or macro- (intercommunity) level in order to ascertain whether program and policy goals are being met.[43] Policy management adds equity considerations to the traditional concern of administrative analyses with efficiency. An accurate assessment of impact, in turn, requires not only adequate technologies but also multiple sources to minimize information error. Computers and surveys by themselves cannot fully meet policy management needs. In addition, the informational aspect of policy management requires channels for citizen participation and feedback. This feature dovetails closely with the assessment dimension of policy management.

As a potentially quite powerful tool for comparative urban research, the urban management concept strives to reorient scholars and practitioners alike away from their traditional concerns. Instead of "who has power" and "who makes decisions," "how to get things done" (and done well) emerges as the dependent variable of major interest. From this perspective, the extent and intensity of managerial transformation is the principle concern. For purposes of analysis, "managerial transformation" signifies a range of changes that bring urban administration into close approximation to the ideal type described by the urban management syndrome already outlined. In concrete terms, managerial transformation takes shape along the following lines: the emergence of more and better resources (resource management); the development of a work milieu that facilitates the coordination and integration of problem-solving activities (program management); and improvements in information sources and processing techniques (policy management) with an eye to providing more accurate assessment of outputs and outcomes, including equities and inequities. This study proposes to explore the relationship between the managerial transformation of urban bureaucracies and the outcomes of administrative operations along broadly comparative lines, focusing on recent Soviet and U.S. experiences. As a general proposition for the study, we suggest that managerial transformation varies directly with city size and automony and inversely with the fragmentation of power within the urban community. But before refining and examining these relationships further, it is first useful to distinguish urban management from urban administration as abstractions suitable for empirical investigation.

Two major characteristics set urban management apart from urban administration: the premium that management places on horizontal coordination and the ability of management as an "open system" to respond innovatively and in complex ways to changes occurring in the environment.[44] The study of urban management further stresses the importance of tools for innovation while recognizing the effect of resources, information, and organization on problem-solving capability. By contrast, studies of administration concern themselves with the intricacies of bureaucratic politics and with the interplay between informal power arrangements as determining specific policy outcomes.[45] Viewed another way, the study of urban administration looks at administrative processes, such as planning, budgeting, staffing, and decision making, largely in terms of separate and discrete problems, each with its own logic and demands.[46] An urban management approach, on the other hand, takes these same dimensions of administration but reconceptualizes them in terms of strategic choices (integrated versus segmented planning, needs assessment versus standard unit measurement, professional versus political appointments). The ways in which the choices are made and implemented make urban bureaucracies more or less managerial while also shaping policy outcomes and future problem-solving capacities.

As applied to comparative research, the shift from the analysis of administration to the study of management promises several important theoretical and empirical breakthroughs. Unlike existing ad hoc studies of administrative reform, the urban management focus provides a single, comprehensive yardstick for assessing all sorts of administrative changes. Equally important, it provides a means for locating such changes (comparatively) along a continuum running from bureaucratic administration to "pure" public management. Such a yardstick enables those concerned with the fate of cities to do more than simply note or describe such changes; it points the way to conclusions regarding the direction of change and permits comparison of changes across a wide range of social, cultural, and political settings.[47]

From a theoretical perspective, the urban management framework generates hypotheses relating the scope and rate of changes in urban bureaucracies to four distinct aspects of urban life: unit size, unit complexity, unit fragmentation, and unit autonomy.[48] "Unit size" refers to the demographic dimension of urban life; a larger population leads to more numerous and more complex demands on administration and a need for greater coordination of administrative activities to cope with the variety.[49] "Unit complexity" refers to the amount of socioeconomic heterogeneity within the urban environment and to the degree of interdependence that characterizes the milieu within which an urban bureaucracy operates. As the element of variety in the ethnic, social, and occupational profiles of the city population increases, so does the number of conflicting demands on administrators. Such conflict, in turn, makes integrated policy implementation across a wide range of problem areas and target populations all the more difficult to achieve. Likewise, differentiation of the city's economic base increases the problems administrators face in coordinating those policies that affect the production and allocation of resources relevant to urban services. The problem is compounded when control over these resources lies in the hands of a variety of government or private units.

"Unit fragmentation," the third variable, refers to the competition for control (pluralism) and potential for conflict that exists within and without an urban bureaucracy. This variable finds expression in the relative concentration of resource control, a question of authority and power within the organizational setting. To the extent to which urban government rests on a foundation characterized by a large number of competing, crosscutting, or simply ill-defined jurisdictional boundaries among administrative subunits or metropolitan actors, it follows that conflict is likely to take precedence over cooperation, and bureaucratic empire building ("imperialism") over comprehensive approaches to problems and tasks.[50] "Unit autonomy," the fourth variable, refers to the dependency of city government on other government levels. Autonomy, in turn, is determined by the relative centralization and decentralization of the national power structure. Within this context, center-periphery linkages shape and control administrative opportunities, management resources, and the role orientations of individual administrators. The focus on unit autonomy underlines the fact that administrative capacity without opportunities remains meaningless.

The empirical study that follows examines the four hypotheses that emerge logically from the definition of urban management. Given increasing size and complexity:

1. Managerial transformation varies directly with the amount of *unit autonomy* within a political system. For example, within a unitary system (such as France and the USSR) some cities command more authority than others. These should also display higher levels of urban management. (The more unit autonomy, the more likely it is that managerial transformation will occur.) Across systems, cities in decentralized systems should display more management characteristics than those in centralized systems. (Across systems, the more centralization, the more likely managerial transformation.) In general, urban management traits should cluster near the decentralization pole of a centralization-decentralization continuum.[51]

2. The managerial transformation of urban administration varies inversely with *unit fragmentation*. Urban bureaucracies that resemble fractured mirrors will be highly resistant to management transformations. (The more concentrated control is within an urban bureaucracy, the more likely managerial transformation.) From this perspective, management traits cluster near the concentration pole of a concentration-fragmentation continuum.

3. *Unit complexity* and managerial transformation co-vary in the same direction. The more complex the urban milieu, the more pressures exist for urban management to move to the fore. (The more complex the urban setting, the

more likely managerial transformation.) While the transition from homogeneity to heterogeneity is frequently the product of rising levels of urbanization and increases in unit size that accompany it, this is not always the case. For example, in the United States (in which the majority of the urban population resides in units of 50,000 inhabitants or less) the trend to metropolitanization, coupled with the pressures of intergovernmental financing and programs, produces problems of complexity and scale without increases in city size.[52]

4. Managerial transformation for city bureaucracies become imperative with increases in *unit size*. Large cities require more urban management, and, hence, both within systems and across them, these units should experience managerial transformation first and with the greatest impact.

In brief, large unit size, great complexity, and high levels of decentralization create real pressures for the introduction of urban management. Conversely, the deconcentration of resources within the city (unit fragmentation) acts as a barrier to such a transformation. Other things being equal between systems, we would thus expect that a system in which there are large, relatively autonomous, and complex cities would display the most urban management traits. Among different cities within a single system, the same rule should hold; administration in the largest, most independent, and most complex should appear the most managerial. Finally, we suspect that in cross-national comparisons, the fragmentation of resources within urban systems (which are otherwise dissimilar) will cancel the controlling influence of the other variables.

The hypotheses promise significant improvement in what to date have remained unfocused and somewhat chaotic discussions of administrative change. More important, they provide a way to link up discussions of changes in urban administration with predictions of changes in urban political processes more broadly defined. In place of ad hoc listings of alterations in a previously existing state of affairs (an approach that assigns a leading role to change by default), the hypotheses generate reasonably precise scenarios of cities' probable as well as possible administrative-political "futures." A schematic representation of the alternatives is provided in Figure 1. The matrix of this figure assumes high complexity and/or large size. Therefore, the transformations depicted will probably describe most accurately the kinds of changes occurring in either large or highly developed cities in a given political system. It should also be stressed that the typology presents transformations in terms of continua rather than endpoints; cities do not suddenly "pass" from one cateogry into another. Likewise, the typology purports to describe only the prevalent mode within a given system, while recognizing at the same time that within-system variations among different kinds of cities occur. Small cities and company towns will not necessarily correspond to the norm described by the general type, regardless of whether the discussion centers upon existing or future arrangements.

With its combination of fragmented resources and information, coupled with the centralized flow of power and authority through the channels of hier-

FIGURE 1

Urban Management: Present and Future

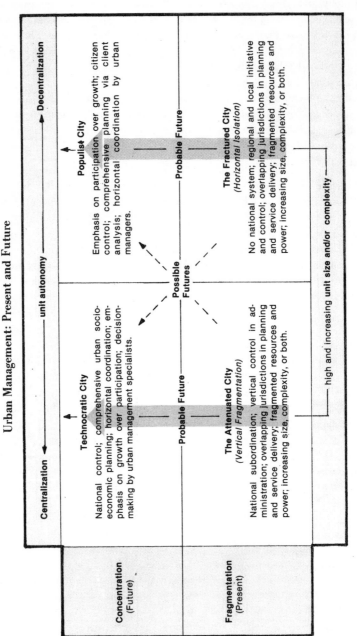

Source: Compiled by the authors.

archically organized bureaucracies and the Communist party, the Soviet city to-day resembles the "attenuated city," the local expression of a national regime type (autocratic), which Samuel Huntington links to the early stages of national development.[53] The U.S. counterpart displays a somewhat different pattern of political decentralization and concentration of administrative control. Here the fragmentation of resources and jurisdictions (what is commonly termed "picket fence federalism") is accompanied by the retention of substantial autonomy at the local level. In terms of its competitive political dynamic, coupled with the socioeconomic dominance of the middle class, the U.S. city as a "fractured city" resembles the local component of Huntington's bourgeois regime-type variant.[54]

From the perspective of administrative futures for U.S. and Soviet cities, the typology distinguishes between possible and probable variants. Insofar as the Soviet political leadership might seek to minimize the political costs of adminis-trative change, the management transformation of Soviet urban administration would lead toward a "technocratic fix" and, thus, in the direction of the "techno-cratic city" category.[55] Alternately, there may be evidence of movement toward a mirror image transformation, a state of affairs characterized by decentraliza-tion, concentration, large size, and complexity (the "populist city"). In the So-viet case, such movements would radically reverse existing political trends at the national level (central control, sectoral implementation). Given prevailing values, the management transformation of the large U.S. city will most logically move it in the direction of the populist variant. But management transformation might also exert a compelling logic of its own, one that would transform (or con-verge) both U.S. and Soviet variants toward some approximation of the "techno-cratic" type (a nationwide computer network, social engineering through social planning, the centralization of intergovernmental relations, the orientation of local officials toward national constituencies). We will return to a discussion of these questions and present trends in the concluding chapter, drawing on the em-pirical data presented in this study.

The investigation of Soviet urban management is organized around macro-level as well as microlevel issues. The first two chapters examine the ways in which both barriers and inducements to urban management emerge as a product of the overall management environment along the cultural, the social and demo-graphic, the organizational, and the political dimensions. The meaning of histori-cally and ideologically derived conceptions of "the city" (and urban life more generally) take on special significance in this context. Proceeding from this dis-cussion of macrolevel, environmental issues, the study moves to an investigation of the organization, allocation, and production of those resources (personnel and finances) that define the resource management dimension of the management syndrome. Chapter 3 looks at the ways in which Soviet city governments train, equip, advance, and control their personnel, and at the differential distribution of these human resources across types of cities.

Chapter 4 continues this theme with a focus on fiscal resources and budgetary constraints. The ways in which budgetary processes (national resource management) shape implementation (urban policy management) are of particular interest. As in Chapter 3, the fiscal aspects of management capacity will be explored across cities of different types. Chapter 5 examines the program management dimension of administrative change in Soviet cities. It focuses on efforts and results in the area of social planning. Chapter 6 discusses trends in the area of policy management, with particular reference to new information technologies, professional training, and the devices utilized to improve the responsiveness of officials and agencies. A concluding chapter will once again raise the question of urban futures, assessing the validity of the initial hypotheses on the basis of the evidence the study has generated.

To claim that the challenge of urban government in the USSR and United States alike is the challenge of management hardly entails either a denial of the ongoing importance of the urban political process or a complete rejection of what has traditionally been the cutting edge of urban inquiry in both the Soviet and U.S. settings.[56] To do so is, however, to recognize and attach the appropriate weight to recent claims from the Soviet side that the management dimension of urban affairs has not been sufficiently appreciated: "urban forms of settlement have now brought to the forefront a complex of serious problems whose solution is possible only within the framework of better city management and through a strengthening of the regulatory role played by management functions."[57] These claims are especially compelling if one accepts the broad definition of politics that Lasswell provides. Having made the case for the comparative study of cities from a management perspective, it remains only to demonstrate how it can be operationalized and to analyze the results.

NOTES

1. Barbara Ward, *The Home of Man* (New York: W. W. Norton, 1976), p. 3.

2. As quoted in David Harvey, *Social Justice and the City* (London: Edward Arnold, 1973), p. 195.

3. M. V. Posokhin, *Cities to Live in* (Moscow: Novosti Press, 1974), pp. 15-16.

4. John Walton, "Problems of Method and Theory in Comparative Urban Studies," *Urban Affairs Quarterly* 11 (1975): 5.

5. Jane Jacobs, *The Death and Life of Great American Cities* (New York: Vintage Books, 1961), pp. 29-140.

6. Among the many treatments of these characteristics see, for example, Louis Wirth, "Urbanism as a Way of Life," *American Journal of Sociology* 44 (1938): 1-24; Lewis Mumford, *The Culture of Cities* (New York: Harcourt, Brace & Co., 1938); C. A. Doxiadis, *Anthropopolis: City for Human Development* (New York: W. W. Norton, 1975), p. 212; and, for a discussion of their effects on urban analysis, see Anthony J. Catanese, *Scientific Methods of Urban Analysis* (Urbana: University of Illinois Press, 1972).

7. On the ecological approach to the study of the city, see Leonard Reissman, *The Urban Process: Cities in Industrial Societies* (New York: Free Press, 1970), pp. 105-21.

John Walton argues that urban life is more "politicized" in Walton, op. cit., p. 8. Social cleavage and social conflict characterize urban life and political behavior in the view of Michael Aiken, "Urban Social Structure and Political Competition: A Comparative Study of Local Politics in Four European Nations," *Urban Affairs Quarterly* 11 (1975): 82-116. See especially Charles Tilly, "The Chaos of the Living City," in *Comparative Community Politics*, ed. Terry N. Clark (New York: John Wiley, 1974), pp. 203-27.

8. Nor are Soviet cities immune to the threat of disorder. For instances of urban violence and disruption related to ethnic and religious conflict, see Rudolph L. Tokes, ed., *Dissent in the USSR* (Baltimore: Johns Hopkins University Press, 1975), pp. 221-23, 382; and Donald S. Carlisle, "Uzbekistan and the Uzbeks," in *Handbook of Major Soviet Nationalities*, ed. Zev Katz, Rosemarie Rogers, and Frederic Harned (New York: Free Press, 1975), p. 310.

9. Francine F. Rabinovitz and Felicity M. Trueblood, *Latin American Urban Research* (Beverly Hills, Calif.: Sage, 1973); Francine F. Rabinovitz, "Urban Development and Political Development in Latin America," in *Comparative Urban Research: The Administration and Politics of Cities*, ed. Robert T. Daland (Beverly Hills, Calif.: Sage, 1969), pp. 88-123; and Mark Kesselman, "Research Perspectives on Comparative Local Politics: Pitfalls, Prospects and Notes on the French Case," in Clark, *Comparative Community Politics*, pp. 352-81.

10. John Friedman, "The Role of Cities in National Development," *American Behavioral Scientist* 12 (1969): 13-21.

11. Rabinovitz, "Urban Development and Political Development," in Daland, op. cit., pp. 88-123; and Kesselman, op. cit., pp. 352-81.

12. Harvey, op. cit., p. 16.

13. Ibid., p. 304; Alexei Gutnov et al., *The Ideal Communist City*, trans. Renee Neu Watkins (New York: George Braziller, 1968), p. 11; Enzo Mingione, "Sociological Approach to Regional and Urban Development: Some Methodological and Theoretical Issues," *Comparative Urban Research* 4 (1977). Ivan Szelenyi, "Urban Sociology and Community Studies in Eastern Europe: Reflections and Comparisons with American Approaches," *Comparative Urban Research* 4 (1977): 11-20.

14. For statistics on Soviet urban population, see Chapter 1.

15. Henry Morton, "The Soviet Urban Scene," *Problems of Communism* 26 (1977): 74.

16. Michael Aiken and Manuel Castells, "New Trends in Urban Studies—Introduction," *Comparative Urban Research* 4 (1977): 7-10; and Robert G. Jensen, "Urban Environments in the United States and the Soviet Union," in *Urbanization and Counterurbanization*, ed. Brian Berry (Beverly Hills, Calif.: Sage, 1976), p. 31.

17. Walton, op. cit., p. 3; Aiken and Castells, op. cit., pp. 7-10; and Paul B. Dornan, "Whither Urban Policy Analysis? A Review Essay," *Polity* 9 (1977): 503-27.

18. Ivan Trufanov, *Problems of Soviet Urban Life*, trans. James Riordan (Newtonville, Mass.: Oriental Research Partners, 1977), p. 23. The original was published by Leningrad State University in 1973, as *Problemy byta gorodskogo naseleniia* SSR.

19. J. R. Thornley and J. B. McLoughlin, *Aspects of Urban Management* (Izmir: Organization for Economic Cooperation and Development, 1976).

20. U.S., Congress, House, Subcommittee on the City, Committee on Banking, Finance and Urban Affairs, *Success Abroad: What Foreign Cities Can Teach American Cities* (Washington, D.C.: Government Printing Office, April 1977).

21. See Claire W. Gilbert, *Community Power Structure: Propositional Inventory, Tests and Theory* (Miami: University of Florida Press, 1972); Michael Aiken and Paul E. Mott, eds., *The Structure of Community Power* (New York: Random House, 1970); Terry N. Clark, ed., *Community Structure, Power and Decision-Making* (San Francisco: Chandler,

1968); and Claire W. Gilbert, "The Study of Community Power: A Summary and a Test," in *The New Urbanization*, ed. Scott Greer et al. (New York: St. Martin's Press, 1968), pp. 222-45.

22. "The problems of the city are not of a local character, and they are extremely urgent." Main Scientific Research Computer Center of the Moscow City Soviet Executive Committee, *Description of the Management System of the City of Moscow*, Report on the scientific research performed according to the Intergovernmental Agreement of 1972 for Scientific and Technological Cooperation between the USSR and USA, Topic no. 3, Project no. 1 (uncirculated draft report; Soviet source document unverified by independent research) (New York: Columbia University, Graduate School of Business, Center for Government Studies, c 1975), p. 9.

23. Brian Berry, "On Urbanization and Counterurbanization," and "The Counterurbanization Process in Urban America," in Berry, op. cit., pp. 7-14, 17-30.

24. Jack Fisher, "Urban Planning in the Soviet Union and Eastern Europe," in *Taming Megalopolis*, ed. H. Wentworth Eldredge, 2 vols. (New York: Anchor Books, 1967), 2: 1081-82; and Jensen, op. cit., pp. 31-42.

25. Dan Dimancescu, "Managing High Density Living," in U.S., Congress, House, Subcommittee on the City, Committee on Banking, Finance and Urban Affairs, *Toward a National Urban Policy*, committee print (Washington, D.C.: Government Printing Office, April 1977), pp. 109-16.

26. For the comparative advantages and disadvantages of the two approaches, see Adam Przeworski and Henry Teune, *The Logic of Comparative Social Inquiry* (New York: John Wiley, 1970), pp. 31-46.

27. William Taubman, *Governing Soviet Cities: Bureaucratic Politics and Urban Development in the USSR* (New York: Praeger, 1973), p. 10.

28. Morton, op. cit., p. 75.

29. Reissman, op. cit., p. 2. Reissman stresses "the sheer technical knowledge and skill required to keep a relatively large number of people alive under urban conditions," especially given the problems of social organization and economic distribution.

30. Frederick O. Hayes, "Changes and Innovation in City Government," in *Improving the Quality of Urban Management*, ed. Willis D. Hawley and David Rogers (Beverly Hills, Calif.: Sage, 1976), pp. 129-36. For a classical statement and elaboration on city government as city politics, see Edward Banfield and James Q. Wilson, *City Politics* (New York: Vintage Books, 1973), pp. 1-2, 7, 339-42. See also Taubman, op. cit., pp. 3-6, 15-17.

31. Hayes, op. cit., p. 137.

32. Grover Starling, *Managing the Public Sector* (Homewood, Ill.: Dorsey Press, 1977), pp. 7, 317-23. In New York City, top officials of the Economic Development Council, an association of 185 large employers founded in 1965 to contribute a series of task forces to help improve the operations of municipal agencies, have persistently attributed many of the city's problems to bad management. David Rogers and Willis Hawley, "The Mismanagement of Cities," in Hawley and Rogers, op. cit., pp. 431, 443-45.

33. Robert L. Lineberry, *Equality and Urban Policy: Distribution of Municipal Services* (Beverly Hills, Calif.: Sage, 1977), pp. 79-80.

34. Harold Lasswell, *Politics, Who Gets What, When, How* (New York: P. Smith, 1950).

35. Willis Hawley and Frederick M. Wirt, eds., *The Search for Community Power*, 2d ed. (Englewood Cliffs, N.J.: Prentice-Hall, 1974), esp. pp. 272-370; and Robert Dahl, *Who Governs* (New Haven, Conn.: Yale University Press, 1961).

36. Lineberry, op. cit., pp. 79-80.

37. Robert C. Fried in a review of Delbert C. Miller's *International Community Power Structure* in *Midwest Journal of Political Science* 5 (1971): 630-31. See also John Walton,

"Structures of Power in Latin American Cities: Toward a Summary and Interpretation,"
in *Urban Latin America: The Political Condition from Above and Below*, ed. A. Portes and
John Walton (Austin: University of Texas Press, 1976), pp. 136-68. See also Jack Goldsmith
and Gil Gunderson, eds., *Comparative Local Politics: A Systems-Function Approach* (Boston: Holbrook Press, 1973), pp. 6-15, 191-92. A concise summary of such concerns in the
literature of the 1960s can be found in Robert T. Daland, "Comparative Perspectives of Urban Systems," in Daland, op. cit., pp. 15-54.

38. In the seminal study by Annemarie Walsh, *The Urban Challenge to Government*
(New York: Praeger, 1969), pp. 7-29, the author stresses the importance of outputs, while
treating them largely as the product of structure (political organization) and power (the political process). A more recent series of cross-national studies on urban housing policy and
development analyzes outcome from the standpoint of class structure, political process, and
urbanization patterns while ignoring the dimension of implementation in favor of a focus on
policy formation. See Louis Masotti and John Walton, "Comparative Urban Research: The
Logic of Comparisons," in *The City in Comparative Perspective*, ed. John Walton and Louis
Masotti (Beverly Hills, Calif.: Sage, 1976), pp. 9-15. The emphasis in this collection is on
patterns of participation, resource competition, systemic causation, historical patterns of urbanization, and the political economy of systems structures. An exception to the neglect
of outcomes remains the work of Jeff Pressman and Aaron Wildavsky, *Implementation:
How Great Expectations in Washington Were Dashed in Oakland* (Berkeley: University of
California Press, 1973). See also Frances Fox Piven, "The Urban Crisis: Who Got What and
Why," in *Cities in Change*, ed. John Walton and Donald Carns, 2d ed. (Boston: Allyn and
Bacon, 1977), pp. 415-33.

39. For a general description of the role of administrative and organizational factors
as they shape outputs, see Hayes, op. cit., pp. 138-49; and Rogers and Hawley, op. cit., pp.
15-25. The executive director of the ICMA has observed that urban management is such an
integral part of the process of government that it becomes a major source of success and
failure in goal attainment. James M. Banovetz, ed., *Managing the Modern City* (Washington,
D.C.: International City Management Association, 1971), pp. i, iii, 40-43. See also Stanley
Powers et al., *Developing the Municipal Organization* (Washington, D.C.: International City
Management Association, 1974), pp. 12, 20-21.

40. *Strengthening Public Management in the Intergovernmental System: A Report for
the OMB* (Washington, D.C.: U.S. Government Printing Office, 1975), pp. 5-6.

41. Ibid., p. 6.

42. Ibid., p. viii, 5. In the United States, only program management has become the
target of any sustained attention and efforts at improvement to date. This is due largely to
a functional approach to service delivery at the national level and a reluctance to institute
any measures that would raise the overhead costs of local government. According to one estimate, by 1975 overhead costs had reached 50 percent of all state and city budgets, excluding fringe benefits. See Starling, op. cit., pp. 368-69.

43. For an application of distributional analysis in the Soviet setting, see Chapter 4.
See also Peter Zwick, "Socioeconomic Policy and National Integration in the USSR," and
Carol Nechemias, "Soviet Housing Policy," papers delivered at the 1978 Southwestern Social Sciences Association Convention, Houston, Texas.

44. *Strengthening Public Management*, pp. vii, viii, 3; Walsh, op. cit., p. 224 (Chart
12). See Powers et al., op. cit., pp. 14-15, 20-21, 26-35, for the distinction between administration and management as it relates to individual roles and organizational structures (matrix
organization, consociated model, system four model). Gerald Zaltman et al., *Innovation and
Organizations* (New York: John Wiley, 1973), pp. 123-46, relate innovation and openness to
the differences between mechanistic and organic structures and their impact on implementation outcomes.

45. Studies that illustrate this point from the perspective of urban management include Starling, op. cit.; John R. Russell, *Cases in Urban Magement* (Cambridge, Mass.: MIT Press, 1974); and Harold Gortner, *Administration in the Public Sector* (New York: John Wiley, 1977). For the administrative perspective, see Francis E. Rourke, *Bureaucratic Power in National Politics*, 2d ed. (Boston: Little, Brown and Co., 1965); Ira Sharkansky, *Public Administration: Policy-Making in Government Agencies* (Chicago: Markham, 1970), pp. 1-13; George J. Gordon, *Public Administration in America* (New York: St. Martin's Press, 1978); and Fred A. Kramer, *Dynamics of Public Bureaucracy* (Cambridge, Mass.: Winthrop, 1977).

46. Starling, op. cit., pp. 448-49; Gortner, op. cit., pp. 152-53; and Powers et al., op. cit., pp. 69-74.

47. The disadvantages of an ad hoc approach are well illustrated by Gerald Caiden's *The Dynamics of Public Administration* (New York: Holt, Rinehart and Winston, 1971).

48. These correspond to the central concerns of classical urban theory; see Reissman, op. cit., pp. 69-149; Wirth, op. cit., pp. 1-24; and Mumford, op. cit.

49. The difference between "needs" and "demands" underlines the political implications of urban management. See David Easton, *A Systems Analysis of Political Life* (New York: John Wiley, 1965), pp. 37-56.

50. On bureaucratic empire building, see Matthew Holden, Jr., "'Imperialism' in Bureaucracy," in Rourke, op. cit., pp. 97-213. For the manner in which differentiated organizational structures promote conflict, see Zaltman et al., op. cit., pp. 148-55.

51. As John Walton has suggested, the future of the city may lie between autonomy and democratic fragmentation. See John Walton, "The Vertical Axis of Community Organization and the Structure of Power," in *Community Politics: A Behavioral Approach*, ed. Charles M. Bonjean et al. (New York: Free Press, 1971), pp. 188-97.

52. John C. Bollens and Henry J. Schmandt, *The Metropolis: Its People, Politics and Economic Life*, 2d ed. (New York: Harper & Row, 1970), p. 112; and *Strengthening Public Management*, op. cit., p. 9.

53. Samuel P. Huntington and Joan Nelson, *No Easy Choice: Political Participation in Developing Countries* (Cambridge, Mass.: Harvard University Press, 1976), pp. 17-27; Kenneth Newton, "Community Decision-Makers and Community Decision-Making in England and the U.S.," in Clark, op. cit., chap. 2.

54. On picket fence federalism, see Starling, op. cit., pp. 54-55; and *Strengthening Public Management*, p. 13.

55. For evidence that the current Soviet political leadership is indeed oriented to a technological fix, see John P. Hardt and George Holliday, "Technology Transfer and Change in the Soviet Economic System," in *Technology and Communist Culture*, ed. Frederic J. Fleron, Jr. (New York: Praeger, 1977), pp. 211-18; and Erik P. Hoffmann, "Technology, Values and Political Power," in ibid., pp. 423-29.

56. Walsh, op. cit., pp. 16-29. For alternative approaches to Soviet urban dynamics see, among others, Taubman, op. cit.; Bernard M. Frolic, "Non-Comparative Communism: Chinese and Soviet Urbanization," in *Social Consequences of Modernization in Communist Societies*, ed. Mark Field (Baltimore: Johns Hopkins University Press, 1976), pp. 149-61; David T. Cattell, *Leningrad: A Case Study of Soviet Urban Government* (New York: Praeger, 1968); and Ronald J. Hill, *The Soviet Political Elites* (New York: St. Martin's Press, 1977).

57. A. S. Gruzinov and V. P. Riumin, *Gorod: upravlenie, problemy* (Leningrad: Lenizdat, 1977), pp. 4, 6-7, 20-23. For Soviet definitions of urban management, see *Management System of Moscow*, pp. 2, 5, 234-35; and Main Scientific Research Computer Center of the Moscow City Soviet Executive Committee, *Experimental Development of Automated City Management Systems for the City of Leningrad*, Preliminary report on scientific re-

search performed in accordance with the Government Agreement of 1972 for Scientific and Technological Cooperation between the USSR and USA, Topic no. 3, Project no. 2 (New York: Columbia University, Graduate School of Business, Center for Government Studies, November 1975), pp. 9, 15-16.

1

THE MANAGEMENT ENVIRONMENT OF
SOVIET CITIES:
FROM MYTH TO MIGRATION

A CULTURAL PERSPECTIVE

The idea of the city as a "system" has led students of urban dynamics to stress the importance of converging and conflicting social values as important aspects of urban problems and policy solutions.[1] These discussions of values, however, have shown little concern for conceptions of "the city" as critical parameters that limit the policy options of those responsible for managing the urban milieu. Analysis of the "urban environment" still turns around the twin issues of urban social structure and the economic setting.[2] Cultural factors are treated as phenomena of generally secondary importance and are usually viewed simply as a clash between rural or small-town values and the demands of life in a modern metropolis.[3] Cross-national, comparative studies of urban systems share this bias. The issue of "culture" in such research refers only to the kinds of urban communities that can be fruitfully compared, most frequently from the perspective of political process rather than policy outcomes.[4] Thus, while studies in urban history have demonstrated that the idea of the "city" has remained neither constant across time nor consistent as among societies, these insights have generally been ignored in the study of urban politics and policies.[5]

Equally important, when the concept "culture" has been introduced into urban research, there has been a clear tendency to focus on it chiefly as a mass phenomenon.[6] It is the values that hypothetically shape the behavior of the urban citizenry—and not those that define the world of urban decision makers—that usually provide the frame of reference. This is evident from the conceptual dichotomies most frequently utilized: "public-regarding versus private-regarding ethos," "conflict or consensus," "integration or cleavage," "participatory versus subject political orientations."[7] By contrast, understanding urban management demands a rather different approach to the subject of culture. It requires that the inventory of culture-related issues be expanded to deal with such subjects as the purpose of the "city," the functions of urban structures and institutions, and the "proper" or legitimate relationship between the city and the national organs of power. It demands as well some historical perspective on official views regarding the city, plus a consideration of the role played by new ideologies in reshaping these views over time. Only when this richer, more diverse approach to the study of "cultural" issues is employed in urban research can comparative analysis fully grasp the cultural factors shaping the decisions of urban managers. In this context, Robert Alford's observations regarding the role of "culture" in urban affairs takes on a special significance: "cultural factors . . . infuse a structure with meaning, provide political actors with justifications for their actions, and legitimate various types of groups and their demands."[8] This definition of the functions of "culture" applies as much to the operative political orientations of urban decision makers as it does to political beliefs at the mass level.

In the Soviet setting, the absence of reliable, systematic data on the political-cultural orientations of either masses or elites makes it all the more useful to approach the subject of culture and the urban environment from the perspective of those kinds of urban outlooks that have prevailed among Russian elites historically. As the investigation indeed reveals, it is these outlooks, overlaid with certain Marxist canons and ideological requirements, that continue to dominate official thinking today. To demonstrate this, we focus on the pervasiveness of traditional Russian concepts of the city in the Soviet period and not on the nature of the Russian or Soviet city per se. In short, the analysis of the management environment begins with an exploration of the contemporary meaning of Russia's urban past as reflected both in official policy toward the city and official pronouncements about the city in both the tsarist and Soviet eras.

Until well after the emergence of a centralized, national government, the term "city" (*gorod*) in the lexicon of the Russian state meant little more than a fortified settlement.[9] Despite the fact that the sixteenth century Russian city already possessed a social order and spatial stratification, it was not until the legislative code of 1649 that urban organization acquired recognition (and, by inference, institutionalization) by government fiat. The idea of an urban class (or "estate," *soslovie*) occupying a fixed place in social and political arrangements and exercising limited electoral rights did not emerge as an element of national policy until 1721, when Tsar Peter the Great enacted the Order of the Magistracy. Later, with the Urban Charter of 1785, the central government took upon itself the right to define and control the formation of cities, while simultaneously reemphasizing their favored status within the political structure of Catherinian Russia.[10] By contrast to its Western European counterparts, however, the privileges of the Russian city remained extremely limited. From 1800 until the present, these developed only as a function of the limited benevolence of the central political authorities.

Almost from the very outset, the relationship between city and state in Russia was defined almost exclusively in fiscal and economic rather than political terms. The city appeared as a prime source of revenue for state development, an outlook that required the state to step in and protect the taxable population against princely encroachments. This focus on the city as an economic resource also encouraged the state to freeze the urban inhabitants in their existing places of residence, while protecting them in their trade, handicrafts, and other economic pursuits. Although still isolated islands in a vast agrarian sea, by the end of the 1600s Russian cities already provided roughly 45 percent of all state revenue. They included, however, only 18 percent of the country's inhabitants.[11] Thus, urban policy emerged as a fiscal policy colored by the perceived needs of the central authorities.

A loss of revenue and political autonomy accompanied state recognition of the cities' strategic role. The spontaneous grouping of certain occupations within or near the city's boundaries led to the aggregation and segregation of economic functions and social roles. In Mumford's terms, the Russian city functioned as a class envelope.[12] And, as was the case with the shift from medieval localism to baroque centralism in the West, a loss of autonomy occurred even as the cities' strategic importance increased. Meanwhile, "suburban sprawl"—in the shape of proliferating, extra-urban settlements with autonomous tax systems—deprived the city proper of indigenous resources. The tax burden on the remaining urban population increased steadily from the middle of the sixteenth century onward. Skilled administrative personnel moved outward and upward; then, as now, expanding national bureaucracies attracted the most able into higher-level military and civilian posts.[13] Resource scarcity was intensified by the fact that Russia's industrial development began and continued largely outside the boundaries of urban settlements. This deprived cities of capital investment and an export base, thus hindering the emergence of a commercially oriented middle class.[14]

Lacking the feudal nexus that had supported the autonomy of post-medieval cities in the West, Russian cities were quickly submerged by the developing political autocracy. Throughout the seventeenth century the Russian city was valued by the political elite chiefly as a source of national revenue. It remained wholly dependent upon the central political authorities for the shape and direction of its development.[15] The image of the city that emerged among the elite downplayed the city as a repository of individual rights and freedoms even as it denied legitimacy to the interplay and conflict of social forces.[16]

The eighteenth century marked an important watershed in the growth of the urban concept in Russian culture. Cities took on added importance as mechanisms for political control and as local agents for the state bureaucracy. In addition to supplying economic resources, Russian cities were also seen as providing an important setting in which national goals could be enforced. The concept of the administrative city thus emerged along with the notion of a service state.

The city was to be used both as an instrument for political rule and as a device for "rationalizing" the world in the Weberian sense. Henceforward (and up to the present, as Chapter 2 shows), cities were assigned places and functions in a strictly organized national hierarchy. Urban administration meanwhile was reduced to a device for imposing homogeneity on the diversity of a multinational empire.[17] The state awarded urban status to settlements more and more according to its own administrative needs.[18] Then as now the importance of a city lay not so much in its size but in its territorial subordination and political proximity to the centers of power.[19]

The legislative record of the eighteenth century also testifies to the strong influence of Enlightenment perspectives and to the gradual emergence of a concept of urban life best expressed by the term "city of reason."[20] The Magistracy Reform of 1721 charted urban development so as to promote the growth of a hierarchy among cities; it also reinforced earlier trends toward the nationalization of urban power structures and the emergence of vertical administrative forms. "Reason" dictated that only strong vertical subordination could serve to realize national goals at the lowest level. A "rational" hierarchy meant that waste in urban administration would be eliminated and a perfect flow of information, resources, and compliance obtained. "Rationalization" also dictated some effort to eliminate the many competing jurisdictions that, for historical reasons, still exercised a strong hold over Russian municipal life.[21] Order, regularity, coordination, and design were all to characterize a "new" urban environment through the rigorous application of statutes and rules. The city emerged as the symbol of light and order, the only place in a backward, agrarian society where a "rational" (that is, Western) life was possible.[22]

Although frequently aborted, the urban reforms of Catherine II later in the century marked further progress in the identification of "reason and modernity" (Westernization) with the idea of the city. The provisions for the election of *urban* deputies to Catherine's commission on legal codification (1766) represented an admission that urban officials could indeed possess both an identity and interest apart from whatever social class to which they belonged. But these early attempts to offset the traditional estate principle with a new, urban principle were soon to collapse. Thereafter, "estates" remained the defining social unit according to which urban policy was framed right up until 1917.[23] Indeed, when added to the variety of existing estate jurisdictions in the area of courts, voting rights, and tax privileges that already governed the lives of urban dwellers, the newly recognized social and legal category of "urban citizens" (*meshchan'e*) effectively precluded any possibility of dealing with urban problems in a holistic fashion. It also hindered the emergence of that shared urban culture that historically has accompanied the development of urban networks elsewhere.[24]

The influence of eighteenth century rationalism on urban perspectives among political elites and intellectuals was to remain an integral part of the Russian tradition until the revolutionary era (as Andrei Belyi's depiction of the geo-metric city in his fin-de-siecle novel, *Saint Petersburg*, so eloquently testifies). The Age of Enlightenment induced an approach to urban planning that viewed cities as abstractions and, in a favorite rationalist metaphor, as physical geome-tries of shapes and planes to be rearranged and engineered at will.[25] An unques-tioning faith in the salacious effects of structural and legal change led to a reli-ance on organizational reform and institutional rearrangement as the major tools of urban policy. These were all that were required to produce a perfect city. Hence, concern for proper spatial organization took precedence over interest in the problems associated with the provision of services or the development of an adequate economic base. Despite some interest in *blagoustroistvo* (public wel-fare) in the late 1860s, Russian planning concepts attached little significance to servicing the needs of the urban population. In Odessa, some early attempts to reverse this trend soon gave way under the general reaction of the 1890s.[26]

For the reasons just outlined, nineteenth century Russian perspectives on the city display marked differences from the images of the city that were then taking hold in the West.[27] Despite a spurt of industrial growth and urbanization after the emancipation of the serfs in 1861, the idea of the city of reason never gave way to the "city of progress"—or to the image of the "industrial city" that flourished in the West during this period. "Without design," a key slogan in much Western social theory of the late nineteenth century, failed to strike a responsive chord in Russia. Certainly, the belief in laissez-faire principles and the value of unrestricted competition as a source of rational, cooperative order remained a minor theme in Russian elite thinking. That mythic "struggle for existence" that provided the Social Darwinist justification for an urban-centered, profit-seeking middle class in the West was viewed with unabashed disdain by Russian revolu-tionaries and reactionaries alike.[28]

In contrast to the West, cities remained fragile, hothouse creations in Rus-sia. This occurred not because of a misplaced belief that a thousand unorches-trated efforts could somehow yield coherent social and political patterns. Rath-er, the explanation lay in the strength of the eighteenth century legacy, espe-cially the belief in the efficacy of central control, rational planning, and deliber-ately engineered development for cities. Indeed, with the passage of the 1892 counterreform, the feeling crystallized that local authority ought to be re-stricted to specific statutory grants within a narrow range of competence. Fur-thermore, neither citizen participation nor government responsiveness was as-signed a positive role in urban problem solving.[29] After the turn of the century, urban strikes and political protests initiated by urban-based and city-educated professions (the third element) encouraged a single view among conservative gov-ernment officials: urbanization by definition represented an ongoing threat to traditional social values and political loyalties.[30]

Broad divisions within what constituted articulate, nonofficial public opin-ion in Russia—the schism between the Westernizers and the Slavophiles—pre-

vented the emergence of any single, well-articulated alternative to official thinking regarding the city. Westernizers on the whole applauded the growth of cities
as the repository of all that was modern, progressive, liberal, and enlightened in
the Russian environment. Yet some supporters, such as Alexander Pushkin, were
alert to the fact that urbanization and modernization could subordinate human
values and concerns to the twin idols of change and progress ("The Bronze
Horseman"). Among the political intelligentsia, those numbered among the fore-
runners of the revolutionary Marxist tradition, including Herzen, Belinsky, Lavrov, and Chernyshevsky, can be classified as largely prourban in their theories of
historical progress and social development. Despite Herzen's romanticization of
the peasant commune, he nevertheless continued to look to an urban setting and
urban forces as the guarantee of Russia's future (*From the Other Shore*). Chernyshevsky meanwhile maintained that an urban commune would recreate a lost
sense of community, while embracing all of the advantages of the division of industrial labor (*What Is to Be Done?*).[31]

A contrary position emerges from the works of the Slavophiles. From the
outset they regarded many of the institutions that defined the nineteenth century city as foreign borrowings, designed either to fail or to produce monstrous
results when transplanted onto Russian soil. In addition to idolizing the peas-
antry and agrarian life as the chief source of virtue, the Slavophiles regarded the
rationalist, rule-making thrust of city government with a good deal of suspicion.[32] Their ideal city was one of independent, autonomous communities, the
members of which come together in a citizens' meeting to provide a consensual
basis for decision making. The "good" city would require a minimum of social
regulation and bureaucracy so as to leave the individual and, more particularly,
the community free for self-regulation.[33] But only in their most extreme ver-
sions (such as Gogol's "Nevsky Prospekt" and Raskolnikov's vision of the city in
Dostoevsky's *Crime and Punishment*) did Slavophile urban visions see life in the
city as an unmitigated force for evil and corruption, a mechanical monster run
amok and bent on destroying Everyman (Gogol's "The Overcoat").[34] From the
standpoint of contemporary Soviet views, it is the Westernizer's prourban bias
coupled with a strong dose of nineteenth century Marxism's faith in the city as
the locus of economic development and social progress that ultimately has prevailed.

The most interesting aspect of these various perspectives on the Russian
city is that none of them managed to capture the unique kinds of urban transformations that were, in fact, occurring. In reality, Russian cities had not developed
along the lines of the industrial city, the image that Westernizers (and later Soviet Marxists) applauded as a symbol of progress. The lure of Russian cities lay
not in opportunities for industrial employment, such as were found in the mill
towns of the Western variant, but in a demand for personal services and unskilled
day labor. Thus, urban growth remained largely the product of peasant in-migration; by the end of the nineteenth century, almost 53 percent of all city dwell-

ers had only recently arrived from the villages.[35] The economic strains such rapid transformation occasioned for city budgets were further aggravated by the stinginess of the national authorities who effectively controlled most fiscal resources. Budget difficulties were reinforced by industrialists' propensity to locate and expand their enterprises outside the cities' boundaries, thus avoiding taxes and levies.[36] As a result, Russian cities became neither the beehives of industrial activity nor the centers of squalor, overcrowding, and social misery that were represented by cities such as Manchester and Birmingham. Industry remained strongly rooted in a rural environment. According to the 1897 census, of the 4.2 million persons engaged in manufacturing less than one-half (48 percent) resided in the cities of the Empire. The province of Moscow, with over 20 percent of its total population urbanized, still had only 57 percent of all its industrial workers located in its cities.[37] In the textile and garment sectors (which gave rise in the nineteenth century to industrial cities in both the United States and in England) the majority of factories remained in rural areas until 1917.[38]

For such reasons, the negative connotations of the industrial city remained a minor theme in Russian urban thinking until the eve of the Bolshevik assumption of power. Although occasionally articulated by political conservatives and by thinkers of the Slavophile or populist schools, theories of urban deterioration and degeneration never gained the solid foothold they acquired in the West. Poverty and other social problems were attributed by the conservatives to individual deficiencies and by the radicals to systemic failings; the urban environment was cited as a "cause" only infrequently.[39] Likewise, since the Russian city did not experience the sharp, highly visible social and economic polarization that characterized nineteenth century New York and London, the Russian city was probably better integrated structurally than its Western counterparts.[40]

Conceptually and practically the legacy passed on to the Soviet regime in October 1917 thus proved to be complex. On the debit side of the balance sheet, the combination of an inadequate tax base and the systematic starving of municipal services in favor of overriding national needs gave rise to an incipient urban crisis. This was further fueled by the crushing obligations Russian cities undertook during the war years and by inflation. By 1917, Russian urban expenditures lagged behind those of every other European power, regardless of size or international importance.[41] Out-migration from the cities and a breakdown in the national food distribution network during the years of civil war exacerbated conditions further, and the crisis atmosphere in Soviet cities persisted until well into the 1920s.[42]

In addition, the predominantly peasant character of Russia's cities and the genuine rootlessness of their still transient labor force made these urban centers a questionable power base for any development strategy predicated on industrialization. These same conditions inhibited the emergence of the kind of proletarian power base that the stabilization of Bolshevik rule demanded. Against such a backdrop it is hardly surprising that the new rulers failed to reverse a centuries-old tradition that minimized ruling the city in the interests of its inhabitants, a tradition that conceptualized urban organization as chiefly a product of complex, vertically ordered linkages. In administrative terms, tsarist practice since the eighteenth century had had the effect of splitting cities into competing hierarchies of functions. Whether intentional or not, the net effect was to "divide and rule" and, simultaneously, to push power continually upward toward the center. Such practices were hardly original to the system of government that Stalin was to institute in the late 1920s.[43]

On the credit side of the ledger, the new Bolshevik rulers also inherited a generally positive orientation toward urban life and city settlements from their tsarist predecessors. Russia's failure to develop real industrial cities, with all of their attendant problems, probably served to reinforce certain prourban strains that were also present in Marxist ideology. With respect to its ability to provide a reasonably clear ground for the emergence of a new urban policy, Russia's backwardness may have proven a blessing in disguise. In its most negative aspects, Marx's Manchester metaphor (which depicted the city as the source of the proletariat's degradation as well as liberation) simply did not apply to Russia. Even as a warning, it failed to offset a long tradition of official thinking, shared by much of the revolutionary intelligentsia that, on balance, regarded the city in a favorable light. In short, Marxist-Leninist ideologues inherited a cognitive and cultural tradition that regarded the city as a positive force for national development. The way thus seemed clear for a coherent, ideologically justifiable urban policy to emerge.

It is all the more striking, therefore, that some 60 years of Soviet power have failed to provide conclusive evidence of any distinctly Soviet Marxist approach to urban development or management. Nevertheless, Soviet urban practitioners still maintain that "a society's approach to urban planning [is] determined by both the ideology and the social system of that society," as if to suggest that a distinctly Marxist-Leninist scheme for urban development exists.[44] Western specialists reply with the counterassertion that Marxist-Leninist ideology "is probably of less practical value today in formulating and implementing substantive policies . . . than ever before."[45] Insofar as any net assessment of ideology's influence involves certain assumptions about human behavior and motivations, evidence of any real impact of Marxism-Leninism on Soviet choices becomes extraordinarily difficult to establish.[46]

The image of the city that Marxist doctrine provides points in a number of directions simultaneously, not all of them mutually compatible.[47] On one side, there stands the image of the city as a revolutionary center, as a bastion of proletarian defense against the forces of the reactionary bourgeoisie with their peasant armies (the Paris Commune of *The Eighteenth Brumaire of Louis Bonaparte*). On the other, there emerges a picture of the city as a source of oppression, alienation, and degradation for the proletariat—the brutality and poverty that Engels describes in *The Condition of the Working Class* and *The Housing Question*.

Neither Marx nor Engels ever made it clear whether urban life was a distinctive but historically transient feature of the presocialist era. Alternately, was there a "socialist city" and "communist city" that would emerge over time and that would embody distinctively new and revolutionary forms of social and economic organization?[48] Consequently, Bolshevik city planners and officials lacked a single, clear-cut model of urban organization to provide them with a set of guidelines and choices for urban reorganization in the 1920s. Marxist doctrine remained clear on only one underlying point: industrialization represented a progressive trend in world historical development and the industrial milieu, of necessity, had to be urban.[49] Only modern industrial cities could sustain social and economic progress and guarantee political revolution.[50]

It is far less evident, however, exactly what would constitute the ideal socialist city. Was the future development of Russian socialism to resemble the urban agglomeration described by Fritz Lang's metropolis, the garden city of Howard, or the linear city proposed by Miliutin? Each "solution" concealed a basic ambiguity, stemming from the opposing pro- and antiurban thrusts of Marxist thought. From one perspective, limiting the size of cities—a canon of Soviet planning for half a century—might seem to point in the direction of a positive, urban orientation. From another, however, such a position may have concealed a latent ruralism, deriving from Marx's enthusiasm for the hunter-fisherman-poet as the prototype of nonalienated man. If the call of the *Manifesto* for an end to the distinction between city and country means the industrialization of rural areas, as Soviet textbooks maintain, are the corollaries of such a postulate pro- or antiurban (deconcentration of city populations, decentralization of productive capacity, spatial and density limits for urban development)?[51]

The opposing thrusts of a Marxist formulation are evident even if we accept the claim that current Soviet planning practice is in some way uniquely Marxist. For example, satellite cities and suburban zones, both characteristic of Soviet planning, can either be viewed as policy outcomes aimed at the extension of high density urban agglomerations *or* as an attempt to inject a distinctly rural atmosphere into the nation's urban future. How is all this to be reconciled with yet another strain in Marxism, that is, praise for the efficiencies of scale provided by large factories and large political and economic units? In terms of planning, Marxist ideology left the Bolshevik regime clear on another major point: a competitive market system, as one of the negative aspects of bourgeois economic development, could not be used to either value or allocate the urban land fund.[52] But as no alternative mechanism was specified, bureaucratic actors in the political marketplace have provided an answer by default.

Soviet Marxism, in short, serves chiefly to limit the debate about urban futures in the USSR. While it provides little structure or clarification for different and opposing arguments, it does set the agenda for discussions of urban policy in a general kind of way (the "other face" of power).[53] It has not, however, provided concrete guidelines for specific policy choices.

It is therefore hardly surprising that Soviet views of the city that emerged after 1917 combined diffuse elements of the Marxist scenario with specifics drawn largely from the legacy of prerevolutionary Russia. A review of the early planning debates and proposals reveals a consensus only with respect to the city's social, economic, and political importance. The creation of a socialist state and economy required a new kind of city, while the "city-as-progress" image supported arguments on behalf of measures to resettle an agrarian population in middle-sized towns.[54]   Early Soviet views echoed the rationalist and centrist thrust that had long been a part of the Russian picture: cities should be deliberately created, engineered, built, organized, funded, shaped, and controlled from the top down. And all this was to be accomplished against the limits imposed by national needs and the superior "rationality" exercised by a central leadership. Early Soviet city planning displayed this same mechanistic bias, with strong roots extending back to the revivalist and neoclassical planning movements of fin-de-siecle Russia.[55]

Simultaneously, the holistic view of the urban environment, which stressed its social and economic as well as physical attributes, represented something new to the Russian setting. Indeed, until the advent of rapid urbanization (1929), the separation of urban planning from other types (1933), and the announcement that all existing Soviet cities were automatically "socialist" by virtue of being Soviet (1931), the city remained a laboratory, an environment in which various ways to deal with the problems of building socialism were to be tested.[56] Marxism thus can be said to have contributed substantially to a more holistic approach to urban problems and to an increased recognition of the national importance of urbanization and urban development.

The advent of Stalinism, however, meant that comprehensive urban planning in practice took a backseat to planned economic development and forced industrialization. Increased preoccupation with political control and the consolidation of power meant that order, uniformity, and physical demonstrations of the "greatness of socialism" through massive investments in elaborate public buildings became the order of the day. Earlier views of cities as administrative and political centers for control once again moved to the fore.[57]

From the 1930s on, Soviet views of the city reached beyond a Marxist orientation in their expressed antipathy to bigness and sprawling metropolises. In part, such conditions are treated ideologically as the source of inhumane conditions existing in the major cities of the capitalist world.[58] Limiting urban growth is currently touted as a major objective of Soviet city planning, one which is to be implemented by locating new industry only in small (under 50,000 population) or medium-sized (up to 100,000 population) cities.[59] Recently, some Soviet urbanists have shown signs of a partial volte-face in this regard. M. L. Strogina, a sociologist, welcomes the absorption of nonurban areas into agglomerations and the emergence of functionally specific zones as valuable tools for creating what she terms "a hidden urban population." In this way, she sees an urban agglomeration as providing the means for "the intensive injection of an urban-industrial culture into the countryside."[60] This position has acquired support among some Soviet geographers who regard the large city as the appropriate core for such an agglomeration.[61] At the same time, demographers such as Viktor Perevedentsev criticize certain earlier assumptions regarding optimal city size.[62]

Soviet perspectives on the city also have gone beyond Marxism in recognizing that "community" must be deliberately fostered in the city rather than left to emerge automatically. The reduction of feelings of group separateness and the provision of access equity has been equated with the emergence of homogeneity among internally heterogeneous microdistricts, the *mikroraiony* of Soviet planning.[63] By delimiting and constructing "self-contained units with local service areas based on an estimated norm of service personnel per thousand population," Soviet planners have sought urban uniformity and equality within a high density environment. Integration of services within a residential area promotes standardization and paves the way for a "socialist" city center with political and administrative rather than economic functions.[64] This conception has its genesis not in any distinctly Marxist rejection of the capitalist business district. Rather, it flows directly from the idea of the administrative city that arose in Russia with the reforms of Peter the Great and from the city of reason of the eighteenth century.

In broad perspective, it thus appears that the role played by Marxist doctrine in shaping the management environment of the Soviet urban decision maker has been far less significant than one might intuitively suppose. This conclusion does not deny that in particular policy areas Marxist thinking may play a role in delimiting a range of alternative courses of action. Rather, it supports the proposition that the lessons of historical experience, traditional Russian outlooks, and ad hoc theoretical accretions exercise considerably greater influence. Kaganovich's ex cathedra pronouncement of 1931—"a socialist city is a city in the Soviet Union"—provides one among many corroborations for the minimal influence of any structured ideological perspectives.[65] To counter, as some analysts have done, that a model for a "socialist city" can be defined by centrally planned allocations, subordination in a bureaucratic state structure, the abolition of private property in land, and a state monopoly on urban services is to confuse descriptors of Soviet outcomes with a model derived from ideologically sacrosanct Marxist goals.[66]

In the Soviet Union today, those strains of Marxist thought that describe the city as "the chief social-spatial forum for the organization of society," and "the center of all economic, social, political, and cultural development" have prevailed.[67] Very much in contrast to a pronounced preference for rural and small-town life in the United States, it is the city in the USSR that is hailed as the optimum setting for promoting the desired social values of family, community, sense of place, and political participation.[68] The city remains an embodiment of the rational (and probable) future for the "new Soviet man," the framework for the spread of reason to every sphere of life via the mechanism of planning.[69] Better urban planning, in conjunction with restrictions on urban growth, is regarded as the solution to urban problems.[70] Most important, the elimination of urban problems is widely regarded as among the main achievements of Soviet society.

How professionals and decision makers view the city describes only part of the management environment. The urban myth that has captured the imagination of the majority of the Soviet population is most dramatically conveyed by the way in which this population "votes with its feet." In this case, the rapid movement of a large proportion of the rural population into the cities suggests that to the popular mind as to the official mind, urban life represents a desirable future. The picture drawn by demographic data bears out this conclusion.

A DEMOGRAPHIC PERSPECTIVE

Urbanization has transformed Soviet society. Consequently, the relatively recent, rapid, and large-scale population shift has also altered the management environment in important ways, especially since the responsibility for meeting the daily needs of an increasingly large proportion of the population falls on the shoulders of urban managers (see Table 1 and Figure 2). The magnitude of this transformation becomes apparent from a profile of Soviet urbanization, for example, the changes in the urban population relative to the total population. The extraordinary pace of such change has been well documented by geographers and demographers. Indeed, since the turn of the century, Soviet urbanization has been far more rapid than the global average.[71] According to the 1970 Soviet census, already 56 of every 100 Soviet citizens were living in cities and towns. By 1975, natural increase and in-migration had increased their numbers to 153 million (Table 1).

As the urban population has come to dominate the society, the number of cities has increased.* There were 2,029 city soviets listed in 1977, compared with 2,006 in 1975 and 1,910 in 1969.[72] Today, well over half of all Soviet cities are young ones (the "new towns"), created since 1917.[73] The totals include many different types of cities, which may be distinguished by function, size, density, complexity, age, socioeconomic structure, and other variables. In collecting data for the 1970 census, Soviet statistical agencies employed size and functional criteria; a settlement with a primarily nonagricultural work force and a few thousand inhabitants was classified as a city.[74] Consequently, the label

---

*The term "urban" is employed in this study to reflect size, complexity, and functional criteria. "City" is used more narrowly to designate formal administrative units with a city soviet or council. The two are not necessarily coterminous.

TABLE 1

Soviet Urbanization and Urban Growth

City Size (population)	Number of Cities			Population (millions)			As Percent of Urban Population	
	1959	1970	1975	1959	1970	1975	1959	1970
Over 1 million	25 }	33 }	39 }	10.5	19.1	44.6 }	10.4	14.0
500,000-999,999				13.7	18.2		13.6	13.4
100,000-499,999	123	188	201	24.4	38.3	43.1	24.2	28.2
50,000-99,999	156	189	222	11.0	13.0	15.4	25.1 }	20.3 }
20,000-49,999	444	556	581	14.1	17.3	18.1		
To 19,999	931	969	970	9.3	10.4	10.6	9.2	7.6
Urban-type settlements	2,940	3,570	3,739	17.0	19.7	21.3	17.5	14.5
Total	4,619	5,505	5,752	100.0	136.0	153.1	100.0	98.0

Sources: Tsentr nauchno-tekhnicheskoi informatsii po grazhdanskomu stroitel'stvu i arkhitekture, *Gradostroitel'stvo SSSR (obzor)* (Moscow: TsNTI po grazhdanskomu stroitel'stvu i arkhitekture, 1976), p. 5; and Kiev NIIP gradostroitel'stva, *Sotsial'nye osnovy razvitiia gorodov (sotsial'nye problemy rasseleniia)* (Moscow: Stroiizdat, 1975), p. 20.

FIGURE 2

Soviet Cities at the Censuses, 1959 and 1970

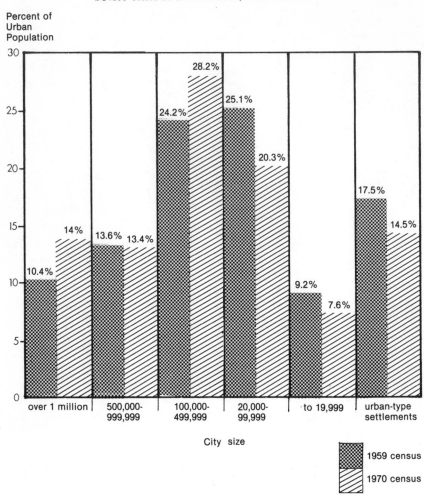

City size

Sources: Tsentr nauchno-tekhnicheskoi informatsii po grazhdanskomu stroitel'stvu i arkhitekture, *Gradostroitel'stvo SSSR* (obzor) (Moscow: TsNTI po grazhdanskomu stroitel'-stvu i arkhitekture, 1976), p. 5; and Kiev NIIP gradostroitel'stva, *Sotsial'nye osnovy razvitiia gorodov (sotsial'nye problemy rasseleniia)* (Moscow: Stroiizdat, 1975), p. 20.

"city" embraces a diverse group of communities, ranging from "great cities" (with a million or more inhabitants, complex economies, and complicated administrative structures) to small, economically insignificant towns.

To differentiate Soviet cities by criteria other than size, it is important to note subgroups of administrative types. Administrative rank (subordination) and administrative role (province capital, regional capital) in turn incorporate certain unspecified economic and political variables. Rank corresponds only imperfectly to a pure size criterion. For example, both Sverdlovsk and Minsk contain approximately the same overall population, but they occupy different ranks in the USSR's administrative hierarchy. Sverdlovsk operates under province control, while the authorities in Minsk report directly to republic-level superiors. Unfortunately, Soviet data does not provide information on density criteria or other information that would correspond to the kinds of distinctions the U.S. SMSA definition employs.*

Urban growth also shapes the management work environment inasmuch as urban managers have to cope with absolute increases in the urban population. In his landmark study, Chauncy Harris concludes that urban growth in the Soviet Union proceeded from 1926 to 1939 at an average annual rate of 6.5 percent, a rate of increase unequaled in either the earlier history of Russia, later periods in the Soviet Union, or in the history of other countries before World War II.[75] As much as sheer numbers, spatial concentration has characterized Soviet urban growth (and has distinguished it from the U.S. experience). In the USSR today, large cities of 100,000 inhabitants or more account for over one-half the urban population and almost one-third of the total population (Table 1 and Figure 2). By 1975, 44.6 million individuals were living in cities of 500,000 or more. These represented 29.1 percent of the urban population, compared to 24 percent in 1959 (Figure 2). Nor does such growth show any signs of abating. Large Soviet cities continue to grow more rapidly than smaller ones; the largest proportional increase between the last two censuses (182 percent, 1959-70) occurred in cities of over one million population.[76] These trends lend credibility to Soviet claims that the rate of urban growth rises in proportion to absolute increases in the size of the population base. According to one estimate, by January 1974, 15.9 percent of the urban population (or 9.5 percent of the total) resided in 11 of the great cities of the USSR.[77] This figure shows a pronounced increase over the proportion living in great cities in 1959. According to this estimate, 30 cities will have populations of 1 million or more by the end of this century.

Two republics occupy the leading positions in rates of urbanization and urban growth, a fact that underscores the importance of administrative relationships for classifying Soviet cities. According to Table 2, the RSFSR (Russian Republic) and the Ukraine account for 68 percent of all Soviet cities and 78 percent of the urban population. These republics contain 9 of a total of 13 cities

---

*Standard metropolitan statistical area of the U.S. Office of Management and Budget.

TABLE 2

Urban Patterns in the Soviet Union

	USSR	RSFSR	Ukraine
Urban population (millions)	149,589	88,231	28,195
As percent of urban population	100	59	19
As percent of republic population	n.a.	56	55
Number of cities	1,999	984	392
With 1 million or more inhabitants	13	6	3
At or above province subordination	872	524	117
Number of urban districts	583	323	109

n.a. = not available.

Sources: SSSR, administrativno-territorial'noe delenie soiuzhykh respublik (Moscow: (Izvestiia, 1974); and Viktor Perevedentsev, "Goroda-millionery," *Literaturnaia gazeta* 18 (April 30, 1975): 10.

with populations of 1 million or more, and they will claim 15 of the 19 such cities that demographers project for 1980. Their cities include 80 percent of all Soviet urban districts (*gorodskie raiony*), indicating the complex administrative structures of these cities. In the RSFSR, the proportion of the population living in cities of 100,000 inhabitants or more increased from 51 to 59 percent between 1959 and 1970, while the proportion of those living in small and medium-sized cities dropped from 33 to 28 percent.[78] In short, the patterns of urban growth and spatial concentration for these dominant republics mirror national patterns.

It is evident from the population statistics that the urban management environment, in addition to being a "big city" environment, is also a new environment. In 1926, there were only 31 cities with populations of 100,000 or more in the fledgling Soviet state.[79] By 1959, there were already 148 such cities, while 240 appeared on the map by 1975 (Table 1). Therefore, in the USSR, the large city represents a new mode of human organization and a relatively recent kind of administrative arrangement.

Urban residents in the USSR are themselves relative newcomers to urban life. Each year, natural increase and in-migration add millions of individuals to the Soviet urban population. Average annual in-migration accounts for 3 million new urban residents, a net increase of 1.5 million.[80] Such statistics suggest that most adults living in Soviet cities today were probably born in rural areas. But this has not prevented the emergence of social relationships that are diverse, competitive, and functionally oriented; in the contemporary Soviet city, social status is derived from occupation and education rather than from history or genealogy. Thus, Soviet cities resemble neither large "urban villages" nor the peasant cities described in this chapter. Having been transformed themselves, the new urban dwellers of the USSR in turn are transforming Soviet society.[81]

One of the most important of these changes has occurred in an occupational structure that evolves to reflect growth in urban-related functions. In the larger cities, the proportion of the population employed in "nonproductive" occupations has been increasing, with local government, social services, scientific research, education, communications, entertainment, and the arts showing relative gains.[82] Such national patterns are repeated in individual cities and republics. In the Ukraine the greatest relative increase has occurred in the service and trade sectors, with science, education, and health showing the second largest relative increases. As this republic has become increasingly urbanized, such changes have occurred primarily at the expense of the agricultural work force, which declined from 1960 to 1971 from almost half to less than one-third of the republic's total.[83] All the same, large Soviet cities confront an endemic labor shortage that strains the cities' ability to provide various services to a changing labor force by directly inflating service demands and by affecting labor recruitment and turnover in city agencies.

The changes described by the seemingly innocuous term "urbanization" carry in their wake a host of management ramifications. Urban managers must grapple with the effects of changes in such areas as age structure, household composition, and education levels. Among other things, urbanization and urban growth in the USSR have meant an increase in inhabitants' leisure time, which (as Soviet time-budget research suggests), in turn, stimulates demand for city-run services (recreational, sports, and entertainment facilities, plus inter- and intra-city transport).[84] The number of passengers carried by already overloaded transport systems continues to grow.[85] From all perspectives, then, the physical redistribution of the Soviet population into cities and the concomitant social transformations have changed the urban management environment.

Ultimately, it is the objective situation that provides the more influential elements affecting the choices open to the Soviet urban manager. Compared to these "objective" elements, "subjective" conceptions such as beliefs about the city probably play a secondary role—and Marxist ideology, except in its justificatory functions, an altogether insignificant one. The choices of the urban manager are also shaped by structural and organizational determinants of authority and power in the urban setting as well as by the leadership role and catalytic functions of the Communist party. It is to these aspects of the management environment that we now turn.

NOTES

1. John C. Bollens and Henry J. Schmandt, *The Metropolis: Its People, Politics and Economic Life*, 2d ed. (New York: Harper & Row, 1970), pp. 40-46; J. J. Palen, *The Urban World* (New York: McGraw-Hill, 1975), pp. 3-38; Louis Wirth, "Urbanism as a Way of Life," *American Journal of Sociology* 44 (July 1938): 1-24; Scott Greer, *The Emerging City: Myth and Reality* (New York: Free Press of Glencoe, 1962), pp. 677-706; Albert H. Cousins and Hans Bagpaul, eds., *Urban Man and Society: A Reader in Urban Sociology* (New York: Alfred A. Knopf, 1970), pp. 129-35. On the "city as system," see Robert L. Lineberry and Ira Sharkansky, *Urban Politics and Public Policy* (New York: Harper & Row, 1971), pp. 4-15. For a critique of this approach, see Douglas Yates, *The Ungovernable City: The Politics of Urban Problems and Policy Making* (Cambridge, Mass.: MIT Press, 1977), pp. 12-16.

2. Although many studies of local politics and policies have built in environmental consideration by using "background variables" to explain policy outputs, those studies have several shortcomings. First of all, they define environment very narrowly: social structure, level of economic development, interparty competition among the U.S. states. Demand patterns and decisional systems are assigned little importance and no attention is paid to values of decision makers as affecting policy choices. See, for example, Thomas R. Dye, "Executive Power and Public Policy in the States," *Western Political Quarterly* 22 (December 1969): 926-39; Richard Hofferbert, "Socio-Economic Dimensions of the American States, 1860-1960," *Midwest Journal of Political Science* 12 (August 1968): 401-18; Robert Salisbury, "The Analysis of Public Policy: A Search for Theories and Roles," in *Political Science and Public Policy*, ed. Austin Ranney (Chicago: Markham, 1968), pp. 151-78. The authors wish to thank Valerie Parker, Boston University, for bringing these references to their attention. The most notable exception to the tendency to exclude cultural factors remains Lewis Mumford's *The City in History* (New York: Harcourt, Brace and World, 1961); and his *The Culture of Cities* (New York: Harcourt, Brace & Co., 1938).

3. "The Urban Crisis," in Cousins and Nagpaul, op. cit., pp. 53-82; "The Social Consequences of Urban Life: Life Styles," in *Urbanism, Urbanization and Change*, 2d ed., ed. Paul Meadows and Ephriam H. Mizruchi (Reading, Mass.: Addison-Wesley, 1969), pp. 222-95; Raan Weitz, ed., *Urbanization and the Developing Countries: Report on the Sixth Rehovot Conference* (New York: Praeger, 1973), pp. 17-65; Bollens and Schmandt, op. cit., pp. 47-99. On problems of adaptation to city life in the USSR, see Evelina Karlovna Vasil'eva, *The Young People of Leningrad; School and Work Options and Attitudes*, trans. Arlo Schultz and Andrew J. Smith (White Plains, N.Y.: International Arts and Sciences Press, 1976), pp. 152-69. Originally published as *Sotsial' no-professional'nii uroven' gorodskoi molodezhi* (Leningrad: Leningrad University Press, 1973).

4. Robert Daland, "Comparative Perspectives on Urban Systems," in *Comparative Urban Research*, ed. Robert Daland (Beverly Hills, Calif.: Sage, 1969), pp. 24-26, 29, 51-53. Conversely, the literature stressing the importance of "political culture" in political systems fails to deal with urban politics and policies. See, for example, Edgar Morin, *The Red and the White: Report from a French Village*, trans. A. M. Sheridan-Smith (New York: Random House, 1970); and Richard Rose, *Politics in England: An Interpretation* (Boston: Little, Brown and Co., 1964). For national bias in the political culture literature, see the discussion of the approach in James A. Bill and Robert L. Hardgrave, Jr., *Comparative Politics: The Quest for Theory* (Columbus, Ohio: Charles E. Merrill, 1973), pp. 85-116.

5. Andrew Lees and Lynn Lees, eds., *The Urbanization of European Society in the Nineteenth Century* (Lexington, Mass.: D. C. Heath, 1976), pp. 47-116; B. I. Coleman, ed., *The Idea of the City in Nineteenth Century Britain* (London: Routledge and Kegan Paul, 1973); Henri Pirenne, *Medieval Cities: Their Origins and the Revival of Medieval Trade*

(Princeton, N.J.: Princeton University Press, 1969); Gideon Sjoberg, *The Preindustrial City: Past and Present* (New York: Free Press of Glencoe, 1960), pp. 323-32.

6. See, for example, Robert E. Agger, Davie Goldrich, and Bert E. Swanson, *The Rulers and the Ruled: Political Power and Impotence in American Communities* (New York: Wiley, 1964), pp. 18-32. An exception to this orientation is the study by Robert Alford and Harry Scoble, *Bureaucracy and Participation in Four Wisconsin Cities* (Chicago: Rand McNally, 1969), esp. pp. 5-10, 138-54, 159-73, 181-82. See also Lawrence B. Mohr, "Determinants of Innovation in Organization," *American Political Science Review* 69 (March 1969): 111-26; and the City Council Research Project findings as partially reported in Robert Eyestone and Heinz Eulau, "City Councils and Policy Outcomes: Developmental Profiles," in *City Politics and Public Policy*, ed. James Q. Wilson (New York: Wiley, 1968), pp. 37-65.

7. Daland, op. cit., p. 42; Martin Plax, "The Use and Abuse of Political Ethos for the Study of Urban Politics," *Urban Affairs Quarterly* 11 (March 1976): 375-86.

8. Robert Alford, "Explanatory Variables in the Study of Urban Politics," in Daland, op. cit., p. 273.

9. Thomas Stanley Fedor, *Pattern of Urban Growth in the Russian Empire during the Nineteenth Century* (Chicago: University of Chicago, Department of Geography, 1975), p. 3.

10. Ibid., pp. 3-4, 6.

11. J. M. Hittle, "The City in Muscovite and Early Imperial Russia" (Ph.D. diss., Harvard University, 1969), pp. 62-70, 82-83; Gilbert Rozman, *Urban Networks in Russia, 1750-1800 and Premodern Periodicization* (Princeton, N.J.: Princeton University Press, 1976), p. 72.

12. Mumford, *City in History*, op. cit., pp. 105, 347.

13. Hittle, op. cit., pp. 17-18, 25-26.

14. Ibid., pp. 41, 46-47.

15. Lawrence Langer, "The Medieval Russian Town," in *The City in Russian History*, ed. Michael Hamm (Lexington: University of Kentucky Press, 1976), pp. 11-31; David Miller, "State and Society in Seventeenth Century Muscovy," in Hamm, op. cit., pp. 44-45, 47-48.

16. Ibid., pp. 49-50.

17. Ibid., pp. 121-22.

18. Fedor, op. cit., p. 7. According to Rozman, op. cit., pp. 247, 254, 272, both Russia and Japan in the premodern period had 90 percent of their urban population in cities with administrative functions.

19. Fedor, op. cit., p. 10.

20. The discussion that follows draws on Hittle, op. cit., pp. 90-103.

21. J. M. Hittle, "The Service City in the Eighteenth Century," in Hamm, op. cit., p. 59; Hittle, "The City in Russia," op. cit., pp. 91-94, 113, 124-25.

22. Ibid., pp. 118-19.

23. Ibid., pp. 133-34, 138. On the "estate principle," in the pre-Revolutionary Russian state, see G. B. Slozberg, *Dorevoliutsionnyi stroi Rossii* (Paris: Imprimateur Pascal, 1933); N. N. Semenov, *Samoderzhavie kak gosudarstvennyi stroi* (St. Petersburg: n.p., 1905), pp. 46-47; M. Pokrovskii, "Vneklassovaia teoriia razvitiia russkogo samoderzhaviia," *Vestnik sotsialisticheskoi akademii*, no. 1 (November 1922), pp. 59-63.

24. For a different interpretation, see Rozman, op. cit., pp. 130-58, 276-83. Rozman fails to recognize, however, that the growth of an urban network in a culturally operative sense continually faced strong institutional obstacles to which the central government lent the full weight of its authority and resources. With the promulgation of the Charter of the Nobility in 1785, the tsarist autocracy decisively reaffirmed its preference for estate and

rural interests over urban ones. Such a rural bias persisted until 1917. See Hittle, "The City in Russia," op. cit., pp. 144-45, 155-56; Stephen S. Sternheimer, "Administration and Political Development: An Inquriy into the Tsarist and Soviet Experiences" (Ph.D. diss., University of Chicago, 1974), chap. 2.

25. Andrei Belyi, *St. Petersburg* (New York: Grove Press, 1969). This translated into the primacy accorded purely physical arrangements and a belief in the linkage between physical structure and human behavior. Such ideas reflected in Baroque as well as modern Soviet planning concepts. See S. Frederick Starr, "The Revival and Schism of Urban Planning in Twentieth Century Russia," in Hamm, op. cit., pp. 222-42.

26. Frederick W. Skinner, "Trends in Building Practices: The Building of Odessa, 1794-1917," in Hamm, op. cit., pp. 141, 152.

27. Mumford, *City in History*, op. cit., pp. 452-54. For Russian views, see George Fischer, *Russian Liberalism* (Cambridge, Mass.: Harvard University Press, 1958); N. Berdiavev, *Leontiev*, trans. George Reavy (Orono, Me.: Academic International Press, 1968); Arthur Mendel, *Dilemmas of Progress in Tsarist Russia* (Cambridge, Mass.: Harvard University Press, 1961).

28. Walter Hanchett, "Tsarist Statutory Regulation of Municipal Government in the Nineteenth Century," in Hamm, op. cit., p. 91.

29. Ibid., pp. 102-3, 106-7.

30. Sternheimer, op. cit., pp 142-202.

31. On the Slavophile-Westernizer controversy, see Andrzej Walicki, *The Slavophile Controversy. A History of Conservative Utopia in Nineteenth Century Russian Thought* (Oxford: Clarendon Press, 1975). See also Alexander Pushkin, *The Poems and Prose and Plays by A. Pushkin*, trans. Adan Yarmolinsky (New York: Modern Library, 1936); A. Herzen, *From the Other Shore and the Russian People and Socialism*, trans. M. Budberg and R. Wollheim (London: Weidenfeld and Nicolson, 1956); Martin Malia, *Alexander Herzen and the Birth of Russian Socialism* (Cambridge, Mass.: Harvard University Press, 1961); Peter Lavrov, *Historical Letters*, trans. James Scanlon (Berkeley: University of California Press, 1967); N. Chernyshevsky, *What Is to Be Done: Tales about New People*, trans. Benjamin R. Trucker (New York: Vintage Books, 1961); Norman G. Periera, *The Thought and Teachings of N. G. Chernyshevsky* (The Hague: Mouton, 1975).

32. Hittle, "The City in Russia," pp. 121-23; Nicolas Riasnovsky, *Russia and the West in the Teachings of the Slavophiles* (Cambridge, Mass.: Harvard University Press, 1952).

33. The ideal resembled neither the participatory commune of contemporary anarchist thought nor the solitary engaged urban village described by Herbert Gans. See Paul Goodman, "People or Personnel," in *Participatory Democracy*, ed. Terence Cook and Patrick Morgan (San Francisco: Canfield Press, 1971), pp. 49-56; Herbert Gans, *The Urban Villagers: Group and Class in the Life of Italian-Americans* (New York: Free Press of Glencoe, 1962).

34. Nicolai Gogol, *Tales of Good and Evil*, trans. Rosa Portnova (London: Sylvan Press, 1945); Adele Lindenmeyr, "Raskolnikov's City and the Napoleonic Plan," *Slavic Review* 35 (March 1976): 37-47.

35. Richard H. Rowland, "Urban In-Migration," in Hamm, op. cit., pp. 116-17.

36. Fedor, op. cit., p. 11; Roger L. Thiede, "Industry and Urbanization in New Russia from 1860 to 1910," in Hamm, op. cit., p. 126.

37. Fedor, op. cit., pp. 130-31 (Figure 2), 139.

38. In 1897, textile workers accounted for 25 percent of the population engaged in manufacturing and industry. But 67 percent of this fraction lived and worked in rural areas rather than cities. As of 1897, only 10 percent of all Russian cities had over 40 percent of their urban population engaged in trade, manufacturing, or industry. Ibid., p. 143.

39. For a more extensive discussion of the positive as well as negative aspects of Russia's peasant cities as they influenced official thinking regarding social welfare policy and ur-

ban policy generally, see Joseph C. Bradley, Jr., "Muzhik and Muscovite: Peasants in Late Nineteenth Century Urban Russia" (Ph.D. diss., Harvard University, 1977), pp. 1-2, 5, 181-83, 194, 207, 211-12, 238-42.

40. Ibid., pp. 243, 255-57, 276-79. For a contrary assessment of the political impact of peasant cities in Russia before 1917, see Leopold Haimson, "The Problem of Social Sta-bility in Urban Russia, 1905-1917 (Part One)," *Slavic Review* 23 (December 1964): 619-42; Leopold Haimson, "The Problem of Social Stability in Urban Russia, 1905-1917 (Part Two)," *Slavic Review* 24 (March 1965): 1-22.

41. Michael Hamm, "The Breakdown of Urban Modernization," in Hamm, op. cit., pp. 185-86, 196-98.

42. Ibid., pp. 183-84.

43. Hittle, "The City in Russia," pp. 339, 341, 343, 348.

44. Mikhail Vassil'evich Posokhin, *Cities to Live in* (Moscow: Novosti Press, 1974), pp. 7, 15.

45. Eric P. Hoffmann, "Soviet Information Processing: Recent Theory and Experi-ence," *Soviet Union* 2, pt. 1 (1975): 47.

46. Alfred E. Meyer, "The Functions of Ideology in the Soviet Political System," *So-viet Studies* 17 (January 1966): 273-85; Peter Reddaway, "Aspects of Ideological Belief in the Soviet Union," *Soviet Studies* 17 (April 1966): 473-83; and David Joravsky, "Soviet Ideology," *Soviet Studies* 18 (July 1966): 2-18.

47. One result was the conflicting pro- and antiurban strains that ran through the de-bate about urban development during the 1920s in the USSR. In some respects this debate still continues. For example, see Alexei Gutnow et al., *The Ideal Communist City*, trans. Renee Neu Watkins (New York: George Braziller, 1968), preface; and Robert J. Osborn, *So-viet Social Policies: Welfare, Equality, and Community* (Homewood, Ill.: Dorsey Press, 1970), chap. 1.

48. David Harvey, *Social Justice and the City* (London: Edward Arnold, 1973), p. 306; and Karl Joseph Kansky, *Urbanization under Socialism; The Case of Czechoslovakia* (New York: Praeger, 1976), pp. 274-75.

49. Recognizing the problematic role of the city in communist doctrine, John Lewis argues that Mao's formulation is not antiurban but rather redresses the balance between the city and the countryside; Lewis concludes that the aim of the Chinese leadership at the be-ginning of the 1970s was the urbanization of the countryside. John Wilson Lewis, "Intro-duction: Order and Modernization in the Chinese City," in *The City in Communist China*, ed. John Wilson Lewis (Stanford, Calif.: Stanford University Press, 1971), pp. 1-26. See also Karl Marx, *Das Kapital*, vol. 1, sec. 10, pt. 4.

50. See Bernard M. Frolic, "Soviet Cities in Transition," unpublished manuscript, chap. 1.

51. G. Kh. Shakhnazarov et al., *Social Science: A Textbook for Soviet Secondary Schools* (Washington, D.C.: Department of Commerce, JPRS, January 1968), p. 226. First published as *Obshchestvovedenie* (Moscow: Gospolitizdat, 1963).

52. Osborn, op. cit., chap. 1; and Harvey, op. cit., chap. 5.

53. Peter Bachrach and Morton S. Baratz, "The Two Faces of Power," in *The Bias of Pluralism*, ed. William E. Connolly (New York: Atherton Press, 1969), pp. 51-66.

54. Milka Bliznakov, "Urban Planning in the USSR: Integrative Theories," in Hamm, op. cit., p. 243.

55. Starr, op. cit., pp. 236-40.

56. Bliznakov, op. cit., pp. 243-52.

57. William Blackwell, "Modernization and Urbanization in Russia: A Comparative View," in Hamm, op. cit., pp. 321, 323-24.

58. Jack Fisher, "Urban Planning in the Soviet Union and Eastern Europe," in *Tam-ing Megalopolis*, 2 vols., ed. H. Wentworth Eldredge (Garden City, N.Y.: Anchor and Co., 1967), 2:1080-81. See also Chapter 5 of this study.

59. Robert G. Jensen, "Urban Environments in the United States and the Soviet Union," in *Urbanization and Counterurbanization*, ed. Brian Berry (Beverly Hills: Sage, 1976), pp. 34-35. See also Chapter 4 of this study.

60. M. L. Strogina, "Problemy razvitiia bol'shikh gorodov i agglomeratsii," *Sotsial'noe issledovanie* 4 (1970): 50.

61. Ibid., pp. 58, 60; Jensen, op. cit., pp. 36-37.

62. Ibid., p. 36. For Soviet views on the relative efficiency of large cities, see Jeff Chin, *Manipulating Soviet Population Resources* (London: Macmillan, 1977), pp. 48-50, and Chapter 4 of this study. Perevedentsev remains the most prominent supporter of the "larger is better" position.

63. Jensen, op. cit., pp. 38-39; Fisher, op. cit., pp. 1081-82, 1096; B. M. Frolic, "The Soviet City," *Town Planning Review* 34 (January 1964): 300-2. Although the *mikroraion* concept in planning is generally assumed to have passed out of fashion in the USSR today, it has reappeared, thinly camouflaged, as urban "nuclear units of settlement (NUS)." Within a region, each NUS has a standard social and spatial structure and is designed to fill all of the needs of its inhabitants. The web-like network of NUS would also have a center designed to fulfill primarily administrative, research, and control functions. See Gutnov et al., op. cit., pp. 105-10.

64. Jensen, op. cit., pp. 34-35.

65. Bliznakov, op. cit., p. 252.

66. Phrased somewhat differently, the ideological contribution becomes a purely negative one: features different from those in the West are declared "socialist." See Ivan Szelenyi, "Urban Sociology and Communist Studies in Eastern Europe: Reflections and Comparisons with American Approaches," *Comparative Urban Research* 4 (1977): 11-20. Many Soviet statements about the "nature of the socialist city" have little substantive content. To say that the socialist city centers around the individual rather than around property, and that the abolition of private holdings, coupled with planned development, is sufficient to create a socialist metropolis and a new milieu for urban architecture is, indeed, to say very little. See Gutnov et al., op. cit., pp. 26-28. Similarly, Posokhin asserts: "The great October Socialist Revolution in Russia has opened up new paths of urban development. The abolition of private landownership and the introduction of economic planning have made the architect's work altogether different from what it was before." Posokhin, op. cit., foreword.

67. A. S. Gruzinov and V. P. Riumin, *Gorod: upravlenie, problemy* (Leningrad: Lenizdat, 1977), pp. 5, 7.

68. Jensen, op. cit., p. 33; Chin, op. cit., pp. 2, 11-16.

69. For Soviet concepts of the "new man," see Joel J. Schwartz, "The Elusive 'New Soviet Man,'" *Problems of Communism* 22 (September-October 1973): 39-50. An excellent satirical account that draws startling parallels between Soviet conceptions of the "new man" and the faith in mechanistic reason and physical engineering of eighteenth century thought appears in the short story by Yurii Olesha entitled "Envy." See *Envy and Other Stories*, trans. Andrew R. MacAndrew (Garden City, N.Y.: Anchor Books, 1967).

70. Jensen, op. cit., p. 34. According to one Marxist observer, it is the presence of the long-term plan, representing a scientific understanding of urban needs and social dynamics, that distinguishes Soviet cities from their Western counterparts. See Mike Davidow, *Cities without Crisis* (New York: International, 1976), pp. 33-36.

71. Chauncy D. Harris, *Cities of the Soviet Union: Studies in Their Function, Size, Density, and Growth* (Chicago: Rand McNally, 1970), p. 229.

72. That is, the number of administrative units in which elections to city soviets were held, as reported in biennial press accounts of local elections. See also *Narodnoe khoziastvo SSSR* (Moscow: Statistika, published periodically).

73. Soviet new towns are treated extensively in I. M. Smoliar, *General Plans for New Towns* (Moscow: Stroizdat, 1973); and Jack Underhill, *Soviet New Towns, Housing and National Growth Policy* (Washington, D.C.: U.S. Government Printing Office, 1976).

74. See discussion of census categories in James Riordan, "Introductory Note," in Ivan Trufanov, *Problems of Soviet Urban Life*, trans. James Riordan (Massachusetts: Oriental Research Partners, 1977), pp. iv-vi.

75. Robert A. Lewis and Richard H. Rowland, "Urbanization in Russia and the USSR, 1897-1970," in Hamm, op. cit., p. 206.

76. Kiev NIIP Gradostroitel'stva, *Sotsial'nye osnovy razvitiia gorodov (sotsial'nye problemy rasseleniia)* (Moscow: Stroizdat, 1975), p. 20.

77. Viktor Perevedentsev, "Goroda-millionery," *Literaturnaia gazeta* 18 (April 30, 1975): 10.

78. Kiev NIIP Gradostroitel'stva, op. cit., pp. 20-23.

79. Harris, op. cit., p. 1.

80. Viktor Perevedentsev, "Novishok v gorode," *Molodoi kommunist* 7 (1971): 91-96.

81. The urban mode of life has been defined in terms of the association between levels of modernization and changes in values and beliefs in society. See Francine F. Rabinovitz, "Urban Development and Political Development in Latin America," in Daland, op. cit., p. 90. The classic statement remains Louis Wirth, op. cit. In the Soviet case, urbanization has been associated with changes in family structure (including birth and divorce rates), social stratification, personal relationships, and marital and occupational preferences. See, for example, Vasil'eva, op. cit.; Trufanov, op. cit., pp. 70-71; and A. G. Volkov, "The Influence of Urbanization on Demographic Processes in the USSR," *International Journal of Sociology* 5 (1975): 107-32.

82. L. N. Kogan and V. I. Loktev, "Sociological Aspects of the Modelling of Towns," in *Town, Country and People*, ed. G. V. Osipov (London: Tavistock, 1969), p. 110.

83. Kiev NIIP Gradostroitel'stva, op. cit., p. 12.

84. Trufanov, op. cit., p. 104.

85. For prognoses on the growth of mass transit, see Kiev NIIP Gradostroitel'stva, op. cit., p. 53; and Tsentr nauchno-tekhnicheskoi informatsii po grazhdanskomu stroitel'stvu i arkhitekture, *Gradostroitel'stvo SSSR* (obzor) (Moscow: TsNTI po grazhdanskomu stroitel'stvu i arkhitekture, 1976), pp. 30-33.

2

THE MANAGEMENT ENVIRONMENT:
A BUREAUCRATIC STAGE,
A POLITICAL SCRIPT

THE ORGANIZATIONAL MILIEU

The urban manager, like the public administrator, more generally is, above all, an individual involved in the "coordination of all organized activity, having as its purpose the implementation of public policy." The manager functions within and provides leadership for a complex organization, one which consists of a formally structured system of roles and functional relationships "designed to accomplish preordained goals."[1] As an individual the manager operates within positions and is guided at least in part by the role(s) attached to that position. The organization, in short, provides both demands on and opportunities for the urban manager, even as it defines a set of structured commitments aimed at guiding the manager's behavior in concrete situations. Put another way, urban management like public administration remains highly contextual at the concrete level. Thus, we would expect Soviet urban officials to operate somewhat differently from their U.S. and Western European counterparts simply because the organizational context that shapes their role orientations and role expectations is so different.[2]

Such differences take shape along a number of lines, providing the Soviet urban manager with a wide range of constraints and commitments. As in other national systems, the organization of city administration in the USSR bears the responsibility for meeting the everyday needs of the city's residents. This emphasis on the service delivery and economic development functions of the urban manager, in turn, encourages him to assume an activist perspective on his own role.[3] But, unlike his counterparts elsewhere, the Soviet manager operates within

Sections of this chapter have been adapted from "Managing Soviet Cities," *Municipal Year Book 1978* (Washington, D.C.: International City Management Association, 1978), pp. 84-91. Reprinted with permission.

an organizational framework encompassing an extremely broad range of services and operations: most urban housing, all surface transport, dining and amusement facilities, consumer services (laundries, repair shops, and service establishments), and enterprises producing consumer goods. In the USSR, the role of government organization both nationally and locally tends to be pervasive and entrepreneurial, in contrast to the rather reactive and restrained role assigned local and national administration in the United States. This is evident in a formal description of the responsibilities of urban managers prepared in a Soviet study of the city of Moscow. According to the study, urban officials

> implement on location the policy of the Party and the government. They must decide all problems dealing with the improvement of public services, the complex development of the economy of the districts and cities, the coordination of work of the enterprises and the organization of different administrative departments in the fields of . . . municipal construction . . . consumer service, social and cultural projects, [and] the production of goods for the public.[4]

At the same time, the monopoly that the city's organizational structures exercise in the USSR can also mean that some residents enjoy fewer or inferior services by comparison with those in other Soviet cities or urban inhabitants elsewhere. In part, this stems from the fact that urban managers frequently lack the power or resources to fulfill their organizational mission; in part, it follows from the absence of private alternatives to pick up the slack or provide choices.

The national orientation of Soviet urban administration represents a second important difference. Given the fact that all land in Soviet cities is state property, theoretically, land use is completely subject to a uniform state plan for physical allocation and utilization. It would follow that the siting of industrial plants and housing complexes could be coordinated so as to limit economic growth and to prevent the overconcentration of urban populations. Finance and economic planning, through which resources are distributed, are also subject to central control. Features such as these make Soviet urban managers actors on a bureaucratic stage constructed around national needs and national hierarchies. In this respect, they operate rather unlike their counterparts in the United States.

The stage itself rests upon a foundation composed of elected city councils (soviets), one that encompasses every Soviet city. In June 1977, nationwide elections to 50,602 local soviets (urban and rural) brought 2.2 million individuals into office.[5] The size of the soviet depends on a variable formula that sets the ratio of deputies to voters according to a given territorial unit's formal rank in the national administrative structure (subordination). Individuals are selected in recognition of their personal achievements and contributions to society, with particular attention to ethnic, class, age, occupational, and sex distributions.[6] Deputies are directly elected every second year from single-member districts.

Winners are determined by a simple majority in elections that are usually uncontested.[7]

Although legislative authority is constitutionally vested in the soviet, in practice they do not function as policy-making bodies. This is not to deny that they perform meaningful functions within the political system. Soviets operate as forums to publicize current policy, to elicit information, to mobilize popular support, and to generate praise for past achievements of the regime. Elections, although uncontested, register great success in mobilizing the population to the high levels of participation characteristic of a modernized, developed society.[8] Elections emphasize political consensus and reinforce the appearance of social solidarity, a fact underscored by biennial announcements of near-perfect voter turnout. Western electoral processes, by contrast, are geared to giving the appearance of aids in conflict resolution and in managing competition for resources.

When convened in session, deputies elected to the soviet proceed to select (in actuality, rubber stamp) an executive committee from among their number. This body, the *gorispolkom*, remains formally accountable to the entire soviet. Such procedures resemble Western parliamentary systems of government in which the separation of powers and direct election of executives are absent. In practice, however, accountability is limited to periodic reports, usually annually, by the executive committee to plenary sessions of the soviet. These are supplemented by the limited ability (or interest) of individual deputies in checking on executive implementation of soviet decisions. As we shall see later in this chapter, the executive committee, in turn, confirms its members, other deputies, or even nondeputies as agency chiefs or department heads and deputy heads. Together, their units comprise the administrative structure of Soviet city government.[9] It is these departmental executives and heads of boards who represent potential urban managers. Local policy-making power resides in their hands, and in the hands of individual members of the *gorispolkom* who, in their "supervisory" (*kuriruiushchie*) roles, oversee the operations of both line and staff units. The linkages within this urban organizational network, together with its ties to a national system of administration, are presented in Figure 3.

Soviet urban managers operate through multiple chains of command and must please not one but several sets of superiors. Most fundamentally, a city's rank in the national administrative hierarchy either contributes to or detracts from the power that individual administrators exercise within their respective departmental hierarchies organized in a national chain of command. Each member of a city bureaucracy derives his status in large part from the rank of the city unit within which he operates. In the United States, by contrast, no such formal hierarchy exists; relations among city officials and their national counterparts vary according to shifting configurations of partisan politics at national and subnational levels.

The principle of dual subordination (similar to *dosage* in the French system) adds another chain of command to the picture.[10] As Figure 3 suggests, this

FIGURE 3

Soviet Administrative Structure

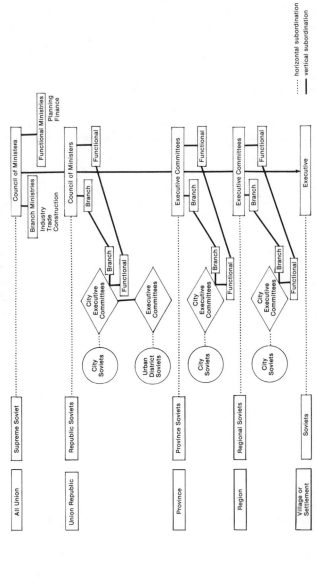

Note: There are approximately 82 city soviets at the republic level, 700 at the provincial, and 1,000 at the regional level of subordination. There are approximately 600 urban districts. There is usually no city finance department in cities subordinate to regions.

Source: Compiled by the authors.

27

makes city executive committees answerable both to the soviet that nominally elects them and to their superior executive organs on the higher rungs of an essentially bureaucratic ladder. In the final analysis, however, a vertical chain of command dominates the decision process; the Leninist model of organizational discipline (democratic centralism), the hierarchical organization of appointment and promotion procedures, and the role orientations of the administrators themselves effectively combine to guarantee that directives flow downward rather than upward.

Various subordination possibilities for cities emerge from the broad administrative framework described by Figure 3. In reality, more than half the "cities" are small, economically insignificant towns whose executive committees report to region-level units. Over 1,000 cities are subordinate to province authorities, the next rung up on the administrative ladder. At the third step, 82 executive committees answer to the most important level of subnational administration, republic governments.* These cities generally include the larger, well-established, more socially heterogeneous and economically complex centers. Such arrangements, in effect, provide urban managers in the larger cities with the most unencumbered access to decision makers at the top levels of power.†

In discussing the administrative hierarchy within which city bureaucracies function, it is important to remember that population alone does not determine subordination.[11] For cities with a million or more inhabitants, 7 of the total of 13 are subordinate to republics; the others report to province authorities. Soviet sources indicate that a city's rank depends on a combination of factors, for example, the complexity of its economy and its physical development as well as the size of its population. Political and strategic factors probably enter into the calculation as well.[12] Given that the subordination of cities fluctuates over time, changes display important practical consequences for the allocation of financial and personnel resources. In addition, a city's administrative structure—including the number and type of departments and the number of positions allowed on departmental staff lists—also depends on the city's administrative standing.

In the USSR, no national legislation details the administrative structure for cities of various ranks. Thus, the general uniformity that cities of comparable

---

*There are 15 republics in the Soviet administrative system. The Russian Republic (RSFSR) dominates the country demographically, geographically, politically, culturally, and by economic measures, including industrial production. Its administrative structure is the most complex.

†Some city leaders may be affiliated with superior units as well. V. V. Grishin, head of Moscow's city Party organization, is also a member of the Central Committee and Politburo; while M. V. Posokhin, chief architect of Moscow, is a long-term member of the Moscow city soviet and has been a deputy to several sessions of the USSR Supreme Soviet. Multiple political memberships for city leaders provide the city with access to and representation in superior administrative and political units. Besides contributing to intergovernmental coordination, this offers individual recognition for achievement.

size and complexity display must stem from informal agreements or, more likely, unpublished national administrative regulations. In practice, there are usually 7-13 members of the *gorispolkomy* in cities of region or province subordination, and 15-25 executive committee members for cities under republic control.[13] If Tiraspol, a city of some 106,000 inhabitants in 1970, is any indication, medium-size cities usually contain the following kinds of departments: finance, communal economy, trade, education, health, social welfare, general affairs, militia, capital construction, architecture, organizational-instructional, housing, and planning. These departments are assisted by various commissions, such as ones for control, administration, minors' affairs, and wardship.[14] In theory, only the city soviet itself can initiate changes in the administrative structure of the city's bureaucracy, although complaints regarding procedural violations indicate that in reality this has not always been the case.[15]

Descriptions of the administrative apparatus for Soviet cities of differing sizes or administrative ranks provide us with a more complete picture of the organizational environment. In the mid-1960s, the Estonian city of Tallin, operating under republic subordination and with a population of over 300,000, had an executive committee made up of a chairman, three deputy chairmen, an administrative secretary, and 12 other members (17 in all). Its administrative subdivisions included agencies devoted to housing, communal economy, the militia, capital construction, culture, and consumer services. Additional departments dealt with architecture, planning, finance, education, health care, and personnel work.[16] At the same time, the Belorussian city of Gorky, under province control, had an executive committee of 15 individuals. The branch apparatus included 14 major subunits. The chairman acted as the "responsible supervisor" for the most important functional departments, that is, planning and finance, as well as those concerned with trade, consumer services, and civil defense. His first deputy supervised housing, communal enterprises, public transportation, utilities, and sanitation. Another was responsible for capital construction, architecture, and public places, while a third concentrated on education, sports, and entertainment. The secretary supervised general administrative and organizational-instructional work.[17] In Gorky, as in other cities, such supervisory responsibilities are allotted to executive committee members over and above the specific managerial assignments they carry.[18]

The administrative structures of the "great cities," most notably Moscow, do not conform to these "typical" pictures. As the nation's capital, the capital of the Russian Republic, the center of Moscow province, and the economic, political, and cultural heart of the country, Moscow occupies a very special place in Soviet national life.[19] A contemporary commentary suggests that "the example of Moscow illustrates all functions of the largest cities of the USSR in their most developed form."[20] Moscow also fulfills an important symbolic role owing to its designation as a model communist city.[21]

The designation "model communist city" conveys another important function of this Soviet metropolis; it represents a laboratory in which various urban management innovations can be tested and analyzed. New management ideas are frequently developed and implemented on an experimental basis within the city's complex and relatively sophisticated management structure. Moscow also contains many of the nation's institutes devoted to policy-oriented research. Thus, modes of operation or organization currently applied in Moscow might suggest the paths along which other Soviet cities will develop in the future.

Moscow's urban managers operate over an extraordinarily broad range of functional, branch, and housekeeping activities.[22] Organized into 50 subunits (27 boards, 9 departments, 14 commissions and committees), these managers are responsible for about 600 types of services. These range from repair shops, custom furniture making, and tailoring to laundries and equipment rental. The administrative network runs enterprises, utilities, public dining facilities, health care agencies, entertainment centers, retail trade outlets, and other services. Urban managers oversee the construction of highways and bridges, housing, sports facilities, and cultural institutions, such as libraries and movie theaters. They also are responsible to some degree for employment, since the city operates job placement centers and maintains computerized records of vacancies.[23] All ground passenger transport, about 900 drugstores, and many youth activities are run through the city. All told, over 40,600 people work in lower-level management positions within the branch agencies run by the city. Although it has about the same population as New York City, the city of Moscow carries between four and five times the number of employees—1.4 million—on its payroll.

At the top of Moscow's management structure sits the presidium of the city executive committee. The executive committee, with 25 members, meets in full session only every other week. In the interim, policy responsibilities fall to the presidium. The chairman, the secretary of the executive committee, and nine other individuals who make up the presidium coordinate city services and the work of the departments.[24]

In Moscow, as in other Soviet cities, dual subordination is a basic fact of administrative operations. All line departments operate under multiple chains of command, as does the entire executive committee. The departments of consumer services and housing are responsible both to the city's executive committee and to the republic ministry of communal economy. In the same fashion, enterprises under the city's control (such as those charged with clothing manufacturing and repair) answer to at least two chiefs, one in the appropriate city department and the other in the ministry of consumer services. From this perspective Soviet structural arrangements involve three types of departments: those that are locally accountable, those that enjoy mixed accountability, and those operating under a highly centralized control system.

Planning and finance departments, two of the most important in a city, are among the centralized type. Annual plans and budgets are passed down through the planning and finance hierarchies. After formal review and approval procedures are undertaken by the city soviet and its executive committee, these documents become law. Meeting the goals expressed in these documents becomes a legal obligation, with organizational and individual penalties linked to noncompliance.

From the standpoint of urban management, it appears that many major decisions ordinarily bypass the city executive entirely. So long as a department's resources and targets originate outside the city administration, city officials are deprived of an important source of management control over both their subordinates and city operations. This dynamic becomes clearer in a comparative context. Federal activities and funding procedures developed for U.S. cities during the years of the "Great Society" gave rise to charges of excessive federal interference in local development and complaints of a loss of management control by city hall.[25] Western observers often interpret this combination of horizontal and vertical chains of command as control devices utilized by higher authorities to limit the options of city administration. By contrast, Soviet sources claim that the mix guarantees a flexible combination of national and local resources in urban decision making. Dual subordination is depicted as an opportunity rather than a limitation for local management.

The Soviet interpretation should not be dismissed casually. Dual subordination does enable national power to be used to enhance the managerial capacity of the city. In an era of heightening interdependencies among government units, there exist real trade-offs between fading local autonomy and the ability of city bureaucracies to achieve the goals and objectives for which they have been formed. Linkages to the national level do provide cities with enhanced ability to service the needs of the urban population and with additional control over the urban environment. Formal linkages aimed at intergovernmental coordination become all the more important when they involve planning and finance departments. Only since 1966 have RSFSR planning commissions been accountable to local executive committees as well as to superior planning bodies. By all accounts, finance and planning directors, as chiefs of field offices of the national bureaucracy, have always been most sensitive to the demands of their superiors and less concerned with their municipal colleagues. Indeed, this is precisely what one would expect from a successful incentive system aimed at encouraging contributions from individual members to a highly centralized organization. But the heads of planning and finance departments are also members of the city executive committee. Such direct incorporation into the city's management structure means that other agency heads enjoy both formal and informal contacts with agents of national offices, a clear advantage when it comes to obtaining resources and to participating in the development of national urban policy.

Dual subordination thus contributes to the integration of national and subnational policies at the point of implementation, the city. The U.S. experience underscores the fact that intergovernmental coordination emerges as a generic problem in urban management elsewhere; frequently, entire projects have been undermined by disorganized implementation efforts.[26] Despite efforts to come to grips with coordination, Soviet cities have not escaped such problems altogether; scholars and practitioners alike frequently complain about "departmentalism" and its negative consequences. In the Soviet setting, the problem stems from four major features of the urban environment: fragmented resources, dispersed authority, the difficulties inherent in coordinating activities of different economic branches, and decades of low allocations. The organizational sources of the coordination problem are sketched out by Figure 4, which depicts vertical fragmentation in Soviet cities. The conflict between vertical (branch) and horizontal (territorial) modes of organization continues to pose an obstacle to coherent urban programs. Urban policies require more than money for effective implementation.

Managers in the larger Soviet cities are probably in a better position to deal with these conditions than are their colleagues in smaller cities. Leningrad and Moscow possess politically powerful main boards to oversee city services. Here the city acts as the single client, aggregating both the demands and the resources involved in housing construction. Urban managers in other cities have been pressing for comparable rights for over two decades. Recent efforts to improve coordination among agencies have relied on expanding the executive committee's approval authority rather than on awarding it direct, total, and unambiguous control over a policy area. Such moves may complicate other management matters, such as personnel control, at least as much as they expand interagency coordination. And it certainly increases the number of approvals and sign-offs needed to move ahead in an already complex organizational environment.

Structural complexity provides another source of coordination difficulties. Insofar as they involve a large number of individuals from whom timely action is required for an entire program to move ahead, complex structures generally work against coordination.* Recent experiences in U.S. cities indicate that the greater the number of agencies involved in a particular program, the less likelihood there is of successful implementation. Under such conditions, it is easier to block programs than to implement them.[27] But Soviet and U.S. experiences alike suggest that increasing the number of individuals and organizations involved in a particular project remains the customary solution to the problems generated by fragmented resources, dispersed authority, and overlapping jurisdictions. Instead of curing the problems of complexity, however, this practice only adds to them.

For some policy areas, Soviet strategies enjoy an advantage over U.S. strategies. In a manner reminiscent of a Rube Goldberg device, U.S. urban policy (as in housing) is supposed to emerge through a process relating a large number of substeps into a coherent program.[28] In a more straightforward fashion, Soviet housing strategies dictate that cities or industrial employers will contract directly

---

*This parallels the cybernetic rule of thumb that structures and processes should no more than match the complexity of the problems for which they are designed. Better yet, structures and processes ought to be designed to reduce the problem's overall complexity.

FIGURE 4

Simplified Schema of Vertical Fragmentation

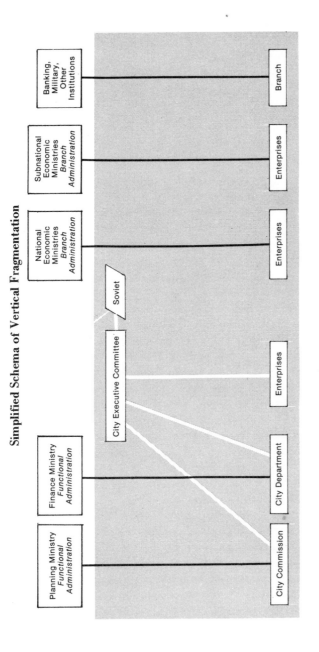

Source: Compiled by the authors.

with construction trusts to build urban housing. Such strategies improve chances for success, for in the complex, highly vulnerable urban environment, the likelihood of successful implementation is already quite low.

The organizational environment in which urban managers operate produces both conflict and modes of conflict management. Agencies over which managers have little control make capital investment decisions about housing construction, roads, sewage systems, and the like. Local enterprises subordinate not to the city but to republic and national ministries participate in developing the city and providing goods and services that enterprises controlled by other ministries consume. In order to draw upon an established infrastructure, enterprises (and their ministerial superiors) still pursue plant expansion and construction in large cities, although such activities have been prohibited for decades.[29] A concern with maximizing production output fosters a predatory attitude toward city resources and an apparent disregard for city plans.

Such attitudes put the city bureaucracy in the position of a general service agency for industrial development. They fail to allow for the city bureaucrat's responsibilities, which include at least a formal commitment to balanced and harmonious urban development. This leads to friction and sometimes even bitter disputes, not unlike those protestations against federal and state interference in urban affairs found on the U.S. scene.

Some of the conflict reflects a longstanding tension between the two divergent planning models, the vertically organized model employed by branch ministries and the horizontally integrated, territorial model used by local authorities. The numerous enterprises operating in a large city necessarily pursue vertically consistent but territorially conflicting production indexes that urban managers, despite their good intentions, frequently cannot align. A city official further finds himself caught between competing demands from different plant directors for the service for which he is responsible. Noncity enterprises may also pursue production goals that adversely affect city enterprises or services. Facing powerful industrial giants and their own superiors, urban managers emerge as relatively powerless individuals who are seldom victorious in these conflicts.[30]

Soviet urban managers thus strive to avoid conflict. Relations among city and economic officials tend to be pragmatic and highly flexible, appearing very different from the highly structured relations that join urban managers to their own superiors in the government hierarchy. Using persuasion, officials hope to strike bargains with industrial managers who make rubles and other resources available. Such bargains frequently require that plant directors agree to subsidize capital construction or services operated under city jurisdiction. Local officials have gone on record as stating that the actual ruble income of the city budget is insufficient to support the goods and services the city must routinely provide. Budgetary increases fail to keep pace with population growth, rising costs, and increasing demands; the resulting financial squeeze places urban managers in the role of "beggar bureaucrats."[31] Numerous accounts relate how the development of the city's economy requires a higher level of expenditure than the budget can support; the remaining funds are contributed by industrial enterprises.[32] The fact that mobilizing interbranch resources for the city is an important function of urban management is evident from the fact that poor performance in this area was criticized by a March 1971 Central Committee resolution.[33]

Still, the signals from the national leadership remain ambiguous on this point. They seem to point to efforts to achieve a judicious balance, not to over-zealous pursuit of industrial resources to channel accumulated riches into urban services. General Secretary Brezhnev underscored this point in a 1970 address at the Kharkov Tractor Plant:

> In some places the following practice is employed[.] In circumvention of existing legislation and in violation of the state's interests, local executives oblige enterprises of all Union and republic subordination to bear great expenditures for the construction of various municipal facilities. Then these expenditures are attributed to the unit cost of output. It is quite clear that it is necessary to wage a resolute struggle against such instances.[34]

This suggests that some regard economic managers as being frequently too cooperative in agreeing to support urban improvements.

The dependency is to some degree mutual, for the city, too, has something to offer. Plant directors rely on city officials for utilities, zoning privileges, truck routes, school services, public eating facilities, and the smooth operation of the other services on which their workers depend. Whether achieved grudgingly or willingly, cooperation becomes necessary if both plant directors and urban officials are to meet their respective goals.

In any case, it is clear that while the complex organizational environment provides a general framework for urban management, particular relationships and roles are likely to take shape according to the goals, preferences, and political orientations that individual managers embrace (and that are discussed in Chapter 3). Activities and relationships are far less routinized and regularized than an emphasis on the organizational context alone would suggest. In particular, urban management does not simply reduce to a set of administrative formulas; nor will administrative activities lead to the implementation of national policies without some form of political guidance and control.

THE POLITICAL DIMENSION

The managers of Soviet cities operate in an environment in which the Communist Party of the Soviet Union (CPSU) plays a major part. In a variety of ways, the Party works to shape those roles and role orientations that, in turn, influence the manner in which city bureaucrats execute the tasks assigned them by virtue of their places in the urban administrative structure.[35] The "role" of the Party in Soviet urban management can be understood in two ways: in terms of the rights of general leadership and direction that the Party monopolizes and in terms of the overall organizational reach (overlapping membership, recruitment powers, supervisory and watchdog functions) of Party units into the city's administrative agencies. Party roles and administrative roles may either complement or contradict one another, depending on the circumstances under which they come into play within the Soviet city. Role reinforcement, role conflict, and role ambiguity—each of these relationships describes an important dimension within the overall linkage between Party and government structures in the Soviet city.[36] Such sublinkages, in turn, bear a strong resemblance to those between urban political machines and city bureaucrats in the U.S. setting. The play of tensions between political roles and values, on the one hand, and administrative—professional orientations, on the other, is hardly unique to the Soviet management environment.[37]

The formal guidelines laid down for urban Party organizations direct them to do "everything necessary" to insure that each and every administrative unit will be maximally effective when addressing the general problems of urban life. Local agencies, like their national counterparts, work under "the direction and guidance of the Party" so that, in theory, the possibility of bureaucratic resistance and fragmented policy implementation does not arise.[38] Along these same lines, a 1968 report by the first secretary of the Minsk Party committee observed that "the Party organs bear the responsibility for everything that happens in a city."[39]

A complex network of structural linkages between Party units and city government provides institutional reinforcement for such directives. Approximately 40 percent of Soviet cities (and all important cities) have a sufficient number of Party members among the population to warrant the organization of a city Party committee (*gorkom*).[40] These are organized along both functional and branch lines, with departments and other subunits paralleling those of the city government. Primary Party organs (PPOs) and Party groups (PGs) complete the picture. PPOs under the *gorkom* are organized within the city's departments, boards, and commissions and embrace all Party members who are full-time city employees. The Party group (PG), by contrast, ties the Party committee to city soviets and standing commissions, that is, to the legislative rather than to the administrative subunits of city government. The PG functions like a political caucus and is distinguished by the fact that its members, by virtue of their regular employment elsewhere, also belong to PPOs at their places of work.[41] In many cases, both the PPO and the PG are headed by a secretary who simultaneously performs the functions of a professional Party worker (*apparatchik*) in a superior Party organ.[47] For those administrative units in which there are insufficient Party members to warrant a PPO, a Party group cutting across several departments will be organized.

Both the PPO and the PG are responsible for discipline within administrative agencies, for the timely fulfillment of directives handed down by higher Party bodies such as the *gorkom*, and for the attainment of targets delineated in plans for the city's economy.[43] The principle of democratic centralism that governs organizational life in Leninist parties precludes the formation of horizontal linkages among the numerous lower-level Party units operating within Soviet city government. Each reports separately and individually only to the *gorkom*, the initial level at which coordination and concentration of powers occurs.[44] At the same time, the overlap in membership between the *gorkom* and the executive committee of the city soviet (*gorispolkom*) creates interlocking directorates. Secretaries of the *gorkom* sit on the *gorispolkom*, while the head of the *gorispolkom* is a *gorkom* member. Such overlap minimizes the possibilities for institutional conflict, although it may exacerbate the conflict between professional and political values already mentioned.[45]

Ideally, Party units work hand in hand with city authorities and agencies even when the membership of the two is not identical.[46] In contrast to the role of the Party in industrial management, the operation of Party and government units in the urban milieu is characterized by a sharing of functions that, in turn, promotes coordination.[47] While the operational direction of city enterprises, trading establishments, and service functions is left to line officials, Party plena devote more attention to the state of the urban economy, including service performance, than to any other issue.[48] Under such circumstances, the Party is expected to concentrate its attention on long-term development and policy issues rather than on the daily routines of urban administration.[49]

This sharing of functions means that Party units, like those of city government, bear responsibility for policy outcomes. These are usually measured as the fulfillment of specific economic indexes based on material output, financial expenditures, and productivity increments.[50] Within the framework provided by the Party's organizational network, members participate in verification and review of city programs, not unlike the various watchdog commissions and private research organizations that track city government operations in many U.S. cities.[51] Party members in city agencies are required to report back regularly to the *gorkom* regarding both the current status of department programs and the kinds of improvements that will enhance performance.[52] PPO members within departments periodically caucus independently from the department as a whole, reviewing particular problems and reports. The caucus then makes its own recommendations to the agency's administrative leadership. Party rules also instruct PPOs to distribute concrete assignments among individual members in order to further the achievement of programmatic objectives and goals. Frequently PPOs and PGs also convene *after* meetings of departmental collegia or after sessions of the *gorispolkomy*, a process generally overlooked in the Western literature on Soviet local government.[53] Such occasions are then utilized by the Party units to work out specific assignments or work programs for individual administrators-cum-Party members.[54]

Party units measure the effectiveness of their work in implementing urban policy in a variety of ways. Chief among these is the number of complaints about an agency's operation that citizens bring before the *gorispolkom*, the city soviet, or the *gorkom* itself.[55] When the imprecations of the *gorispolkom* prove ineffective in moving departments off dead center regarding a given task (as occurred in the Department of Transportation in Rostov), the *gorispolkom* can appeal directly to the *gorkom*. The latter, in turn, responds by obligating individual Party members directly, ordering them to carry out the *gorispolkom*'s directives promptly.[56] Failure to carry out what is now a Party assignment could result in a reprimand from Party superiors, a permanent blot on the individual's Party record, or other disciplinary measures. Dismissal from one's post or expulsion from the Party itself can be invoked in cases of flagrant abuse of power or obstructionism.

Like all sanctions, however, even these procedures are far from foolproof. One account in Azerbaidzhan notes the "reshuffling of failed executives from one post to another," apparently with the acquiescence of local Party leaders.[57] Along similar lines, in 1970 the Minsk province Party organization criticized lower-level Party units and, in particular, urban district Party committees and department PPOs for insufficient diligence in overseeing and coordinating the work of those Party members involved in Minsk city administration.[58] The Party organization of the Moldavian republic echoed these same complaints in 1969 and again in 1970.[59]

The relative strength of the Party in the management environment thus emerges as a function of two critical factors. The first of these, role overlap, involves the reach of Party recruitment and penetration, the "saturation levels" it achieves within city administration through PPOs and PGs. The second, role definition, flows from the Party's directive staffing powers, its *nomenklatura* (selection and sign-off) authority in administrative personnel matters. While these factors have operated over many decades of Bolshevik power in the USSR, like other structural features of the system their dynamics and importance have altered somewhat over time.

With respect to organizational reach and role overlap, the 1960s represented a period of real expansion. From the final years of the Khrushchev era on into the early 1970s, the national leadership launched a systematic campaign to upgrade the role of the Party in local administration. It was during this time that PPOs and PGs acquired much of their statutory authority for supervising urban administration. This period also witnessed the introduction of the practice of having PPOs and PGs deliver formal reports to the *gorkom* on the operations of the administrative units they supervised. By contrast, until 1963 the *gorkom* had only been interested in the work of the PG among deputies to the local soviet and in the results of its presession caucuses. Close supervision of the performance of individual Party members and their fulfillment of administrative responsibilities dates from this time.[60]

In the mid-1960s, the Party leadership also undertook a number of measures to improve the quality of Party cadres working in city administration. The Party introduced special training seminars under *obkom* (province Party committee) auspices for Party secretaries in all urban PPOs. These seminars were run by the department heads of the Party's own apparat. For cities of lesser importance, seminars were organized and operated under the auspices of city or regional Party committees.[61] Concurrently, the Party's organizational reach was extended by drawing larger numbers of urban administrators into its political network. Politicization through targeted membership drives and professionalization through special training represented two sides of the same coin; both contributed to redefining the Party's role so as to enhance urban management.

Party strength as a function of its ability to reach or "saturate" the ranks of Soviet local officials also developed rapidly after 1960. Prior to this time, political recruitment of state administrators had concentrated at the national, republic, or province levels; frequently, no more than 10-30 percent of city bureaucrats wore the twin hats of administrator and Party member.[62] Part of the explanation for this circumstance lay in the fact that for Party members as well as their non-Party counterparts, urban administrative work remained financially unappealing. Wage levels for comparable technical and administrative positions in the industrial sector were traditionally much higher. In addition, during the early years of Khrushchev's leadership, the Party concentrated primarily on expanding its organizational controls over those working in industrial management. As a result, by the end of the 1950s, Party control in urban administration still resembled a "commanding heights" situation, one that first prevailed under Lenin's leadership during the years of civil war (1918-20). But such a situation impeded rather than facilitated coordination within city administration.

Evidence pertaining to cities in Russia's Rostov province indicates that changes in the Party's position within urban bureaucracies occurred after 1961. Party units began to assign more members to work in city government or to recruit more actively those already performing administrative tasks into the Party's ranks. The data is summarized in Table 3. At the same time, *gorkomy* throughout the USSR began to take a more active part in the selection of subdepartmental-level personnel, such as bureau heads and section directors.[63]

Within Rostov province, the Party's efforts met with considerable success. For the province as a whole at all levels (province, city, town, village), the number of administrative agencies lacking any Party members fells from 63 in 1961 to 6 in 1969. Urban administrative agencies, however, all had Party organizations in the form of PPOs by 1969.[64] Even when the overall number of administrators in the province declined as a result of Khrushchev's "war against bureaucracy," the number of Party members working in these agencies nevertheless doubled, as Table 3 indicates.[65]

The province's average for political saturation of administrative agencies at all levels remains somewhat low when compared to the total penetration of ad-

TABLE 3

Party Saturation of State Administration, Rostov Province
(all levels)

Year	Number of Administrators	Number of Party Members	Percent Party Saturation*
1961	20,043	1,403	7.0
1963	15,000	1,800	12.0
1965	10,530	2,000	19.0
1967	10,500	2,200	21.0

*CPSU members as percent of total number of administrators.

Source: A. S. Bezmat'ev, "Sovershenstvovanie partiinogo rukovodstva mestnymi Sovetami deputatov trudiashchikhsia (1961-1967 gg na materialakh Rostovskoi oblastnoi partiinoi organizatsii)" (Master's thesis, Rostov State University, 1971), p. 139.

ministrative departments in the "great cities" of the USSR (see Chapter 3). But the increase in Party penetration in 1960-68 nevertheless remains impressive. Table 4 charts the expansion of the Party's organizational hold within both executive committees and administrative departments for various levels of government within Rostov province. As already indicated, part of the increase can probably be accounted for by the assignment of existing Party members to administrative posts. In other cases, however, it is likely that "the best and the brightest" from among those already employed were invited to join the Party's ranks.[66] In any case, the Party's hold over city administration in both an individual and a collective sense was substantially strengthened. The data in Tables 3 and 4 also suggest that Party members in administrative agencies have enjoyed preferential treatment during periods of personnel cutbacks; indeed, Party membership may be attractive to Soviet state administrators precisely because it functions as a kind of insurance policy, aiding in promotion and protecting against dismissal.

In addition to its recruitment powers, the Party plays a direct role in personnel management in city government. It commands considerable staffing controls that reinforce its power to shape the roles and performance of urban managers. These powers include the right to hire and fire, to promote, evaluate, and confirm appointments made by government units.[67] In general, administrative positions in city government are staffed through a routine set of procedures defined by the nomenklatura, a list of jobs for which specific Party units select the appointees. These nomenklatura powers expanded considerably during the latter part of the 1960s. Since 1961, in addition to its basic nomenklatura powers, the gorkom has also wielded what Soviet sources label powers of an "accounting-

TABLE 4

Growth of Party Organizational Strength in Local Government: Rostov Province, Increases, 1961-68

	1961[a]		1963		1965		1967	
	Number	Percent	Number	Percent	Number	Percent	Number	Percent
A. Total administrative units (departments, boards)	788	100.0	788	100.0	788	100.0	816	103.6
B. Primary Party organs								
Executive committees								
City and county	67	100.0	67	100.0	67	100.0	72	103.7
Villages	50	100.0	58	116.0	87	129.9	98	189.2
Departments and boards, all levels	60	100.0	72	120.0	63	105.0	97	156.0
Total	177	100.0	197	111.3	237	133.9	267	145.6
C. Party groups								
Executive committees								
Village	—	—	—	—	78	100.0	355	455.1
Departments, boards	—	—	65	100.0	138	212.3	196	301.5
Total	—	—	65	100.0	216	332.3	551	847.7
Total Party organizational strength (B + C)	177	100.0	262	148.0	453	255.9	818[b]	462.1[b]
Party penetration (B + C/A)	—	22.5	—	33.2	—	57.5	—	100.0[b]

[a] Equals 100 percent.
[b] The error here is unexplained by the data source. The figure of 100 percent for Party saturation is therefore an approximation.

Source: A. S. Bezmat'ev, "Sovershenstvovanie partiinogo rukovodstva mestnymi Sovetami deputatov trudiashchikhsia (1961-1967 gg na materialakh Rostov-skoi oblastnoi partiinoi organizatsii)" (Master's thesis, Rostov State University, 1971), p. vii (Appendix) (table 11).

control" *nomenklatura*. These embrace the right to check and review individual administrative performance in certain offices and to veto appointments by other agencies. In these cases, however, the Party exercises no direct staffing authority. Following Khrushchev's downfall, the Party also took on itself the right to create reserve pools of administrative manpower, called the "cadre-reserve *nomenklatura*." In so doing, it extended its control to the prerecruitment stage as well.[68]

In practical terms, the local *nomenklatura* operates according to routine procedures. The *obkom* staffs the positions of chairmen of city and region (*raion*) executive committees when these units are under province jurisdiction. It also recruits deputy chairmen, secretaries, and department heads for provincial government agencies. City and regional Party committees (*gorkomy* and *raikomy*) appoint the deputy chairmen of city executive committees, the secretaries of these committees, and department heads for city agencies.[69] These procedures define the basic *nomenklatura*. The accounting-control *nomenklatura* operates for a number of other local government positions where the Party does not select the appointee but, instead, retains veto privileges. For example, the *gorkom* exercises accounting-control *nomenklatura* rights with respect to deputy chairmen, executive secretaries, and department heads in executive committees for urban districts. But the actual appointment power rests with either the city soviet or, in some cases, with the province government.

The cadre-reserve *nomenklatura*, unlike the others, is defined in terms of individuals rather than positions. Since 1964, local Party organizations have pinpointed groups of individuals already working in Party and government offices. The Party unit involved then monitors their performances closely over a period of time. Such formalized procedures provide a strong foundation on which the Party can exercise its basic *nomenklatura* authority. It insures the selection of individuals who have already demonstrated the kinds of skills, style, and political commitment that the Party seeks. As a result, it can now shift cadres around more freely than formerly, without worrying about the difficulty of replacements. By 1971, Rostov province possessed a *nomenklatura* reserve for every important administrative post down to the level of department heads for urban districts. All members of this pool had a complete secondary education and also possessed some specialist qualifications.[70]

Despite the complex network of controls, coordinating devices, and shared functions that characterize Party-government relationships within the city, the work environment of the urban manager is far from frictionless. Overzealous Party members can generate a great deal of trouble in a situation in which the line dividing the responsibilities of the *gorkom* from those of city agencies is unclear at best. Party leaders are frequently reminded that their object is "to lead but not to supplant" (*rukovodit' no ne zameniat'*); an updated (1968) version reformulated this classic exhortation as "to influence but not to replace."[71]

By the same token, too little Party involvement also poses problems for urban management. The record suggests that Party organizations are sometimes negligent in the performance of their control and coordination responsibilities. One account from the late 1960s complained that the PPO of the *gorispolkom* of Alma Ata, a major Central Asian city, had paid practically no attention to the operation of the executive committee for some time. Indifference to citizen complaints, delays in program implementation, and unnecessary complications in the processing of documents were cited as a few of the results. PPOs in cities in another case were cited for failing to provide Party members within city agencies with individualized assignments or programs. Elsewhere, city and regional Party committees have been criticized for failing to exercise adequate leadership over their subordinate PPOs and PGs.[72] Similar problems occur within the urban district as well, as a November 1966 session of the Party committee in the Leningrad district of Moscow makes clear. Party cadres were subjected to severe criticism on the grounds that they had ignored defects in the work of their departments, had failed to prevent breaches of state discipline, and had overlooked corruption and nepotism in departmental operations.[73]

The political environment of the Soviet city forces the urban bureaucrat to wear several hats simultaneously. Like all Party members who hold responsible posts, his Party hat defines him as a kind of conductor. In such a capacity he is expected to orchestrate, coordinate, check, and control the performances of a large variety of instruments that, in turn, are executing quite specialized and complicated tasks. All this must be done in accordance with the "score," the Party line handed down by the higher-level political authorities. From the perspective of the Party and political control, such arrangements possess a number of advantages. Chief among them is the city administrator's "insider" status in matters of local politics, together with his familiarity with the day-by-day operations of city administration. In his role as a coordinator for a complex organizational system, the Party member-cum-administrator is expected to perform as an urban manager in the literal sense of the term.

The administrative hat that the same individual wears, however, gears him to a somewhat different role. His job is defined in terms of specific task assignments. Equally important, his abilities are judged in terms of the particular successes—or programmatic failures—of the agency in which he functions. Performance defined as agency outputs—rather than management defined as a coordinating process to expedite policy outcomes—provides the yardstick by which his work is evaluated. Meeting goals and attaining targets becomes more important than the methods whereby this is achieved. Agency outputs take over planning or program management.

When combined, these organizational and political features of the urban environment in the USSR render it simultaneously supportive and destructive of the emergence of real urban management. The bureaucratic stage and the political script frequently fail to provide the kind of harmonious setting in which administrative actors could realize their full dramatic potential. In their capacity as Party members, city administrators can and do participate in the writing of the script. But in their capacities as administrators, they are forced to follow the stage directions of others who may lack the functional skills, specialist knowledge, and professional commitments that successful performance requires. Political control does indeed provide the concentration and horizontal coordination that urban management as defined in the Introduction demands. At the same time, however, political control reinforces the kinds of centralization and vertical fragmentation that inhibit adequate administrative responses to local needs and local problems. In brief, neither the bureaucratic stage nor the political script guarantees urban management processes top billing in the contemporary Soviet city.

NOTES

1. Harold Gortner, *Administration in the Public Sector* (New York: John Wiley, 1977), pp. 3, 4.

2. See, for example, Jerry F. Hough, "The Soviet Concept of the Relationship between the Lower Party Organs and State Administration," *Slavic Review* 24 (June 1965): 215-40.

3. This activist perspective was made clear to the authors repeatedly in their interviews with Soviet city officials and urbanists over the course of 1975-77. For an analysis of activist perspectives in U.S. city planning, see J. Vincent Buck, *Politics and Professionalism in Municipal Planning*, Administrative and Policy Studies Series, 3 (Beverly Hills, Calif.: Sage Professional Papers, 1976).

4. Main Scientific Research Computer Center of the Moscow City Soviet Executive Committee, *Description of the Management System of the City of Moscow*, Report on the scientific research performed according to the Intergovernmental Agreement of 1972 for Scientific and Technological Cooperation between the USSR and USA, Topic no. 3, Project no. 1 (New York: Columbia University, Graduate School of Business, Center for Government Studies, ©1975), p. 38. Uncirculated draft report; Soviet source document unverified by independent research.

5. "Soobshchenie ob itogakh vyborov v mestnye sovety deputatov trudiashchikhsia," *Izvestiia*, June 25, 1977, pp. 1-2. In comparison, there are approximately 78,000 local governments in the United States, including 6,304 cities of which 30 have more than 125,000 inhabitants. "Inside the Yearbook," *Municipal Yearbook 1977* (Washington, D.C.: International City Management Association, 1977), unpaged.

6. Ronald J. Hill, *The Soviet Political Elite* (New York: St. Martin's Press, 1977), pp. 17, 37-57.

7. Max Mote, *Soviet Local and Republic Elections* (Stanford, Calif.: Hoover Institution, 1965); Howard R. Swearer, "The Function of Soviet Local Elections," *Midwest Journal of Political Science* 5 (1961): 129-49; Everett M. Jacobs, "Soviet Local Elections: What They Are, and What They Are Not," *Soviet Studies* 22 (1970): 61-76; and Jerome Gillison, "Soviet Elections as a Measure of Dissent: The Missing One Percent," *American Political Science Review* 62 (1968): 814-26.

8. L. G. Churchward, "Soviet Local Government Today," *Soviet Studies* 17 (1966): 446-50. On the linkages between political mobilization and political development, see J. P. Nettl, *Political Mobilization: A Sociological Analysis of Methods and Concepts* (New York: Basic Books, 1967), pp. 123-61; and Samuel P. Huntington and Joan Nelson, *No Easy Choice: Political Participation in Developing Countries* (Cambridge, Mass.: Harvard University Press, 1976), pp. 17-41.

9. See Chapter 3, this study. There are no legal requirements that city department heads or chairmen (of main boards or administrative directorates) sit as elected deputies to the council. According to data for the city of Tiraspol, 1950-67, during each two-year term from one to five department heads of the council were not elected deputies. Hill, op. cit., p. 21.

10. Mark Kesselman, *The Ambiguous Consensus, a Study of Local Government in France* (New York: Alfred A. Knopf, 1967); and idem, "Political Parties and Local Government in France: Differentiation and Opposition," in *Comparative Community Politics*, ed. Terry Nichols Clark (New York: John Wiley, 1974): 111-38. Not surprisingly, the centralized French system bears significant similarities to the Soviet: *tutelle*, denoting legal subordination in a centralized administrative system; and *cumul*, denoting the multiple affiliations of officials at the national and city level, and which provides direct access to central decision-making units. See note bottom of p. 28.

11. On the other hand, certain types of mass transit networks are provided primarily according to population configurations. Subway systems, a case in point, are only considered for cities with at least 1 million inhabitants. Author's notes of discussion at the Institute of Town Planning, Lithuanian Gosstroi, Vilnius, June 1977.

12. Carol W. Lewis, "The Harvard Conference on Soviet Urban Research," *Comparative Urban Research* 5 (November 1977): 72-76.

13. Boris Nikolaevich Gabrichidze, *Gorodskie sovety deputatov trudiashchikhsia* (Moscow: Izd. Iuridicheskaia literatura, 1968), chap. 5.

14. Hill, op. cit., pp. 12, 21-23; A. S. Gruzinov and V. P. Riumin, *Gorod: upravlenie, problemy* (Leningrad: Lenizdat, 1977), pp. 50-55.

15. Gabrichidze, op. cit., p. 182.

16. Ibid.

17. Ibid.

18. Ibid.

19. For a description of the economic role of the city of Moscow and its surrounding region, see F. R. Ian Hamilton, *The Moscow City Region*, Problem Regions of Europe (London: Oxford University Press, 1976).

20. *Management System of Moscow*, p. 5.

21. For example, "This task of building a model communist city, posed at the Twenty-Fourth Congress of the Soviet Communist party, will be carried out in every field of endeavor not only by the Muscovites but by the entire Soviet people." Mikhail Vassil'evich Posokhin, *Cities to Live in* (Moscow: Novosti Press, 1974), p. 128.

22. This description of Moscow's structure and functions is based upon the following sources: *Management System of Moscow*, sec. 2; T. A. Selivanov and M. A. Gel'perin, *Planirovanie gorodskogo khoziaistva (na primera Moskvy)* (Moscow: Ekonomika, 1970), pp. 14-20; and G. B. Poliak and E. V. Sofronova, *General'nyi plan i biudzhet Moskvy* (Moscow: Finansy, 1973).

23. Author's notes of discussion at Main Scientific Research Computer Center of the Moscow City Soviet Executive Committee, June 1977.

24. *Management System of Moscow*, sec. 2.

25. On the fiscal aspects of intergovernmental relations in the United States today, see *Significant Features of Fiscal Federalism*, 1976-77 ed., 3 vols. (Washington, D.C.: Advisory Commission on Intergovernmental Relations, 1976-77). For a comparison of the principal features of federal aid programs of the 1960s with those of the 1970s, see Lawrence Susskind, "Revenue Sharing and the Lessons of the New Federalism," *Urban Law Annual* 8 (1974): 33-71.

26. Bernard J. Frieden and Marshall Kaplan, *The Politics of Neglect* (Cambridge, Mass.: MIT Press, 1975); Erwin C. Hargrove, *The Missing Link: The Study of the Implemen-*

tation of Social Policy (Washington, D.C.: The Urban Institute, 1975); and Jeffrey L. Pressman and Aaron B. Wildavsky, *Implementation: How Great Expectations in Washington Were Dashed in Oakland* (Berkeley: University of California Press, 1973).

27. Pressman and Wildavsky, op. cit.

28. For a history of U.S. housing policies, see Jewel Bellush and Murray Hausknecht, *Urban Renewal: People, Politics, and Planning* (Garden City, N.Y.: Anchor Books, 1967).

29. In discussions, Soviet urban managers and planners without exception pointed to the expansion of industrial facilities as the single most important cause of continued growth in large cities. Author's notes of discussions in Kiev, Vilnius, Moscow, and Leningrad, June 1977.

30. For a further discussion of political conflict of this sort, see William Taubman, *Governing Soviet Cities: Bureaucratic Politics and Urban Development in the USSR* (New York: Praeger, 1973); and Carol W. Lewis, "Politics and the Budget in Soviet Cities" (Ph.D. diss., Princeton University, 1975). chaps. 7, 8. The picture of Soviet city leaders combating industrial giants, with money and power on the side of the latter, appears disconcertingly familiar in light of U.S. experience. While both the city and national politics underlying this picture are quite different, management outcomes, by contrast, are not.

31. Carol W. Lewis, "The Beggar Bureaucrat: Linking National and City Politics in the Soviet Union," Paper delivered at the annual conference of the American Society for Public Administration, Washington, D.C., April 1976.

32. S. Voroninskii, "Den'gi liubiat khoziaina," *Izvestiia*, February 9, 1968, p. 3; P. Demidov, "Poisk," *Izvestiia*, July 5, 1975, p. 3.

33. Central Committee, CPSU, "O merakh po dal'neishemu uluchsheniiu raboty raionnykh i gorodskikh sovetov deputatov trudiashchikhsia," *Pravda*, March 14, 1971, pp. 1-2.

34. Leonid Il'ich Brezhnev, "Rech' tovarishcha L. I. Brezhneva," *Pravda* April 14, 1970, pp. 1-2. The quote is translated in "Brezhnev in Kharkov: The Economy," *Current Digest of the Soviet Press* 22 (May 12, 1970): 7.

35. For a discussion of the theoretical problems involved in applying the concept of "role" and "role orientation" to the study of administration, see Richard Price, *Society and Bureaucracy in Ghana* (Berkeley: University of California Press, 1974), pp. 14-18.

36. See Eric P. Hoffmann, "Role Conflict and Ambiguity in the Communist Party of the Soviet Union," in *The Behavioral Revolution and Communist Studies*, ed. Roger E. Kanet (New York: Free Press, 1971), pp. 233-34, 236. Price, op. cit., pp. 16-17; Eric P. Hoffmann, "Social Science and Soviet Administrative Behavior," *World Politics* 24 (April 1972): 449.

37. Buck, op. cit.; John C. Bollens and John C. Ries, *The City Manager Profession: Myths and Realities* (Chicago: Public Administration Service, 1969); and Richard J. Stillman, Jr., "The City Manager: Professional Helping Hand or Political Hired Hand," *Public Administration Review* 37 (November-December 1977): 659-70.

38. Iu. M. Kuznetsov, "Povyshenie roli i otvetstvennosti mestnykh sovetov," in *Kommunisty i ekonomicheskaia reforma* (Moscow: Izd. Mysl', 1972), p. 325. Stated simply, in the words of another Soviet source, "our Party, as the leading and guiding force of Soviet society, answers for all that goes on in the country, including the work of the [s]oviets." I. M. Orlov, *Deiatel'nost' KPSS po povysheniiu roli Sovetov v stroitel'stve kommunizma* (Moscow: Vyshaia shkola, 1970), p. 90.

39. I. Poliakov, "Vliiat', a ne podmeniat'," *Izvestiia*, February 29, 1968, p. 3.

40. The number of city Party committees has increased, as has the number of cities. In 1967, there were 747 *gorkomy*, and in 1969 there were 760; by 1973, 780 were reported. Gabrichidze, op. cit., p. 183; and *Itogi vyborov i sostav deputatov mestnykh sovetov deputatov trudiashchikhsia, 1969 g. and 1973g. (statisticheskii sbornik)* (Moscow: Izvestiia, 1969 and 1973).

41. Interviews, Law Faculty, Department of Soviet State Development, Moscow State University, 1975-76.

42. Ibid.

43. A. S. Bezmat'ev, *Sovershenstvovanie partiinogo rukovodstva mestnymi sovetami na etape razvernutogo kommunizma* (Rostov-on-Don: Izd. Rostovskogo gosudarstvennogo universiteta, 1971), pp. 16, 19.

44. Ibid., pp. 18-19.

45. Hill, op. cit., pp. 105-8.

46. S. Sabaneev and G. Konovalov, "Ruka ob ruku," *Izvestiia*, May 17, 1967, p. 3.

47. Two members of Moscow University's Law Faculty have traced the formal system of specific functional overlap to the Eleventh Party Congress in the spring of 1922, when the Communist party was declared the "leading force" in all sectors and its sphere extended explicitly to all activities undertaken by local soviets. G. Barabashev and K. F. Sheremet, "KPSS i Sovety," *Sovetskoe gosudarstvo i pravo*, November 1967, pp. 31-41. Several other Soviet sources point to the Eighth Party Congress, March 1919, for the formalization of Party-state relations. It was then that the local Party committees formally were given roles in policy making in a territory and supervisory responsibilities over local administrative units at corresponding levels in the hierarchy. See, for example, Orlov, op. cit.

48. See reports on *gorkom* plenum agendas in *Partiinaia zhizn* 15 (August 1974): 63-64. For a summary of topics considered at city executive committee and city soviet meetings, see D. A. Bykovskii, *Organizatsiia raboty ispolkomov mestnykh sovetov* (Moscow: Izd. Iuridicheskaia literatura, 1968), pp. 9-12. For a report on the Moscow *gorkom*'s responsibilities, see N. Liaporov, "Vperedi god boevoi, napriazhennoi raboty (c plenuma Moskovskogo gorkoma KPSS)," *Pravda*, December 24, 1974, p. 2.

49. There are numerous cases in which Party members working in the bureaucracy of the city Party committee have themselves actually run city services or important economic institutions. The roots of such practices stretch back to 1919 when Party units were accused of making decisions that should have been left in the hands of the *gubernaia* executive committees. See Efrim Grigor'evich, Gimpel'son, *Sovety v gody inostrannoi interventsii i grazhdanskoi voiny* (Moscow: Nauka, 1968), p. 119.

50. One discussion of the concepts "outcomes" and "outputs" is Frank S. Levy, Arnold J. Meltsner, and Aaron Wildavsky, *Urban Outcomes; Schools, Streets, and Libraries* (Berkeley: University of California Press, 1974), pp. 2-8.

51. The Twenty-Fourth Party Congress extended the rights of PPOs with respect to the verification of Party directives and the monitoring of personnel policies. "KPSS v tsifrakh," *Partiinaia zhizn'* 14 (July 1973): 9-26. As the first secretary of the Central Committee of the Georgian Communist Party said with reference to the situation in Tbilisi, "In the Party apparatus, in the state apparatus and in public life, no person should be outside our control, in the best, most direct and most global sense of the word." E. A. Shevardnadze, "Sovershenstvovat' sistemu kontrolia i proverki ispolneniia v svete reshenii xxix s"ezda KPSS," *Zaria vostoka*, November 15, 1974, pp. 1-5.

52. *Problemy Sovetskogo stroitel'stva gosudarstvennogo upravleniia i pravovogo vospitaniia na sovremennom etape* (Ufa: Izd. Upravleniia delami soveta ministrov, BASSR, 1975), p. 110.

53. A. S. Bezmat'ev, "Sovershenstvovanie partiinogo rukovodstva mestnymi sovetami deputatov trudiashchikhsia (1961-1977 gg. na materialakh Rostovskoi oblastnoi partiinoi organizatsii)" (Master's thesis, Rostov State University, 1971), pp. 147-48.

54. Ibid., p. 149.

55. Ibid., pp. 150-51.

56. Ibid., pp. 145-47.

57. G. A. Aliev, "O zadachakh partiinoi organizatsii Azerbaidzhana po dal'neishemu uluchsheniiu podbora, rasstanovki i vospitaniia kadrov v svete trebovanii xxix s"ezda KPSS," *Bakinskii rabochii*, July 31, 1975, pp. 2-6.

58. F. G. Apostol, "Partiinoe rukovodstvo mestynym sovetam v ravitom sotsialisticheskom obshchestve" (Master's thesis, Moscow State University, 1973), pp. 28-29.

59. Ibid., p. 23.

60. Bezmat'ev, *Sovershenstvovanie partiinogo rukovodstva*, pp. 11-13.

61. Bezmat'ev, "Sovershenstvovanie . . . (1961-1967),", pp. 154-55.

62. Ibid., p. 139.

63. Ibid., p. 140.

64. Ibid., p. 142.

65. See George Breslauer, "Khrushchev Revisited," *Problems of Communism* 25 (September-October 1976): 18-33, on the "war against bureaucracy."

66. Bezmat'ev, "Sovershenstvovanie . . . (1961-1967)," p. 143.

67. *Stil', metody i kul'tura raboty gosudarstvennogo apparata: materialy nauchnoprakticheskoi konferentsii sovetskikh rabotnikov Primorskogo kraia* (Vladivostok: Dal'nevostochnoe knizhnoe izdatel'stvo, 1974), p. 13.

68. Interviews, Law Faculty, Department of Soviet State Development, Moscow State University, 1975-76; Institute of State and Law, Academy of Sciences, USSR, 1976.

69. Bezmat'ev, "Sovershenstvovanie . . . (1961-1967)," pp. 92-93.

70. Ibid., pp. 84-95, 97; P. G. Ablakova, "Deiatel'nost KPSS po dal'neishemu povysheniiu roli mestnykh sovetov v usloviiakh stroitel'stva kommunizma (na materialakh partiinykh organizatsii Kazakhstana, 1965-1968 gg)" (Master's thesis, Kazakhstan State University, 1969), p. 108.

71. Poliakov, op. cit., p. 3.

72. Ablakova, op. cit., pp. 188-89.

73. Ibid., pp. 174-75.

3

URBAN ADMINISTRATIVE PERSONNEL: FROM COMMISSARS TO MANAGERS

THE PROFESSION OF URBAN MANAGEMENT

The management capacity of urban government is neither more nor less than the sum total of the managerial capacity of those officials who supervise the departments that provide the city with goods and services. Environmental constraints, including cultural values, structures of roles, and political controls tell only a small part of the story. The ultimate success of government in any jurisdiction rests primarily on the quantity of outcomes, and these are far from fully determined by environmental factors. In many instances, it is the administrators, who expand, elaborate, implement, and even propose the programs and policies that lie behind outcomes, who play the leading roles.[1] Environmental factors only provide the setting within which the urban management capacity can grow and develop. It is personnel factors that constitute a central dimension of resource management within the initial formulation of the components of urban management as described in the Introduction. In contrast, however, to the relatively well-developed literature linking management capacity to personnel variables at the national level in the comparative study of political systems, relatively little attention (in either theory or practice) has been directed to the operation of these same factors at the subnational level. Even in the United States, the personnel function, in the words of Robert Golembiewski, "has had to struggle for its place in the organizational sun."[2] Private business has traditionally shown a much keener appreciation for the importance of personnel management than has been true of either federal or city agencies.

The authors wish to thank the editors of *Comparative Politics* for permission to reprint several of the tables appearing in this chapter.

The literature on public administrators in the United States has traditionally dealt with personnel questions within the context of the pendulum swing between staffing systems based on merit and those centered around political patronage. Job classification, compensation schedules, recruitment procedures, certification, evaluation, or policies related to promotion and transfer are commonly discussed from a single vantage point: to what extent and why do achievement criteria predominate over ascriptive criteria and to what effect?[3] Studies of personnel issues in a comparative, cross-national framework likewise display a preoccupation with merit-versus-patronage concerns. In many instances, such studies focus on the extent to which a given personnel system approximates the standards of the bureaucratic model.[4] In neither instance have scholars systematically directed their attention to such matters as job design, work motivation, the impact of career patterns, the role of processes, or the impact of recruitment procedures on administrative professionalization.[5]

These, as well as other considerations, indicate that the managerial transformation of urban administrative personnel necessarily occupies a prominent place —and a hithertofore neglected one—in any study of the transition from urban administration to urban management. At the most general level, urban bureaucracies (like other organizations) depend on their manpower to produce a given mix of goods and services. Hence, policies that have as their outcome the incorporation of particular political perspectives and skills into the upper ranks of city agencies act as fundamental prerequisites for administrative performance geared to the attainment of policy and programmatic goals. "Performance" in this context emerges as a function of many factors, including the degree of expertise officials command, the amount of political commitment that the urban bureaucracy embodies, and the "goodness of fit" between administrators' values and those that policy makers strive to maximize.[6] The transformation of personnel traits and values becomes all the more important when, as in the Soviet case, sustained socioeconomic growth remains an important policy objective. It becomes clear from other studies that, particularly at the local level, the absence of managerial capacity seriously hinders successful attainment of development objectives, in fact as much as poor planning or inadequate fiscal resources.[7] Clearly, then, programs that aim to upgrade administrative skills or to enhance managerial perspectives in the city exercise a multiplier effect. They well may yield more effective payoffs than increased investments in individual policy areas or programs.[8]

The management transformation of urban administration also exercises an important influence on government performance in light of an urban bureaucracy's ability to adapt and innovate in the realm of problem solving. A number of studies have indicated that bureaucracies are, by their very nature, conservative and conserving forms of organization.[9] On the other hand, as the initial discussion of the twin issues "why cities?" and "why urban mangement?" make abundantly clear, the very diversity, complexity, size, and fragility of the urban system increase both the necessity for and likelihood of organizational innovation —if the needs of the system are to be met. Innovative activity within organizations generally emerges as a function of two variables: the diversity of the organization's task structure plus the complexity of an incentive system organized around performance rather than time-in-grade. At the same time, the situation urban bureaucracies confront is a paradoxical one; the very fact of complexity, according to one interpretation, renders the adoption of innovations problematic. This means, in turn, that the sum of innovative efforts must exceed the level of innovation required, a finding that lends added weight to the importance attributed to personnel systems in urban bureaucracies.[10]

Thus, from the standpoint of the kinds of responses public management demands, it becomes important for an urban bureaucracy to generate large numbers of innovative proposals. Within this context, there is already evidence (from the study of U.S. state administration) to suggest that the probability of innovation varies directly with the professionalization of administrative personnel.[11] Professionalization contributes to urban management as an innovative form of city administration precisely because professionals enter a bureaucracy with some immunity against its homogenizing and conservatizing effects. By virtue of their specialized skills and training in a body of abstract, specialized knowledge, professionals possess a sense of separate ethos, collegial responsibility, and relative freedom from lay judgments about the quality of service rendered. Such characteristics render them elitist (a frequent charge) as well as extraordinarily capable of devising new ways to accomplish traditional ends.[12] Professionals manifest "common ways of perceiving and structuring problems and of attacking and solving them" that may not have been previously utilized within the organization.[13] They are true "cosmopolitans" who, in contrast to the "locals," have not acquired all of their knowledge and expertise from conventional ways of doing things or from within the organization itself.[14] They themselves emerge as the chief product of that change in staffing that we have included as a component of managerial transformation. Being more educated and more autonomous in their values and goals, and possessing more skills than their nonprofessional counterparts, professionals bring new and different hierarchies of preferences to the urban organization. These, in turn, leave them more open to changing environmental influences than are their counterparts, the organization men.[15]

A number of quite specific factors render the management transformation of administrative personnel particularly important in the study of Soviet cities. In the first place, studies of the role of Soviet elites, while stressing patronage networks, have traditionally failed to address the existence and significance of local-national differences within these networks. And yet, there is considerable evidence that even in extremely hierarchical systems, lower-level actors can and do exercise considerable influence on policy outcomes.[16] Second, as Chapter 2 demonstrates, the prevailing organizational structure and political control system sets limits that, under Soviet circumstances, preclude many of the alternate routes to organizational innovation, such as decentralization, participatory management, flexible incentive structures, or competitive bidding for resources.[17]

Under such circumstances, the quality of staff assumes increased importance. Indeed, the extent to which Soviet city administration today approximates the "model" of urban management elaborated in the Introduction will depend in large part on whether the participants in such administration—in particular, top executives, such as department heads and agency chiefs—have successfully effected the transition from political commissar to urban manager.[18] The spread of urban management in the USSR presupposes that those running city agencies are already socialized to patterns of behavior that embody a preference for change, adaptation, and flexibility. It would also require that the backgrounds of top administrators, considered collectively, provide the kinds of skills and expertise that the operation of large-scale and complex units in a fragmented system demands. These questions warrant further empirical examination, given that the linkage between administrative outlooks and policy outcomes in other settings has proved to be an important one. Empirical investigation into the attitudes and preferences of top administrators in the health departments of 94 Canadian and U.S. cities has shown that different value preferences and role orientations correlate significantly with different kinds of policy outcomes.[19]

An examination of changes occurring over time in the profiles of Soviet city administrators may also be instructive from a comparative perspective. Recent reassessments of the value of merit recruitment systems in the United States suggest that it is problematic that a recruitment policy heavily infused with a political component will always be destructive of public policy goals. As Chapter 2 has demonstrated for the USSR and as other studies have shown for the United States, all public personnel systems operate within a political environment, and, in part, mirror its impact.[20] In the United States at present, the "political" component of administration certainly shows every sign of increasing as equity considerations, client-oriented advocacy, and affirmative action move to the fore as major administrative concerns.[21]

At the same time, the notion that merit systems by themselves contribute to the achievement of policy goals through administration has come under fire. Indeed, some of the major failings of the U.S. civil service today, with its 13 million employees, have arisen precisely because of the rigidities and lack of managerial discretion that a system of merit-oriented personnel procedures engenders. Cities as diverse as Chicago and Minneapolis have abolished their civil service boards and switched hiring, firing, and promotions back to the hands of elected officials, while 100 other state, county, and local governments have overhauled their systems so extensively that the label "merit system" scarcely applies.[22] On the basis of the experience of cities such as New York, a strong argument can even be made that merit staffing may actually adversely affect the "merit" of subsequent policy outcomes. As early as 1963, a Brookings Institution report criticized the quality of professional, technical, and managerial personnel in the bureaucracy of New York City, a charge repeated throughout the 1960s and 1970s. The number of city employees for the various municipal services (police, fire, sanitation, education, transportation) constantly rose, even as the quantity of service outputs dropped and costs increased.[23] To this it can be added that merit systems are seldom truly open, given the "inside track" phenomenon in hiring. They also encourage excessive fragmentation and complexity in job structuring. Finally, the examination procedures that lie at their cores have yet to justify themselves in terms of the performances of the individuals actually recruited.[24] In brief, a merit system easily transforms itself into its opposite, a closed and meritless mode of public service recruitment.

When the problems of management transformation are viewed from this perspective, it would appear that the obstacles to urban administrative professionalization loom just as large in the United States as in the USSR.[25] In all fairness, it should be noted that opinion among U.S. specialists is far from unanimous as to whether public administration can or ought to constitute a profession in the narrow sense of the term. Professionalization requires that a number of conditions be met: special techniques acquired through protracted, preentry training; a sense of collegial responsibility; independent self-regulation; and the existence of an organization that licenses practitioners and enforces ethical standards.[26] If, as Don Price notes in *The Scientific Estate*, the social role of the public administrator is, by definition, closer to that of the politician than to that of the scientist or professional, it may be more fitting to regard administration in the United States primarily as part of the policy process than as an emergent profession.[27]

Obstacles can be cited for the Soviet case as well. Conventional wisdom on communist administration has it that the political ties of administrators are so strong that the boundary between administrator and politician is hopelessly blurred.[28] Indeed, as the preceding chapter suggests, the partnership idea linking administrative officials to local Party leaders in Soviet cities would seem to render the probability of an emergent professionalism all but nonexistent. At best, we might anticipate that urban administrative elites would show signs of coalescing as a career or occupational grouping—but one that is incapable of becoming a true profession.[29] Although no more than 4 percent of all "responsible" officials in the United States at present possess degrees in public administration, not a single administrator as yet possesses such a degree in the USSR.[30] To date, the Soviet setting provides no schools or programs devoted to public administration as a generic course of study (there are courses in "Soviet state development" that function as adjunct programs within faculties of law). Nor are there professional associations such as the American Society for Public Administration or the International City Management Association to link city and national personnel. At present, the situation in the USSR appears to be such that what we would expect to emerge under optimal circumstances is some form of the "administrator technician," the presence within the ranks of city administrators of large numbers of scientists, engineers, economists, and planners who are recruited into administrative posts on the basis of their technical expertise.[31]

Such individuals already figure prominently among the top ranks of the federal civil service in the United States. According to census data, between 1960 and 1976 the percentage of "professional, technical and kindred" employees in the civilian labor force rose to 40 percent in federal, state, and local posts combined. For local units alone, the proportion of the total employment accounted for by this group in 1976 stood at 42 percent.[32] At the same time, however, analysis of the increasing importance attributed to U.S. city managers indicates that they remain a "Janus-faced occupation," one that strives toward professionalism while simultaneously remaining intensely political in its concern for community-oriented responsiveness and accountability.[33]

The complex and interactive nature of the process we have labeled management transformation makes it all the more difficult to apply the yardstick of professionalism to changes occurring in Soviet urban administration. Our task is further complicated by the absence of systematically descriptive or analytic studies of Soviet administrative elites at the local level. The Western literature on Soviet urban politics and government seldom focuses on questions pertaining to administrators. When it does so, it usually (and erroneously) refers to statistics relating to the overall executive committee (*gorispolkom*) of the Soviet city. Accurate data cannot be retrieved from these statistics, given that the *gorispolkom* typically includes many individuals who neither head city departments nor perform the functions of administrative executives. It usually includes local military commanders, directors of major factories, Party officials, trade union executives, and its own support personnel.[34] In addition, the absence of any survey research data collected by Soviet scholars and dealing with the attitudes and perceptions of elites at any level forces us to infer these perceptions from career profiles, socialization experiences, and demographic variables. The situation thus provides a less rigorous methodology than we would like.[35] At the same time, however, it is possible to utilize career data on urban elites narrowly defined and to look at this data both longitudinally (across time) and latitudinally (across different types of cities). This approach generates clues to emergent leadership styles and differences in orientations among various categories of Soviet urban executives. Given the demonstrated importance of such differences in leadership styles and orientations among urban elites in the United States, the importance of marshaling additional data within a cross-national framework becomes all the more compelling.[36]

The analysis that follows is addressed to the nature, extent, and meaning of changes in Soviet urban elites as they pertain to management transformation and the role of personnel policy in that transformation. The analysis proceeds from the assumption that different skill levels, recruitment patterns, and demographic characteristics do, in actuality, affect administrative behavior and that such behavior, in turn, plays a role in shaping policy outcomes.[37] More narrowly, we inquire whether such transformation occurs in precisely those cities our hypothesis would suggest: the largest, most complex, most fragmented, and most autonomous. We are particularly interested in the patterns of allocation for resource management, since "rewarding the rich" need not apply to financial strategy and budgetary allocations alone (see Chapter 4).

Alternatively, if the distribution of personnel resources runs counter to our hypothesis, then perhaps at best a brief can be made for official claims that redistributive goals and the objective of balanced growth shape all policy decisions in urban affairs.[38] If this is indeed the case, administrative executives in small and medium-size cities should display levels of skills, orientations, degrees of political commitment, and the kinds of flexibility (measured by career experiences) that are on a par with those of their great-city counterparts. Last, it is also possible that the kinds of personnel characteristics that would make an urban bureaucracy managerial are absent altogether. Then we would expect to find political patronage as the sole recruitment criterion. This would reflect in low and constant levels of skill and training for executives across various types of cities, coupled with fairly constant levels of political penetration into administrative ranks. Furthermore, no significant differences in demographic characteristics would surface among administrative cohorts across time or city type. Which of these three alternative pictures most accurately describes the current state of urban administration in the USSR can be decided on the basis of the analysis of the data provided below.

PATHWAYS TO POWER

In recruitment to top-level administrative posts, the Party is formally assigned a leading role by virtue of the *nomenklatura* (staffing) powers already discussed in Chapter 2. In a city, the designation of particular individuals for specific posts usually comes from the city Party committee (*gorkom*), frequently in the form of a Party assignment for the individual involved.[39] In great cities, the assignment is likely to come directly from the province level or higher. Recommendations from trade unions and from the Party's youth organization, the *Komsomol*, may also be taken into account. In any case, it is assumed that the Party unit involved is thoroughly familiar with the candidate's skills, past performance, and political record.[40] In recent years, the increasing complexity of administrative tasks and the higher skill levels required have led the Party to introduce a "cadre-reserve *nomenklatura*." This represents an important step in the institutionalization of professionalism within administrative ranks.[41] Only after the Party has made a de facto selection do local soviets enter the picture, confirming (in every case with which the authors are familiar) the Party's choice. Given that only a small number of urban administrators appear to have served as city soviet deputies, and given the binding authority of Party recommendations, the role of the city soviet appears relatively unimportant, even as part of the sign-off process.[42]

The preceding description makes it clear that the pathway to power for top city bureaucrats in the USSR does not pass through any formal procedures (such as grade examinations or educational certification) designed to certify merit. Indeed, it was only after 1965 that job descriptions and position classifications that are periodically updated were even introduced into urban administration (the qualifications handbooks). Even then, these applied only to lower-level and technical posts. Uniform compensation schedules have been worked out probably at the national level. These are published in limited editions and as "eyes only" documents in the form of *Unitary Salary Schedule Handbooks*.[43]

Interestingly enough, such merit devices were introduced into Soviet public administration at about the same time that analogous mechanisms were coming under increasing fire in the United States. The use of position classification has been criticized for leading to overclassification, for failing to measure real merit, and for representing a tool that is largely irrelevant to effective public management.[44] A rank-in-person approach has been advanced as one alternative; in many respects, this produces the same outcome that Party-controlled staffing in the USSR presumably accomplishes. Likewise, public employee compensation schedules in the United States are increasingly being held up to the mirror provided by private enterprise, beginning with the national Salary Reform Act of 1962 and continuing through the Co-ordinated Federal Wage System introduced in 1968. Like classification procedures, compensation plans have become subject to increasing criticism for overrewarding certain categories of personnel and for underpaying top executives.[45]

It is important to remember, however, that even as traditional merit procedures have gained increasing acceptance in the USSR since 1965, as of 1976 the scope of such regulations still had not been extended much beyond the technical and service personnel employed in city bureaucracies.[46] Despite much discussion in the academic literature regarding the advantages of *attestatsiia* (a system of personnel review to certify merit before promotion or transfer), such procedures, based as they are on formal examinations, are still applied chiefly in Soviet industrial management; and even here they operate only for promotion, not initial recruitment. When the city of Voronezh introduced *attestatsiia* in 1972, it did so only for its lower echelon specialists and technicians; executive and managerial personnel in city agencies were deliberately excluded.[47]

In terms of the career patterns that Soviet urban administrators might pursue, both the scholarly literature and interviews with Soviet urban specialists suggest that the pathway to power follows a zigzag or crossover pattern. Administrative practitioners are described as moving across Party, Soviet, industrial, and agricultural bureaucracies even as they move up the managerial ranks to a larger city or factory, a more powerful department, or a post in a higher-level Party unit.[48] This pattern would make the Soviet urban bureaucrat, like the U.S. counterpart, an "in-and-outer." If accurate, it would also indicate that local elites in the USSR, much like their national colleagues, increasingly resemble the co-opted type of leader. Their presence, as Western observers have argued for almost a decade now, may signify a fundamental transformation of the Soviet system of rule.[49]

Whether this transformation is managerial remains to be seen. If indeed management transformation is proceeding apace, then we would also expect: (1) some evidence of increased prominence for co-opted types across time; (2) a differential distribution of co-opted officials in favor of large cities or great cities; and (3) evidence that co-optation operates very broadly. For the last point, such evidence would include some indication that executive experience within the Party plays as important a role in the career background of the urban executive as does experience in industrial management or local government. To the extent that such relationships fail to emerge from actual data on Soviet officials, the reality of urban management transformation in the USSR is called into question.

In order to investigate these relationships, statistical profiles for top-level administrators—chief executives of departments and agencies—have been compiled. The absence of a large number of cases or controls unavoidably weakens our arguments. But such a methodology is still preferable to reliance on the kinds of institutional description and episodic data that so often prevents the inclusion of the Soviet experience in any systematic, comparative studies.[50] Our analysis makes distinctions among communities by city type: great city; large, medium, and small cities; and the large urban district that resembles the medium-sized city.[51] The data is drawn from Moscow, from cities in Rostov province, RSFSR, and from the Moscow district in Leningrad. Administrative profiles within a city's bureaucracy can be differentiated according to the relative "rank" of the agencies involved, thereby allowing subcommunity distinctions. For such purposes, main boards are ranked as the most influential, since they are likely to have more financial and personnel resources as well as more direct access to the upper reaches of the administrative structure of the city. The main boards are followed by other boards and, finally, by administrative departments. The use of such a rank ordering to uncover differences in administrative careers also expands the explanatory power of a study relying on a single time-cut.

Table 5 presents data on Moscow's administrative elite. It suggests as well the kind of urban managers the "model communist city" of the future presumably will employ. The Moscow data indicates that the most important and powerful administrative posts go to those officials who are older, possess a long affiliation with the Party (*stazh*), have the most previous work experience (that is, more co-opted career patterns), and who have some experience as urban deputies. Conversely—and in contrast to the initial hypothesis labeling Soviet urban executives as "in-and-outers"—there also emerges an inverse correlation between

TABLE 5

Pathways to Power: Department Heads and Agency Chiefs, Moscow, 1975, by Category of Administrative Agency

	Main Boards (N = 13)	Boards (N = 27)	Departments (N = 12)	Total (N = 52)
Age (percent)				
Under 19	0.0	0.0	0.0	0.0
20-29	0.0	0.0	0.0	0.0
30-39	0.0	3.7	8.3	3.8
40-49	15.4	29.6	25.0	25.0
50-54	15.4	18.5	33.0	21.2
55-59	23.1	29.6	8.3	15.4
Over 60	38.5	18.5	25.0	23.1
$\bar{X}$[a]	56.9	55.0	53.3	54.3
SD[b]	6.5	6.9	7.9	7.2
Party membership				
Age when joined				
$\bar{X}$	27.2	25.0	29.5	26.0
SD	7.3	3.5	10.4	5.3
Years in party				
$\bar{X}$	29.8	28.7	26.4	28.5
SD	6.9	7.2	7.8	7.4
Education (percent)				
Higher	84.6	96.3	91.7	92.3
Secondary	7.6	3.7	8.3	5.8
Unknown	7.6	0.0	0.0	1.9
Specialization (percent)				
Engineering	15.2	37.0	25.0	28.8
Education	7.6	3.7	0.0	3.8
Health	7.6	0.0	0.0	1.9
Law	0.0	0.0	8.3	1.9
Economics	7.6	0.0	16.7	5.8
Arts	7.6	0.0	0.0	1.9
Other	38.5	55.5	50.0	50.0
None	15.4	3.7	0.0	5.8

Years of work experience			
$\bar{X}$	20.0	17.4	18.4	18.3
SD	10.6	5.9	5.5	7.3
	(N = 12)	(N = 25)	(N = 10)	(N = 47)
Area of work experience (percent)[c]			
Party	7.7[d]	40.0	50.0	33.3
Soviet	30.8	28.0	50.0	33.3
Trade union	0.0	4.0	20.0	6.3
Economic	53.8	64.0	33.0	54.2
Cultural	15.4	0.0	10.0	6.3
	(N = 13)	(N = 25)	(N = 10)	(N = 45)
Administrative experience (percent by area)			
Party	30.8	37.0	41.7	36.5
Soviet	23.1	51.9	33.3	40.4
Economic	46.2	51.9	33.3	48.1
Combined	38.5	44.0	41.7	42.3
Other or not specified	7.7	11.1	25.0	19.2
	(cult.)	(unknown)		
Tenure (years in present post)			
Under 1[e]	0.0	0.0	16.7	3.8
1-3	46.2	37.0	50.0	40.4
4-6	7.7	14.8	8.3	13.5
7-10	30.8	22.2	8.3	21.2
Over 10	15.4	25.9	16.7	21.2
$\bar{X}$	6.5	7.3	5.7	6.8
SD	5.3	10.1	6.9	8.2
Current deputy roles (percent)	100.0	88.8	66.7	86.5

a$\bar{X}$ = average.

bSD = standard deviation.

cParty and soviet.

dPercentages do not add up to unity owing to overlap.

eFor calculation, counted as 0.5.

Source: Spravka o rukovoditeliakh glavnykh upravlenii, upravlenii i otdelov Mosgorispolkoma (Moscow: Izd. Mosgorispolkoma 1975). Calculated only for heads of agencies.

the rank importance of posts and the amount of Party work or executive experience within the Party that top-level city officials command. Put another way, while the administrative elite is likely to have a long affiliation with the Party in terms of length of membership, responsible work within the Party's bureaucracy at any level does not seem to account for a significant proportion of its previous work experience. In 1975, only 36.5 percent of Moscow agency heads had served as Party *apparatchiki* (paid workers). The same holds true for administrative experience in city government (40.4 percent) as opposed to that conferred simply by virtue of membership in the city council as an elected deputy (86.5 percent). Overall, in terms of both work experience in general and prior executive experience in particular, the pathway to power leads through involvement with Soviet industry as opposed to either executive or nonexecutive work in the Party, trade union, or cultural or municipal bureaucracies. Work in a factory (54.2 percent) or managerial experience in industry (48.1 percent) smooths the way to the top in cities that are themselves the most important in the national urban hierarchy.

The data from the Moscow case supports the management transformation hypothesis of the Introduction only in a highly qualified fashion. Certainly in terms of their high levels of education (92.3 percent with higher education), substantial preentry work experience (18.3 years), prior exposure to the workings of an industrial economy (54.2 percent with work experience, 48.1 percent with management experience), and relatively stable tenure in their posts (6.8 year average), these Moscow bureaucrats qualify as "professionals" and "managers." By the same token, however, we fail to find any systematic interagency correlation between the intensity of the managerial demands particular agencies impose and the qualities of the executives they actually recruit in Moscow. More concretely, the main boards—by virtue of the large number of subdivisions they utilize, the reach of their administrative operations, the complexity of their agency mission, and the fragmentation of responsibility that these factors engender—should, if the hypothesis is to hold, recruit individuals of the following profile: the best educated, the most experienced in Party and economic work, those having the greatest amount of prior executive experience, and those with the highest levels of exposure to the workings of Soviet local government. A quick glance at Table 5 reveals that this is not the case. Further, the recruitment advantages that age and length of Party affiliation confer suggest that seniority and political patronage still play a prominent role in personnel practices. Such data fit our picture of how a "managerial type" should look only with some difficulty.[52]

The emergence of the managerial administrator in the Soviet city has been limited by yet another important consideration: the relatively short tenure of even those administrative executives who occupy the most important urban posts in the entire country.[53] In view of the standard deviation that accompanies the mean of 6.8 years in office, it is hardly surprising that the proportion of great-city officials with less than three years in office ranges from 46 to 50 percent. On the one hand, these figures might be cited as supporting the hypothesis that management transformation is, indeed, the wave of the future for Soviet cities. After all, the modern manager is presumably fresh and flexible in his outlook and representative of all that is new in a society. The fact of short tenure would seem to argue decisively that these urban bureaucrats are not organization men but, instead, are circulating rapidly through the ranks. But when the tenure data is coupled with the age data, the picture changes dramatically. The "new blood" is basically a recycled product ("old wine in new bottles") as was true of the more general transition from tsarist to Soviet administration in the 1920s.[54]

From the standpoint of the probable values of the administrative cadre, the age data is particularly revealing. In 1975, the city of Moscow was run by a generation that grew to physical, social, and, political maturity in the 1930s, the height of Stalinism. They entered the Party at a period when those concepts of commandism, authoritarian rule, and strict hierarchical organization, which were to bear the label "Stalinism," already provided the defining principle of Party and government life in the Soviet Union. While it certainly cannot be assumed that their leadership styles and organizational values have remained frozen since that time, there is little evidence to suggest that they represent a totally new and different managerial type of official, one whose attitudes, approaches, and orientations differ significantly from those of his predecessors. Political conservatism seems to march hand in hand with technical proficiency in the model communist city.

This detailed investigation of career characteristics of Moscow agency chiefs can be placed in a broader perspective by a review of the profile of the city's entire administrative staff. From 1960 onward, that proportion of the city's working population employed in administrative organs (even including management personnel in city-run hospitals, enterprises, amusement facilities, and other institutions operated on a cost accounting basis) has grown steadily.[55] By 1975, administrative employment covered as many individuals as did work in health care facilities or in housing management and consumer services combined. The same proportions of the work force were employed by city agencies as there were in retail trade operations or urban surface transport (including road maintenance) (see Table 6, columns A).[56] Equally striking, the number of administrative personnel exceeded those employed by public dining facilities, by communications institutions, and by various technical services. Even during the heyday of Khrushchev's much-touted "war against bureaucracy," the number of city administrators in Moscow increased by 31.2 percent (1960-64). The Brezhnev-Kosygin diumvirate rejected Khrushchev's attack on the public bureaucracy as just another example of his "harebrained scheming" and "subjectivist"approach to policy formulation. Nevertheless, the initial period of the new leadership witnessed a further increase in the city's administrative staff of 55.5 percent. As a result, by the end of the decade and across the span of two leaderships differing radically in their public conceptions of bureaucracy, the administrative staff of Moscow had almost doubled in size, increasing 86.7 percent since 1960.[57]

TABLE 6

Average Yearly Distributions of Labor Force and Percentage Increments, Moscow, 1965-75

	1960	1965		1970		1971		1972		1973		1974		1975	
	A	A	B	A	B	A	B	A	B	A	B	A	B	A	B
All workers and employees, city of Moscow	100.0	100.0	100.0	100.0	114.4	100.0	113.4	100.0	115.7	100.0	117.8	100.0	119.5	100.0	121.3
Industry	36.4	33.2	100.0	30.3	101.5	29.6	100.9	28.9	100.7	28.5	101.0	28.1	101.1	27.8	101.4
Transport, total	8.9	8.4	—	8.1	106.6	8.1	107.6	7.9	108.8	8.0	111.0	8.0	112.1	8.0	114.2
Surface (bus, auto, truck)	4.8	5.0	100.0	5.0	110.6	5.0	112.2	4.9	113.5	5.0	116.6	5.0	118.0	5.0	120.6
Railroad	2.9	2.4	—	2.1	99.2	2.1	99.5	2.0	99.4	2.0	99.7	2.0	100.1	2.0	102.3
Communications	1.4	1.5	100.0	1.4	102.9	1.4	110.5	1.5	115.7	1.5	117.7	1.5	119.6	1.5	120.3
Construction	7.6	6.1	100.0	6.6	121.6	6.8	127.9	7.1	136.1	7.1	137.7	7.1	139.1	7.0	139.6
Project design, construction	2.6	2.8	100.0	3.1	124.8	3.2	128.5	3.2	131.6	3.2	133.7	3.1	133.6	3.0	133.1
Trade	4.8	5.4	100.0	5.4	110.2	5.4	113.3	5.3	112.7	5.3	114.0	5.2	115.2	5.2	115.3
Public dining places	2.3	2.5	100.0	2.7	122.2	2.7	125.4	2.7	126.6	2.7	129.4	2.7	131.3	2.7	132.2
Housing, consumer services	5.7	5.0	100.0	5.1	113.2	5.2	116.6	5.1	119.0	5.0	117.9	5.0	120.4	5.0	121.4
Health	4.4	4.3	100.0	4.5	118.3	4.6	121.7	4.7	125.8	4.7	129.5	4.9	136.8	5.0	142.0
Culture and education	5.3	5.7	100.0	6.0	117.9	6.0	119.0	6.0	121.2	6.0	123.8	6.1	126.3	6.1	129.0
Scientific institutes	12.4	17.0	100.0	17.6	115.4	17.8	118.7	18.2	123.6	18.5	128.3	18.7	131.9	19.0	135.8
Credit and insurance agencies	0.4	0.5	100.0	0.5	110.0	0.4	108.1	0.5	113.4	0.5	115.4	0.5	126.3	0.5	134.9
Administration	—	3.7	100.0	4.7	142.3	4.7	146.2	4.8	150.1	4.8	155.3	4.9	159.4	5.0	164.5
Administration, 1960 base	3.1	—	131.2	—	186.7	—	n.a.	—	n.a.	—	n.a.	—	n.a.	—	n.a.

n.a. = not available.

Note: A columns indicate percentage of yearly total; B columns indicate percentage of 1965 base.

Sources: Moskva v tsifrakh, 1971-1975 gg (Moscow: Izd. Statistika, 1976), pp. 79, 81; *Moskva v tsifrakh: kratkii statisticheskii sbornik* (Moscow: Izd. Statistika, 1972), pp. 66, 67.

The proportion of women employed in Moscow's administrative ranks rose as well. From 57 percent of the total staff in 1965, it rose to 64 percent in 1975, an increase of 13 percent of the 1965 base.[58] The "feminization" of the bureaucracy slightly exceeded the 55-56 percent average for the working population of the city as a whole. It also represented the highest rate of feminization for any single branch of city employment.[59] In general, the overall growth rate for administrative personnel of either sex was higher than in any other branch of the economy, standing at 42.3 percent for 1965-70 and 64.5 percent for 1965-75.[60] The most rapid increases occurred between 1965 and 1970.[61]

Additional comparisons of the tenure of Moscow city administrators with that of employees in other branches of the urban economy paint a picture of remarkable continuity. As of 1967, fully 46 percent of Moscow's municipal employees had been working in some post in the city bureaucracy for at least 20 years, that is, since 1947. Of the total, 31.6 percent entered city agencies during the early years of World War II.[62] These figures suggest that the "old wine in new bottles" phenomenon that we found at the upper ranks of city administration may include the "Indians" as well as the "chiefs."

The educational qualifications of Moscow's administrative staff have increased as well over the years. But the absence of raw data in Soviet sources makes calculation of percentage increments impossible. For the years 1965-75 administrative employment ranked third among all branches of the city's economy employing specialists with higher education (72,600 in 1965, 100,400 in 1975).[63] As was true for changes in the proportion of the work force employed in administration, the absolute increase in the number of specialists working within city agencies was greater than for the proportion working in any other branch.[64] Among the branches of the city economy that employed specialists with only a secondary specialized education, city administration consistently ranked fourth.[65] Such a picture of the rising skill qualifications among Moscow's administrative personnel mirrors those changes occurring among elites in other types of communities (see Tables 7 and 8). By 1975, 12.4 percent of all city personnel in Moscow had some sort of specialist qualifications.

Our second set of data on urban administrators describes the personnel situation in large, medium, and small cities. We draw upon data available solely for Rostov province (RSFSR) and then only in aggregate form.[66] Further distinctions among communities could be made by letting the large urban district stand as representative of cities of medium size (see Table 8).

The Rostov data shown in Table 7 presents a sharp contrast to data in Table 5 in those categories for which comparisons are possible. In contrast to their metropolitan colleagues, officials in Rostov's cities are less likely to be Party members. They are also, on the average, less educated, less specialized in their training, and enjoy a longer tenure in office. These observations hold even for straight-line projections of the 1961-67 changes to 1975, thereby matching the time frame for the Moscow data.

TABLE 7

Pathways to Power: Department Heads and Agency Chiefs in Large, Medium, and Small Towns,[a] Rostov Province,[b] 1961 and 1967

	Planning		Culture		Education		Finance		Welfare		Trade		Public Order		Municipal Economy		Total[c]	
	1961	1967	1961	1967	1961	1967	1961	1967	1961	1967	1961	1967	1961	1967	1961	1967	1961	1967
N	11.9	17.3	11.7	14.7	13.9	18.7	19.0	22.0	14.4	17.3	13.0	13.0	6.1	17.0	4.6	6.0	403[d]	388
Party penetration (percent)	80.9	80.8	84.1	96.2	100.0	100.0	100.0	100.0	97.4	98.4	100.0	100.0	100.0	100.0	77.7	100.0	93.8	96.7
Education (percent)																		
Higher	31.9	32.7	20.6	44.2	98.7	98.5	26.7	42.4	7.7	13.1	14.3	42.9	45.5	66.1	22.2	33.3	37.0	49.5
Unfinished higher	10.6	5.8	15.9	21.2	1.3	1.5	12.0	0.0	2.6	3.3	7.1	0.0	12.1	11.9	0.0	11.1	7.9	6.7
Total	42.5	38.5	36.5	65.4	100.0	100.0	38.7	42.4	10.3	16.4	21.4	42.9	57.6	78.0	22.0	44.4	44.9	56.2
Secondary	42.6	53.8	41.3	34.6	0.0	0.0	58.9	57.6	37.2	50.8	42.9	50.0	0.0	22.0	22.2	33.3	35.5	36.3
Unfinished secondary	14.9	7.7	22.2	34.6	0.0	0.0	2.7	0.0	51.3	32.8	21.4	7.1	0.0	0.0	55.6	22.2	18.9	7.5
Total	57.5	61.5	63.5	34.6	0.0	0.0	61.6	57.6	88.5	83.6	64.3	57.1	0.0	22.0	77.8	55.5	54.4	43.8
Elementary	0.0	0.0	0.0	0.0	0.0	0.0	0.0	0.0	1.3	0.0	14.3	0.0	9.1	0.0	0.0	0.0	0.7	0.0
Specialization (percent)																		
Engineering	2.1	9.6	0.6	0.0	0.0	0.0	1.3	0.0	0.0	0.0	0.0	7.1	9.1	3.4	22.2	44.4	2.2	4.1
Education	4.3	1.9	0.0	0.0	100.0	100.0	4.0	4.5	1.3	1.6	7.1	0.0	12.1	0.0	11.1	11.1	21.8	18.8
Health	0.0	0.0	0.0	0.0	0.0	0.0	0.0	0.0	0.0	0.0	0.0	0.0	0.0	0.0	0.0	0.0	0.0	0.0
Law	0.0	0.0	0.0	0.0	0.0	0.0	1.3	1.5	5.1	14.1	0.0	0.0	45.5	78.0	0.0	0.0	5.0	14.4
Economics	31.9	40.4	0.0	0.0	0.0	0.0	66.7	83.3	1.3	1.6	7.1	14.3[e]	0.0	3.4	0.0	0.0	16.6	20.9
Arts	0.0	0.0	22.2	46.2	0.0	0.0	0.0	0.0	0.0	0.0	0.0	0.0	0.0	0.0	0.0	0.0	3.5	6.2
Other[f]	34.0	32.7	0.0	19.2	0.0	0.0	8.0	10.6	0.0	3.3	14.3	35.1	0.0	3.4	0.0	0.0	6.2	9.8
None	27.7	0.0	77.7	34.6	0.0	0.0	18.7	0.0	92.3	78.7	71.4	42.9	33.3	11.9	66.6	44.4	44.9	24.5

Years in present post

Under 1	19.1	9.6	33.3	5.8	16.0	6.1	12.0	10.6	23.1	18.0	35.7	14.3	21.2	8.5	44.4	22.2	22.4	10.7
1-3	17.0	23.1	34.9	15.4	20.0	9.1	18.7	4.5	11.5	13.1	21.4	42.9	6.1	13.6	44.4	44.4	20.4	15.4
4-6	6.4	13.5	23.8	9.6	16.0	18.2	22.7	22.7	3.8	14.8	14.3	7.1	24.2	6.8	11.1	22.2	15.6	14.8
7-10	29.9	32.7	3.2	36.5	24.0	30.3	33.3	24.2	42.3	23.0	14.3	14.3	24.2	39.0	0.0	0.0	25.6	28.9
Over 10	17.0	21.2	4.8	32.7	24.0	33.3	13.3	37.9	19.2	31.1	14.3	21.4	24.2	32.2	0.0	0.0	16.1	30.2

[a] According to official Soviet statistics for the period under scrutiny, Rostov cities distributed as follows:

	Population	1961	1967
Great cities	Over 1 million	1	1
Large cities	100,000-500,000	4	4
Medium cities	50,000-100,000	4	4
Small cities	10,000-50,000	10	10

Narodnoe khoziaistvo Rostovskoi oblasti (Rostov: Izd. Statistika, 1961), p. 22.; *Rostovskaia oblast' za 50 let* (Rostov: Izd. Statistika, 1967), p. 21.

[b] In order to convert raw data on all administrative executives within the province to weighted Ns for urban units alone, correction factors (C.F.) were devised on the following grounds: the proportion of all administrative units that were urban times the estimated distribution of each type of agency among territorial divisions. The C.F.s look as follows:

Agency	1961	1967
Planning	.253	.333
Culture	.185	.283
Education	.185	.283
Finance	.253	.333
Welfare	.185	.283
Trade	.923	.938
Public order (police)	.185	.283
Municipal economy	.253	.333

As these do not reflect on the assumption of equal distribution of administrative characteristics between urban and nonurban units, they have been applied only to the Ns. Soviet sources detailing actual percentage of rural administrators are unreliable for discussing the functional distribution of personnel. Many executives of rural territories live in cities, and the rural figures typically include collective farm managers and cooperative personnel in the totals. *Narodnoe*, p. 7; *Rostovskaia oblast'*, p. 7; I. A. Azovkin, *Mestnye sovety v sisteme organov vlasti* (Moscow: Iur. lit., 1971), pp. 137-38.

[c] The "totals" as percentages are uncorrected.

[d] Uncorrected.

[e] Entirely in trade professions.

[f] Indicates specializations in agriculture and health fields.

Source: A. S. Beznat'ev, "Sovershenstvovanie partiinogo rukovodstva mestnymi Sovetami (1961-1967 gg na materialakh Rostovskoi oblastnoi partiinoi organizatsii)" (Master's thesis, Rostov State University, 1971), p. vi (Appendix), table 10.

TABLE 8

Pathways to Power: Top-Level Administrators[a] in an Urban District, Moscow District, Leningrad, 1961-67

	Year			Percent of Increase/Decrease
	1962	1964	1966	
Age				
$\bar{X}$	47.2	48.6	47.4	—[b]
SD	8.1	8.0	8.7	—
Party membership penetration (percent)	88.8	90.4	95.4	+6.6
Years ($\bar{X}$)	12.3	13.2	11.5	—
Years (SD)	4.0	4.0	5.0	—
Education (percent)				
Higher	50.0	32.0	36.4	-13.6
Unfinished higher	0.0	4.6	4.5	-0.1
Total	50.0	36.6	40.9	-9.1
Secondary	40.0	54.2	54.6	+14.6
Unfinished secondary	0.0	4.6	0.0	-0.4
Total	45.0	58.8	54.6	+9.6
Elementary	5.0	4.6	4.5	-1.5
Years of preentry work experience				
$\bar{X}$	10.7	10.3	8.2	-2.3
SD	5.3	5.6	5.5	
Work experience by area (percent)				
Party and Komsomol	15.0	15.7	17.7	+2.7
Trade union	0.0	0.0	3.6	0.0
Municipal units	20.0	21.8	20.9	+0.9
Economic administration	5.0	3.5	4.3	-0.7
None, cultural affairs, other	60.0	59.0	53.5	-6.5
Previous executive experience by area (percent)[c]				
Party and Komsomol	2.3	2.9	3.2	+0.9
Trade union	0.0	0.0	0.7	+0.7
Municipal units	3.0	4.0	3.8	+0.8
Economic administration	0.8	0.7	0.8	0.0

Years of urban administrative experience (in present post)				
X̄	6.8	6.3	6.2	—
SD	5.8	6.3	2.2	—
Years of urban administrative experience (in any post)				
X̄	6.8	6.3	6.2	—
SD	5.8	6.3	5.2	—
Special preparation for present post (percent)				
Individual courses	15.0	18.2	18.2	+3.2
Polytechnical education	5.0	4.6	4.5	−0.0
Secondary specialized education	15.0	27.3	27.3	+12.5
Unfinished higher education	0.0	4.6	4.5	−0.1
Higher education	50.0	31.8	36.4	−13.6
Type of preentry work experience (percent)				
Worker	10.0	4.6	4.5	−5.5
Intelligentsia[d]	55.1	59.1	63.7	+8.6
Employee	34.9	36.3	31.8	−3.1
Levels of political activism (percent)				
Political education	25.0	1.4	22.7	−2.3
Workers control	0.0	0.0	0.0	0.0
Deputy	20.7	27.3	27.3	+6.6
Social activist	5.0	9.1	22.7	+17.7
Total	50.7	37.8	72.7	+22.0

aAs recalculated from the original tables, top-level "administrators" include all agency heads, their deputies, and the heads of sectors or divisions. Given the fact that deputy heads regularly move up into the top posts of their agencies and the fact that the number of sector heads involved is likely to be quite small, the data base of Table 8, while seemingly broader than for the other tables, becomes comparable to that for elite levels of urban administration in other Soviet communities.

bDashes indicate increase/decrease value not significant.

cCalculated by multiplying the percentages with work experience in an area by the percentages listed as leaders.

dThe distinction between "intelligentsia" and "employee" remains vague in the original, despite an involved explanation. Presumably the former category refers to those with some sort of professional skills, while the latter refers to white-collar work of a more general sort. See table source, pp. 181-85.

Note: X̄ = mean, SD = standard deviation. The increase/decrease was calculated according to the following formula:

$$(\bar{X} + SD) - (\bar{X} - SD) - (SD\ 1966 - SD\ 1962)$$

If $SD > \bar{X}_1 - \bar{X}_2$, then the difference is "not significant."

Source: B. D. Lebin and M. N. Perfil'ev, Kadry apparata upravlenniia v SSSR (Leningrad: Izd. Nauka, 1970), pp. 176, 186, 188, 197, 198, 221, 224, 235, 238. According to the authors (pp. 166-67), this district is a "typical" one among those in large Soviet cities in terms of its demographic structure, the level of economic development and the like. One of the most striking features of this "typical" bureaucracy lies in the way in which it discriminates against women in top posts. Between 1961 and 1967, the proportion of female executives declined from 63.1 to 40.0 percent (and from 87.2 to 82.9 percent of all specialists and instructors). For the district as a whole, women comprised 58.8 percent of the population in 1959. See pp. 173, 176.

Among the top administrators described in Table 7, differences by area of policy specialization also are important. Despite the overall importance of planning commissions in the urban decision-making framework (see Chapter 2), the levels of Party penetration among these administrators remain lower than for other agencies.[67] A similar situation prevails in the departments of culture and social welfare. Interagency differences are also apparent with respect to levels of skill and technical preparation. The most educated administrators head the departments of security, culture, municipal economy, trade, and finance, in that order. Again, the educational levels of planning and welfare administrators are quite low. In welfare and municipal economy agencies, moreover, a sizable proportion of administrators still lacked a complete education as late as January 1968.[68] In terms of the average for agency heads with some amount of higher education, those in planning, finance, welfare, trade, and municipal economy fall below the average. The picture that emerges does not speak strongly for the management transformation hypothesis: high skill components associated with a managerial type of executive concentrate in agencies devoted to political supervision and ideological control. Conversely, these components remain heavily discounted in such crucial areas as planning, municipal economy, and finance.

In certain important respects (and contrary to our hypothesis), we can conclude that the urban administrator in this second cluster looks more managerial than his great-city counterpart. Table 5 indicates that top Moscow administrators are drawn heavily from the engineering field, followed by economics and law. Fully half of them had no specialization entered in their official biographies. By contrast, those of Table 7 possess substantially more preparation in the field of economics, followed by education and law. Engineering backgrounds— and the technique-oriented, efficiency concerns that presumably predominate among great-city administrators—have all but vanished from the picture.[69] Again, it appears that administrators with appropriate backgrounds are the least likely to be recruited for the urban environment most in need of modern management skills and orientations.

With respect to personnel turnover, cities in this second category share some of the same problems as the great cities. The proportion of administrators having served three years or less is substantially lower (26.1 percent), as opposed to the 44.2 percent in Moscow. At the same time, however, cities in Rostov province experienced almost a doubling of the proportion of officials serving for more than a decade in the years 1961-67. If this trend is projected forward to 1975, well over half of the administrators in Table 7 will show a decade or more of experience in the same post. The profile then mirrors the profile of Moscow's administrative staff as a whole. Here again, we find that Soviet cities experience real problems in developing a core of experienced but flexible managers, a cadre that would have a tenure averaging 4-9 years.

Data pertaining to a third set of officials—top administrators of Moscow district in Leningrad—make possible further comparisons among communities.

The group described by Table 8 are younger than those of Table 5, indicating that the path to power in Soviet urban administration may well lead through an urban district early in the official's career. Like our second cluster of bureaucrats in Table 7, not all of those represented in Table 8 are Party members. At least at the level of the great city, a filtering out on the basis of political affiliation does occur. Along similar lines, the length of Party affiliation is lower for urban district agency heads than for those already in Moscow. This fact reinforces the impression that some measure of political commitment is employed as individuals move up the ladder of posts in the national urban hierarchy. Nor is this merely a function of differing time frames. If the political *stazh* of the 1967 cohort of urban district administrators is projected forward to 1975 (assuming no bias in favor of age but only a normal aging process), then the average *stazh* for the great-city elite administrator should be only 20 years. In point of fact, the average for the Moscow cohort of 1975 stood at 26 years, indicating that the length of Party affiliation is an active factor in the selection process.

In other respects, the urban district administrator of Table 8 compares unfavorably to both his great-city and to his medium-to-small-city counterpart when the yardstick of managerial transformation is applied. These findings, in turn, do support the argument of a differential distribution of skills in the initial hypothesis. Educational levels among these top-level executives are substantially lower. This suggests that, measured simply in terms of the amount of training the recruitment process enlists, those cities most likely to face management problems *do* recruit a more qualified administrator. By comparison with the Moscow group, urban district administrators also have less preentry work experience (in 1966, 8.2 years on the average in the urban district, as against 18.3 years in Moscow), less experience in Party work (17.7 percent against Moscow's 33.3 percent), less industrial work experience (4.3 percent of all urban district administrators), and less management experience in industrial enterprises (0.8 percent).

The data thus yields a mixed set of findings that support the management transformation hypothesis only with certain very real and important qualifications. Moscow's administrators resemble management professionals only in some limited respects, for political patronage still figures very prominently in selection procedures for the top urban posts. Furthermore, the picture that our data sketches with respect to age, turnover, and skill qualifications among top-level administrators across different types of communities hardly suggests that any kind of "iron law" of management transformation is at work in Soviet urban affairs. The data also reveals an important aspect of change in the Soviet system. Personnel changes appear at once "modernizing" in a technical sense (education, skills, work experience) and "conservatizing" from a political perspective (Party penetration, period of political commitment, the political generational affiliation of administrators).[70] In terms of the schema of city futures presented in the Introduction, the data on Soviet urban administrators argues strongly in favor of the "probable" as opposed to the "possible" alternative; to judge on the basis of the personnel component, the technocratic city rather than the populist one is the more likely outcome. If Moscow indeed represents the wave of the future, the case for the technocratic city becomes all the more compelling.

How does the Soviet urban administrator as an emergent manager look by comparison with his U.S. counterpart? Comparisons remain difficult because comprehensive and systematic personnel data are missing on both sides. If the profile of U.S. city managers is used as a functional analogue for comparative purposes, some general similarities and differences can be pinpointed.

Similarities do exist. The fact that a sizable body of U.S. scholarly opinion argues that the city manager is not a purely autonomous professional but a "'politician for hire'" and a major actor in community decision making strengthens rather than vitiates our comparison.[71] Today, 2,665 U.S. city managers or chief administrative officers in cities with a total of more than 100 million population share with their Soviet colleagues the problem of fragmented authority.[72] It arises in the U.S. setting directly out of the cross-pressures engendered by the complexity of intergovernmental "marble cake" relationships and out of the growing demands for increased participation in administrative decision making from various constituencies.[73] But, whereas a large number of Americans reside in communities employing city managers of chief administrative officers, the overwhelming majority of these are relatively small and homogeneous. Although we are using a formal (rather than functional) definition of "urban manager" for the U.S. case, the personnel data here also calls into question the real impact of an urban management transformation. In the United States as in the Soviet Union, the type of cities most in need of management capacity still appear the least likely to command a management-oriented cadre of urban administrators.

The contrasts between the two groups are important as well. Engineering, still the preferred training for Soviet great-city administrators, is steadily declining among U.S. city managers (from 77 percent in 1934 to 18 percent in 1977).[74] Equally important, interviews with Soviet urban administrators, coupled with a survey of the monograph literature, suggest that an attitudinal shift away from a concern with "the techniques of municipal management" (the title of the 1958 flagship volume of the International City Management Association's Municipal Management Series) toward that broader appreciation of human, social, and organizational skills required in "managing the modern city" (the 1974 edition of the same volume) has yet to be effected.[75] If the ICMA 1975 survey of city managers is employed as a baseline for comparison, the U.S. cohort appears better educated on the average (76 percent with bachelor's degrees, and 48 percent with advanced degrees).[76] As we shall demonstrate in Chapter 6, generalist management training has not yet taken hold for Soviet city officials as a matter of national policy.

Comparison is also useful along other dimensions. In theory, administrative recruitment in the USSR is designed to ensure that the Soviet urban administrator is an "in-and-outer," an administrative generalist who is co-opted from other fields of employment through a zigzag pattern of recruitment and promotion across several kinds of local bureaucracies. In practice, however, this procedure is not universally applied. In the United States, by contrast, the informal shape that career patterns of city managers have assumed increasingly favors the "in-and-out" pattern. In 1977, 29 percent of U.S. city managers had previous experience in government service, 16 percent had prior experience in business management.[77]   In both settings, urban officials appear to take an activist view of their policy roles, seeing themselves as career professionals (75 percent on the U.S. side).[78]   At the same time, personnel turnover in the USSR, at least in the great cities, remains somewhat higher than in the United States, where tenure averages five years.[79]   Finally, Soviet urban administrators lack any professional association, newsletter, or journal devoted to their concerns as urban administrators. Professional organizations, however weak they remain as licensing and governing bodies in the United States, still represent an important first step in professionalization of an occupational or career grouping. The step has yet to be taken in the Soviet Union.[80]

MATERIAL INCENTIVES

Money as a motivator has long seemed one of the most efficacious solutions to problems of morale and productivity in both the public and private sectors in the United States. The importance of a compensation plan that is both equitable and geared to the performance of public employees is traditionally described as a pillar of "good" administration, whether local or national[81] Increasing interest in the dynamics of public management has been accompanied, however, by a growing realization that monetary incentives are not the only ones to which administrators respond. Indeed, it has become characteristic of the public management as opposed to public administration literature that U.S. administrators are now regarded as no more captive of a "Midas syndrome" than are their counterparts working in the private sector.[82]

All the same, the importance of material incentive plans as a mechanism whereby capable individuals are attracted to and retained by public service cannot be entirely discounted. Nor can the role played by financial rewards in improving performance be disregarded. Payment must be adequate for the individual official to achieve his material, psychological, and social goals. Over and above such considerations, money may also exercise considerable power as a symbol, especially in the United States. Studies of federal administrators in the United States have shown that the twin issues of pay and security figure prominently among the full panalopy of incentives available to those working in administrative positions. Other needs and drives that, according to the psychologist Abram Maslow, fall at the upper end of a hierarchical continuum still rank higher as motivators.[83]

In the absence of any firsthand information about the full complex of drives that probably motivate Soviet urban administrators, our discussion of ways to maintain the quality of personnel resources in the USSR is necessarily limited to a discussion of material incentives.[84] Soviet city bureaucrats work for a fixed salary that varies from agency to agency and among cities of various ranks. There is no evidence that any of the variations in incentive arrangements employed in the United States—such as the cost-savings plan currently employed in New York or some form of the Scanlon Plan occasionally employed by local government—have yet appeared in the Soviet city.[85] In the USSR, the absolute amount of an official's salary still depends on the territorial subordination and the hierarchical rank that a given city occupies (see Chapter 2) and on pay scales developed nationally. But the variance for individuals in the same area of administration performing essentially the same tasks seldom exceeds 50 rubles a month.

According to information available, the salaries of urban executives look as follows. Department heads generally earn some 200 to 250 rubles a month, with the monthly salary increasing up to 250 or 300 rubles a month in the great cities. Legal consultants earn about 100 rubles a month, while organizational instructors (personnel administrators) are paid 150 rubles monthly. Other specialists earn somewhat less than what they would for the same tasks and skill qualifications in Soviet industry.[86] Moving out of the cities, we find that the salaries of rural administrative officials are somewhat lower and the officials themselves far fewer. Predictably, salaries for provincial and regional authorities are greater: 400 rubles a month for the chairman of the provincial executive committee, 300 rubles for the administrative assistant, 170 rubles for personnel administrators.[87]

To put these figures in some perspective, it is important to note that since 1971 the minimum wage in the USSR has stood at 70 rubles a month. Likewise, the average monthly industrial wage rose from 154 rubles in 1974 to 161 rubles in 1975.[88] According to Soviet economists, the "material welfare minimum budget" for a typical family of four (two adults, two children) stood at 205.6 rubles a month in 1976, or 51.4 rubles a person.[89] On an all-union basis, the average monthly wages of industrial workers and white collar employees were 96.5 rubles monthly in 1965, 122 rubles in 1970, 146 rubles in 1975, with a rise to 170 rubles projected for 1980.[90] In 1974, white collar employees generally earned an average of 126 rubles monthly; engineers and technicians, 193 rubles (200 rubles by 1975); and professional managers, some 205-50 rubles or more.[91]

Information on salaries for administrative staffs and officials at all levels and across types of cities is, unfortunately, still lacking. Information on Moscow alone, while undoubtedly inflated vis-a-vis a national urban average, does, however, provide some indication of possible prevailing patterns. Between 1970 and 1975, the average monthly wage of all workers and employees in the city rose by some 14 percent, with the largest increase occurring between 1974 and 1975.[92] All the same, administrative salaries remained consistently higher than those for most other branches of the city's economy, rising from 156.2 rubles monthly in

1970 to 160.6 rubles in 1975. Salaries for Moscow's administrative personnel were also considerably higher than average administrative salaries at the national levels. By 1975, the national average stood at 124 rubles a month for administrative wages at levels within the sum of all territorial jursdictions.[93] In Moscow, according to Table 9, only the wages of contruction personnel and employees in surface transport were higher for any given year.

How representative this rather precise breakdown is for other cities and hierarchical levels still remains unclear. A 1974 study of wage differentials by Perevdentsev (see Table 10) presents a somewhat different national picture. On an all-union basis, administrative wages registered the smallest total gain (18 percent) of any branch of the Soviet economy between 1965 and 1973. But actual salary levels for administrators fell below the national average in only one year, 1973. A similar picture prevailed throughout Rostov province for overall administrative salary increases.[94]

Whether and to what extent such remuneration is "adequate" as an incentive for high administrative performance is difficult to assess. Certainly, the picture for Moscow suggests that, as in other areas (see Chapter 4), the great cities command more resources than do others. The data indicate that, whatever equity and redistributive goals the political leadership may profess, these retreat into the background when it comes to rewarding administrators. At the same time, Soviet sociological studies have shown that the service sector generally is regarded as undercompensated by Soviet standards and as an occupation of low prestige. In studies conducted among secondary school graduates in the cities of Novosibirsk (1963), Leningrad (1965), and Lvov (1968), employment in city services always placed near the bottom in occupational rankings.[95] While such studies do not speak to the position of top administrators, they do suggest that there exist real problems in recruiting, motivating, and adequately compensating those lower-echelon line employees who constitute the overwhelming majority of the city's employees.

Comparisons of Soviet administrative salaries and patterns of change with those in the United States are as difficult as they are tempting. In 1975, full-time municipal employees in the United States earned more on the average than other state and local employees.[96] A 1976 survey of 26 different types of municipal administrators in almost 5,000 U.S. cities indicated an average salary increase of 7.4 percent over 1975, while police and fire officials led the list for the entire previous five-year span. For city managers and finance directors, the total increases in the 1971-76 period amounted to 41 percent and 44 percent, respectively. Overall, large salary differentials continue to exist between central city officials and those in the suburbs of the SMSAs, as well as between those in large and small municipalities.[97] Thus, there are large differentials within and among U.S. cities. Our Soviet data suggest that an analogous situation exists in the USSR, although it follows a different pattern and for rather different reasons.

On the whole, the Soviet data available raise serious doubts regarding official Soviet claims that administrative expenditures have been held down to only

TABLE 9

Average Monthly Wages, Workers and Employees, Moscow
(rubles)

	1970	1971	1972	1973	1974	1975
Average for the Moscow city economy	137.1	140.2	143.5	146.5	151.0	156.6
Industry	137.6	142.1	146.4	149.9	154.2	158.0
Transport average	144.2	149.9	155.3	158.0	163.5	168.7
Surface (bus, auto, truck)	157.9	160.2	163.0	165.5	173.0	179.2
Railroad	117.3	129.0	140.5	144.1	147.0	148.6
Communications	116.9	121.8	123.9	126.0	129.2	134.4
Construction	165.6	167.4	169.9	171.3	176.1	180.0
Project design, construction	145.1	147.5	150.5	152.7	155.2	156.2
Trade	105.8	108.2	111.1	113.1	115.3	116.3
Public dining establishments	120.3	122.6	125.0	126.7	129.6	132.4
Housing and consumer services	101.7	102.8	104.0	105.3	107.9	108.8
Health	104.3	105.1	108.5	112.6	123.6	124.5
Culture and education	128.7	129.1	133.4	139.1	141.3	142.2
Scientific institutes	145.0	148.9	151.4	154.3	160.2	160.2
Credit and insurance agencies	117.6	121.1	122.8	127.3	131.3	137.7
Administration	156.2	157.1	158.5	158.8	160.6	160.6

Source: *Moskva v tsifrakh, 1971-1975* (Moscow: Izd. Statistika, 1976), p. 90.

TABLE 10

USSR Average Monthly Wages
(rubles)

Branch	1965	1970	1973
Industry	104.2	133.3	147.3
Agriculture	75.0	101.0	118.5
Housing, municipal economy, consumer services	79.0	92.0	99.0
State administration and social (mass) organizations	105.9	122.2	125.0
National average	96.5	122.0	135.0

Source: Viktor Perevedentsev, "Zarabotnaia plata," *Zhurnalist*, August 1974, pp. 79-80.

1-2 percent of total city budgets.[98] The official Moscow city budget for 1975 put administrative outlays at only 0.6 percent of the total.[99] This figure conceals salary costs hidden in the subordinate budgets of those city agencies and institutions that have been placed on cost accounting, a major objective of Soviet local authorities since the economic reforms of 1965. As a result, it is difficult to say whether or not administrative outlays have actually risen or fallen in this period. Rather, it is probably true (as Gertrude Schroeder has demonstrated convincingly for the national level) that Soviet statistics greatly underestimate total personnel costs in public bureaucracies, in large part because the published statistics employ an institutional rather than a functional definition of administration.[100] Our data suggest a similar conclusion, at least for the city of Moscow. The evidence shows that administrative salaries are high by comparison with those in other sectors and have risen steadily, as has the number of administrators employed. If the proportionate costs of administration are falling, this can only be due to greater outlays in other sectors, or to the conversion of administrative costs into personnel expenditures listed within other categories.

The track record for policy outcomes in the area of Soviet administrative salaries in cities provides us with reason to believe that the spread between Moscow and other Soviet cities may be on the rise. Some salary increments were introduced in 1968, but these were not, according to Soviet interviewees, applied across the board. Officials in the Department of Justice, for example, received no raise, and most of the increments were assigned to the woefully underpaid rural personnel in villages and county units.[101] This is in line with tradition dating back to the late 1920s, which has been used periodically to strengthen the hold of the national government over the local level.[102] Rural administrative cadres were also the major but not exclusive beneficiaries of a 1968 statutory provision whereby all members of soviet executive committees were to be automatically compensated at their former levels when they left other, better-paid posts for administrative duties.

In the late 1960s, the central leadership also introduced a premium system that, in theory, was designed to improve administrative compensation plans. This was part of a larger effort to link plan fulfillment to direct material incentives, another product of the 1965 economic reforms. But the material base provided by these reformed plans remains very narrow. In departments of finance, for example, both employees and executives are eligible for quarterly premiums as follows: 20 percent of base salary for plan fulfillment (that is, cases processed, savings effected, revenues collected, levels of profitability attained in subordinate enterprises) and 0.05 percent for the first 1 percent by which the plan is overfulfilled. For additional increments to the planned output above this 1 percent, the size of the premium rises to 30 percent of the base salary of the individuals deemed responsible. But for departments with no direct link to the production sector—such as education, planning, police, and social welfare—material incentives and premiums are far more restrictive, not exceeding 0.05 percent of the total wage fund in any case. In practice, this means that a department with a wage fund of 1 million rubles would have at best only about 500 rubles a year to distribute among some 50 employees. In such cases, the motivational impact of the "new" system, if any, must be purely symbolic.[103] In addition, such provisions were applied at first only to bureaucrats at the national level, being extended to city agencies in 1968 and rural agencies in 1971.[104] The plan apparently was not applied to all cities; Moscow remained a notable exception as late as 1974. Elsewhere, accounts indicate that the criteria for plan fulfillment were frequently so nebulous as to make the motivating force of premiums quite negligible.[105] The failure of the incentive system to achieve its objective is indicated most dramatically by the continuing high rate of personnel turnover in city agencies.[106]

Personnel skills and performance incentives still represent only one among several kinds of resources that Soviet urban bureaucracies command in order to effect a managerial transformation of city administration. To fully understand the management implications of current practices, we must look at material as well as human resources. Even the most highly skilled, well-trained, attitudinally flexible, and demographically "new" kind of administrators must still operate within the constraints of budgetary processes, outputs, and outcomes that limit and define their spheres of activity. Managers without sufficient monies are just as constrained as urban bureaucrats who do not know how to apply their resources constructively. Thus, it is to the question of financial resources—how they are generated, allocated, and to what effect—that we now turn our attention.

NOTES

1. Harold Gortner, *Administration in the Public Sector* (New York: John Wiley, 1977), p. 301.
2. R. Golembiewski, ed., *People in Public Service: A Reader in Public Personnel Administration* (Itasca, Ill.: F. E. Peacock, 1970), pp. 29-66.
3. Gortner, op. cit., pp. 268-74; N. Joseph Cayer, *Public Personnel Administration* (New York: St. Martin's Press, 1975), pp. 15-55; Nicholas Henry, *Public Administration and Public Affairs* (Englewood Cliffs, N.J.: Prentice-Hall, 1975), pp. 187-96; Grover Starling, *Managing the Public Sector* (Homewood, Ill.: Dorsey Press, 1977), chap. 13; George J. Gordon, *Public Administration in America* (New York: St. Martin's Press, 1978), p. 235-44.
4. Cayer, op. cit., pp. 141-50; John Armstrong, *The European Administrative Elite* (Princeton, N.J.: Princeton University Press, 1973), pp. 73-96, 201-27; Fred Riggs, *Administration in Developing Countries* (Boston: Houghton Mifflin and Co., 1964), pp. 272-78; Gerald Caiden, *The Dynamics of Public Administration* (New York: Holt, Rinehart and Winston, 1971), pp. 199-211, 256-72. A recent criticism of this approach to comparative administrative recruitment can be found in B. Guy Peters, *The Politics of Bureaucracy: A Comparative Perspective* (New York: Longman, 1978), pp. 74-76. Peters argues that the real issues in administrative recruitment are not the merit-versus-patronage or representative-bureaucracy debates but the dynamics of the institutions themselves. It may be these more than social background or recruitment methods that shape behavior and hence policy. See ibid., pp. 103-5.
5. For the differences in the two perspectives, see Starling, op. cit., p. 368 and chap. 14.
6. See armstrong, op. cit., pp. 47-71 for the importance of the value systems of administrative elites for national economic development policies in Europe. For a discussion of performance, see ibid., pp. 275-98.
7. Jack Koteen, "Key Problems in Development Administration," in *Administrative Issues in Developing Economies*, ed. Kenneth Rothwell (Lexington, Mass.: Lexington Books, 1972), pp. 62-64.
8. Chi-Yuen Wu, "Public Administration in the 1970s," in Rothwell, op. cit., pp. 222-23. Current international technical assistance projects reflect such thinking so that behavior modification ranks ahead of institutional transformation as a major goal of development administration programs today. See, for example, Dwight Waldo, ed., *Temporal Dimensions of Development Administration* (Durham, N.C.: Duke University Press, 1970), especially selections by Peter Savage, Warren Ilchman, and Frank Sherwood. For earlier perspectives, see Jay Westcott, "Governmental Organization and Methods in Developing Countries," in *Development Administration: Concepts and Problems*, ed. Irving Swerdlow (Syracuse, N.Y.: Syracuse University Press, 1963), pp. 45-67.
9. Gerald Zaltman et al., *Innovations and Organizations* (New York: John Wiley, 1973); Ralph P. Hummel, *The Bureaucratic Experience* (New York: St. Martin's Press, 1977), pp. 83-90.
10. James Q. Wilson, "Innovation in Organization," in *Organizational and Managerial Innovation*, ed. Lloyd A. Rowe and William Boise (Pacific Palisades, Calif.: Goodyear, 1973), p. 35.
11. Ibid., pp. 40-41. For a preliminary definition of professionalization as applied to U.S. public administration, see Cayer, op. cit., pp. 155-56; Henry, op. cit., pp. 195-96.
12. Richard L. Schott, "Public Administration as a Profession," in *Current Issues in Public Administration*, ed. Frederick S. Lane (New York: St. Martin's Press, 1978), pp. 273-74.
13. Frederick C. Mosher, "Professions in Public Service," *Public Administration Review* (hereafter PAR) 38 (March-April 1978): 147. For the impact of professional standards

and norms on urban outputs and outcomes, see also Frank S. Levy et al., *Urban Outcomes: Schools, Streets, and Libraries* (Berkeley: University of California Press, 1974), chaps. 2, 3, and 4.

14. Wilson, in Rowe and Boise, op. cit., p. 41.

15. Ibid., pp. 43-44; William H. Whyte, Jr., *The Organization Man* (Garden City, N.Y.: Anchor Books, 1956), pp. 36-68, 201-24, 225-68. For a brief critique of Whyte's views, see D. S. Pugh et al., *Writers on Organizations* (Hammondsworth, England: Penguin Books, 1971), pp. 164-67.

16. Stephen Sternheimer, "Modernizing Administrative Elites: The Making of Managers for Soviet Cities," *Comparative Politics* (forthcoming, 1979).

17. Wilson, in Rowe and Boise, op. cit., pp. 44-47.

18. For a discussion of the meaning and historical significance of the political commissar role in Soviet administration generally, see Stephen Sternheimer, "Administration for Development: The Transformation of the Soviet Bureaucracy, 1920-1930," in *Russian Officialdom from the Ninth through the Twentieth Centuries: The Bureaucratization of Russian Society*, ed. Walter Pintner and Don K. Rowney (Chapel Hill: University of North Carolina Press, forthcoming, 1979).

19. Lawrence B. Mohr, "Determinants of Innovation," in Rowe and Boise, op. cit., pp. 55-57 (tables 1 and 2).

20. Cayer, op. cit., pp. 3-12; Henry, op. cit., pp. 208-19.

21. John Rehfuss, *Public Administration as Political Process* (New York: Scribners, 1973), pp. 224-27; David Stanley, "What's Happening to the Civil Service," in Lane, ed., op. cit., p. 251.

22. Starling, op. cit., p. 373.

23. Ken Auletta, "A Reporter at Large: More for Less," *The New Yorker*, August 1, 1977, pp. 28-48.

24. E. S. Savas and S. G. Ginsburg, "The Civil Service: A Meritless System," in Lane, ed., op. cit., pp. 260-63.

25. See Schott in Lane, op. cit., pp. 273-77 on obstacles in the United States.

26. Ibid., p. 273.

27. Don Price, *The Scientific Estate* (Cambridge, Mass.: Harvard University Press, 1965), pp. 120-269; Stanley Powers et al., *Developing the Municipal Organization* (Washington, D.C.: International City Management Association, 1974), pp. 14-18.

28. See, for example, A. Doak Barnett, "Mechanisms for Party Control in the Governmental Bureaucracy in China"; Carl Beck, "Party Control and Democratization in Czechoslovakia"; Ezra F. Vogel, "Politicized Bureaucracy: Communist China"; all in *Frontiers of Development Administration*, ed. Fred W. Riggs (Durham, N.C.: Duke University Press, 1970), pp. 415-36, 437-58, 556-68; Merle Fainsod, "Bureaucracy and Modernization: The Russian and Soviet Case," in *Bureaucracy and Political Development*, ed. Joseph LaPalombara (Princeton, N.J.: Princeton University Press, 1963), pp. 233-67.

29. Schott, in Lane, op. cit., p. 274; H. Wilensky, "The Professionalization of Everyone," *American Journal of Sociology* 70 (September 1964): 138-39.

30. Schott, in Lane, op. cit., p. 275.

31. Ibid., pp. 277-78; Henry, op. cit., pp. 196-99.

32. Frederick C. Mosher and Richard J. Stillman, Jr., "Introduction: The Professions in Government," *PAR* 37 (November-December 1977): 631.

33. Richard J. Stillman, Jr., "The City Manager: Professional Helping Hand or Political Hired Hand," *PAR* 37 (November-December 1977): 666.

34. See M. Azovkin, *Mestnye sovety v sisteme organov vlasti* (Moscow: Izd. Iuridicheskoi literatury, 1971). This statistical error mars a number of otherwise excellent studies of local elites by Western scholars, among them B. M. Frolic, "Decision Making in Soviet Cit-

ies," *American Political Science Review* 66 (March 1972): 38-52; and Ronald J. Hill, *The Soviet Political Elite* (New York: St. Martin's Press, 1977), pp. 72-75.

35. William A. Welsh, "Introduction: The Comparative Study of Political Leadership in Communist Systems," in *Comparative Communist Political Leadership*, ed. Carl Beck et al. (New York: David McKay, 1973), pp. 10-11.

36. For an analysis of leadership styles among urban elites in the United States, see Sandra P. Schoenberg, "A Typology of Leadership Styles," in Rowe and Boise, op. cit., pp. 177-79; Alvin Toffler, "Organizations," in Rowe and Boise, op. cit., pp. 333-49.

37. For a detailed discussion and critique of this assumption, see Daryl J. Bem, *Beliefs, Attitudes and Human Affairs* (Belmont, Calif.: Brooks-Cole, 1970), pp. 54-69.

38. On redistributive goals and Soviet public policy, see Peter Zwick, "Socioeconomic Policy and National Integration in the USSR," Paper delivered at the Southwestern Social Science Association Conference, Houston, Texas, April 1978.

39. Interview, Department of Justice, Leningrad *gorispolkom*, 1976.

40. Interview, Institute of Philosophy, Leningrad Branch, Academy of Sciences, USSR, 1976.

41. "O rabote obkoma Volgogradskoi oblasti (September 1968, Central Committee, CPSU)," *KPSS v resoliutsiiakh i resheniiakh (1966-1968)*, 10 vols. (Moscow: Politizdat, 1972), 9: 469-71.

42. I. Moskalev, *Sovershenstvovanie deiatel'nosti mestnykh sovetov* (Moscow: Mysl', 1975), p. 77; interview, Institute of Philisophy, op. cit.

43. Unfortunately, these were not available to the authors. Hence, all salary data have been pieced together from interviews and other sources.

44. Cayer, op. cit., pp. 60-62.

45. Ibid., pp. 67-71.

46. V. I. Remnev, *Problemy NOTa v apparate upravleniia* (Moscow: Nauka, 1973), pp. 95-96 (fn. 70). See also *Kvalifikatsionnyi spravochnik dolzhnostei sliuzhashchikh* (Moscow: NII Truda, 1970 and 1972).

47. I. A. Rozenbaum, "O spetsial'noi podgotovke upravlencheskikh kadrov," *Sovetskoe gosudarstvo i pravo* (hereafter *SGiP*), no. 1 (1976), pp. 57-58; G. V. Iakovlev, *Apparat upravleniia* (Moscow: Izd. Iuridicheskaia literatura, 1974), pp. 217 (fn. 2), 218 (fn. 2); E. K. Tsiukina, "Problemy sovershenstvovaniia apparata," in *Problemy nauchnoi organizatsii truda v apparate*, ed. V. S. Osnovin (Voronezh: Izd. Voronezhskogo gosudarstvennogo universiteta, 1974), p. 62.

48. R. G. Ablakov, "Diatel'nost KPSS po dal'neishemu povysheniu roli mestnykh sovetov" (Master's thesis, Kazakhstan State University, 1969), pp. 94-97. Interviews: Faculty of Law, Leningrad State University, 1975; Faculty of Law, Moscow State University, 1976; and Institute of State and Law, Academy of Sciences, USSR, 1976.

49. Frederic J. Fleron, Jr., "System Attributes and Career Attributes," in Beck et al., op. cit., pp. 43-79; idem, "Co-optation as a Mechanism of Adaptation to Change," in *The Behavioral Revolution and Communist Studies*, ed. Roger E. Kanet (New York: Free Press, 1971), pp. 125-50.

50. See, for example, David T. Cattell, *Leningrad: A Case Study of Soviet Urban Government* (New York: Praeger, 1968); T. H. Friedgut, "Community Structure, Political Participation, and Soviet Local Government: The Case of Kutaisi," in *Soviet Politics and Society in the 1970s*, ed. Henry Morton and Rudolph Tokes (New York: Free Press, 1974), pp. 261-98; B. M. Frolic, "Municipal Administration, Departments, Commissions, and Organizations," *Soviet Studies* 22 (January 1971): 376-93; Henry Morton, "The Leningrad District: An Inside Look," *Soviet Studies* 20 (October 1968): 206-18; William A. Taubman, *Governing Soviet Cities: Bureaucratic Politics and Urban Development in the USSR* (New York: Praeger, 1973).

51. Tables 5, 7, and 8 also appear in Sternheimer, "Modernizing Administrative Elites."

52. Soviet great-city officials probably have about the same average tenure in office as do city managers in the United States—five years. But they are generally older than their U.S. counterparts (early forties) by almost a decade. Like them, however, Soviet officials tend to belong to the dominant ethnic group (Russian) and are overwhelmingly male. For the data on U.S. cities, see Stillman, "The City Manager," pp. 663-64; Laurie S. Frankel and Carol A. Pigeon, "Municipal Managers and Chief Administrative Officers: A Statistical Profile," *Urban Data Service Reports* 7 (Washington, D.C.: International City Management Association, February 1975).

53. See also Frolic, "Decision Making," p. 51 (n. 32); Cattell, op. cit., pp. 53-54 (tables 8, 9).

54. Sternheimer, in Pintner and Rowney, op. cit.; Barrington Moore, Jr., *Soviet Politics: The Dilemmas of Power* (New York: Harper & Row, 1965), pp. 277-96.

55. In 1960, administrative personnel in Moscow constituted 3.2 percent of the city's labor force; in 1965, 3.7 percent; in 1969, 4.6 percent; and in 1970, 4.7 percent. See *Moskva v tsifrakh, 1966-1970: kratkii statisticheskii spravochnik* (Moscow: Izd. Statistika, 1972), p. 65.

56. Soviet official statistics deal chiefly with percentages and proportional rates of increase. According to the deputy mayor of Moscow, the city had 1.4 million employees in 1975. John Kaiser, "The Use of Computer Systems by Local Government in the Soviet Union," Paper presented at the Fourteenth Annual Conference of URISA, Atlanta, Ga., August-September 1976, p. 11.

57. *Moskva v tsifrakh: 1966-1970*, p. 67; George Breslauer, "Khrushchev Revisited," *Problems of Communism* 20 (September-October 1976): 18-33.

58. According to another source, women accounted for 55.5 percent of city administrative personnel in January 1960, 55.3 percent in January 1965, and 58.8 percent in January 1967. In 1960, the proportion of female administrative employees was slightly below the demographic norm (55.8 percent female) for the entire city population. *Moskva v tsifrakh za gody Sovetskoi vlasti* (Moscow: Izd. Statistika, 1967), p. 58.

59. *Moskva v tsifrakh: 1966-1970*, p. 80.

60. Ibid., p. 81.

61. Ibid., p. 82. Between 1965 and 1970, the rate of growth for administrative personnel exceeded that for the other 18 branches of the city's economy. Between 1971 and 1975, the rate of growth for administrative personnel ranked sixth out of the 19 branches. Ibid., p. 83.

62. Ibid., p. 69. For all branches taken together, the average proportion of the work force with over 20 years' service was less (32.3 percent).

63. Comparable figures for Leningrad are available only for 1963. These put the number of specialists with higher education working in city administration at 7,900 individuals. Thus, while the city as a whole had a population slightly less than half that of Moscow (2.9 million versus 6.04 million, 1960), the number of specialists in city administration in Leningrad was disproportionately smaller, being only slightly more than one-tenth that of Moscow. Here as in other sectors of Soviet urban life, the "rich get richer." *Leningrad i Leningradskaia oblast' v tsifrakh* (Leningrad: Lenizdat, 1964), pp. 13, 69; *Moskva v tsifrakh: 1966-1970*, p. 5.

64. Ibid., p. 88.

65. Ibid., p. 89.

66. A comparison of the statistical profile of Rostov province to that of the USSR as a whole (levels of industrialization, urbanization, political saturation of the population, and demographic characteristics) argue for the representativeness of the case in its aggregate

form. See *Narodnoe khoziaistvo Rostovskoi oblasti: statisticheskii sbornik* (Rostov: Izd. Statistika, 1971), inter alia; *Narodnoe khoziaistvo SSSR v 1970 godu* (Moscow: Izd. Statistika, 1971), inter alia.

67. On city planning commissions, see Frolic, "Decision Making in Soviet Cities," pp. 42-44.

68. Given the difficulty in adjusting for rural-urban differences, it could be argued that the table is biased in favor of low educational qualifications owing to the proportion of rural administrative personnel, which the figures would reflect. But given the small number of full-time administrators working in rural offices, the distortions involved are probably negligible. By 1970, only 18 percent of all administrative personnel in the province served in rural areas. See *Narodnoe khoziaistvo Rostovskoi oblasti*, p. 140.

69. On the limitations of engineering preparation as a background for public management, see Stillman, "The City Manager," p. 663.

70. Jeremy R. Azrael, *Managerial Power and Soviet Politics* (Cambridge, Mass.: Harvard University Press, 1966), pp. 152-72.

71. Stillman, "The City Manager," p. 659.

72. Ibid., pp. 659, 662.

73. Ibid., p. 662.

74. Ibid., p. 663.

75. Ibid.

76. Ibid. In the United States, 34 percent of city managers with B.A.s majored in government, while almost 80 percent of those with advanced training received it in the field of public administration. The significance of such training for job performance, however, has been called into question in discussions of "the great training robbery." See Henry, op. cit., pp. 198-99.

77. Stillman, "The City Manager," p. 664.

78. Ibid., pp. 665-66.

79. Ibid., p. 664.

80. Ibid., pp. 664-65; Schott, in Lane, op. cit., pp. 274, 276.

81. Cayer, op. cit., p. 64; Peters, op. cit., pp. 87-91; Fred A. Kramer, *Dynamics of Public Bureaucracy* (Cambridge, Mass.: Winthrop, 1977), pp. 103-5.

82. Gortner, op. cit., pp. 231-35; Cayer, op. cit., pp. 92-105; Starling, op. cit., pp. 333-63; Stanley Powers et al., *Developing the Municipal Organization* (Washington, D.C.: International City Management Association, 1974), pp. 84-95; Peters, op. cit., pp. 87-91.

83. Gortner, op. cit., p. 233. See Peters, op. cit., pp. 87-91, for a comparative perspective. See also Franklin P. Kilpatrick et al., *The Image of the Federal Civil Service* (Washington, D.C.: Brookings Institution, 1964); David T. Stanley, *The Higher Civil Service* (Washington, D.C.: Brookings Institution, 1964). On Maslow's needs hierarchy, see Starling, op. cit., pp. 337-40; Gortner, op. cit., pp. 222-24 (esp. table 7, p. 223).

84. Soviet sociological studies of worker and employee motivation, job satisfaction, and performance have yet to deal with administrative and executive work in the USSR. See, for example, G. V. Osipov, ed., *Industry and Labor in the USSR* (London: Tavistock, 1966).

85. Powers et al., op. cit., pp. 90-91.

86. Interview, Law Faculty, Moscow State University, 1976.

87. Ibid. A village mayor earns 120-30 rubles a month.

88. Leonard Kirsch, *Soviet Wages: Changes in Structure and Administration since 1956* (Cambridge, Mass.: MIT Press, 1972); L. Blykhman and O. Shkaratan, *Man at Work* (Moscow: Progress, 1977), p. 178; Ludmila Rzhanitsyna, *Soviet Family Budgets* (Moscow: Progress, 1977), pp. 62 (table 10), 63.

89. Ibid., p. 128 (table 23).

90. Ibid., p. 42 (table 5).

91. Ibid., p. 178.

92. *Moskva v tsifrakh* (Moscow: Izd. Statistika, 1976), p. 11.

93. Rzahnitsyna, op. cit., p. 59.

94. *Rostovskaia oblast' za 50 let* (Rostov: Izd. Statistika, 1967), pp. 141-42. Between 1960 and 1970, salaries for administrative personnel at all levels in the province rose by 42.8 percent, a figure somewhat below the average for provincial salary increases for all categories of personnel combined.

95. Murray Yanowitch, *Social and Economic Inequality: Soviet Union* (New York: M. E. Sharpe, 1977), pp. 105-6; *Current Digest of the Soviet Press* 29 (August 3, 1977): 8.

96. Carol W. Lewis, "Managing Soviet Cities," *Municipal Yearbook: 1977* (Washington, D.C.: International City Management Association, 1978), p. 90.

97. Stanley M. Wolfson, "Salaries of Municipal Officials for 1976," *Urban Data Service Reports* 8 (Washington, D.C.: International City Management Association, 1976).

98. Carol W. Lewis, "Politics and the Budget in Soviet Cities" (Ph.D. diss., Princeton University, Princeton, N.J., 1975), pp. 23 (table 9), 24-26 (table 10).

99. *Biurdzhet goroda Moskvy na 1976* (Moscow: Mosgorispolkom, 1975), p. 24. See also V. A. Pertsik and A. I. Kazaniuk, "O povyshenii effektivnosti," in *Voprosy sovetskogo gosudarstvovedeniia: trudy*, 71 vols. (Irkutsk: Izd. Irkutskogo gosudarstvennogo universiteta, 1970), 71: 77, for administrative expenses in the Bratsk city budget.

100. Gertrude E. Schroeder, "A Critique of Official Statistics on Public Administration in the USSR," *Association for Comparative Economic Studies Bulletin* 18 (Spring 1976): 34-43.

101. *Pravovye voprosy raboty mestnykh sovetov* (Moscow: Izd. Iurdicheskoi literatury, 1974), p. 243; interviews, Law Faculty, Moscow State University, 1976.

102. Sternheimer, in Pintner and Rowney, op. cit.; Stephen Sternheimer, "Administration and Political Development: An Inquiry into the Tsarist and Soviet Experiences (Ph.D. diss., University of Chicago, 1974), pp. 338-501.

103. *Kak organizovat' upravlencheskii trud* (Moscow: Izd. *Izvestiia*, 1971), p. 50.

104. *Pravovye voprosy*, p. 243.

105. Ibid., pp. 242-43.

106. A. I. Limarenko, "Problemy sovershenstvovaniia organizatsionno-instruktorskogo apparata mestnykh sovetov (na materialykh Ukrainskoi SSR)" (Master's thesis, Lvov State University, 1972), pp. 131, 132.

4

REWARDING THE RICH

THE ALLOCATION OF FINANCIAL RESOURCES

Financial resources constitute the second major component of that ability to generate, coordinate, and appropriately allocate resources we have termed "resource management." The initial step in assessing the current and prospective status of financial resource management is an examination of the budget process. Then those resources devoted to the urban sector, to individual cities, and to their subcommunities are considered. The relative concentration of control over resources becomes a critical factor in assessing management capacity. That concentration discloses the urban managers' ability or inability to implement decisions. Whether these decisions be their own or their superiors', the success of urban programs and individual careers depends on successful implementation. Furthermore, since planning for economic factors is a program management component (as laid out in the Introduction), we will consider some of the major developmental as well as cost implications of Soviet urban resources management.

According to Charles Beard, "The history of urban civilization could be written in terms of appropriations, for they show what the citizens think is worth doing and worth paying for."[1] When applied to Soviet cities, however, budget analysis illuminates not city policies but regional (republic) and, more particularly, national policies. All evidence suggests that in the great majority of cities, almost all budget outputs of consequence are generated outside the urban arena.[2] Most adjustments and accommodations that show up as changes in a Soviet city's budget can be traced to decisions taken at higher administrative levels.

Parts of this chapter are adapted from "The CPSU and Urban Management," Paper delivered at the annual conference of the Northeastern Political Science Association, November 1976.

To provide the financial basis for implementing Party and government policy, the top national leadership distributes allocations to leading members of competing bureaucratic hierarchies. These allocations are central to city operations, since all financial resources of any magnitude flow through the unified state budget and economic plans. There exist no significant independent sources of revenue. Therefore, in an operating, national, and highly centralized budgetary system of the Soviet variety, city revenues and expenditures represent outputs of the national system, whereas at the city level they represent inputs. At the outset, then, the average level of autonomy in urban resource management is so low as to inhibit management transformation. The system provides resources, the absolute amount and distribution of which lie largely beyond the control of city leaders.

Outputs from the national system constitute critical management resources for the Soviet city. Since all human activity has associated costs (although all costs may not be accurately translatable into monetary units), the budgetary process and its outcomes play a pivotal role in all activities and organizations. A Soviet city budget, like city government itself, is central to a greater range of activities and institutions than is the case for cities in the United States.[3] Representing the only integrated, territorially based financial plan for the city as a whole, the Soviet city budget reflects both the broad scope of activities pursued by city administrators and the means provided them by their superiors to pursue these activities. From this perspective, distribution patterns evident in city budgets describe the differential distribution of management resources by the center to urban communities and their managers.

The professed as well as operative goal in Soviet budgetary practice is a single, integrated system in which the budget is drafted from the bottom up by the finance apparatus and approved from the top down by the Soviet hierarchy. Each budget includes those of subordinate units, so that, for example, the budgets of cities of republic subordination are included in the budget of the corresponding republic. In effect, a city's budget is approved by the executive unit to which the city is subordinate as well as by the city soviet and its own executive committee.[4]

The budget for each city is drawn up on the basis of departmental requests, routinely calculated from prior expenditures and justified increments. In this way, Soviet city spending in any given fiscal year becomes largely a function of past allocations. Departmental requests are developed in accordance with guidelines and directives provided by the city's finance department in its role as a field office of the national finance ministry. Moreover, budgeting is heavily circumscribed by departmental procedures, staff norms and pay schedules, and legal and administrative constraints. Chief among these are the absolute impermissibility of deficit spending and an inviolable rule precluding cities from borrowing. A city budget is well insulated by this process from demands generated and articulated in the city. In sum, Soviet city budgeting is characterized by hierarchical patterns and executive dominance without a great deal of flexibility, maneuverability, or discretion at the city level.

In the United States, budgetary decision making in cities also operates under highly constrained circumstances. State legislation often specifies and limits revenue sources, mandates certain expenditures, and requires a particular format and a balanced operating budget.[5] Borrowing, while permitted, is regulated by state law; debt service (along with employee pension funding) presents a significant uncontrollable expense. In addition to these environmental constraints, other constraints are induced by the internal workings of the budgetary process. Several case studies in large U.S. cities indicate that city budgeting tends to be "incremental," with departments generally requesting last year's appropriations plus an increase.[6] In conjunction with the requirement for a balanced budget, this produces a process in which new allocations become a function of past decisions. These case studies also indicate that under routine circumstances, executive dominance characterizes the process of piecemeal adjustment. Municipal legislatures and interest groups commonly do not play an effective role.

From a comparative perspective, it becomes apparent that neither Soviet nor U.S. budgeting is a distinctive response to unique circumstances. In both cases, budgeting for urban jurisdictions uses similar, specific decision-making techniques. One case in point, applicable to both U.S. and USSR cities, is the fact that legal provisions drawn up at higher levels create pressures for a balanced budget, a requirement that induces local officials to aim for a surplus.[7] Again in both cases, budgeting usually involves routine decisions, and these decisions endure over the short term Budgeting operates less as a focus of conflict within the city than as a process for confirming and recording bureaucratically induced continuity.

Budgetary decision making with a strong historical bias is a response of bureaucratic administration to problems confronting complex organizations. Decision making that relies heavily upon prior decision suits a situation in which a large quantity and variety of information must be processed and in which a great number of decisions must be made. Too much information about too many activities enters the agencies and the system as a whole for decisions to be made anew in each round of budget.[8] Economizing becomes even more important where coordination among bureaucratic units emerges as a major challenge and when timely response is necessary. Predictability—as introduced through budgeting techniques that foster continuity—reduces the level of uncertainty with which managers have to deal. The use of precedent reduces conflict among agencies and activities by applying past settlements to current conditions.[9] Given that only a small fraction of the current budget is susceptible to change within a given budget round, the price of reducing conflict is the loss of flexibility in the short run. By projecting the past into the city's future, budgeting of this type ranks as a major conservative mechanism in both Soviet and U.S. cities, where, in effect, leaders deal primarily with the past.

In the postwar era, Soviet and U.S. city leaders have seen an absolute increase in financial resources flowing into their cities. But since local revenues have not kept pace with the growth in local expenditures, the budget process in both countries serves to redistribute resources among government units. As a result, financial interdependencies among government levels have increased, as has the complexity surrounding financial decision making.

In contrast to the rise in federal aid to U.S. cities, direct intergovernmental subsidies account for a decreasing and quite small proportion of aggregate revenue in Soviet cities.[10] Yet the Soviets, like their U.S. colleagues, exhibit an increasing reliance on nonlocal revenues. Whereas in the United States intergovernmental payments play an increasing role as city population increases, the opposite pattern holds true for Soviet cities.[11] Since the larger Soviet cities tend to have jurisdiction over those economically profitable enterprises from which revenues can be drawn into the budget, the more economically developed cities (and, hence, usually more populous cities) can rely heavily on local revenue sources.

In considering the question of taxes, the revenue-generating capacity of certain taxes is a critical question in the U.S. system. This is not the case in Soviet cities where, over time, the amount of revenue is largely independent of specific sources. Adjustments are made to keep revenues and expenditures aligned as the requirement of a balanced budget is met. The largest single source of total Soviet city revenue since 1960 has been the turnover tax (*nalog s oborota*). This tax, part of the deductions from state tax and revenue accounts, is calculated as a fixed proportion of a commodity's price and paid mainly by consumer, food, and light industries. By 1973, it was generating 28 percent of all city revenue.[12] Although the turnover tax approaches the property tax in relative weight, it is specifically not a local tax. It is different from the property tax also in that its productivity is related to national and urban development (although the amount retained by the city need not be). Consequently, the Soviet tax structure builds in the possibility of the city's adjusting to long-term economic changes in a way foreclosed by the property tax system used for U.S. municipalities.

Over the years, Soviet cities have been drawing increasingly upon another nonlocal tax, the tax on population (*nalog s naseleniia*). By 1973, this direct tax was providing 16 percent of all city revenue in the country. However, it is less important in Russian cities, particularly in the highly developed ones, such as Moscow and Leningrad.[13]

Some tax features are shared by the two systems. In both countries, national and local tax structures are quite different from each other. Individual and corporate income taxes and the payments from profits accounts, respectively, generate more than half of all federal receipts in the United States and more than half of the national revenue in the Soviet Union. But these taxes are less significant at the city level.[14] There are also appreciable differences in both countries among cities as well as among regions in tax and revenue structures.

Although financial pressures and budget constraints remain part of the daily life of any urban manager, expenditures through Soviet city budgets have increased almost 1,400 percent from 1940 to 1974.[15] This increase, however, has yet to make up the sacrifice of urban services and amenities that has accumulated over the years. The sacrifice itself originated in the exigencies and economics of all-out industrial development. While much of the increase in city budgets can be traced to housing and its associated costs, health and education have continued to dominate aggregate city spending in the entire postwar period. Currently, health and education account for approximately three-fifths of the over 15 billion rubles spent annually through city budgets.[16]

While nationwide generalizations are valid and interesting, they obscure the fact that the pace and substance of urban development differ among republics, provinces, and within as well as among metropolitan regions. Rudimentary observation provides vivid confirmation of this point. Yet, what distinguishes Soviet development is not the fact of variation per se. In most systems, a dominant and preferential position is held by particular cities, of which primate cities and national capitals are common examples.[17] In Italy and the United States, there is clear evidence of variations on a north-south axis.[18] What distinguishes the Soviet case are the specific patterns of variation and the influence these exercise on national and urban development processes.

By looking at city budgets, it is possible to confirm and specify some variations in the differential distribution of management resources among cities. To the extent that city budgets are descriptive rather than normative documents, budget data allows us to separate rhetoric from reality. Although questions have been and must continue to be raised about the utility of city budgets for political analysis, they remain among the best statements summarizing the distribution of urban resources.[19] Nonetheless, it is advantageous to supplement budget data by other types of documentation: speeches, agenda and press reports, plans, interviews, observations, and, where available, social survey data. This is no less the case for Soviet cities.

Using budgets introduces certain problems. Some, such as availability and reliability issues, are chronic to any study of the Soviet Union. Others are associated more specifically with the urban context in all systems. Most serious among these is the problem of accounting for off-budget resources coming into the cities. In Bratsk, for example, the city budget amounts to 21 million rubles, whereas enterprises in the city spend five times that on capital construction and municipal services alone.[20] Of the 150 million rubles spent on urban development in Vilnius, only one-third is covered by the city budget.[21] Even in Moscow, the city budget finances only two-thirds of all capital construction in the city.[22] City budget figures report only those financial resources administered through the city's executive committee. By estimating off-budget resources, we can place a city in its proper place on the concentration-fragmentation continuum. Accordingly, in order to draw an accurate picture, city budget data should be supplemented by a record of other resource flows such as housing and industrial investments. These, along with government financing through budgets, define the core resources underlying urban development opportunities. What is made of these opportunities rests with management capacity.

Modes of program evaluation demonstrate at length and in detail that budget analysis is limited.[23] While budget analysis has the advantage of using objective, quantitative data, subjective and qualitative considerations are omitted; alone it fails to address either needs or preferences. Specifically, it is unable to take participant perceptions of service outputs and urban outcomes into account systematically. This shortcoming becomes important when one remembers that individuals act on the basis of their understanding of reality rather than on the basis of the budget figures themselves. Indeed, it is possible that both city leaders *and* citizens perceive the distribution of resources in the city to be different from the actual distribution set forth in the budget. Budget analysis is no more useful when it comes to analyzing objectively service outputs and urban outcomes. Increasing expenditures may represent more or better services, growing inefficiencies, or perhaps a continuing but increasingly unsuccessful effort to meet changing demand curves.[24] Furthermore, research in the U.S. locale has shown that performance (service outputs) may not be tied to inputs.[25] Thus, expenditures do not represent approximate measures of outputs nor of their distribution. One is compelled to concur that expenditures are "poor surrogates for services delivered."[26]

Budget amounts, on the other hand, do represent resources available to urban managers for application to urban programs. The capacity to transform inputs (to the urban milieu from the national system) into city government performance and desirable long-term effects (outputs and outcomes, respectively) stands as a central facet of overall management capacity.

It has been argued that the distribution aspects of urban services are relevant only at the subcommunity (or micro) level of analysis. According to Robert Lineberry: "The principal issue of service distribution is not the overall quality of public services in a city, but their differential allocation—or, more exactly, the suspicion of differential allocation— to various neighborhoods."[27] Very possibly this is the case from the point of view of individual residents relying on prompt and adequate city services. Alternatively, the case may be overdrawn, and at least partially an artifact of an approach that assumes that individuals perceive service advantages or disadvantages in terms of proximate surroundings.

It is in these authors' understanding that variations within a city are not the only distribution patterns relevant to development outcomes and notions of equity. Nor is subcommunity analysis of outputs and outcomes the only type relevant to urban services. Over two decades ago, Charles Tiebout argued that migration within metropolitan areas can be traced to cost and service differences among urban jurisdictions.[28] The same factors may come into play in interregional migrations. Relatively unacceptable levels of urban services and housing are frequently cited as a cause of Soviet labor turnover and reverse migration. Indeed, Soviet suburbanites have been characterized as the "urban poor of Soviet society."[29]   In addition, intercommunity (or macro) differences lie at the very core of the push-pull dynamic of rural-urban migration. As so much of the modernization literature suggests, variations among communities are likely to become increasingly important as educational levels rise and long distance communications (radio, television, telephone, travel) become widespread.

Variations in services within cities may not be critical ones, measured either by objective or subjective criteria. In fact, satisfaction with one's neighborhood may have little to do with either objective service levels or subjective citizen assessments of government performance. A few examples serve to clarify these points. If residents in one neighborhood receive more or better services than those available elsewhere in the city, they still may be only moderately well-off compared with residents in extremely well-serviced cities. Neighborhoods at the bottom of the service scale in one city may be preferred to neighborhoods at the top of the scale in another city insofar as residents' preferences are determined by communitywide considerations. There can be status considerations associated with living in a certain suburb widely regarded as wealthy, although the service level falls far below that of other, less prestigious communities. Or there may be status, employment, or other advantages to living in the most poorly serviced area in Moscow compared with the best serviced neighborhood in Ufa. Soviet apartment exchange listings, often offering more living space in return for locational preferences, suggest that this is in fact the case.

This is not to deny that subcommunity differences exist and are important in Soviet cities, although ethnic and income variations among neighborhoods are far less visible than in U.S. cities. Time-budget research, sometimes employed in planning the development of communal and cultural facilities and services, has established the existence and importance of variations in standards of living and modes of life among urban residents.[30] To an observer, the most visible difference is probably that between the core (city center) and periphery. Core areas appear to have more public facilities, more services, and, frequently, the more desirable housing. Observation of retail outlets within cities indicates that more and more varied goods are to be found in the center (a fact confirmed by descriptions of shopping habits).[31] Lags in developing urban infrastructure in the USSR are described as a frequent problem.[32]

A distribution pattern favoring the center is not unique to Soviet cities. Considering only the distance dimension in the distribution of parks, fire protection, and public libraries (all services with a fixed location) in San Antonio, Lineberry concludes that it is "only the older, near-to-core areas that are consistently most proximate to public facilities."[33] However, spatial distribution assumes an additional importance in a context wherein distributional patterns in urban services are not offset (or exaggerated) by private sector patterns. In the Soviet context, physical mobility still depends primarily on access to public transit rather than on private transport purchase. Hence, physical mobility bears little relation to socioeconomic characteristics of the residents. The Soviet case suggests that mobility can be used as an objective measure of need; clearly, the interplay of location and mobility should be taken into account in discussing the differential distribution of government outputs. This would be analytically most valuable when populations concentrated in one neighborhood are relatively immobile compared to other city residents. This holds true, for example, in impoverished neighborhoods in U.S. city centers.

Serious questions must be raised about the usefulness of an inquiry into subcommunity distribution considered independently from problems of control.[34] Certain inequalities within and among cities cannot be attributed to decision making in the cities themselves. As already discussed, urban allocations are not among the functions of city management in the Soviet Union, and distributional outcomes in Soviet cities are tied less to decisions made by city leaders than to the national arena. The same argument, furthermore, can also be made for the distribution of services affected by categorical grants-in-aid in U.S. cities, for state-mandated expenditures, and for limitations induced by uncontrollable changes in the macroeconomic environment (for example, steep cost increases in a service sector affecting a particular target group). Where control over distribution falls largely outside the city, more than subcommunity analysis is necessary for a comprehensive statement about the distribution of benefits and burdens.

Be they explicit or implicit, formal or informal, distribution rules of some sort necessarily are applied to the provision of government services. Numerous possible distribution standards can be posited for public services.[35] Some possibilities involve consideration of recipients' abilities, such as ability to pay (a market princple) or to contribute (a merit principle). Others involve notions of efficiency or equity. For our purposes, it bears noting that the appearance of homogeneity constitutes one possible definition of equity, one that strongly takes subjective factors into account.

In the Soviet case, social homogeneity is incorporated into the very definition of proper and fitting urban life. As the discussion of urban microdistricts in Chapter 2 indicates, homogeneity, that is, outcome equity, has been put forth as a professed goal of urban planning. Furthermore, policy pronouncements and critical articles in the press suggest a commitment to remedial action against recognized developmental imbalances between the urban and the rural sectors, among communities, and within communities.[36] Speaking of the development of Moscow, Posokhin writes in this regard:

A model communist city is not just one kind of urban development; it has to do with the life of a socially homogeneous body of people, multimillion strong, in all its breadth and diversity, under the most progressive form of organization.[37]

A report prepared by the Ukrainian State Building Committee (*Gosstroi*) amplifies this point by specifying "the necessity of achieving the uniformity of socioeconomic conditions of life for the whole population under minimum expenditure."[38] Under conditions of heterogeneity, then, any differential distribution should foster the achievement of this goal of homogeneity. This establishes the underlying analytic principle.

This is not to deny the fact of inequalities, any more than a statement as to a U.S. commitment to choice (making alternatives available to citizen-as-consumer preferences) denies the fact that broad segments of the U.S. urban population are excluded effectively from service alternatives because of economic limitations on their participation in the market. What it does suggest, however, is that subcommunity distributional questions may not be considered appropriate under circumstances in which homogeneity is emphasized. As Chapter 5 will show, there is little evidence to date to support a claim that the Soviets seriously have undertaken or applied the findings of client analysis or subcommunity distributional analysis. Often Soviet analysts use a highly aggregated approach, which obscures differentiation among and within cities. As a case in point, two Soviet urbanists estimate that economic expenditures aimed at satisfying the needs of urban residents amounted to 3 billion rubles between 1971-75, and are projected at 11 billion rubles (an increase of almost 400 percent) over 1976-80.[39] As they are coupled with inadequate analytic tools and primitive measures, standards are transformed into standardization. In housing, this has led to defining social equity as output uniformity. In the distribution of apartments among urban residents, equity is thereby reduced to an operational standard whereby households of like size receive identical accommodations.[40]

THE DISTRIBUTION OF FINANCIAL RESOURCES

Our analysis of Soviet circumstances begins with the choice of a distribution rule by which to compare resources in various cities. Input equality, defined as equal per capita expenditures, is conceptually (although perhaps not administratively) the most rudimentary way to go about distributing management resources. Since we agree "the concept of equality is not easily applied to any social phenomenon, most assuredly including urban public policy," we choose the "simple-first" strategy as a practical starting point.[41] Moreover, our concern with the equity aspect stems logically from the regime's professed egalitarian norms and its purported objective of promoting social homogeneity and balanced development. Expenditures are examined because they refer to the money allotted and used to fulfill the tasks faced by urban managers. Revenue categories merely record monies formally received. The per capita measure of financial resources is only rarely applied by Soviet analyses, while it is common in analyses of U.S. city budgets.[42] Thus, this measure becomes even more interesting from a comparative standpoint.[43]

Total expenditures and per capita expenditures for several cities are shown in Table 11 and Figure 5. The figures are displayed according to the two dimensions along which important variations occur: by rank in the hierarchical administrative structure and by republic. An allocation index devised on the basis of this data and shown in Table 12 measures the direction and magnitude of variation from the national average. The allocation index identifies the major beneficiaries of the budget process at the city level by expressing per capita expenditures in each city as a percent of per capita expenditures in all cities nationally. By comparing what cities spend through the city budget to the national average, the allocation index establishes a yardstick for assessing how well or poorly certain cities fare.

The index should be used in a cautious fashion. The notes with Table 11 describe the limitations of the data. In some cases, figures drawn from different years are used to establish the position of a single city. Relying on the balancing in formal accounts, we calculate some figures from revenue data and make adjustments for budget surpluses. In each case, the size of the allowed surplus understates the magnitude of the variation. Without a time series, it is always possible that the data describe a fortuitous circumstance, such as, for example, an attempt to compensate for relatively low expenditures in previous years. Given Soviet budgeting processes, this circumstance is unlikely. Furthermore, the reader is reminded that only three of the 15 republics are included.

Table 12 indicates that the distribution of budget resources among cities does not proceed on an equal per capita basis. Historically, the RSFSR has dominated urban expenditures, and Russian cities are still "overrewarded." They spend a disproportionate share (more than three-fourths) of all city budget resources. Put another way, Russian cities spend 148 percent of the national average (148 percent of what they would be spending were the equal per capita distribution rule applied). Thus, they emerge as major beneficiaries in the budgetary process.

Cities in Kazakhstan clearly are not doing as well on the average as are Russian cities. There are fewer city residents in the whole of Kazakhstan than there are in the city of Moscow. Less than half the republic's inhabitants are "urban," even if one includes all urban units down to and including urban settlements. The capital, Alma-Ata, has a population of somewhat over 800,000, and none of the republic's cities has over 1 million residents. The republic fairs poorly on the index, which shows Kazakh cities spending 84 percent of the average for the nation.

Yet, to speak of a republic as a whole obscures some of the variations that the index highlights. Disaggregation of the Russian data is necessary so that the distribution among the republics is not masked by the inclusion of a special case. Patterns can be skewed considerably by the mere presence of Moscow, which accounts for 13 percent of all Soviet city expenditures, 16 percent of all Russian city expenditures, and almost 6 percent of the Soviet population living

TABLE 11

Expenditures in Soviet Cities

	Subordination	Population (thousands)	Ruble Expenditures (thousands)	Per Capita Ruble Expenditures
USSR	872 at province or higher	129,500[a]	15,552,000[b]	120
Kazakh SSR	49 at province or higher	5,500[c]	557,650[d]	101
Lithuanian SSR, Vilnius[e]	Republic	460	50,000	109
RSFSR	524 at province or higher	67,300	12,000,000[f]	178
Moscow	Republic	7,368	1,989,603[g]	270
Leningrad	Republic	3,786	910,186[g]	240
Krasnodar	Krai	519	47,679[h]	92
Leningrad province[i]	4 cities subordinate to the province (of 17 total)	214	18,413	86
Volkhov	Province	48	3,783	79
Vyburg	Province	69	7,674	111
Gatchina	Province	70	6,179	88
Sosnovyi Bor	Province	27	777	29

aPopulation figures as of January 1974 for the 872 cities are available in *SSSR, administrativno-territorial'noe delenie soiuznykh respublik* (Moscow: Izvestiia, 1974).

bG. V. Darkov and G. K. Maksimov, *Finansovaia statistika* (Moscow: Finansy, 1975), p. 49. The figure is for 1973.

cThis figure omits two very small cities.

dI. L. Kim, *Sovershenstvovanie poriadka sostavleniia biudzheta* (Moscow: Finansy, 1975), p. 15. Since the figure is specified for income, and there is balancing in formal accounts, an allowance for a subsidy is necessary to convert the figure into expenditures. To avoid understating the position of cities in Kazakhstan, allowance is made for a 5 percent surplus only.

ePopulation and expenditures figures from notes of discussion with chairman of the executive committee of Vilnius city soviet, June 1977.

fCalculated from data in V. S. Demchenkov and M. F. Uzhvenko, *Regulirovanie mestnykh biudzhetov* (Moscow: Finansy, 1975), p. 73. Information given is that subsidies to Russian city budgets amount to .15 percent of total budget resources, or 20 million rubles. Allowing for a surplus, the figure is converted into expenditures (formal account). In order to avoid overstating the position of Russian cities, allowance is made for a 10 percent surplus. The budget figure refers to 1971.

gO *gosudarstvennom biudzhete RSFSR na 1975 god i ob ispolnenii gosudarstvennogo biudzheta RSFSR za 1973 god* (Moscow: Finansy, 1975).

hThis figure is from Demchenkov, op. cit., p. 75-76. The four city district budgets are included.

iIbid., pp. 48-51.

Source: Compiled by the authors.

93

FIGURE 5

Soviet per Capita City Expenditures

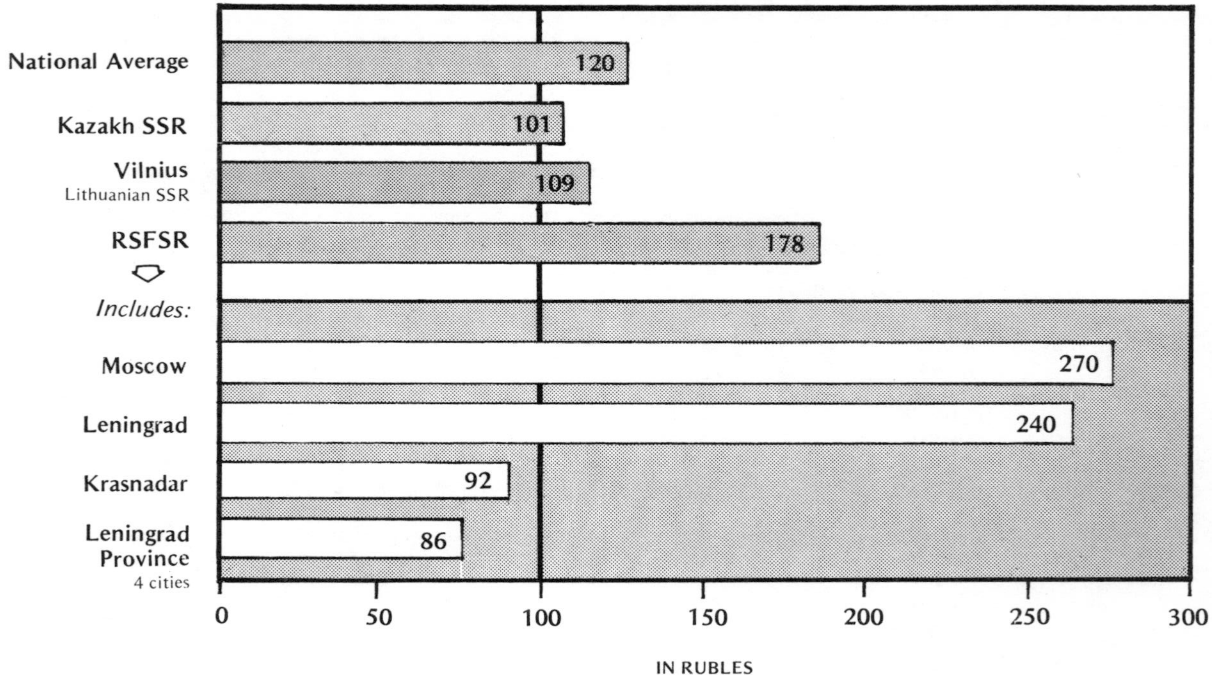

National Average — 120

Kazakh SSR — 101

Vilnius
Lithuanian SSR — 109

RSFSR — 178

Includes:

Moscow — 270

Leningrad — 240

Krasnadar — 92

Leningrad
Province
4 cities — 86

IN RUBLES

0   50   100   150   200   250   300

Source: Compiled by the authors.

TABLE 12

Soviet Urban Allocations

	Population as Percent of USSR City Total[a]	Expenditures as Percent of USSR City Total[a]	Allocation Index[b] (percent)
Kazakh SSR	4.20	3.8	84
Lithuanian SSR,			
Vilnius	0.40	0.3	91
RSFSR	51.97	77.0	148
Moscow	5.70	12.8	225
Leningrad	2.90	5.9	200
Krasnodar	0.40	0.3	77
Leningrad province			
(for four cities)	0.17	0.1	72

[a]Includes cities at or above province subordination only.
[b]The allocation index is: 100 (per capita expenditures for city/per capita expenditures for USSR cities).

Source: Calculated from data in Table 11.

in cities (see Tables 11 and 12). Disallowing for Moscow, expenditures for the Russian republic come to 167 rubles per capita, compared to 178 rubles with Moscow included. Without this privileged city, the Russian position on the index falls from 148 percent to 139 percent. Although Moscow's index is higher than Leningrad's, both cities enjoy a special status in the society, as reflected in the spread between these two cities and the republic as a whole. A heavily disproportionate share of all city resources are spent in these cities, as Figure 5 shows graphically. When clarifying the republic's position by disallowing for *both* cities, per capita expenditures in Russian cities fall to 162 rubles and the index to 135 percent. This still indicates an important comparative advantage for the republic as a whole.[44] Clearly, then, Russian cities and particularly Moscow and Leningrad enjoy a relatively larger share of the financial resources underlying management capacity.

An alternative interpretation is possible as well and must be explored. Rather than a difference among republics, the Russian advantage may reflect a difference among cities under circumstances in which cities of a certain type are concentrated in a particular republic. Russian cities' claim to superior resources may reflect the presence of a large number of cities with urban districts and, hence, a special budgetary status.[45] Managers in a city with urban districts are responsible for implementing the allocation of resources among the districts and therefore have broader budget responsibilities and resources than they would otherwise command. Since urban districts are, in turn, a function of size, this amounts to a test for a simple distribution rule whereby cities with large populations are granted higher per capita expenditures. However, the case of Krasnodar undercuts this possibility. In this category, by virtue of its four urban districts, Krasnodar spends at a level (index: 77 percent) well below what would be expected were resources distributed to the benefit of these cities. This suggests that the distribution involves more than population, and that the preeminent position of Russian cities is not attributable simply to the large number of cities with urban districts.

Within the RSFSR, rank in the national administrative hierarchy or subordination is the best indicator of the relative level of budget resources. Moscow and Leningrad, both subordinate to the republic, stand on the index at 225 and 200 percent, respectively; in contrast, Krasnodar and the cities subordinate to Leningrad province stand at 77 and 72 percent, respectively. To some extent this is expected, since some spending (such as staff size and salaries of the city's executive committee) is directly related to the city's position in the formal state hierarchy. However, the magnitude of variation cannot be accounted for by staff expenses alone.

The macrodistribution rule of administrative rank suggests that resources are distributed within the RSFSR according to a functional criterion, whereby larger and economically complex cities are rewarded for the functions they fulfill for the society. Distributing resources on the basis of rank rewards cities directly for administrative position and indirectly for economic complexity and population growth. This reward structure is in accord with the proposition, based on research in Czechoslovakia, that top-level leaders in socialist systems view the urban system and individual cities as centers of industrial production.[46] This argument is supported by the fact that the economic plans called for the government budget in 1975 to receive from turnover taxes 5 billion rubles from enterprises and organizations in Moscow.[47] This reward structure further fits the picture of the "administrative city" as drawn in Chapter 2.

However, subordination is less useful for predicting the index value across republics, since Vilnius, the republic capital of Lithuania, stands at only 91 percent on the index. It should be noted, however, that Vilnius is being rewarded for what looks to be, in these authors' eyes, its administrative function. This feature surfaces through a comparison of Vilnius with Krasnodar, both of which have populations of roughly one-half million. Both cities are very close in per capita expenditures, and both spend what amounts to 0.3 percent of all city expenditures nationally. Significantly, however, Vilnius stands at a higher level on the allocation index than does Krasnodar (91 compared to 77 percent, respectively). Thus, a variable other than population affects the distribution of budget resources, and that is administrative rank.

We turn now to off-budget resources for the purpose of establishing whether these large variations in budget resources are counterbalanced or magnified by other resource flows. This methodology is particularly important in light of the formal policy of smoothing developmental imbalances among cities by altering the allocation patterns in industrial investments. Almost invariably, industrial growth is pinpointed as the single most critical factor stimulating and sustaining urban growth in the established urban centers.[48] The impact of industrial location on urban development is perhaps most dramatic in the case of Togliatti, in which the step from a hydroelectric plant to the Volga automobile plant created a city of almost one-half million residents. With the growth of new enterprises, new jobs are created and additional workers attracted into the area. Therefore, it should be possible to restrain urban growth by distributing industrial investments in favor of the small- and medium-sized cities.

Industrial investments over the two decades suggest an unbroken tradition in Soviet investment practices—that of channeling capital investments into the larger cities. Industrial investments can be evaluated according to two yardsticks, each measuring investments differently but suggesting similar conclusions.* Measuring investments by the number of new enterprises, it is found that the Ninth Five-Year Plan slated more than half of all new industrial enterprises for cities with less than 100,000 inhabitants. In the Eighth Plan period, three-quarters of all new enterprises were planned for cities with populations under one-quarter million.[49] Yet, more than 1,000 enterprises were built or reconstructed over the Ninth Plan period just beyond the jurisdictional limits of major industrial centers in the RSFSR.[50] They thus contributed to the growth of the metropolitan area, including the center. Measuring investments in terms of ruble value, the first three years of this plan saw more than half of the total investments made in the RSFSR by the three most important national construction ministries flowing into large cities. Small- and medium-sized cities received approximately 17 percent.[51] Clearly, the greatest ruble share of investments went to industrial facilities in or near relatively developed cities.

According to several city planners, continued industrial development is the main reason Moscow, Leningrad, Kiev, and Vilnius keep growing, despite prohibitions on in-migration and restrictions on industrial expansion written into the territorial plans.[52] The construction of new industrial enterprises and the expansion of existing facilities are forbidden in many cities, including Russian cities with one-quarter million inhabitants or more. But the construction continues, sometimes beyond the city's immediate administrative boundaries, and sometimes under a category that relates the investment to modernization and re-equipment rather than to new or additional productive facilities. The consequence for small cities has been that plans for urban investment (that is, con-

---

*Other criteria also can be applied to industrial investment. One pertinent to the issue of growth is the number of jobs created.

struction) and services went unimplemented in most cases during much of the Eighth and Ninth Five-Year Plan periods.[53]

State ownership of urban land alone, therefore, does not seem to engender automatically the capacity to direct urban development. This capacity is related as well to control over land use and to the concentration of urban resources in managers' hands. In the Soviet case, described in Chapter 2, vertical fragmentation of resources and authority inhibits management control of urban development and management transformation. In addition to industrial investments, other financial and material resources from branch ministries also engender fragmentation and even political conflict. One effect has been to forestall reliable budget forecasting, as a city executive committee chairman complains: "Give us 300 million rather than 542 million rubles . . . but let it be a firm, planned sum that does not change 18 times."[54] Furthermore, it is less than easy for the city to get those funds allocated to it, although city administrators sometimes view enterprises as ready sources of off-budget subsidies for city services and facilities.[55] The 1971 reforms, formally aimed at giving urban officials more control over urban resources, are not being implemented in a timely or wholehearted fashion. Since implementation would require reducing the role of branch ministries in urban affairs, this is less than surprising. Generally, the larger cities at higher rank are in a better position regarding these "departmental" resources. These cities enjoy special budget rights, often contract for all housing construction in the city, and depend less on departmental financing than do the smaller cities. The "descending chain" of developmental disproportions and the advantage held by administrators in cities at high administrative levels is described by another city executive committee chairman this way:

> The ministries give money for construction of municipal service facilities in the region to the Kazakh Republic Council of Ministers. . . . Some of it doesn't reach its intended destination. . . . The pruned funds arrive in the province center, and the bulk of this money is used in Pavlodar facilities. The other cities in the territorial complex get what is left over.[56]

Even for these large, highly ranked cities, industrial expansion is not without costs to the city. The growth of enterprise and the attraction of new workers into the city immediately increase consumption of services supported by the city budget. These include surface transport, retail trade outlets, public dining facilities, and health and other services. The expansion of cultural, administrative, and other "nonproductive" institutions does not generate commensurate funds to compensate the budget for the additional costs it bears. On the other hand, some of the industrial growth involves city enterprises, which are geared to supporting the daily needs of the residents. Growth in this area may bring in additional revenues. For example, in Moscow approximately half the city's revenue is derived from over 2,400 enterprises and organizations under the city's jurisdiction.[57] Growth of nonsubordinate enterprises may or may not benefit the city's immediate service picture, depending on the bargaining talents of the individuals involved. But because budget resources are related to administrative rank, and rank is related to economic development, a city is rewarded indirectly for industrial development and population growth. Thus, budget considerations encourage a concentration on the growth of productive capacity.[58]

Urban housing is another resource flow by which urban development is channeled and subsidized. It involves a meaningful proportion of the resources devoted to the urban sector; the total value of housing and communal facilities under local soviet jurisdiction in the RSFSR is over 2 billion rubles, which amounts to approximately one-fifth of the republic's fixed assets.[59] For this reason, distribution patterns in housing should be examined alongside those of budget allocations and industrial investments.

Not all resources devoted to housing are off-budget, however. Some housing is financed directly through city budgets. The state budget finances about 65 percent of total investments in housing construction and, in 1974, USSR ministries allocated more than 200 million rubles to local soviets for municipal construction. For 1975, 310 million rubles were planned (an increase of more than 50 percent); much of this sum involved housing.[60] In Moscow, housing amounts to over half of all city-financed capital investment (and one-quarter of all investment in the city).[61] The possibility should be considered, then, that housing resources represent budget allocations in a different guise. Should this be so, the distribution and fragmentation arguments, with their implications for managerial transformation, would be caught in an analytic snare wrought by the problem of fragmented resources. The analytic problem is even more important in view of the policy decisions, formalized in the March 1971 resolutions and decrees, to transfer gradually state urban housing to the executive committees of city soviets, which would act as "sole clients" for housing management in the city.

Approximately 60 percent of all urban housing still belongs to ministries and departments outside city jurisdiction (and, by and large, the city budget).[62] A February 1975 editorial in *Pravda* pointed out that in the Uzbek, Georgian, Lithuanian, and Moldavian republics, as well as in some territories and provinces within Russia, the Ukraine, and Kazakhstan, the number of buildings under ministerial jurisdiction had actually increased since 1971.[63] It becomes evident under these circumstances that few, if any, city administrators have the exclusive line management responsibilities for housing suggested in the "sole client" phraseology. City budgets may even be slipping in their relative positions. Housing jurisdiction apparently has more to do with funding sources than with efficient construction, management, and maintenance.[64] Therefore, although poor housing conditions may be ameliorated somewhat through the city's budget, housing cannot be declared a direct product of that budget alone. In sum, housing may be considered as a separate resource flow.

The distribution of housing parallels that of budget resources and industrial investments. Housing (measured as square meters of living space per capita) varies by republic, economic region, and city (see Table 13). Cities with over 1 million inhabitants average 12.6 square meters per person, compared to the national average for all cities of 11.6 square meters per capita (or 11.4 square meters, excluding the large cities). Cities in the RSFSR stand at 103 percent of the national average for all city residents, while Moscow alone can claim 122 percent, the highest in the country. Cities in Kazakhstan, on the other hand, fall below the national average in living space per capita, just as they did in budget resources. The republic capital, Alma-Ata, does better than the republic as a whole, a fact that fits the distribution rule of administrative rank. Since there is more living space per capita in larger cities than in smaller ones, and per capita housing space increases by 0.2 square meters annually, Viktor Perevedentsev, the Soviet demographer, concludes that large cities benefit from what amounts to a six-year lead on housing conditions.[65] While this permits us to say at the community level of analysis that nationally formulated housing policies still favor the larger, higher ranked cities, the data say nothing about the distribution at the subcommunity level. Suffice it to note that highly subsidized, low rent scales have not obviated the "relation between housing accommodations and stratification in Soviet society."[66]

There are efficiency implications as well as equity effects in distributing resources through national processes that reward and encourage growth.[67] In considering efficiency, the likelihood that the costs of urban services are related to the size of the city's population is widely discussed, but as yet the discussion about optimal city size remains inconclusive. Davidovich found that per capita expenditures in larger cities are higher than per capita expenditures in smaller ones; total capital outlays and per capita operating expenditures increase with increased population size.[68] Others counter that expenditures increase only 3-4 percent once service variations are taken into account.[69] Even were the question of costs borne by city government resolved, this single component would not end debate over optimal city size, for it is not only the amount that figures into investment calculations. It is also a question of who pays. For purposes of industrial siting, the larger cities continue to be considered more efficient from the point of view of branch ministries that can maek use of the established infrastructure, labor supply, and services provided through the cities' budgets.[70]

Failure to resolve the question about the relative efficiency of cities of different population sizes suggests that costs are related to other factors as well. If we conceive of the relationship between service costs and city size as a dynamic one, then changes in population size and demographic structure suggest themselves for consideration.[71] A physical redistribution of the population follows the distribution of housing, jobs, and adequate support services. Population shifts imply the abandoning of residential, service, and other facilities and the building of new facilities in other locations. Housing shortages, inadequacies in

TABLE 13

Living Space in Selected Republics and Large Cities

	Per Capita Living Space (in square meters)	*Housing Index (percent)**
National average		
Urban	11.6	—
Excluding large cities	11.4	—
RSFSR	12.0	103
Ukraine	12.2	105
Kazakhstan	10.0	86
Moscow	14.2	122
Kiev	12.9	111
Leningrad	12.4	107
Alma-Ata	10.8	93
Average for cities with 1 million residents or more	12.6	109

*The housing index is: 100 (per capita living space in jurisdiction/per capita living space for USSR cities).

Source: Viktor Perevedentsev, "Zhilishcha," *Zhurnalist*, October 1974, pp. 76-77.

the delivery of basic city services (such as mass transport), and uncoordinated service delivery in new residential areas have been attributed to rapid urban growth, that is, the change in population size.[72] Furthermore, the costs of maintaining services are related to a slackening off of growth. Thus, policies that foster population shifts and demographic changes alter the urban sector's cost structure and the distribution of costs within and among cities.

Changes in population size introduce new cost considerations into urban management. For example, high investment costs combined with rapid urban growth have led to the adoption of high density standards in residential construction.[73] In the large cities, the centers are growing more slowly than the outlying areas. In Moscow, while overall density increased from 1959 to 1970, density within the Garden Ring (city center) dropped.[74] New housing with adequate facilities by Soviet standards is being built for multimember families on the city's outskirts. In consonance with these developments, reverse commutation flows and multistep commuting from the suburban areas have increased, along with the interest shown in adaptive reuse of public buildings.[75]

Demographic changes affect both operating and capital costs. These costs are related to characteristics of the populations being served as well as to their number. If the city government is to respond to developing service needs, new institutions and new services are needed; some are being provided.[76] In this regard changes in the age structure are particularly important, since according to both Soviet and Western thinking on the matter, changes in the life cycle are extremely influential in daily routine and hence on consumption of urban services.[77] Thus, as the distribution of the age structure in a city alters, so do the demands placed on urban services. Nor is it to be expected that certain cost increases will affect all cities in the same way or to the same extent. In this regard it should be noted that the proportion of pensioners in Moscow climbed from 13.7 percent of the population in 1959 to 19.5 percent in 1970, and the city budget bears much of the related expense.[78] Homes for the disabled and aged require absolute increases in city outlays, as the costs for maintaining each individual mount.[79] The aged are also heavy consumers of medical services, which are increasingly expensive for the city to provide. Rising personnel costs, growing support staffs, and higher capital costs push up the per capita costs of certain services, including hospital care, at the very same time as consumption promises to increase as a result of changes in the population structure.[80]

The fact that the urban infrastructure is characterized by relatively high, fixed, operating costs magnifies the impact of changing population size and structure on services and overall resources.[81] It is very difficult to hold down cost increases, since a large proportion of the costs are attributable to employee wages and salaries. As one recent Soviet assessment sums up the problem: "The economy of the big cities is one of the most complex systems managed by man. The traditional methods and the increase . . .[in] management personnel do not lead to any improvement . . . [in] efficiency.[82]

Not only is it very difficult to hold down cost increases but there is very little reason to do so. More efficient operations by city enterprises are supposed to be rewarded through incentive funds and above-plan profits. In the long term, efficient operations reflected in cost reductions work against the overall city budget since, as it now stands, profits are automatically incorporated into the next plan. ("The greater the profit, the more challenging that plan will be."[83]) Only above-plan profits redound directly to the city's budget, and the amount involved is so small that the short-term gain is insignificant. Moreover, the retention of incentive funds in those city enterprises on cost accounting has further fragmented resources in the city by removing them from the city budget.

By distributing housing investments, industrial investments, and budget allocations according to a standard that incorporates rank, development, and size, large, high-ranking, Russian cities continue to be rewarded for past developmental and political successes. Even within the RSFSR, allocation and investment processes foster interurban variations that are self-perpetuating and that increase over time. These "preferred" cities keep growing on the basis of a chain reaction to their own development. Having achieved an initial level of development and a high administrative position, these cities then are given through preferential allocations and investments the means by which to secure and sustain further opportunities for development and growth. These cities receive additional resources (in effect, capital transfers) over and above the national average, and these resources are important factors in shaping the speed and substance of city development.[84] Furthermore, the fact that all three resource flows parallel each other undermines any attempt to link the distribution pattern to the distribution of needs among Soviet cities.

Thus, Soviet urban development reflects national and regional economic growth to a greater extent than it reflects the general plans, and the mechanisms aimed at containing urban growth succumb to developmental processes beyond the control of city leaders and planners. By and large, the beneficiaries of the differential distribution are those very cities deemed by official policy to be out of bounds for further growth. Loud lamentations in the Soviet press and Western analyses describe and decry urban sprawl and the disproportions introduced into urban development on national and metropolitan scales. These problems are traced to a variety of factors: historical and geographic conditions; sectoral planning leading to the fragmentation of decision making and responsibility; and rapacious economic managers whose interests in professional advancement dictate plan fulfillment. But these conventional explanations suggest that developmental disproportions are the results merely of breakdowns or gaps in planning and management processes. They imply that if the Soviets were to turn their management efforts in this direction, the phenomena would fade. Our distributional analysis, by contrast, suggests that these phenomena are the logical outcomes of a set of coherent, mutually supportive policies favoring the larger, higher ranking Russian cities. The fact that the resource flows reinforce each other multiplies their individual impacts.

The differential distribution of resources has several predictable developmental consequences. These resources secure and sustain disproportions among republics. The current patterns of regional domination are being projected into the future, as past developmental successes are rewarded with additional resources through government investments and allocations. Developmental differences among regions have been attributed variously to socialist urbanization in general, to the socialist system as a redistributive system, and to class exploitation and underlying social conflict.[85] In the latter view, "The main contradiction is no longer the classical opposition of town and country but rather the imbalance between the center and periphery and between developed and underdeveloped areas."[86] These imbalances could exacerbate the nationality problem; minimally, regional distributional preferences fail to ameliorate the problem.

These distributional outcomes would be less important in generating domestic political conflict were the share of the nation's wealth devoted to the urban sector increasing significantly. (They also would be less important were private sector alternatives to urban government services available.) Despite large absolute increases, this is not the case. Even as cities are responsible for more services, more activities, and a growing proportion of the population, overall expenditures through city budgets show only a small proportional increase relative to all expenditures in the national budget (from 6 percent in 1940 to almost 8 percent planned for 1974).[87] Under circumstances in which the urban sector's share of national resources remains so constant, an increase in resources for some cities necessarily leads to cutbacks in others.

For the smaller cities at the lower levels in the administrative hierarchy, this entails an inevitable relative decline, evn if their leaders manage to sustain the city's position in absolute terms. They are receiving a disproportionately small share of the resources necessary for performing the job they have undertaken. Their problems in resource management are compounded by the fact that resource control in their cities is highly fragmented and lacking in autonomy. Frequently, officials in these small cities depend upon departmental sources for financing city investments and operations. Conversely, resource management in "preferred" cities is more concentrated, as their leaders enjoy more control over more resources. Financial advantages and relatively concentrated resource control are bought through centralization. The opportunity to press claims in the competition for funds is related directly to access to the bureaucratic center, and leaders in cities of higher administrative rank are closer to those making the allocative decisions in the "sequence of iterative coordinations between the subordinate and superior planning organs."[88] Given this opportunity, talented individuals are able to press their claims for constrained resources in the politics surrounding the distribution of resources among bureaucratic leaders. In this way, the distribution of financial and personnel resources is related. But although the picture is somewhat ambiguous and at times contradictory in both cases, financial resources provide a far clearer case for managerial transformation in the preferred cities than do personnel resources.

The distribution patterns also compel the authors to forecast a continued failure to either contain unplanned growth or to smooth out developmental imbalances among cities. This prognosis is made with that caveat common to social science research: all other things held constant. Jane Jacobs argues that "the past development of a city is no guarantee of future development because the city can stop vigorously adding new work into the economy and thus can stagnate."[89] The dominant form of human organization in modern society—the city—depends on growth. Budget allocations, housing investments, and industrial investments, distributed as rewards for past growth, are among the major mechanisms working to sustain and amplify growth. In the event that serious attempts are made to alter the flow of resources (and undertaken successfully), then our prognosis could be proven wrong. In the interim, residency restrictions and policy pronouncements promise little in the way of counteracting the impact of these resources flows.

Differential distribution patterns in the Soviet Union indicate that the generation and redistribution of urban resources through national mechanisms do not guarantee equity or even uniformity among cities. National processes have led to substantial rewards for certain cities to the detriment of others. In the Soviet case, these processes have produced one policy outcome, which some observers view as positive (and which U.S. processes have not produced): resources flow into the major urban centers. This is the other aspect of developmental unbalance, for it serves to designate and then support major cities as privileged centers within the society. In the Soviet case, the differential distribution of urban resources has led to the rich growing richer and the large growing larger still.

NOTES

1. Charles Beard, *American Government and Politics*, as quoted in Robert L. Lineberry and Edmund P. Fowler, "Reformism and Public Policies in American Cities," in *Community Politics: A Behavioral Approach*, ed. Charles M. Bonjean, Terry N. Clark, and Robert L. Lineberry (New York: Free Press, 1971), p. 286.

2. The general description of Soviet city budgeting is based upon Carol W. Lewis, *The Budgetary Process in Soviet Cities* (New York: Columbia University, Graduate School of Business, Center for Government Studies, 1976), and idem, "Comparing City Budgets: The Soviet Case," *Comparative Urban Research* 5 (November 1977): 46-57.

3. Despite the greater range of activities and operations undertaken by Soviet city governments, they have few, if any, specific areas of functional specialization. This characteristic they share with their U.S. counterparts. Theodore Lowi, *The End of Liberalism* (New York: W. W. Norton, 1969), pp. 44-45. While Soviet city governments enjoy more of a monopoly over some services because there is no competing private sector, they compete with other providers in the branch and territorial hierarchies.

4. The city budgets of Moscow and Leningrad represent, respectively, the largest and second largest entries in the budget of the Russian republic. *O gosudarstvennom biudzhete RSFSR na 1975 god i ob ispolnenii gosudarstvennogo biudzheta RSFSR za 1973 god* (Moscow: Finansy, 1975).

5. Only nine states place no limits upon municipal taxing or spending powers. John Shannon and L. Richard Gabler, "Tax Lids and Expenditure Mandates: The Case for Fiscal Fair Play," *Intergovernmental Perspective* 3 (Summer 1977): 7-12. See also Eileen Shanahan, "Control over City Budgets Is Extensive in Some States," New York *Times*, June 8, 1975, p. 1.

6. John P. Crecine, *Governmental Problem Solving: A Computer Simulation of Municipal Budgeting* (Chicago: Rand McNally, 1969); Robert L. Lineberry, *Equality and Urban Policy: Distribution of Municipal Services* (Beverly Hills, Calif.: Sage, 1977), pp. 151-52; Aaron Wildavsky, *Budgeting: A Comparative Theory of Budgeting Processes* (Boston: Little, Brown and Co., 1975), pp. 114-35. The studies cover Oakland, San Antonio, Cleveland, Pittsburgh, and Detroit.

7. As Wildavsky points out, a balanced budget means that revenue considerations dominate expenditures, and the central focus becomes how much there is to spend rather than how much has to be spent to achieve certain objectives. Ibid.

8. Information issues are considered further in Chapter 6.

9. Other decisional rules (such as the application of professional norms and consumption patterns) to further economize and routinize operations are treated in Lineberry, op. cit., pp. 64-67; and Frank S. Levy, Arnold J. Meltsner, and Aaron Wildavsky, *Urban Outcomes: Schools, Streets, and Libraries* (Berkeley: University of California Press, 1974), pp. 229-37.

10. V. S. Demchenkov and M. F. Uzhvenko, *Regulirovanie mestnykh biudzhetov* (Moscow: Finansy, 1975), p. 73. Subsidies amounted to 0.15 percent of city revenues in the RSFSR in 1971, a total of 20 million rubles. Only 19 city budgets were receiving direct subsidies that year.

11. Thomas Muller, *Growing and Declining Urban Areas: A Fiscal Comparison* (Washington, D.C.: The Urban Institute, November 1975).

12. G. V. Darkov and G. K. Maksimov, *Finansovaia statistika* (Moscow: Finansy, 1975), pp. 48-49.

13. Ibid., and *O gosudarstvennom biudzhete RSFSR.*

14. The deductions-from-profits tax, part of the payments-from-profits account, is calculated as a planned percentage of actual profits and paid according to the enterprise's administrative subordination. The deductions-from-profit tax (*otchisleniia ot pribyli*) has been the most important source of revenue in Moscow since 1965. One readily available source for Moscow budget data is G. B. Poliak and E. V. Sofronova, *General'nyi plan i biudzhet Moskvy* (Moscow: Finansy, 1973).

15. Total city expenditures rose from 1.1 billion rubles in 1940 to 15.3 billion rubles in 1974; the largest increases both proportionally and absolutely occurred prior to the 1970s. Demchenkov and Uzhvenko, op. cit., pp. 18, 30; Darkov and Maksimov, op. cit., p. 48; Nina Aleksandrovna Shirkevich, "Arifmetika biudzheta," *Sovety deputatov trudiashchikhsia,* June 1968, pp. 29-31; and idem, *Mestnye biudzhety SSSR* (Moscow: Finansy, 1965).

16. Darkov and Maksimov, op. cit., p. 48; G. V. Darkov, "Mestnye biudzhety (statisticheskii obzor)," *Finansy SSSR* 43 (January 1969): 28; and Shirkevich, *Mestnye biudzhety,* p. 61.

17. For example, see Charles J. Savio, "Revenue-Sharing in Practice: National-State-Local Subventions in Venezuela," in *Latin American Urban Research,* ed. Francine F. Rabinovitz and Felicity M. Trueblood (Beverly Hills, Calif.: Sage, 1973), pp. 79-96.

18. Robert Reinhold, "Cities in North Face Reduced Federal Aid under Block Grants," New York *Times,* February 13, 1977, p. 1. Also see the series "Sunbelt Region Leads Nation in Growth of Population," initiated by Robert Reinhold, "Section's Cities Top Urban Expansion," and Jon Nordheimer, "Area Spans Southern Half of Country," New York *Times,* February 8, 1976, p. 1, sec. 1. On Italy, see Robert C. Fried, "Communism, Urban Budgets, and the Two Italies: A Case Study in Comparative Urban Government," *Journal of Politics* 33 (November 1971): 1008-51.

19. Ibid.

20. A. Miasnikov, "There Should Be One Master," *Current Digest of the Soviet Press* 24 (September 28, 1977): 8-9, translated from *Ekonomika i organizatsiia promyshlennogo proizvodstva* 4 (July-August 1977): 124-31. According to this author, funds are drawn primarily from three sources: allocations from the state budget, state subsidies earmarked for specific projects, and money from branch ministries with enterprises in the city.

21. Author's notes of discussion with chairman of executive committee of Vilnius city soviet, June 1977.

22. Poliak and Sofronova, op. cit.

23. Leonard Merewitz and Stephen H. Sosnick, *The Budget's New Clothes,* Markham Series in Public Policy Analysis (Chicago: Rand McNally, 1971); Harley H. Henricks and Graem M. Taylor, *Program Budgeting and Benefit-Cost Analysis* (Pacific Palisades, Calif.: Goodyear, 1969); and Carol H. Weiss, *Evaluation Research* (Englewood Cliffs, N.J.: Prentice-Hall, 1972).

24. In his analysis of Soviet housing needs, Henry Morton concludes that the housing deficit has been expanding since 1965. "Who Gets What, When, and How? Housing in the Soviet Union," Paper prepared for delivery at the 1977 Annual Meeting of the American Political Science Association, September 1977.

25. See, for example, Ira Sharkansky, "Government Expenditures and Public Services in the American States," *American Political Science Review* 61 (December 1967): 1066-77.

26. Lineberry, op. cit., p. 19. For a study using aggregate budget expenditures as a measure of outputs, see Terry N. Clark, "Community Structure, Decision-Making, Budget Expenditures and Urban Renewal in 51 American Communities," in Bonjean, Clark, and Lineberry, op. cit., pp. 293-313.

27. Lineberry, op. cit., p. 123.

28. Charles M. Tiebout, "A Pure Theory of Local Expenditures," *Journal of Political Economy* 64 (October 1956): 416-24.

29. Henry Morton, "The Soviet Urban Scene," *Problems of Communism* 26 (January-February 1977): 474.

30. Elizabeth Ann Weinberg, *The Development of Sociology in the Soviet Union* (London: Routledge and Kegan Paul, 1974), chap. 5.

31. Author's notes of discussion with city planners and officials in Leningrad and Vilnius, June 1977. In response to questions about locational preferences, ready access to transportation was mentioned in Leningrad, whereas in Vilnius the nonstandard apartment layouts in the older sections of the city center were given as the determining factor.

32. B. S. Vasilev and A. G. Stolbov, "Ways of Building up the Urban Infrastructure," *Current Digest of the Soviet Press* 24 (September 18, 1977): 9, translated from *Ekonomika i organizatsiia promyshennogo proizvodstva* 4 (July-August 1977). The reasons cited include the lack of both comprehensive planning and reliable leisure time projections.

33. Lineberry, op. cit., pp. 125, 184. He traces his finding to decision rules in urban public bureaucracies that reward consumption and population growth.

34. Levy, Meltsner, and Wildavsky, op. cit., 11. They make the argument that distributional analysis should focus on those variables susceptible to control, so that a policy perspective can be maintained.

35. In Lineberry, op. cit., p. 189, four distribution standards are used: equity, efficiency, demand, and need. In Levy, Meltsner, and Wildavsky, op. cit., p. 12, three are discussed: efficiency, responsiveness, and equity. There are others, including political expediency and economy.

36. This issue is discussed further in Chapters 1 and 4.

37. Mikhail Vasil'evich Posokhin, *Cities to Live in* (Moscow: Novosti Press, 1974), p. 128. Also on the same theme, see Alexei Gutnov et al., *The Ideal Communist City*, trans. Renee Neu Watkins (New York: George Braziller, 1968), p. 152.

38. USSR Gosstroi, Center of Scientific and Technical Information in Civil Construction and Architecture, *Urban Development in the Ukrainian SSR*, Report prepared for the UN Conference-Exposition on Human Settlements, Vancouver, June 1976, p. 4.

39. A. S. Gruzinov and V. P. Riumin, *Gorod: upravlenie, problemy* (Leningrad: Lenizdat, 1977), pp. 3, 77.

40. L. Gordon and E. Klopov, *Man after Work* (Moscow: Progress, 1975), p. 45. For remarks concerning the application of nationwide averages as standards in urban services, see V. Ia. Liubovny and V. K. Savelev, "Russia's Small and Large Cities," *Current Digest of the Soviet Press* 24 (September 28, 1977): 7-8.

41. Lineberry, op. cit., p. 36.

42. The measure of per capita expenditures figures in the debate over optimal city size. Vladimir G. Davidovich, *Planirovka gorodov i raionov* (Moscow: Stroizdat, 1964). See also Viktor Perevedentsev, "The Concentration of Urban Population and the Criteria of Optimality of a City," *International Journal of Sociology* 5 (Summer-Fall 1975): 18-36, translated from *Urbanizatsiia i rabochii klass v usloviiakh nauchno-tekhnicheskoi revoliutsii* (Moscow: Akademiia Nauk SSSR, 1970): 212-30.

43. Suggestively, the per capita measure is rare in Soviet analyses of budget resources but quite common in housing analyses. Possibly financial resources are considered as public

resources with communitywide (that is, collective) significance, whereas housing involves individual interests. On individual interests in housing, see Posokhin, op. cit., p. 8.

44. In the United States, region has been suggested as an important predictor of government expenditures in certain policy areas. See Raymond Wolfinger and John Osgood Field, "Political Ethos and the Structure of City Government," *American Political Science Review* 60 (June 1966): 306-26; and Lineberry and Fowler, op. cit.

45. At the beginning of January 1972, there were 452 urban districts in 141 cities; two years later, urban districts had increased to 538, 60 percent in the RSFSR. Demchenko and Uzhvenko, op. cit., p. 71; and *SSSR, administrativno-territorial'noe delenie soiznykh respublik* (Moscow: Izvestiia, 1974), p. 8.

46. Karl Joseph Kansky, *Urbanization under Socialism: The Case of Czechoslovakia* (New York: Praeger, 1976), p. 239.

47. Main Scientific Research Computing Center of the Moscow City Soviet Executive Committee, *Description of the Management System of the City of Moscow*, Report on the scientific research performed according to the Intergovernmental Agreement of 1972 for Scientific and Technological Cooperation between the USSR and USA, Topic no. 3, Project no. 1 (New York: Columbia University, Graduate School of Business, Center for Government Studies, 1975), p. 140. Uncirculated draft report; Soviet source document unverified by independent research.

48. Author's notes of discussions with Soviet city planners, June 1977.

49. B. E. Svetlichnii, "Planirovanie gradoobrazuiuschchikh protsessov i problemy rasseleniia," *Planovoe khoziaistvo* (September 1974): 140-44.

50. V. Beketov, "Zavod v raitsentre," *Pravda*, September 9, 1975, p. 2.

51. Ibid.

52. Author's notes of discussion, June 1977.

53. V. Baranov, "Problemy razvitiia malykh gorodov," *Ekonomicheskaia gazeta* 40 (October 1974): 9. According to this source, almost all of the 850 small and medium cities in the RSFSR had some sort of general development plan by the beginning of 1974. Considering the inability of territorial planning to do more than slow down urban growth, it is interesting to note that some Soviet urbanists have reversed themselves and have begun to speak of the advantages of great urban centers. See, for example, Gruzinov and Riumin, op. cit., p. 67; Jeff Chin, *Manipulating Soviet Population Resources* (London: Macmillan, 1977), pp. 48-51.

54. Miasnikov, op. cit., p. 8.

55. Ibid.; and the discussion in Chapter 2.

56. M. Poltaranin and V. Sevastianov, "On the Banks of the Irtysh," *Current Digest of the Soviet Press* 24 (August 3, 1977): 7, translated from *Pravda*, July 3, 1977, p. 2.

57. Poliak and Sofronova, op. cit., p. 75.

58. Party and career considerations also foster this kind of concentration. V. V. Grishin, the first secretary of the Moscow *gorkom*, has identified accelerating the city's economic growth as one of his organization's chief tasks. N. Liaporov, "Vperedi god boevoi, napriazhennoi raboty (c plenuma Moskovskogo gorkoma KPSS)," *Pravda*, December 24, 1974, p. 2.

59. I. Miromenko, "Kogda odin khoziain," *Pravda*, June 10, 1975, p. 3. See also Chapter 5, note 84.

60. D. G. Tonsky et al., *Current Trends and National Policy in the Field of Housing, Building and Town Planning in the USSR* (Moscow: Gosgrazhdanstroi, 1976), pp. 11-12, 17; N. K. Baibakov, "Zakliuchitel'noe slovo," *Izvestiia*, December 21, 1974, p. 2. These large sums do not contradict Morton's argument that housing needs are outstripping its provision and that capital outlays have declined proportionally since 1960. Morton, "Who Gets What?" op. cit., p. 5.

61. See the Moscow city budget summary in Lewis, "Comparing City Budgets," op. cit., pp. 52-53.

62. "Zhiloi fond—narodnoe dostoianie," *Pravda*, February 1, 1975, p. 1.

63. Ibid.

64. Tonsky, op. cit., p. 18.

65. Viktor Perevedentsev, "Zhilishcha," *Zhurnalist*, October 1974, pp. 76-77. New housing is described as accounting for only one-half of the current investment in housing; the remainder is devoted to repair and renovation.

66. Morton, "Urban Scene," p. 76.

67. A case for considering both efficiency and equity is given in Anthony Downs, *Urban Problems and Prospects* (Chicago: Markham, 1970), pp. 4-5; and Levy, Meltsner, and Wildavsky, op. cit., pp. 8-9. To the Soviets, efficiency is an important criterion but not the only one; the application of multiple criteria has been cited as the reason why decisions about urban development are made at the highest state levels. Author's notes of discussions at the Central Scientific Research and Design Institute for City Construction (TsNIIP gradostroitel'stva), June 1977.

68. Davidovich, op. cit., p. 30.

69. V. I. Artemchuk, *Metodika opredeleniia stoimosti stroitel'stva i ekspluatatsii gorodov* (Kiev: Stroizdat, 1964), pp. 128-29, cited in Perevedentsev, "Construction of Urban Population," pp. 25-26. In the United States, there are indications that economies of scale do not apply to municipal services. Muller, op. cit.

70. Author's notes of discussion at TsNIIP gradostroitel'stva, June 1977.

71. Population size is related to demographic structure, and changes in population size are related to demographic changes. On the sex-age structure and migration, see Evelina Karlovna Vasil'eva, *The Young People of Leningrad, School and Work Options and Attitudes*, trans. Arlo Schultz and Andrew J. Smith (White Plains, N.Y.: International Arts and Sciences Press, 1976), p. 154. See also on this matter Zh. K. Arkhangelskaia, "Models of Population Reproduction for Long-Term Planning of Housing Construction," in *Town, Country and People*, ed. G. V. Osipov (London: Tavistock, 1969), pp. 100-6. On absolute population size related to the labor force and on changes in population size related to changes in the labor force, see I. Frumin and E. E. Kliushnichenko, *Tekhniko-ekonomicheskie raschety v general'nykh planakh gorodov*, vol. 1 (Kiev: Gosstroi USSR, 1973), pp. 48-51. For an analysis of costs related to density in the United States, see *Real Estate Research Corporation, The Costs of Sprawl: Detailed Cost Analysis* (Washington, D.C.: Government Printing Office, 1974).

72. Thomas J. Anton, *Governing Greater Stockholm: Study of Policy Development and System Change* (Berkeley: University of California Press, 1975).

73. Tonsky, op. cit.; and author's notes of discussion at TsNIIP gradostroitel'stva, June 1977.

74. F. E. Ian Hamilton, *The Moscow City Region*, Problem Regions of Europe (London: Oxford University Press, 1976), p. 20.

75. Prognoses on the growth of mass transit are to be found in Kiev NIIP gradostroitel'stva, *Sotsial'nye osnovy razvitiia gorodov (sotsial'nye problemy rasseleniia)* (Moscow: Stroizdat, 1975), p. 53; and Tsentr nauchno-tekhnicheskoi informatsii po grazhdanskomu stroitel'stvu i arkhitekture, *Gradostroitel'stvo SSSR* (Moscow: Gosgrazhdanstroi SSSR, 1976), pp. 30-34.

76. Perhaps because they are among the most profitable of city services, public dining facilities are being increased rapidly relative to other public services. *Management System of Moscow*, p. 135. See ibid., p. 192, on child care and preschool facilities. On the expansion of public services, see Gordon and Klopov, op. cit., p. 79.

77. Ibid., p. 191; and for use of life cycle as a major theme, see C. A. Doxiadis, *Anthropopolis: City for Human Development* (New York: W. W. Norton, 1975); and Gutnov et al., op. cit.

78. *Moskva v tsifrakh, 1960-1970 gg* (Moscow: Statistika, 1972), p. 140; and *Management System of Moscow*, pp. 14-16.

79. Ibid., sec. 3.

80. In 1967 a hospital bed in Vilnius cost one-third of what it cost in 1977, which is equivalent to two average apartments. Author's notes of discussions at the City Planning and Building Institute, Vilnius, June 1977.

81. See Vasilev and Stolbov, op. cit., for a brief discussion about the relatively high fixed operating costs of Soviet city government.

82. Main Scientific Research Computer Center of the Moscow City Soviet Executive Committee, *Experimental Development of Automated City Management Systems for the City of Leningrad*, Preliminary report on scientific research performed in accordance with the Government Agreement of 1972 for Scientific and Technological Cooperation between the USSR and USA, Topic no. 3, Project no. 2 (New York: Columbia University, Graduate School of Business, Center for Government Studies, November 1975), p. 2.

83. Miasnikov, op. cit., p. 8.

84. Under Eastern European conditions, state subsidies of the urban infrastructure constitute a regressive tax as resources are moved into the urban centers from the lesser towns, suburban areas, and rural regions. In Eastern Europe, as in the Soviet Union, the differential distribution of financial resources and urban services plays an important role in shaping regional and national development. Ivan Szelenyi, "Urban Sociology and Community Studies in Eastern Europe: Reflections and Comparisons with American Approaches," *Comparative Urban Research* 4 (1977): 11-22.

85. Ibid.; Kansky, op. cit., pp. 242-44; Enzo Mingione, "Sociological Approaches to Regional and Urban Development: Some Methodological and Theoretical Issues," *Comparative Urban Research* 4 (1977): 26.

86. Ibid., p. 26.

87. Calculated from data in Demchenkov and Uzhvenko, op. cit., pp. 18, 30; and from Darkov and Maksimov, op. cit., p. 48.

88. *Management Study of Moscow*, p. 111.

89. Jane Jacobs, *The Economy of Cities* (New York: Vintage, 1969), p. 122.

5

SOCIAL PLANNING AND
URBAN MANAGEMENT

METHODOLOGY

> Planning is the process of preparing a set of decisions for action in
> the future, directed at achieving goals by optimal means and learning
> from the outcomes about possible new sets of decisions and new
> goals to be achieved.[1]

The early years of the 1970s witnessed radical new developments in Soviet
approaches to city planning with the turn to social planning for the urban environment. The urban social plan—which Soviet sources describe as "the planned
management of social processes [and] a means of predicting the socioeconomic
consequences of the scientific-technical revolution"—is frequently cited as evidence that the USSR has reached the level of "developed socialism" on a local
as well as national scale.[2] Such inflated ideological claims aside, the "revolutionary" nature of the social planning concept in the Soviet context cannot be
lightly dismissed. The concept conceals several important shifts in traditional attitudes about city planning and urban management in the USSR, which merit
closer attention.

From a theoretical perspective, "social planning" in the Soviet lexicon
means a kind of planning that combines projections of physical, economic, demographic, sociological, and political (attitudinal and behavioral) change in an
urban setting in order to bring the various kinds of transformations into a harmonious relationship with one another and with the goals of urban policy. The
social plan is supposed to express these dimensions as a set of indicators, which
can then be included in a series of equations designed to bring all aspects of city
life into perfect balance. The "social" nature of the plan stresses planning for so-

cial as well as economic factors in an integrated fashion to produce program management. It is embodied both in the plan's concern with the sociological characteristics of the city as a social system and in its rejection of a purely physical approach to planning issues. The descriptive and projective indicators that an urban social plan in theory employs range widely across the many dimensions of urban life: changes in the "social structure" (occupational and skill profiles) of the urban labor force; alterations in the educational and demographic makeup of the population; specification of the optimal relationship between the "city-forming" and "city-servicing" (producing and consuming) sectors of the urban population; and the levels and distribution of service delivery in such areas as housing, health care, retail trade, cultural facilities, and urban transport. Urban social plans are also intended to include base-line data and projected transformations with respect to such factors as the social and political activism of the population, time budgets of the urban population, levels of social deviance and criminal behavior, labor turnover, and labor productivity. In short, the "social plan" is supposed to act as a dynamic, three-dimensional map of the Soviet city that will guide urban decision makers in their efforts to realize successfully policy goals and objectives.

At the most general level, the introduction of the social planning concept into Soviet discussions of urban problems (and urbanism) has carried in its wake a new recognition of the systemic nature of urban life.[3] The idea of the city as a holistic and complex unit, as a setting that can be engineered only in terms of the network of interrelationships (not sectors) that defines it, owes much to Western systems analysis concepts. But it also marks a return to a more fundamentally Marxist orientation toward urban problems, a perspective that disappeared from Soviet city planning discussions with the advent of Stalinism and the faith in physical planning it engendered. The social planning idea requires city planners to model the city in all its complexity. It demands that they identify social as well as economic goals and deal with economic *outcomes* as social *inputs* rather than view economic goals as targets to be achieved for their own sake. Social planning calls for the development of social indexes that can project as well as describe; it treats the sociological dimension of urbanism as a critical concomitant of the economic, cultural, and political objectives that urban decision makers strive to advance.[4] From the perspective of urban management, social planning provides the cornerstone of a new planning edifice based on a regional approach to city planning; at the same time, it rejects the sectoral orientation that, until very recently, dominated all Soviet discussions of city planning. Moreover, the "systems" thrust of the social plan aspires to link the social plans of individual enterprises and institutions (which have become an almost universal phenomenon since 1966) into a comprehensive scheme for social transformation, one that ideally embraces ministry, city, and factory.[5]

The introduction of the social planning concept has been accompanied by renewed attention to the tie between urban planning and urban management. From the assumption that all social processes are *upravlaemye* (subject to direction and mangement) it follows that urban management depends heavily on correct calculations regarding social dynamics.[6] In the process of policy implementation, social dynamics represent inputs as well as outcomes; plans for urban economic development must take these inputs and outputs into account.[7] This runs directly counter to earlier assumptions in Soviet city planning that social problems would "solve themselves" given the proper spatial arrangements and sound economic planning.[8]

The managerial dimension of social planning is also evident in its rejection of traditional assumptions that measure urban administration and urban development strictly in terms of the quantity of inputs involved.[9] Social planning shifts the emphasis away from plans that look to the administration of policy goals by sector toward those that stress the management of programs across constituencies. Coordination acquires a more prominent place in planning discussions.

A survey of the literature on Soviet social planning combined with interviews with those urban specialists for whom the development of operational social plans is a principal concern underlines Soviet social planning's managerial thrust. In short, social planning proceeds from a recognition of the *complexity* of urban problems to calculations in which *city size*, the structural *fragmentation of resources* and *center-periphery linkages* (centralization-decentralization) occupy a prominent place. The social plan, as described by these sources, aspires to combine and coordinate resource planning, policies planning, and program planning in a single matrix. This matrix, in turn, is to provide firm guidelines for implementation decisions. Improved information sources, including empirical sociological investigations, are to serve as a prerequisite to these ends. From an administrative perspective, the effect of the social plan, when implemented, would be to reorient practitioners away from their traditional agency-clientele concerns toward the multidimensional problems that bind them together.

From the perspective of the focal hypothesis of our study, social planning serves as the first and most important step in the introduction of *program management* into Soviet urban life. As such, it marks an important milestone in the transition from administration to management described in the Introduction. In addition, the Soviet social planning idea contains an implicit plea for increased urban autonomy as is evident in recent proposals for the creation of a national ministry of urban affairs within the central government structure. Evidently, Soviet social planning shares many of its concerns and proposed solutions with its U.S. and British counterparts.[10]

To demonstrate that expert opinion in the USSR has moved decisively toward a more managerial perspective on city planning is not enough. It remains to be seen whether such conceptual shifts have registered any practical effect or mobilized political support. Ideas without individuals or groups behind them usually die aborning. Thus, social planning might have remained an intellectual curiosity had not urgent problems provided the impetus necessary to move it off the pages of journals and monographs into the realm of practical development and limited implementation.

Among such problems, the chronic labor shortage that has threatened Soviet cities and urban industrial organizations since 1968 occupies first place.[11] The end of a pool of surplus labor resources (such as farm labor and unemployed females) from which new reserves could be drawn has created a powerful incentive for city planners to seek new ways to increase labor productivity, decrease work force turnover, and better distribute existing labor resources among industries. For cities as diverse as the Russian "new town" of Rubtsovsk founded in 1927, the old industrial-trading cities and province centers of Orel and Sverdlovsk, and Leningrad, one of the country's great cities, the growing tension between the needs of the urban economy and available labor resources has been cited as the chief stimulus to the move toward social planning.[12] Correspondingly, the first attempts at social planning in Nizhnii Tagil, a regional center in Sverdlovsk province, RSFSR, surfaced at a time when a decline in the already low rate of population increase collided with a rising rate of out-migration among the working age population.[13] Here as elsewhere, social planning efforts coincided with a mismatch between labor supply and labor demand that reached crisis proportions. These cases hardly represent isolated incidents; the summary theses of a 1975 conference devoted to urban planning termed the need to eliminate the "labor deficit" the "chief impetus to urban social planning" in the USSR.[14]

The second push for the introduction of social planning came from the accumulating evidence that traditional methods of economic planning were now inadequate to deal with the complex interaction of factors in an advanced urban economy. Already, investigations of excessive labor turnover, absenteeism, low productivity, and other problems made it clear that the poor quality of urban services in many cases translated into costs borne by enterprises and industrial ministries in the urban setting.[15] But social planning went even further, focusing attention on the fact that econometric models used in planning dealt with the issues of industrial siting, plant expansion, and renovation purely from an economic, sectoral perspective. In terms of long-range costs to urban systems, the question was increasingly raised by the late 1960s as to whether it was "rational" to promote further economic development where there already existed a developed infrastructure, skilled labor force, and sophisticated communications network. To continue along the traditional path invariably meant that all plans for limiting city growth notwithstanding, the expansion of the largest and most industrialized urban centers, such as Moscow and Leningrad, would probably continue unchecked.[16]

The shortcomings of traditional modes of physical planning for the Soviet city were equally glaring. City plans (*genplany*), even with their limited aims of controlling and organizing capital construction within the city's boundaries, never came to grips with the basic contradiction between vertically organized national economic planning and the *horizontal* thrust that planning for a city entails.[17] Existing reforms had provided no answer. From 1971 onward, all enterprises located in a city have been required by law to clear their economic plans, including construction projects and work force increments, with the city soviet. In practice, however, clearance has meant little more than ex post facto notification of local authorities of an already accomplished fact. As of 1975, ministries not only reported their capital construction projects after the fact but then did so only to government authorities at the *republic* level.[18] At present, even on paper, the lines of authority between those units engaged in spatial planning (local construction departments and the office of the chief architect) and those responsible for economic planning at the city level (planning commissions) remain extremely fuzzy.[19]

Against such a background, urban social planning has exercised great attraction for two very specific reasons. In the first place, it promises to institutionalize jurisdictional coordination in city planning. Until its introduction, the Soviet city remained the target of a bewildering variety of unrelated plans that governed its numerous and varied functions: the construction targets of the *genplan*, the economic goals of regional and municipal economic plans, the industrial production and labor targets of enterprise plans, and the objectives described in the work plans of administrative agencies and urban service units.[20]

The second reason is that social planning at the city level promises a solution to the difficulties that early efforts at enterprise social planning had encountered by 1973-74. By this time, it had become clear that the idea of a social plan for an entire branch of the economy had failed to gain a foothold. At fault was the indifference or opposition of the branch ministries.[21] "Branch social plans" amounted to little more than limited information sharing among enterprises under a single jurisdiction. In addition, the composite nature of industrial production and the diverse range of products lumped together in the Soviet version of branch economic organization probably make the idea of ministerial social planning more than a little utopian.[22] Early results at the enterprise level have revealed that housing, transport, consumer services, leisure-time facilities, vocational education programs, and other concerns tackled by social plans are hardly amenable to solution within factory walls. These concerns demand a municipal rather than an enterprise response.[23]

The precise stages involved in the introduction of urban social planning remain obscure. In part, this may stem from a desire among many Soviet urbanists to make the phenomenon appear more widespread and successful than our analysis suggests it in fact is. It may stem as well from the political debate that swirls around many of the issues linked to urban social planning, such as factory-city relationships and the representation of cities qua cities within the national bureaucracy. Several sources suggest that plans were "in place" for cities in geographical areas as far flung as the Bashkir Autonomous Republic (Almatevsk, Sterlitanak), the Tatar Autonomous Republic, the Urals (Sverdlovsk, Nizhnii Tagil), Kirgiziia (Dzhalal-Abada), and the Ukraine (Donetsk, Zhdanov) by 1970.[24] This hardly squares with the second thread in the argument, that is, that social plans arose precisely in those urban centers in which social planning at the enterprise level was already most advanced. In that case, Leningrad, Krasnodar, Lvov, Perm, and Sverdlovsk should have led the list.[25] Still other sources date the introduction of social planning from 1971 all-union legislation. These regulations enlarged the formal authority of city soviets, with particular reference to a new grant of jurisdiction to "control and coordinate" the quinquennial plans for *all* institutions and factories located within the city's boundaries.[26]

Actual evidence regarding the development of the first plans remains sparse. In Leningrad in 1969, the province party organization (*obkom*) instructed the Research Institute for Concrete Sociological Investigations (NIIKSI), a research unit attached to Leningrad State University, to begin work on social plans for the city's urban districts.[27] A sample plan had already been drawn up by a district party committee. In response to General Secretary Brezhnev's call for such plans at the Twenty-Fifth Party Congress in 1971, the State Planning Commission (*Gosplan*) issued in 1972 a series of instructions detailing methods for the drafting of "complex plans for the socioeconomic development of Leningrad city and Leningrad province."[28] In the same year, NIIKSI began work on a social plan for Orel, a city in which rapid population growth threatened to outstrip available housing and urban services.[29]

Whether any one of these early efforts really merits the label "social plan" must remain open to question. According to a later estimate by NIIKSI, they stumbled in one or two ways. Some merely generalized the indicators already utilized in enterprise social planning for the city as a whole, ignoring the peculiarities of the urban system involved. Plans for the Leningrad districts Angarsk, Dzhalal-Abada, and Orel belong to this category.[30] Other plans limited themselves to projective descriptions of already-existing trends; the interdependence of various factors, the impact of sociocultural changes on economic prospects, and the search for a fit between the city plan and sectoral plans were ignored.

In any event, a review of the profiles of the cities mentioned reveals no correlation between the peculiar preconditions hypothesized as a catalyst for the urban management syndrome—large size, great complexity, high fragmentation, and relative autonomy—and the kinds of circumstances under which the early urban social plans emerged. Notably, only the social plan for the city of Leningrad, completed in 1976, actually tried to model causally a comprehensive urban future. To do this, it stressed the interdependence of goals and targets, the mutability of indicators, and the variability of the resource base. For Leningrad, this also meant a plan that demanded increased inputs and resources from the national authorities.[31] Instead, one finds many similarities between the diverse political as well as socioeconomic considerations that determine the siting of federal pilot projects (Model Cities) in the United States and the kinds of factors that apparently affect the staging of social planning in the USSR. Urban management calculations per se are rarely in evidence in either case.

Activities in Leningrad took their cues from a December 1971 charge by Brezhnev to city and province units concerning the preparation of a social plan for the 1976-80 quinquennium. In March 1972, the *obkom* issued the appropriate directives. For a number of reasons, Leningrad represented an attractive proving ground: labor shortages compounded by a low birthrate; a lack of industrial diversification as compared to Moscow, Perm, or Sverdlovsk; and factories faced with productivity problems owing to outmoded capital equipment (especially in the chief industry, machine building).[32] May 1972 brought a *Gosplan* resolution obligating all national agencies and ministries to direct enterprises within their hierarchical jurisdiction to develop operative social plans for the workplace by 1976. These were described as the foundation stones for a city-wide plan on which work commenced during 1972-73.[33]

But in Leningrad, as elsewhere, the first drafts of the social plan apparently represented little more than a summation of the social indexes that, by 1973, already had been worked out by many of the city's factories.[34] Nevertheless, the development of such preliminary documents was important, if only to provide the information required for a truly operational municipal plan. According to 1972 *Gosplan* instructions, the provincial government authorities (*obispolkom*) were empowered to set forth a range of problems to be included in enterprise social plans. They were also to coordinate all work in the "preplan period," 1972-75. Accordingly, ministries were no longer to confirm the social plans of their enterprises before communicating them to provincial and city governments. Instead, the Leningrad authorities and the ministries were to cooperate in the development of enterprise social plans. In the final analysis, however, *Gosplan* as a national planning body retained ultimate "sign-off" rights; individual social plans had to correspond with the "complex plan for the socioeconomic development of the USSR" as a whole.[35] After some three years' work on what have been described as "interbranch and social problems," the de facto agenda for urban social planning prepared by the Leningrad authorities, a second draft was ready for Leningrad—and for such cities as Sverdlovsk, Orel, Tallin, and Minsk by 1976.

A closer look at the techniques, organizations, models, and content of social plans reveals both their strengths and weaknesses from an urban management perspective. Analysis of a number of discussions of planning methodologies suggests that plans are drawn up using a system of balances within the framework of an equilibrium model of the particular urban system involved.[36] Despite the traditional philosophical antagonism between equilibrium concepts associated with bourgeois sociology and economics and a dialectical materialist conception of social reality, this conflict has in no way diminished the enthusiasm of Soviet social planning advocates for the idea of a balance. From a macoperspective the determining balance operates between two variables: the "city-forming" population (*gradoobrazuiushchee naselenie*), meaning "employees of all basic industries, transportation and construction enterprises, scientific and medical institutions, and higher level administrative units," and the unit capacities of urban service outputs (*gradoobsluzhivaiushchee naselenie*), as measured by the number of service personnel charged with meeting the needs of the population. The final objective of every social plan is to match up present and projected demands for urban outputs, from education and consumer services to transportation, housing, and leisure-time facilities, with the resource base provided by the city's production potential. Uncovering disproportions in allocations and input deficiencies, especially with respect to labor supply, is regarded as the first step in eliminating them.[37]

Such a macrolevel balance, in turn, requires a whole series of microlevel solutions to equations within a matrix model of the urban system. The matrix itself combines descriptive as well as prescriptive elements and is structured along input-output lines. A descriptive section, composed of columns on the left-hand side of the matrix, reflects the state of affairs at the outset of the planning period. As one's glance moves to the right across the matrix, columns on the far side describe the plan's "goals," that is, how matters ought to stand at the termination of the plan period. The intervening columns represent the cumulative inputs needed to move the city from point A to point B over a designated period of time, usually five years. The matrix also designates a series of policies (*meropriiatiia*) to be utilized to translate the descriptive segments of the model into the prescriptive ones.[38]

Ideally, such a matrix model represents the entire complex of goals those charged with urban decision making and administrative implementation will pursue over a given time period. It promises to bring these into line with the sum total of resources, including both those already available and those that the operation of the plan itself presumably generates. "Balancing" in this context requires that the situation be modeled mathematically, equations solved, and indexes calculated from the standpoint of systemically interdependent rather than linearly additive relationships. Multiple regression techniques rather than simple correlations are presumably employed to trace the impact of various factor inputs on individual outcomes, given that every "relationship" involves two or more independent variables. The subbalances of the plan define a series of urban subsystems, performing input functions for each other as well as for the urban complex as a whole.[39] It is precisely this thrust toward comprehensive modeling, together with the twin drive to overcome resource and decision fragmentation and to compensate for the absence of structural autonomy in urban decision making, that lends the social planning phenomenon its managerial dimension.

Prior to the calculation of a final balance, each plan must measure and adjust for the flow of influence between and among various factors. As in Soviet economic planning, this requires a whole series of trial balances with appropriate policy measures designated. The trial balances then serve as the second round of inputs into additional calculations based on adjustments and trade-offs. This interactive process continues until a final and politically acceptable prognosis for a city's development is achieved. The final plan variant in effect describes empirically a complementary set of goals for urban development across all sectors. These, in turn, are assumed to be realizable, given the proper attention to the complex of intermediate tasks that the plan delineates.[40] But whether the plan balances are meant to be truly directive, as one body of literature and some interviews suggest, or whether (in the words of another study) they signify merely a "probable prognosis of possible outcomes" remains a question on which Soviet specialists themselves express varying opinions.[41]

The rows and columns of the planning matrix perform a wide variety of functions for setting goals and devising implementation guidelines. As already noted, the first column defines the input levels for various factors at the outset of the plan period, for example, the number of workers already in the work force. The next set of columns describes all projected increments to the baseline figures from various sources during the course of the plan; additions to the labor force through in-migration, graduates from educational institutions, new recruits, and demographic increases. A third set designates decreases attributable to various causes: mortality rates, out-migration, labor turnover, and absenteeism. The fourth group expresses the total quantity of resources remaining at the end of the plan period with all negative inputs subtracted. This summary column is then to be compared and balanced against a fifth column, which describes the total demand for a given resource, that is, jobs and job slots in the urban economy. A final column expresses anticipated shortfalls.[42]

The rows of the matrix summarize all resource inputs, outputs, and balances in terms of a diverse, stratified urban population. Reflecting as they do the social, professional, and demographic distinctions existing within the urban population, the rows serve to underline the importance of diversity and complexity in the design of policies and programs. The crosshatching produced by row-column combinations thus represents both a concrete *outcome* and an *input* into many other variables. Matrixes of this kind must be constructed for every single problem that the social plan tackles, ranging from issues such as labor force size, housing, and transport to consumer services and levels of social and political activism. Matrixes must ultimately be "balanced" among themselves to produce a final, comprehensive plan, no mean task given the sheer number of variables involved.

A typical framework for the matrix balances contains the following divisions and subdivisions:[43]

1. Population and Labor Resources. Eight subdivisions including demographic profiles, changes projected through natural growth and immigration, changes in the social structure of the population, changes in ethnic composition, changes in the age profile and sex composition of the population, and labor force turnover.

2. The Municipal Economy. Contains descriptions and projections for growth in industry and other branches of the economy, for capital construction and supply.

3. Standard of Living. Includes data on income and expenditures, services and satisfaction of consumer needs, health care facilities, sports facilities, recreational facilities, and environmental protection standards.

4. Education. Numbers of pupils by level (preschool, primary, secondary, higher) and type (general, specialized secondary, professional-technical).

5. Political Activism and Cultural Development. Targets include numerical increases in the proportion of the population involved in political education, utilization of cultural facilities, increased spatial dispersion of cultural facilities, and reductions in instances of antisocial behavior.

6. Improvements in the Work of Local Administration. No subdivisions specified.[44]

As the number of targets increases, the number of balances required rises, and the problems involved in intersector balancing become quite complex. The quality of information utilized, the suitability of correlational and multiple regression statistical techniques for modeling interdependence causally, and the extent to which the indexes generated accurately reflect real social phenomena—each of these problems poses a real limit to the social plans' ability to provide adequate management guidelines.

Further investigation reveals why, despite the social plans' managerial thrust, they remain captives of fragmented administrative environment. Each social plan includes not one but three gross balances, which, in turn, testify to the continued influence of other planning hierarchies. *Interbranch balances* are calculated to describe the relationship of the plan to the sectoral structure of the urban economy. An *economic balance* describes the overall relationship between labor force demand and the population's demographic structure. Finally, a *socioeconomic balance* depicts the fit between the demand for urban services (calculated on the basis of the social structure of the population) and the units of service available to different strata.[45] In the last case, the difficulties involved in developing anything resembling an overall balance for consumption has led planners to employ the method of "balance by parts." Such a method accepts separate and not necessarily interrelated balances for each kind of consumption.

Ultimately, as social plan proponents stress, the key to a truly integrated plan lies in the formulation of "universal social indicators" (*skvoznye pokazateli*). These would provide common denominators of measurement for all areas embraced by the social plan.[46] At present, the development of such indicators remains an unfulfilled aspiration, although Soviet sociologists avidly follow U.S. efforts to develop "quality of life" indicators for such reasons.[47] To date, however, Soviet social planners have yet to come to grips with the fact that while good social indicators can reveal *how* a program or measure fails, they will not show *why* it has done so.[48]

Despite the practical difficulties that hobble the social planners, Soviet social planning promises improved urban management from several perspectives.

The use of balance techniques within the framework of an input-output feedback system promises to move Soviet city planning away from the linear and sectoral approach to problem solving. Under the traditional system, the planning of physical and economic development proceeded in isolation from one another, while social factors were ignored or treated as residuals. Equally important, social planning requires that both demand and supply be regarded as mutable in the construction of equations. In addition, these terms take on more than simple quantitative significance.[49] For example, "supply" (with respect to the size of labor force reserves) is intended to do more than designate the number of workers with a certain level of skills. It is also meant to reflect workers' aspirations and orientations, emphasizing what some Soviet planners term "social occupations" defined in terms of individual strivings.[50] The labor deficits that cities experience thus become both a subjective as well as an objective problem. Likewise, "demand" now signifies both the needs of the economy and the level of aspirations of the population. Such a reconceptualization coupled with the greater use of survey data in social planning suggests that at least the germ of the idea of client analysis has taken root among social planning techniques. In practice, however, social plans still rely heavily on standardized norms.[51]

To complete the discussion of the methodology of social planning and its managerial potential for administrative decision making, it is important to look at "who signs off" at various stages of the process. As the Leningrad case described earlier suggests, party units play a prominent part. A "council for socioeconomic development" (attached to the *obkom* or to municipal party committees) normally bears the major responsibility for setting the main directions of the plan. As in the case of Leningrad ("Fundamental Directions for the Socioeconomic Development of Leningrad"), this draft is then reviewed and possibly amended by other party and governmental units.[52] Technical details—the development of an information base, indexes, balances, and the structuring of the matrix—are left in the hands of academic sociological centers or ad hoc bodies of specialists.[53]

Despite a number of statutory provisions that enlarged their powers between 1968 and 1974, the units designated as planning commissions within Soviet city government do not appear to be actively involved in social planning. In some respects, solving the problems caused by fragmentation and deconcentration has simply meant substituting one variant of the difficulty for another. Even the 1974 "model charters" for the planning commissions—which provide them with the "right of review" for all city policies—limit their *coordinating* authority to "the development of summary indices for a comprehensive economic plan" for the city. Social plans remain the provenance of the councils attached to the party.[54] Indeed, the fact that city planning commissions are structured according to branch-oriented subunits, each of which coordinates with a superordinate agency within the *Gosplan* hierarchy, means that the commissions' work runs directly counter to that programmatic thrust that social plans presumably encourage. And, as presently constituted, the commissions remain so under-staffed that they are unable in some cases to fulfill even their traditional eco-nomic responsibilities, such as the projection of a demand-supply balance for fuel resources in the case of provincial planning commissions in the RSFSR.[55]

The organizational procedures applied in developing social plans follow a fairly general format. A case study of the process as it unfolded in the Lenin district of the city of Saratov provides an example both typical in its dynamics and significant because of the nature of the assumptions it displays. The plan arose on the foundation provided by social plans in the city's enterprises, all of which had such plans in operation by 1976.[56] Technical details were worked out by a "laboratory for concrete sociological research" operating out of the district "council for socioeconomic development." The latter was an arm of the district party committee. The council consisted of 27 individuals, including the party first secretary, the chairman and deputy chairman from the district executive committee, various department heads, plus representatives from the party's youth branch (*Komsomol*), the trade union organs, and the ranks of local indus-trial executives. After studying the experience of other cities, the council pub-lished a *metodika* (methodological guidelines). This, in turn, provided a frame-work within which the laboratory developed informational "models" to be used to generate a data base for the actual plan. In this fashion, the party's subordi-nate units decisively shaped the techniques applied, the kind of information sought, and thus the plan itself.[57]

In addition to the *metodika*, the council bore the chief responsibility for a statement of plan goals labeled the "Basic Directions for the Socioeconomic De-velopment of Lenin District." After being discussed and confirmed by party bodies within the district and city, this statement then guided further research and determined the actual kinds of balances and forecasts the plan contained. At the third stage of the process, all data generated according to the informa-tional models were collected, codified, and worked into a series of matrixes and balances in the manner described earlier. Once a final variant of the matrix was hammered out, it went once more before the district party committee, the city government, and the city party committee for ratification.[58] In numerical terms as well as strategic placement, it thus appears that party rather than government units dominate the entire spectrum of the sign-off process.

The formulation of a second social plan in the district for 1976-80 added several additional stages and procedures. Planners are now required to evaluate the results of the preceding plan (methods unspecified); to produce a "social geography" of the district together with "cultural passports" (profiles of educa-tional levels, utilization of cultural facilities) of district enterprises; and to work toward closer coordination of district-level and enterprise-level social plans.[59] If, indeed, these represented "new" departures, then they tell us much about the shortcomings of the first plan: the absence of an adequate information base with accurate sociological data, no provisions for evaluation, and a lack of cooperation between the planners in enterprises and those responsible for the city as a whole. Apparently even the formulation of a wide range of informational models —the district employed 14—had failed to overcome those problems of fragmentation, poor measurement techniques, and conceptual shortcomings that hindered the production of an information base adequate to the ambitious goals of social planning. Indeed, the construction of better models took first priority during the second phase of social planning in the Lenin district.[60]

Evidence from other plans can also be cited to suggest some tenuous movement in the direction of two critical tools of public management: management by objectives (MBO) and planning-programming-budgeting systems (PPBS). A review of social planning efforts in Leningrad emphasizes its MBO orientation.[61] Discussions of "how to plan" recommend that goal-oriented and program-focused blocs of indicators be developed to supplement more traditional methods that detail supply and demand simply by the type of input factor involved. Social planning in Sverdlovsk attaches great importance to the development of "cultural passports" for the city and for the province as a whole.[62] Such profiles deliberately ignore the lines of vertical subordination for the agencies involved. They therefore indicate that the provision of integrated programs and services is to take precedence over ministerial accountability in order to highlight distributional achievements and shortcomings. Elsewhere, discussions of the methodology of social planning suggest that program scheduling methods (what Soviet planners term "network graphs") are to be employed in the calculation of social plan targets.[63]

A review of both methodological discussions and descriptions of actual plans also suggests that neither cost-benefit analysis nor program-evaluation-review-techniques (PERT)—both critical ingredients of a PPBS approach to planning—have yet made an appearance in the Soviet city.[64] This indicates, in turn, that the important conceptual shifts needed to make social planning truly operative have yet to occur. Such shifts pertain directly to the problems that arise in shifting resources from one activity to another, in dealing with the "lumpiness" of scheduling activities, and in discounting costs over time. Without cost-benefit analyses, PERT, and critical path analyses, it is impossible to devise optimal ways either to undertake or to "crash" projects and programs. Insofar as neither these issues nor the techniques required have been recognized, much less fully utilized, in Soviet social planning, Soviet balance methods remain weak in the area of choice. In this way, they are also quite different from the processes of optimization modeling increasingly in vogue in Western planning.

Similarly, provisions for choice are neglected in the social plan for the Lenin district. The history of the planning process makes no mention of cost-benefit analysis.[65] Targets are related to implementation only via general statements of goals within the plan itself; *programmatic* thinking and planning remain altogether absent. And while costs, revenue sources, and timetables are attached to the plan, neither this plan nor the *metodiki* developed for other cities provide guidelines to planners as to how to choose among competing goals.[66] For example, it is probable that efforts to raise the skill level of the work force via increased education and training, one of the goals of social plans, will at some point come into conflict with a second objective, that is, increasing the level of political activism among the same population. Similarly, eliminating heavy physical labor, especially for women, may clash with the goal of increasing production or with efforts to improve the manpower pool. In general, planning methods provide no way to handle such a clash of direction and objective, thereby undermining the plan's managerial thrust.

Examination of another plan for an urban district in Minsk reveals that the overall programmatic thrust of the plans remains underdeveloped. "Goal trees" are employed only in the organization of the planning process and do not figure as a device to assist in interrelating and rank ordering the various aspects of the completed plan.[67] Here, too, program scheduling and policy staging along the lines of a PERT network, while familiar enough in U.S. practice, are missing. The same applies to "decision trees" and "relevance trees," both devices that the policy planner utilizes in the United States.[68] Such omissions, in turn, probably leave the Soviet plan victim to the "triple cut," which is required at the final stage of the social planning process at all levels. Planning procedures here dictate that the total set of indexes contained in the social pan be reworked one final time to correspond to branch economic plans, to territorial plans, and to plans for the development of the regional economy. In light of this final "review," it is difficult to imagine how, in the event of conflicts, urban needs can receive due consideration.[69]

ASSESSMENT

The kind of planning just described differs from the newer approaches to social planning advocated in the United States. To be sure, city planning in the United States traditionally has appeared quite similar to contemporary Soviet practice, thus lending some credence to the familiar theories of "lag" in the development of similar processes and functions within all industrial societies. Today, however, Western thinking regarding social planning generally attaches far greater importance to the *decision* dimensions of planning—or what, in the planning literature, is termed "intelligent choice" and "systematic evaluation of consequences." Assessing alternative pay-offs plays a more prominent role than in the Soviet version. Likewise, Western faith in social planning generally is qualified by a suspicion that too much reliance on social indicators can serve as a mask for technocratic elitism.[70] Conversely, guarantees for and enhancement of citizen participation, coupled with moves to preserve a sphere of individual choice, form critical components of the Western but not the Soviet variant.[71] To be sure, Soviet social plans possess a "political activism" component. But this refers only to such activities as attendance at political lectures and political schools, membership in the party, and participation in mass campaign work of one sort or another. It does *not* measure consequences, and it does *not* refer in any way to involvement in the social planning process itself. A comprehensive summary of the similarities and differences is presented in Table 14.

For the outside observer, it remains extraordinarily difficult to gauge the extent to which the social planning phenomenon has passed from the stage of discussion to that of implementation. Too frequently, Western scholars studying aspects of communist systems, particularly local government and politics, tend to generalize from isolated or regionally particular examples of success and failure to the system as a whole. As elsewhere in this study, our approach to Soviet social planning emphasizes combining individual-level and aggregate-level data in order to draw microlevel as well as macrolevel conclusions.

For a study of social planning, such aims have dictated an analysis focusing on projects and operative plans, discussions of methodological issues, the opinions of social planning experts, surveys of *metodiki*, and investigations of varying points of view expressed at conferences. But widely conflicting reports regarding the number of operative plans coupled with a "bandwagon effect" (the relabeling of traditional plans in order to score political points nationally) complicate the task still further. Interviews with local officials and planners in 1976 and 1977 suggest that some sort of social plan is currently operative in Tallin, Vilnius, and roughly 33 other cities in the USSR. These same interviews also revealed little attention to or knowledge of social planning in such large urban centers as Kiev in the Ukraine. Conceptions among construction planners and architects as to what constitutes such a plan vary widely. In some cases, a "social plan" simply means norms for the number of housing units, the amount of green space, the number of cultural facilities, pollution control standards, and the like —in short, the social dimensions of traditional spatial plans.[72] Which (if any) plans actually utilize the techniques and format of the social planning methodologies described above is even more difficult to assess. The plans themselves still remain "eyes only" documents of a classified nature. For such reasons, Soviet evaluations of the scope of social planning provide us with our major source of information to date.

Soviet urbanists provide mixed reports on the impact of the social plan phenomenon. One 1974 account observed that "we are still far from having a social plan for every city." Another noted more specifically that "during the Ninth Five-Year Plan [1971-75], social plans were implemented only in several small towns in the Tatar ASSR and in the Ukraine, remaining at the development stage for both the city of Leningrad and Leningrad province." For Moscow, work even on the preparatory stage of a social plan was described in 1975 as being "scarcely underway."[73] Another 1975 report describes the number of Soviet cities with social plans as "a mere handful."[74]

These evaluations also reveal that many plans remained mere compendia of forecasts, failing to designate any specific measures or agencies for implementa-

TABLE 14

Contemporary Directions in Urban Social Planning

	USSR	United States
Catalysts	1. Labor shortages and declining productivity 2. Limited results with enterprise social plans 3. Failure of sectoral planning to meet urban needs (housing, consumer services, transport)	1. Racial violence, intractable urban poverty 2. Federal planning requirements 3. Shortcomings of physical planning (for example, spot zoning)
Traditional methods	1. Planning for economic branches and spatial development of city 2. Uncoordinated, multilayer planning (region, urban territory, enterprise, city agencies, urban economy); horizontal fragmentation	1. Planning for physical development 2. Planning by agency-client linkages
New planning perspectives	1. Comprehensive and holistic (systems analysis) 2. Directive and preventative	1. Applied empirical sociological investigation; problem-oriented 2. Indicative and curative
Focus and objectives	1. System equilibrium 2. Problem solving, goal attainment	1. Outcomes within context of preserving political pluralism 2. Problem solving

126

	3. Equity (defined as standardization and homogeneity)	3. Selection among alternative strategies (optimization models) and provision for citizen choice
	4. Social harmony (integration)	4. Access equity
		5. Social harmony defined as absence of conflict
Methods	1. Matrix balancing	1. Cost-benefit analysis
	2. Social indicators	2. Linear and systems solutions
	3. Elite planning	3. Objective and subjective inputs and outputs
	4. Standardized norms	4. User-satisfaction planning
	5. Policy measures	5. Needs assessment
		6. Program effectiveness measures
		7. Tentative attempts to shadow price
Obstacles	1. Vertical fragmentation	1. Horizontal fragmentation
	2. Inadequate information	2. Inadequate control over industrial siting
	3. No evaluation tools	3. Privatization of decision making
	4. Conflicting jurisdictions	4. Absence of powerful program constituencies
	5. Inadequate resource base	5. Inadequate resource base
	6. Conflicting development goals (economic growth versus user satisfaction)	6. Conflicting development goals (fiscal balance versus user satisfaction)

Source: Compiled by the authors.

tion.[75] Invariably such reports cast doubt on a 1976 claim that social planning already represented "a nearly universal phenomenon" for Soviet cities and urban districts.[76] One study revealed that two of the "social plans" included in the 1976 assessment (for Valdivostok and Sverdlovsk), in fact, represented the old type of plans for urban economic development with a new label affixed. They became "social"plans simply by virtue of efforts to coordinate projections for service delivery with estimates of shifts in the demographic structure of the city. Both feedback calculations and concern for the transformation of the social structure remained completely absent.[77] In the case of another social plan, this time in Ussursk, the "indexes" represented arbitrarily projected targets for city agencies and administrators. As such, they failed to reflect an empirically derived balance between the possible and the desirable.

In the case of social plans for urban districts, Leningrad and Moscow included, the concern of the social plans focuses chiefly on ways to generate new labor resources. No calculations of social needs, occupational aspirations, or factors not directly affecting productivity have entered into the planning picture.[78] Indeed, analysis of such plans by a NIIKSI team of researchers revealed that only about one-third of those for Leningrad's districts displays sufficient similarity to justify a common label. Some 70 percent of all indexes of the traditional sort (production output, labor force, materials) were identical among the various social plans. But once we look at indexes relating to social problems and administrative inputs, the level of identity falls to 20 percent. The overall structure of these plans remains heavily influenced by social plans drawn up for factories located within the district. Thus, the plans fail to take into account the wide range of problems unique to the districts themselves.[79]

The single most comprehensive gauge to measure the impact of social planning to date remains the proceedings of a 1975 national conference along with an updated overview appearing in the daily press in 1977. At the 1975 conference, participants agreed that all existing social plans fell under two headings. Some simply summed the social indicators developed by enterprises within the territorial unit. Others took as their point of reference that traditional kind of branch plan that, in the past, has always shaped the city's economic, cultural— and, ultimately, social—development. "Social change" appeared only as a dependent variable. Conference reports further observed that even with respect to developing comprehensive balances between labor force requirements and labor resources, social plans still displayed grave deficiencies.[80] The October 1977 update provides further evidence for our contention that most Soviet cities still have attained only rudimentary types of social plans. Only Moscow, Leningrad, and Sverdlovsk qualified as having "complex plans for socioeconomic development" (the current title) as of the article's dateline. This suggests that many of the 35 cities described by other sources as having "social plans" have yet to integrate social *and* economic planning to the extent that the concept actually demands.[81]

In the last few years, a new institute within the prestigious and powerful Soviet Academy of Sciences, the Institute for Socioeconomic Problems in Leningrad, has been charged by *Gosplan* with developing a *metodika* for "large cities" (over 500,000 population) to use in social planning. But its efforts have stalled with attempts to find ways to circumvent or supplement the nonmanagerial kind of serial balancing upon which social planning equations still rely heavily. According to recent interviews, serious problems are posed by the failure to develop methods for accurate quantification and standards for comparison, to say nothing of obtaining reliable information from a wide variety of jurisdictions.[82] The unimpeded and accurate information flows that urban management requires largely remain aspiration rather than fact. Likewise, needs assessment, whether for or by the citizenry, has scarcely begun to replace those traditional planning habits associated with centrally controlled norm-setting ("normativization"). Standard unit measurement techniques of urban administration still prevail over the methods of distribution analysis that urban management demands. On-site inspection of housing projects and discussions with construction engineers revealed that the idea of "one day care center per 1000 inhabitants," a holdover from microdistrict planning, still remains quite strong.[83] Questions pertaining to user satisfaction and alternative preferences seldom seem to arise. Finally, social plan implementation remains firmly subordinate to sectoral decisions at all levels. Ministers continue to ignore even the traditional schemes for horizontal integration (the *genplan*) when siting or expanding their subordinate firms.[84]

The persistent inability of the format and techniques of social planning to win wider acceptance in the Soviet urban environment indicates that much remains to be done to transform city administration into city management. But such an observation ought in no way to obscure the tremendous strides that some seven years of discussion of social planning and limited (experimental?) implementation have made toward injecting a more managerial flavor into urban administrative operations. All the same, it is important to remember that the shortcomings in social planning that we have stressed are *not* merely a function of its brief life, as many Soviet accounts suggest. They stem, rather, from constraints that show few if any signs of disappearing. For purposes of analysis, it is useful to break these down into two categories, the exogenous and the endogenous.

Exogenous constraints range from the simple operational problem of prying information out of institutions over which the city government has little authority (the most important industrial enterprises) to more complex ones, such as the highly centralized manner in which resources are still allocated in the USSR.[85] The social planning literature abounds with recommendations by specialists that more resources be placed under the control of local authorities. The schemes suggest that this be done either through enterprise payments for the use of the city's labor force (a capitation tax) or through reimbursement by factories and institutions for utilization of urban land and services (in effect, a user fee).[86]

A 1977 conference on social planning went so far as to recommend the creation of a national ministry for urban affairs, comparable to HUD but probably stronger. The objective here was to counterbalance the sectoral fragmentation and horizontal insulation engendered by existing administrative arrangements.[87] Such a reform might possibly give Soviet cities an independent channel to the resources of the national budget that they now lack. Equally important, such a measure would increase the cities' overall political clout qua cities. This would represent an important change from the perspective of the national game of bureaucratic politics, which, as elsewhere, shapes macrolevel resource allocation. Such a proposal rests on a new conventional wisdom among Soviet urbanists: from the perspective of national economic development, local units (for example, cities) are now said to represent important and quasi-independent social, economic, and cultural complexes that must be nurtured and supported in their own right. Institutional recognition is deemed highly significant. Conversely, so long as cities rely largely on personal lobbies and individual clout (as in the case of Leningrad and the provincial first secretary, G. V. Romanov, who sits on the party's Central Committee), a systematic policy of urban development that allocates resources among cities by *need* rather than by *political power* will hardly emerge. Instead, the old "permanent factors" in Soviet urban development—decision rules, the organizational ranking of cities, the size of the city's economic base, and personal influence—will continue to operate. Under such conditions, the most well-endowed cities would remain the most favored, irrespective of objective need or requirements.

Exogenous constraints on successful social planning also stem from the strong sense of departmentalism that infuses city administration in the USSR and that impedes managerial transformation. As in other settings, such problems arise largely out of administrative structure and its vertical fragmentation. But in the USSR, in contrast to other unitary, centralized systems such as France and Britain, vertical cleavages are reinforced rather than neutralized by the ways in which local and national politics are linked.[88] Dependency relationships in the Soviet setting tie a city agency to a ministerial superior, not to the national government or party leadership per se. In any event, city agencies here as elsewhere manifest a strong "organizational interest," a natural proclivity to promote the importance and growth of their particularistic functions—construction, maintenance of roads, operation of schools, operation of theaters and cinemas, maintenance of parks and public places. "Good planning" thus comes to be viewed primarily in terms of an agency's ability to consume larger quantities of inputs.[89] Under such circumstances, performance reduces to "how much is produced." Meanwhile, the issues of "who is served" and that of the overall effect on the community fall by the wayside.

Horizontal fragmentation in the urban environment also impedes social planning efforts. It has been frequently noted in comparisons involving continental and British forms of urban government that national authorities in these cases exercise much stronger and more comprehensive regulatory powers over cities than is true in the United States.[90] But there exists an additional dimension to this picture as well, one that, in the Soviet setting, takes shape as a conflict among the various levels of priorities that administrative agencies are called upon to observe. Soviet cities are not closed systems, and city leaders lack control over many of the variables that affect social outcomes. Frequently, it is difficult to reconcile the demand for industrial production and economic growth that dictates the operations of the enterprises located within city boundaries with the call by social planners for integrated and harmonious urban development.[91]

The tension in U.S. cities between public amenity and private gain, or between real estate interests and those of urban dwellers threatened by urban renewal schemes, finds a Soviet parallel in the ongoing battle between the interests of industrial production and those of social plans stressing the delivery of public goods, limited physical growth, and social equity. Further, those decisions in the USSR that most critically affect urban labor resources (for example, job assignments for graduates of institutions of higher learning) are developed with national or regional priorities most prominently in view. Urban needs occupy a backseat. As a result, Soviet city administrators find themselves horizontally isolated or insulated with respect to many important decisions. Consequently, social plans continually fall victim to branch-oriented indicators and priorities, and, thus, the possibilities for a managerial approach to questions of implementation are again diminished.[92] The situation in the USSR today remains one of "layer-cake planning" vis-a-vis the urban environment, and, in all fairness, an integrated, holistic approach to urban problems still appears quite problematic.

Endogenous problems internal to the planning process play an equally important role in limiting the impact of Soviet social planning. Many factors continue to elude social planners' analysis and control, no matter what method of measurement is employed. Social surveys conducted in the city of Perm between 1969 and 1974 revealed considerable disagreement among urban respondents as to what constituted the ideal kind of urban settlement.[93] Such disagreements, in turn, render it difficult to develop plan targets that "satisfice" in Simon's sense. In practical terms, such disagreements pose real obstacles to plans that could control factors such as out-migration or that could enhance levels of satisfaction with urban services. Additional research in Leningrad carried out by NIIKSI reveals that such social problems as a declining birthrate and the ensuing labor shortage are not at all related to the kinds of input variables (income, wages, living conditions, services, amount of housing) that social plans can conceivably manipulate.[94] Indeed, Soviet social planners have yet to consider whether urban outcomes and user satisfaction are necessarily related.

The absence of any universally accepted procedure for rank ordering and reconciling the various goals of social plans constitutes a second kind of problem.[95] Goal conflict is assumed to be nonexistent. Instead, plans proceed from the assumption that an umbrella goal, such as "improving the well-being of the population," simply expresses the sum of all targets relating to specific problems.

One case suffices to illustrate the fallacy in such reasoning. In social plans, the device applied to index urban transport performance focuses upon the number of passengers transported. To increase performance outputs, local transport authorities engage in behavior that undermines rather than complements the plan's larger goal. In order to fulfill social plans, they have shortened routes and created branch lines, thereby increasing the number of transfers travelers make. The resulting figures reflect positively on the operations of the transport system, as transfers double and triple the body count.[96] But this occurs at the expense of system efficiency, time expended by commuters in getting to work, and overall levels of comfort. Nor have goals always been properly coordinated or their interaction carefully charted before embodying them in social plans. As a result, many plans strive to reduce rush-hour traffic by staggering starting hours for factories and institutions without making the necessary adjustments in the working hours of stores and service establishments.[97]

While something on the order of program management or management by objectives would eliminate such difficulties, few steps in this direction are evident. All discussions of funding stop short of formulating true program budgets. Likewise, program evaluation and assessments of effectiveness are still absent from the lexicon of urban social planning. According to one Soviet evaluation of the recent social plan for Leningrad, its "programmatic, goal-oriented approach" remains simply a terminological gloss.[98]

A third type of problem internal to the social planning process turns on the way in which "need" is assessed and targets set. A description of the social plans utilized by the urban districts of Leningrad for 1971-75 reveals that the planners failed to devise standards for establishing adequate performance levels or evaluation criteria. In the words of one Soviet commentator, "do we regard 152 greengrocers, 86 dry goods stores, 58 schools and 109 kindergartens" as adequate or too few to really meet the needs of an urban district?[99] And, further, how does one decide between the creation of beauty parlors and equipment rental centers if the shortage of both appears equally acute? The commentary suggests that the decision rules employed in the Leningrad case strongly resemble projections of standard unit measures rather than targets set according to needs assessment either for individuals or for social groups.

To be sure, it is not the failure of Soviet social plans to raise the issue of personal choice per se that is damning in the Soviet context. Indeed, the political values of the elite as well as the dominant political culture deny the importance of "bourgeois individualistic" choice in planning as in many other contexts.[100] But the failure of the plans to consider choice from *any* perspective, be it collectivist or individualistic, represents a real shortcoming.[101] Further, when a single alternative is singled out and approved, the policy prescriptions appended ("create more day care centers," "raise levels of political activism," "eliminate heavy manual labor") frequently remain slogans rather than prescriptive guidelines.

Other problems plague the social planning movement as well. The absence of specialists in social planning means that the expertise needed to sell the idea to traditional planners is frequently missing. As of 1975, only a single institution, the Leningrad Financial-Economic Institute, had devised a course dealing with social planning for cities and regions.[102] The plans themselves have yet to propose measures in one area quite critical for improved urban management, that is, organizational reform. In theory, every social plan includes a section dealing with "improvements in management," incorporating features such as administrative reorganization, new personnel policies, and changes in operating techniques. In practice, however, all plans merely repeat the well-worn exhortations of a 1971 party-state decree, "On Measures for Strengthening the Material-Financial Base of Regional and Municipal Soviets." To date, juridical changes designed to clarify functions and tasks for city agencies constitute the sum and substance of policy recommendations in this area.[103]

To label urban social planning a failed innovation in the context of Soviet managerial transformation is undoubtedly premature. For one thing, as a new approach to urban planning, its emphasis on coordination, integration, and interdependency displays many of the management features already evident in social planning in the United States. For another, the party leadership itself has made a substantial and long-range commitment to the spread of social planning practices. Such support reflects in the organizational backing provided over the last few years by the powerful Leningrad province party organization. It also emerges from the ideological and political acceptance inherent in the verbal reaffirmation and guiding directives emanating from the first secretary himself.

Equally important, both the Academy of Social Sciences attached to the party's Central Committee and the all-union Academy of Sciences have devoted considerable attention to the problems of social planning.[104] The Academy of Sciences has established a major research organization, the Institute for Socioeconomic Problems already mentioned, specifically designed to focus on the problems of Soviet urban systems. Since it opened in 1975, its chief function has been to render theoretical and methodological assistance to the social planning efforts of local authorities in Leningrad and other Soviet cities. In a similar vein, Soviet sociologists attached to the Academy are currently participating in a joint U.S.-USSR research program to further the development of social indicators.[105] Better indicators, in turn, promise to overcome many of the obstacles that currently impede social planning efforts.

From the vantage point of improving urban management, and despite its apparently limited and experimental nature, the turn toward urban social planning in the USSR promises several real advances in the managerial transformation of urban administration. Our assessment of current practice, however, shows that acceptance remains limited and unenthusiastic at best. On the other hand, descriptions of the research underlying social plans reveal that an awareness of the importance of needs assessment and client analysis has begun to penetrate Soviet planning procedures. Such questions as "what don't you like about life in the city?" while naive and even crude by some survey research standards,

nevertheless represent an important step in the direction of accepting the significance of subjective, attitudinal factors as variables shaping citizen behavior in urban systems.[106] In the long run, it may help move Soviet city government toward
a situation in which responsiveness is viewed as genuinely legitimate and not simply as politically expedient.

Conversely, other features lead us toward a negative balance in any effort
to devise a net assessment. Soviet social planners have yet to appreciate the real
importance of organizational arrangements to the delivery of urban goods and
services. Institutional frameworks give shape to administrative performance,
partly through the incentives and deterrents they employ to structure roles and
partly through the kind of attachments—including a sense of legitimacy and loy-
alty—that institutional rules and organizational values generate. Institutional
frameworks serve either as barriers or as facilitators to innovation, either as channels for information feedback or as layers of bureaucratic insulation against client demands. In an endless variety of ways, often conflicting, institutions help
determine goals, resource flows, information transfers, and role orientations
among administrative actors. These, in turn, affect program implementation. To
date, however, no concern for institutional analysis or design has appeared either
in the literature about social planning or in the plans themselves. Nor do the
plans challenge traditional budgetary procedures. "Measures for financing social
policy goals," like the traditional budget, operate for audit and control purposes
in Soviet social plans but do not help to organize programs. The "sources" listed
simply designate the traditional wellsprings of urban finance.[107] In this way, social plans still rely heavily on a comptroller's accounts rather than on the substi-
tution of a manager's budget.[108]

Our analysis of those social plan approaches and procedures utilized in the
USSR today underlines the accuracy of a 1975 assessment from a volume on urban planning issued by the Institute of Sociology of the Academy of Sciences:
"At the present time, no means for actually determining the effectiveness of social planning exists."[109]   Indeed, the current (1977-78) Soviet preference for a
uniform system of social indexes to be applied to any city coupled with the demand for a single *metodika* to be applied nationwide suggests that social planning proponents may have become less rather than more sensitive to the unique
problems of different kinds of cities and different sorts of urban clienteles. At
any rate, the continued absence of such managerial tools as PPBS, MBO, critical
path analysis, and evaluation research suggests that social planning in the USSR
still underrates the importance of techniques that can institutionalize learning
and feedback in the planning process.[110]   Indeed, by stressing the shape of the
plan document over the way in which the *planning process* is executed, Soviet
attempts at devising social plans suffer from many of the same rigidities that
continue to plague urban planning efforts in other national settings:

It has up to now deceived itself by evading the realities of uncertainty about the future, of change through the passage of time, of

natural errors in forecasting. There has been, both professionally and perhaps politically, a "faith" of planning, a faith in the "omnipotence" almost of plans. The case has been made [but by others] for those involved in planning to take as their starting point that the plans they produce will be wrong, that they will not "work." This is the beginning of the learning system.[111]

Such a judgment in no way precludes the fact that with a shift in political alignments and diminished importance of the branch principle in economic planning (perhaps as a result of the 1973-74 economic reforms), regionally integrated and socially oriented planning for the Soviet city could really take root and flourish. This eventuality, in turn, depends on the success or failure of current efforts to convince the national party leadership that a new organizational format within the Soviet state structure is necessary to encourage urban management, in other words, a ministry of cities. As the history of HUD in the United States indicates, much depends as well on the extent to which such a ministry remains sensitive to the very real differences among the needs of various cities. Otherwise, centralization and the drive to achieve a technocratic "fix" is likely to generate a penchant for comprehensiveness and uniform solutions. Such an outcome may aggravate problems rather than resolve them. At the same time, the fate of the social planning movement rests on the ability of planners to discard their conceptual blinders and to overcome the methodological difficulties that still thwart successful social plan implementation. Until such time, urban social planning in the USSR is likely to continue to promise more as a tool for urban management than it can, in fact, deliver.

NOTES

1. Tony Eddison, *Local Government Management and Corporate Planning* (New York: Barnes and Noble, 1973), p. 23. The authors wish to thank Professors Henry Brady, University of California, Berkeley, and Thomas A. Reiner, University of Pennsylvania, for their helpful comments and criticisms on this chapter.

2. I. M. German and V. I. Mal'tsev, *Sotsial'noe planirovanie v gorodskom raione* (Saratov: Privolzhnoe knizhnoe izdatel'stvo, 1976), pp. 5, 6; A. S. Gruzinov and V. P. Riumin, *Gorod: upravlenie, problemy* (Leningrad: Lenizdat, 1977), pp. 138-39.

3. Ibid., pp. 141-43; E. P. Muraviev and S. V. Uspenskii, *Metodologicheskie problemy planirovanie gorodskogo rasseleniia* (Leningrad: Izd. Leningradskogo gosudarstvennogo universiteta, 1974), pp. 14-24; A. N. Alekseev and O. I. Shkaratan, eds., *Planirovanie sotsial' nogo razvitiia gorodov* (Moscow: Izd. Institut sotsiologicheskogo issledovaniia, 1973), pp. 17-18.

4. Muraviev and Uspenskii, op. cit., pp. 78, 81, 83.

5. Gruzinov and Riumin, op. cit., p. 139; interview, Institute of Social and Economic Problems (hereafter ISEP), Academy of Sciences, USSR, Leningrad, 1976.

6. M. V. Borshchevskii et al., *Gorod: metodologicheskie problemy kompleksnogo sotsial'nogo i ekonomicheskogo planirovaniia* (Moscow: Nauka, 1975), p. 14; German and

Mal'tsev, op. cit., p. 69. Erik P. Hoffmann has pointed out ("The Scientific Management of Society," *Problems of Communism* 26 [May-June 1977]: 62-63) that as used by Soviet analysts today, the term *upravlenie* reflects the conviction that socioeconomic phenomena operate as systems.

7. German and Mal'tsev, op. cit., p. 19. From this perspective, social planning in the USSR represents the response of urban planning as a discipline to the "scientific-technical revolution in human affairs," See, for example, Paul M. Cocks, "Retooling the Directed Society: Administrative Modernization and Developed Socialism," in *Political Development in Eastern Europe*, ed. Jan Triska and Paul Cocks (New York: Praeger, 1977), pp. 55-58.

8. Alekseev and Shkaratan, op. cit., pp. 85-86; E. I. Kornevskaia, *Mestnye sovety RSFSR i territorial'no-sotsial'noe planirovanie* (Moscow: Izd. Sovetskoi Rossii, 1976), pp. 30, 32.

9. Eddison, op. cit., pp. 25-28. Much of the attraction of master plans for cities in the West has lain in the importance they attach to construction and capital expenditures. Both kinds of targets have exercised great attraction for Soviet planners, given Soviet planning's general predilection for physical and quantitative measurements (the *val*) of output rather than those relating to the suitability of the end product (profit, salability, client response). See Robert Campbell, *Soviet Economic Power: Its Organization, Growth and Challenge*, 2d ed. (New York: Houghton Mifflin and Co., 1960), pp. 28-82.

10. For the kinds of problems that have stimulated social planning in the West, see "Approaches to Social Planning," in *Urban Planning and Social Policy*, ed. Bernard J. Frieden and Robert Morris (New York: Basic Books, 1968), pp. 2-4; M. Broady, "The Social Aspects of Town Development," in *Taming Megalopolis*, 2 vols., ed. H. Wentworth Eldredge (Garden City, N.Y.: Anchor Books, 1967), 2: 931-32; Eddison, op. cit., pp. 8-9. Like U.S. social planning, the Soviet variant lays heavy emphasis at the theoretical level on the importance of complex, multidimensional problems in place of agency programs and clienteles. Its management orientation also flows from the fact that goals are emphasized over procedures and methods. The Soviet variant differs, however, in two important respects. First, it is prescriptive rather than descriptive, in contrast to its U.S. counterpart. And, second, the Soviet variant stresses the importance of social inputs into economic growth policies rather than the social outcomes of these policies as its chief concern. See H. J. Gans, "Social and Physical Planning for the Elimination of Urban Poverty," in Frieden and Morris, eds., op. cit., pp. 49-53; Harvey S. Perloff, "New Directions in Social Planning," in Eldredge, ed., op. cit., 2: 879-93; Eddison, op. cit., pp. 84-85, 89, 91-97.

11. Stephen Sternheimer, "Social Planning in the Soviet Factory," in *Industrial Labor in the Soviet Union*, ed. A.Kahan and B. Ruble (forthcoming); N. I. Lapin et al., *Teoriia i praktika sotsial'nogo planirovaniia* (Moscow: Izd. politicheskaia literatura, 1975), p. 151; B. S. Khorev, *Problemy gorodov* (Moscow: Nauka, 1971), pp. 260-81; *USSR: Some Implications of Demographic Trends for Economic Policies*, ER71-10012 (Washington, D.C.: Central Intelligence Agency, January 1977), pp. 7-13; Murray Yanowitch, *Social and Economic Inequality: Soviet Union* (White Plains, N.Y.: M. E. Sharpe, 1977), pp. 165-66, 175.

12. Alekseev and Shkaratan, op. cit., pp. 94-97.

13. V. L. Barsik, "Opyt sotsial'nogo planirovaniia krupnogo industrial'nogo tsentra," in *Aktual'nye problemy sotsial'nogo planirovaniia: Sektsiia "Sotsial'nogo planirovaniia v regione"* (Moscow: Izd. Bashkirskogo obkoma KPSS, 1975), p. 80.

14. A. V. Dmitriev and M. Tiukaev, "Nekotorye voprosy kompleksnogo sotsial'nogo planirovaniia," in *Aktual'nye problemy*, p. 153; N. S. Semeniuk, "Voprosy planirovaniia migratsionnykh potokov molodezhi," in *Aktual'nye problemy*, p. 124; V. D. Popov, "K voprosu o planirovanii razvitiia sistema obrazovaniia," in *Aktual'nye problemy*, p. 47. One-third of all reports at the 1975 conference dealt with the urban labor shortage and with social planning as a solution to the problem. Similar objectives governed the formulation of

social plans for Moscow's urban districts, 1971-75. See Alekseev and Shkaratan, op. cit., pp. 85-86, 98; B. N. Chaplin and N. N. Bokarev, "Sotsial'noe razvitie gorodskogo raiona," in *Planirovaniia sotsial'nogo razvitiia*, ed. D. A. Kerimov (Moscow: Mysl', 1976), pp. 76-81. Despite the importance of the housing shortage in the USSR and its function as a bridge between the social and economic worlds of the city, there is no evidence that this problem made any direct contribution to the onset of social planning. Nor has there been any apparent tie between severe manpower problems in such areas as Siberia and the application of social planning to urban settlements there.

15. David E. Powell, "Labor Turnover in the Soviet Union," *Slavic Review* 36 (June 1977): 272-74. A 1969 social survey conducted in Leningrad revealed that among the reasons for suboptimal use of the labor force, inefficient urban transport ranked at the top of the list of complaints, followed closely by poor planning of consumer services and retail food outlets. See Popov, op. cit., pp. 44-46.

16. Muraviev and Uspenskii, op. cit., p. 74; Borshchevskii et al., op. cit., pp. 13, 156, 160, 162, 163. The statistics on per capita production in the Northwest Economic Region (Leningrad, Pskov, Novgorod, Vologda) indicate that this has already happened. See Muraviev and Uspenskii, op. cit., pp. 64, 76 (table 18).

17. Ibid., p. 65.

18. Ibid., pp. 65-66.

19. Borshchevskii et al., op. cit., pp. 150-51. Many of Herbert Gans' criticisms of physical planning in the United States are equally applicable to the USSR. See his "Planning for People, Not Buildings," in *Urban Administration: Management, Politics and Change*, ed. Alan Edward Bent and Ralph A. Rossum (Port Washington, N.Y.: Kennikat Press, 1976), pp. 152-71.

20. Lapin et al., op. cit., p. 150. For further discussion of the conflict between branch-oriented economic planning and proportional development as a goal, see Khorev, op. cit., pp. 142-43.

21. Sternheimer in Kahan and Ruble, eds., op. cit.; S. F. Frolov, "Planirovanic sotsial' nogo razvitiia na raznykh urovniakh sotsial'noi organizatsii," in *Aktual'nye problemy sotsiologii truda*, ed. V. G. Vasil'ev (Moscow: Institut sotsiologii, Akademiia nauk SSSR, 1975), p. 108.

22. Lapin, et al., op. cit., pp. 154-56.

23. V. P. Polozov, "Napravleniia i ob"ekty sotsial'nogo planirovaniia," in *Chelovek i obshchestvo*, no. 15 (Leningrad: Izd. Leningradskogo gosudarstvennogo universiteta, 1976), pp. 27-29; Frolov in Vasil'ev, op. cit., pp. 106-8; A. S. Pashkov, "Metodologicheskie i metodicheskie voprosy sotsial'nogo planirovaniia," in *Kompleksnoe sotsial'noe issledovanie*, ed. A. S. Pashkov (Leningrad: Leningradskogo gosudarstvennogo universiteta, 1976), pp. 113-14; Popov in *Aktual'nye problemy*, pp. 44-46. A possible input to which the social planning literature does not attach any overt importance is the work of East European urbanists on such issues as the relationship between city size and urban infrastructure (Poland) or the linkage between the decentralization of decision making and the viability of welfare economics (pre-1968 Czechoslovakia). The authors wish to thank Thomas Reiner for bringing these issues to their attention.

24. Frolov in Vasil'ev, op. cit., p. 108; Lapin et al., op. cit., p. 151; Sh. B. Aldasheva, "Opyt raboty gorodskogo soveta po planirovaniiv," in Kerimov, ed., op. cit., p. 96; A. S. Pashkov and M. N. Mezhevich, "Sotsial'noe planirovanie," in *Chelovek*, p. 10.

25. Lapin et al., op. cit., pp. 39-45; Pashkov and Mezhevich in *Chelovek*, p. 10.

26. A. V. Dmitriev and M. N. Mezhevich, "Kompleksnoe planirovanie v gorodakh," *Sotsiologicheskoe issledovanie* 4 (1976): 53-57.

27. N. A. Aitov, "Voprosy teorii i praktiki regional'nogo sotsial'nogo planirovaniia," in *Aktual'nye problemy*, pp. 56-71.

28. M. L. Strogina, "Problemy razvitiia bol'shikh gorodov i agglomeratsii," in *Sotsial' noe issledovanie* 4 (1970): 58.

29. Alekseev and Shkaratan, op. cit., pp. 89-90. Whereas the average annual increment for population increase in urban areas stood at 9.4 persons per 1,000 urban inhabitants (base) for the Central Economic Region for the years 1959-67, it registered at 26.4 persons per 1,000 urban inhabitants for the same period in the city of Orel.

30. "Vvedenie," in *Chelovek*, pp. 5-6.

31. Ibid., p. 6.

32. A. V. Dmitriev, "Rol' Leningradskoi partiinoi organizatsii v razvitii praktiki i teorii sotsial'nogo planirovaniia," in *Chelovek*, pp. 21-25; N. Vasil'evich, "Vozmozhnost' primeneniia programno-tselovogo podkhoda dlia kompleksnogo planirovaniia," in ibid., p. 83; interviews, ISEP, 1976, 1977.

33. Dmitriev and Mezhevich, "Kompleksnoe planirovanie," p. 58.

34. Alekseev, op. cit., pp. 32, 34.

35. Dmitriev and Mezhevich, "Kompleksnoe planirovanie," pp. 58-59.

36. Any generalizations regarding social planning methodology remain tenuous in part because, as one section head in the Leningrad-based Institute for Social and Economic Problems put it in 1976, "Practice has outstripped theory." Even though some three dozen cities were said to have social plans as of 1976, there still existed no universally accepted methodology or format for social planning. At present at least six research centers in the USSR have produced social planning methodologies: Ufa, Novosibirsk, Moscow, Kiev, and two in Leningrad. Interviews, ISEP, 1976, 1977.

37. This represents a major modification of traditional practice in Soviet city planning that calculated urban growth (economic development, social services) as the linear product of increases in the city-forming population. Jack Fisher, "Urban Planning in the Soviet Union and East Europe," in Eldredge, ed., op. cit., 2:1078-79.

38. Muraviev and Uspenskii, op. cit., pp. 122-23.

39. Alekseev and Shkaratan, op. cit., p. 28.

40. Borshchevskii et al., op. cit., p. 167; Muraviev and Uspenskii, op. cit., pp. 123, 125.

41. Borschevskii et al., op. cit., p. 184; German and Mal'tsev, op. cit., pp. 48-51.

42. Borshchevskii et al., op. cit., pp. 186-87 (table 4).

43. V. V. Blinova et al., *Metodicheskie rekomendatsii po kompleksnomu planirovaniiu sotsial'no-ekonomicheskogo razvitiia gorodskogo-administrativnogo raiona* (Leningrad: Nauka, 1971).

44. Polozov, in *Chelovek*, pp. 32-33; *Metodicheskie rekomendatsii po sostavleniiu kompleksnogo plana sotsial'no-ekonomicheskogo razvitiia* (Minsk: Izd. Raikoma KPB, 1975), pp. 13-15.

45. Borshchevskii et al., op. cit., p. 170 and n. 19.

46. M. V. Borshchevskii, "Metodologicheskie problemy," in *Chelovek*, pp. 39, 41-42; Borshchevskii et al., op. cit., pp. 170, 172. Borshchevskii and others have suggested "cost" and "time" as two universal indicators to replace the practice whereby each discipline focusing on urban problems has utilized separate and unrelated indicators as measures of change. See also Ia. I. Gilinskii, "Vremia kak faktor," in *Chelovek*, pp. 63-71. As in the West, program goals tend to be hazy and ambiguous so that measures are needed to translate broad goals into specific figures. See Grover Starling, *Managing the Public Sector* (Homewood, Ill: Dorsey Press, 1977), pp. 248-53.

47. Interview, G. V. Osipov, deputy director, Institute of Sociology, Academy of Sciences, USSR, 1977. On U.S. efforts, see Daniel Bell, *The Coming of Post-Industrial Society* (New York: Basic Books, 1973), pp. 79, 330-36.

48. Starling, op. cit., pp. 248-53.

49. Borshchevskii et al., op. cit., p. 176.

50. Ibid., pp. 174-76.

51. On client analysis, see Paul Davidoff and Thomas A. Reiner, "A Choice Theory of Planning, *Journal of the American Institute of Planners* 28 (May 1962): 108-11. For Soviet variants, see Blinova et al., op. cit., pp. 12-14, 177-83; L. I. Shishkina, "Voprosy proforien-tatsii," in *Chelovek*, pp. 94-97. Soviet practices in the use of standard norms are described in N. P. Frisova and V. S. Ertov, "Sovershenstvovanie systemy torgovli v plane," in *Chelovek*, pp. 88-90; Iu. P. Mosolov et al., "Dukhovnye potrebnosti," in *Chelovek*, pp. 107-8, 110; M. N. Mezhevich, "Sovershenstvovanie upravleniia v gorodakh," in *Chelovek*, p. 44. The Sverdlovsk plan, for example, combined client analysis with the use of preestablished norms to reorient the delivery of cultural services. The norms were developed on the basis of ser-vice delivery levels in use elsewhere, corrected for the assigned amounts of capital construc-tion funds available. See V. P. Mazyrin, "Planirovanie razvitiia uchrezhdenii kul'tury v Sverdlovskoi oblasti," *Sotsiologicheskie issledovanie* 3 (1976): 115.

52. Dmitriev and Tiukhaev in *Aktual'nye problemy*, pp. 151-52.

53. Ibid., pp. 80-81; Blinova et al., op. cit., p. 178. In the case of Moscow's urban dis-trict plans, the division of sociological research operating under the local party committee (urban district) developed the plans in conjunction with the party unit's methodological council (which supervises all major sociological research carried out on the district itself). In general, party clearance is required in the USSR for any research project involving a substan-tial survey. See Chaplin and Bokarev, in Kerimov, ed., op. cit., p. 77. In Leningrad, ISEP has played a key role in the formation of the city's social plan as has the Urals Scientific Center for the Sverdlovsk plan. Interviews, ISEP, 1976, 1977.

54. Kornevskaia, op. cit., pp. 12, 53-55, 57-58; O. E. Kutafin, *Mestnye sovety i na-rodno-khoziaistvennoe planirovanie* (Moscow: Izd. Moskovskogo gosudarstvennogo univer-siteta, 1976), pp. 61-63.

55. Ibid., pp. 41-43, 45, 49-50, 52. In small cities, planning commissions have only a chairman and one or two economists on their staffs. In cities such as Sverdlovsk, two sets of plans have been utilized: the "plan" of the planning commission, which deals with urban economic development, and another plan, which projects social transformations. See Kor-nevskaia, op. cit., pp. 68-69.

56. German and Mal'tsev, op. cit., p. 20.

57. Ibid., p. 22.

58. Ibid., p. 23.

59. Ibid., pp. 24-25.

60. Ibid., pp. 25-29, 31, 33.

61. Vasil'evich in *Chelovek*, pp. 83, 85.

62. Mazyrin, "Planirovanie razvitiia uchrezhdenii," pp. 114-15.

63. Blinova et al., op. cit., pp. 182-86. See p. 184 for a sample network graph.

64. For a summary review of these techniques, see Donald A. Krueckerberg and Ar-thur L. Silvers, *Urban Planning Analysis: Methods and Models* (New York: John Wiley, 1974), pp. 201-25, 231-50.

65. Part of the explanation may lie in the fact that the technique is deeply rooted in neoclassical (that is, capitalist) economic theory. But evidence of Soviet attempts to develop an ideologically acceptable counterpart is still missing. See *Metodicheskie rekomendatsii*, pp. 12, 30-31, 33-37, 45, for the use of correlational and multiple regression analyses as well as linear extrapolations in Soviet social planning.

66. Interviews with planners in TsNIPP gradostroitel'stva Moscow regarding the prob-lem of choice among the values of different utilities drew the response that "this, of course, lies at the heart of the problems we face." Interviews, Moscow, 1977. See also Chapter 6 (note 16) on this issue.

67. *Metodicheskie rekomendatsii*, pp. 7-10.
68. Starling, op. cit., pp. 149-54.
69. Dmitriev and Mezhevich, "Kompleksnoe planirovanie," p. 62.
70. M. M. Weber, "Comprehensive Planning and Social Responsibility," in Frieden and Morris, op. cit., pp. 14-15; "Approaches," in Frieden and Morris, op. cit., p. 6.
71. Weber, in Frieden and Morris, op. cit., pp. 18-22. On citizen participation in urban planning in the West, see also: John Friedman, *Retracking America: A Theory of Transactive Planning* (Garden City, N.Y.: Anchor Books, 1973), pp. 70-84; Peter Loveday, "Citizen Participation in Urban Planning," in *The Politics of Urban Growth*, ed. S. Parker and P. N. Troy (Canberra: Australian National University Press, 1972), pp. 129-48; Bernard Crick and G. Green, "People and Planning," *New Society*, September 1968, pp. 334-35; J. L. Grove and S. C. Procter, "Citizen Participation in Planning," *Journal of the Town Planning Institute* 55 (July-August 1969): 292-95; Martin Rein, "Social Planning in Search of Legitimacy," *Journal of the American Institute of Planners* 35 (July 1969): 233-44.
72. Interviews: Kiev NIIP Gradostroitel'stva, 1977; Moscow, Gosstroi, 1977; Moscow, Gosgrazhdanstroi, 1977; Vilnius *gorispolkom*, 1977; ISEP, 1976, 1977; NIIKSI, Leningrad University, 1976; Leningrad *gorispolkom*, 1976.
73. Muraviev and Uspenskii, op. cit., p. 65; Frolov in Vasil'ev, ed., op. cit., p. 108.
74. Lapin et al., op. cit., p. 151.
75. German and Mal'tsev, op. cit., p. 119.
76. Kornevskaia, op. cit., p. 21.
77. Ibid., pp. 24-29.
78. Ibid., pp. 34-41.
79. Pashkov, in Pashkov, ed., op. cit., pp. 125-27.
80. Mezhevich, in *Aktual'nye problemy*, p. 163; Borshchevskii and Petrov, op. cit., pp. 194-95. See also Pashkov, in Pashkov, ed., op. cit., pp. 115, 122.
81. A. Dmitriev and M. Mezhevich, "Edinii plan goroda," *Izvestiia* (Moscow edition), October 19, 1977, p. 5.
82. Ibid.; interviews, ISEP, 1976, 1977.
83. Interviews, housing projects in Leningrad, Tallin, Moscow, 1977. This type of approach is also rampant in the literature at the operational level in the United States.
84. Dmitriev and Mezhevich, "Edinii plan goroda," p. 5. In recent years in the city of Volgograd, 30 enterprises were constructed in violation of the city's *genplan*. The number stood at 127 in Kharkov. Even in housing, where the need for citywide planning (as opposed to sectoral planning) has long been recognized, roughly one-third of the housing fund remains in the hands of ministerially controlled enterprises in Moscow and Leningrad, despite legislation already two decades old (the 1957 Decree and Program on Housing) that mandated full transfer of the fund to the city governments. See Henry Morton, "What Have Soviet Leaders Done about the Housing Crisis?" in *Soviet Politics and Society in the 1970s*, ed. Henry Morton and Rudolph Tokes (New York: Free Press, 1974), pp. 174-85; Alfred De-Maio, Jr., *Soviet Urban Housing* (New York: Praeger, 1973), pp. 17-20, 64-70.
85. Kutafin, op. cit., p. 139.
86. Borshchevskii et al., op. cit., pp. 158-59, 192-97. According to the authors, approximately 70 percent of the average city's resource base still lay within ministerial jurisdiction as of 1975. See also M. N. Rutkevich, "Nekotorye problemy," in Kerimov, ed., op. cit., p. 30.; Gruzinov, p. 77. The problem is not easily resolved, for the transfer of such "resources" as housing constitutes a new drain as well as an accretion to city budgets in light of the expenses of renovation, repair, and replacement, which rents are not adequate to cover. See N. G. Starovoitov, *Nakazy izbiratelei* (Moscow: Izd. Iuridicheskaia literatura, 1975), p. 63. In this respect, an apparently "beneficent" policy bears a certain resemblance to the impact of federal highway programs on state budgets in the United States.

87. Dmitriev and Mezhevich, "Edinii plan goroda," p. 5; interviews, ISEP, 1977.

88. Arnold Heidenheimer et al., *Comparative Public Policy: The Politics of Social Choice in Europe and America* (New York: St. Martin's Press, 1975), p. 112.

89. Eddison, op. cit., p. 36.

90. Heidenheimer et al., op. cit., pp. 114-15.

91. Borshchevskii et al., pp. 179-83.

92. Ye Polozov, "Sotsial'noe planirovanie: tseli, zadachi, ob"ekt," in Pashkov, ed. op. cit., p. 114.

93. Z. I. Fainberg, "K voprosu o perspektivnykh tseliakh dolgosrochnogo regional' nogo-sotsial'nogo planirovaniia," in *Aktual'nye problemy*, p. 191.

94. V. Boiko, S. F. Buinova, "Problema rozhdaemosti kak sotsial'no-psikhologiche-skaia problema kompleksnogo planirovaniia," in *Aktual'nye problemy*, pp. 171-73.

95. Gruzinov and Riumin, op. cit., pp. 75-76.

96. Ibid., p. 77.

97. Ibid., pp. 77, 79.

98. Vasilevich, in *Chelovek*, p. 85. On program evaluation in social planning in the West, see Perloff in Eldredge, op. cit., 2:892-93.

99. Pashkov, in Pashkov, ed., op. cit., p. 127.

100. On Soviet political culture, see A. Inkeles and R. Bauer, *The Soviet Citizen: Daily Life in a Totalitarian Society* (Cambridge, Mass.: Harvard University Press, 1961); Zvi Gitelman, "Soviet Political Culture: Insights from Jewish Emigres," *Soviet Studies* 29 (October 1977): 543-64.

101. For a discussion of the problems involved in calculating social rationality for so-cial planning, see Bell, op. cit., pp. 299-338.

102. Borshchevskii et al., op. cit., pp. 198-200.

103. Gruzinov and Riumin, op. cit., p. 95.

104. Kerimov, op. cit.; idem, ed., *Problemy sotsial'nogo planirovaniia* (Moscow: Mysl', 1974).

105. Interview, G. V. Osipov, deputy director, Institute of Sociology, Academy of Sciences, USSR, 1977.

106. Barsik, in *Aktual'nye problemy*, p. 82.

107. Interviews, Tallin, *gorispolkom*, 1977.

108. Eddison, op. cit., pp. 37-44.

109. Frolov in Vasil'ev, op. cit., pp. 109-10.

110. Our findings regarding Soviet public management call into question claims by Western specialists on the USSR that MBO, PPBS, and other management tools have been accepted by the political leadership at both the theoretical and practical levels. To date, the only evidence to support such conclusions cited by such authors is in the realm of industrial management. See Cocks in Cocks and Triska, eds., op. cit., pp. 63-66. By Cocks's own admis-sion, the party's desire for stability and its fear of endangering its vanguard role has blunted the drive for "scientific management."

111. Eddison, op. cit., pp. 16-17. Authors' emphasis.

6

INFORMATION AND INNOVATION

INFORMATION NEEDS AND TOOLS

The generation, storage, and processing of data, together with the application of the information obtained to decision making, comprise the information dimension of urban management. Inputs that are too numerous and too varied, however, can turn management efficiency into administrative profligacy. The same applies to information processing techniques. Therefore, some effort must be made to determine information needs more precisely and in line with well-articulated goals. Information must be processed with the tools and techniques most appropriate to these needs if urban management is to be enhanced.

Minimally, information should meet the following criteria. It should be readily accessible to decision makers, appropriate to their requirements, available on a timely and regular basis, and reliable and accurate.[1] Good management also requires that decision makers be able to draw upon many and varied sources as well as types of information. Multiple channels for input, therefore, become critically important in the dynamic and complex urban environment, primarily because they reduce the likelihood of information error and distortion. Conversely, reliance on a single input mode necessarily distorts information as it enters policy management. In this regard, one assessment notes that Soviet information gathering at the local level still remains relatively primitive.[2] The preceding chapter supports such an assessment. Social planning, while well developed in research institutes and universities, is still deficient in practice. Generally, social planning still relies on data generated by bureaucratic or research organizations, that is, "from above." Meanwhile, the data source—the urban population—is consigned to passivity as an object of investigation.

There are many ways to gather empirical data.[3] One method involves provisions for continuous citizen access to administrative decision making in cities.

By itself, however, this participatory mode will also distort information, for it relies exclusively upon participants' subjective views for the data base. If a positive relationship is assumed between citizen access and city government outputs, then activism is being rewarded by shifts in government outputs.[4] By including some complaint mechanisms, citizen access operates as a feedback device that can be used to ensure that city agencies will pursue the goals specified through the political process with minimum untoward consequences. Only then does an urban system emerge as self-regulating; only then do public opinion and the means for determining public needs enter into an alliance that is more than coincidental.[5]

Another way to introduce new information into urban administration is through new kinds of education and professional training for urban bureaucrats. Such training enhances the informational capacities of urban bureaucrats precisely because training involves socialization to new values as well as acclimation to new ways of viewing problems and resolving them. This variant of information input is definitely "elite" rather than participatory in nature, if only because it emphasizes training and expertise for a selected few individuals as the critical variable in transforming administrative policy making. Insofar as "the people who control the information of government tend to control the functions and operations of government," knowledge becomes power—and the power of the urban professionals, not the citizenry at large.[6]

Data on internal and external conditions constitute "the basis of any form of management."[7] Recognition of this fact in the Soviet Union has developed rapidly over the last decade; it began with the compilation and publication (Kharkov, 1968) of the first demographic survey of an individual city undertaken since the 1930s.[8] No doubt, the many earlier conferences and symposia dedicated to the importance of concrete sociological research contributed to this recognition.[9] In any case, the information industry in the USSR is growing as the "scientific-technical revolution" has been extended to the "scientific management of society."[10] One analysis of the impact of modern information processing technology on Soviet politics concludes that Soviet government officials and theorists alike agree that more and better information is still needed.[11]

In planning agencies, research institutions, and universities, the Soviets are devoting a great deal of attention to analytic tools designed to deal with the complex interrelationships of urban life. Using such tools, they strive to organize and process urban data into a comprehensive and comprehensible picture. One such tool is the modeling of large systems through linear programming, optimization models, and simulation techniques. The problem, however, is that linear programming has proved less than satisfactory for dealing with an environment characterized by nonquantifiable variables.[12] The models often ask the wrong question, that is to say, a question whose answer is of little interest to decision makers. Frequently, the models also fail by conceptualizing the urban arena at a level of analysis generally considered inapplicable to concrete problem solving.

These problems are not unknown in the United States, where there is growing recognition of the limited usefulness of different modes of systems analysis.[13] Thus, these analytic tools only occasionally function as real management tools. One exception in the Soviet case is that set of models dealing with the transportation function. These can be and have been used actually to set standards and to plan; in this way they do represent a management tool for decision making.[14]

In Soviet applications of systems analysis, the main thrust now lies with optimization models.[15] The foremost problem with optimal solutions, here as elsewhere, is their narrowness. At present, no method has been devised by which values among different utilities can be compared or nonquantified variables incorporated.[16] The information generated this way is all too often irrelevant to management concerns—and, hence, not helpful for actual problem solving.

The way information is organized establishes categories of thought by structuring the object or issue under study and by defining its components and their interrelationships. This organization affects both the substance of what one is doing and, ultimately, goal formulation. The search for technical solutions to policy problems transforms a possibly broad range of questions for analysis into a narrower collection of queries amenable to solution by the analytic tools at hand. When we remember that problem solving begins with the goals of the organization, it becomes important that the goals appropriate to electronic data processing and systems analysis are necessarily "quantitatively defined according to a given set of indices."[17] These interfaces and the limits they impose have been denied by some Soviet sources but confirmed by others.[18] The salient point here is that the problem is recognized to some degree, as is its effect on changes in information flows in the city.[19] Overall, in the Soviet city there is still a distinct bias toward quantitative data and clearly defined objectives.[20] If anything, this bias serves to reinforce traditional Soviet reliance on quantitative production, on service outputs, and on productivity indexes.

Perhaps the most far-reaching effect of the growing methodological sophistication of Soviet information processing techniques has been on goal formation. Here what appears feasible now overshadows the importance attached to what is desirable. The purpose of "ideal type" planning would be to change urban realities so that they will conform to ideologically derived images rather than to empirically grounded probabilities. By contrast, optimization techniques require the selection of the best alternative, given existing circumstances. In any event, analytic tools of this sort still encourage only small steps, as opposed to the utopian leaps associated with the less methodologically sophisticated 1930s.[21] The same moderation—or "conservatism"—emerges from other features of what we would term the "information environment" in urban management. This refers specifically to the volume of decisions and to their complexities.[22]

The volume and complexity of decisions urban management demands has given rise to yet another tool, automated urban information systems. City planning and management is technically complex, and technological adaptation is necessary. This becomes apparent in efforts to develop national urban development schema that require some forecasting of the distribution of the population and labor resources.[23] It is no less apparent in managing individual Soviet cities. Here the range of operations, services, and functions associated with city government—plus the number of city employees and the complexity of the urban economy—add up to an enormous flow of information.

In Soviet cities, the primary proclaimed purpose of automated urban information systems is the organization of data for use by the city soviet's executive committee.[24] In Soviet no less than U.S. cities, managers are frequently oversupplied with information, although this information is not always appropriate to their decision-making needs.[25] Thus, automated urban information systems are geared to improving the timeliness and reducing the quantity of information urban managers must consider by preprocessing data for their use. However, while *quantity* changes, the *quality* of data on which urban managers base their decisions need not be transformed (or improved!) as a result of computerization. At least in Moscow, the Main Computer Center is said to rely upon data already at the disposal of the local soviets.[26]

It is the weight of this information burden that has encouraged computerization in the United States and the USSR. In both cases, the role of urban information systems has been recognized, at least in theory. In the United States, computers are assigned a vital role in city operations, with the great majority of chief executives of local government finding computers an "essential tool" in the daily operations of their government.[27] For the USSR, controversy still rages over the quality of the Soviet computer industry relative to the United States and to Soviet "needs."[28] Lags in the industry have undoubtedly affected computerization in Soviet cities. But the problem may diminish as the industry develops and as urban information needs are accorded some priority. It was estimated that in 1970 more than 250 computer centers were in operation in enterprises, research institutions, and design offices in the USSR.[29] In 1973, more than 1,250 applications were recorded, but still mostly in the field of economic management.[30] At least 31 operational computers were in use among Soviet city governments as of mid-1973.[31] Two years later, sources suggest that more than 200 different scientific and design organizations were participating in the development of computer applications to Soviet urban management and urban economies.[32]

It is therefore possible to conclude that there is, in fact, some substantial commitment to computerization in the Soviet urban setting. It may well be that computer applications in urban management will develop and expand but only in step with the development and expansion of the computer industry itself in the USSR. The commitment is likely to be costly—and less than universally accepted. This should become increasingly evident as urban officials get caught up in the unanticipated pressures generated by new methods even as they are progressively less swayed by the diminishing prestige associated with initial installation.[33]   Among city employees, the improvements in oversight made possible through computer applications are likely to generate unease and resistance over time.[34]   Likewise, computer systems have not been embraced wholeheartedly or universally in U.S. cities; indeed, problems sometimes offset altogether the perceived benefits accruing to city hall. Serious questions have arisen regarding the provision of information that is really new and the so-called meaningful time savings.[35]   The real test remains whether or not long-term improvements in city government operations can be directly traced to the introduction of automated information systems. Whether these improvements will outweigh the attached political costs in many instances remains to be seen in both settings.

Improvements—meaning improved government services—are most often measured in the United States and in the Soviet Union in terms of the twin criteria of efficiency and economy.[36]   Automation is said to have been introduced into Leningrad administrative operations on the principle of "maximum economic effect."[37]   Presumably this meant, among other things, the potential to decrease markedly administrative costs. In addition to straightforward increases in labor productivity, automation was supposed to free managerial personnel from day-to-day operational activities by pushing decisions concerning minor adjustments down the administrative hierarchy. The management level would retain its hold only over decisions relating to choices among priorities. Here, however, we find that automated information processing has been confused with automatic decision making. "Good" decisions do not invariably flow from computer programs. In point of fact, most of the decisions have already been made during the course of designing and programming the computer system. These are then only fed back into the management system and cannot, with any accuracy, be regarded as its true end product.

Some of the "efficiency" Soviet writings associate with automated information systems is, therefore, probably the product of wishful thinking. Information processing techniques, when applied, can provide only a *limited* source of efficiency, especially insofar as information costs do account for a major part of expenditures in management processes.[38]   If the Leningrad experience is revealing, then there have indeed been some savings in Soviet urban administration; according to one source, computerization in that city provided "a real, annual economy of [sic] administrative-managerial expenditures."[39]

At the same time, it is important to note that a single automated information system, covering urban construction and eight subdivisions of Moscow's city government, was developed at a cost of some 9 million rubles.[40] At this stage in the Soviet computer industry's development—and in contrast to the U.S. situation—"hardware" (equipment) still represents the major portion of a system's overall costs. In the Leningrad computer system for construction management, design costs were said to represent only 10 percent of the system's costs. "Software" expenditures accounted for 30 percent, and hardware the remaining 60 percent.[41] True, hardware costs can be expected to decline as technology evolves in the Soviet electronics and computer industries (or, perhaps, as restrictions on trade with the West are eased). If hardware costs decline, and if urban applications become less sophisticated so as to require only inexpensive design and software expenditures, then the costs of automated information systems in Soviet cities will diminish. With a decline in installation costs, the number of installations could also rise. If, on the other hand, increasingly sophisticated applications are sought, software expenditures will soon absorb hardware savings. As in U.S. cities, the application to which the urban information system is put in the USSR is a critical variable in determining that system's efficiency.

In the USSR, automated information systems are used today for a wide range of functions: servicing the city government, routine housekeeping applications (for example, payroll, billing, purchasing), and servicing the city (for example, housing management, control of retail inventories, public transport scheduling and routing, among others).[42] Computers have been used as well in tracking implementation of executive committee orders through document control. Such systems were initiated in 1973 in Leningrad and a year later in Moscow.[43]

There are other examples of operational information systems, including Moscow's computerized citywide personnel placement service (*AIS trudoustroistvo*). In operation since 1975, this system appears to represent a management system more than an information system, for its output is used in developing labor projections and is related to decisions in education and training.[44] There are 30 district bureaus organized under the City Bureau for Manpower and Information, and each bureau covers enterprises and organizations in its own district and several dozen other nearby employers. Reflecting Moscow's particular problems, separate files are kept for nonresidents of the city and retirees. The overall system is designed to meet specific labor shortages by providing information about 2,100 enterprises and organizations, their workers, vacancies, and summary data on labor resources. Processing is carried out on a MINSK-32. The basic benefits are seen to be shortened unemployment periods and improved labor distribution in the city. The overall annual savings after one year in operation was estimated at 350,000 rubles. Nevertheless, this service still represents a rather routine data processing task. It required little more than a mechanical shift to automated record keeping; comparable *manual* systems still operate in 120 other cities. Less resistance and more immediate results, particularly in time savings, are to be expected from applications such as this one. This holds true because neither administrative procedures nor the type of output are greatly altered as the system is introduced.[45]

According to a 1974 survey of computer usage by 600 municipal departments in 83 cities in the United States, computer usage is most widespread in four departments of city government: accounting and finance; police; public works; and water, sewage, and utilities. Fire, legal, and park and recreation departments exhibit fewer examples of computer application.[46] This pattern, taken in conjunction with usage in Soviet city government, suggests that scheduling and housekeeping functions (representing routine data processing tasks) are among the first to be automated. Thus, it appears that simplicity is the basis on which urban information systems are implemented rather than other priority rules (for example, urgency). Then, too, experimentation is less likely to prove embarrassing when kept internal to city government operations.

It may be thought that changes in the basic organization of city government would follow the introduction of automated information systems. Logically, managerial methods ought to be adjusted to new information demands and to changes in information flows. But a comparison of the organization of automated information systems in Soviet and U.S. cities presents a different picture. In reality, the information system is itself shaped in accordance with the city's preexisting organizational structure.

There are three basic structures by which automated information systems can be organized: centralized, federated, and decentralized facilities. Centralized data processing departments are organized as high-level units in the city's government, are responsible to the chief executive, and are designed and developed by the chief executive or another high-ranking official such as the city budget director.[47] The centralized structure, while accepted as more economical, is also associated with "costs"—problems of empire building and user resistance among city agencies. This was the experience of the first operating urban information system in the United States, Databank in Alexandria, Virginia.[48]

A federated structure tends to encourage cooperation among users by integrating information systems already in place. Although participating agencies may view the structure as a "territorial infringement," they still retain their own data bases and facilities. As individual subsystems, they are joined through an automated information exchange.[49] A major problem with this structure is subsystem compatibility, which is difficult to guarantee on a departmental basis.

In a decentralized structure, data specifications and collection are undertaken by participating agencies. This system may be most appropriate for data gathering rather than analytic or management purposes. The eventual demise of a project developed through a federal demonstration grant to the Tulsa Metropolitan Planning Commission has been traced to the funding problems inherent in a decentralized system and to a lack of cooperation by data collection agencies.[50] In addition, under these arrangements there is relatively little computer sharing with other city departments, although most departments using computers do not own them.[51] In sum, the centralized structure for automated information systems is not a characteristic feature of U.S. cities, and "large-scale centralized computer bureaus in city hall are not too prevalent."[52]

In Soviet cities, the opposite pattern prevails. The pattern is one that is congruent with the overall centralization of city government organization in the USSR. In Moscow, the city's Main Scientific Research Computer Center operates under the first assistant chairman of the executive committee of the city soviet.[53] This computer center has 500 employees working in three locations, and handles approximately 60 percent of the city's computer requirements.[54] A citywide system, named *Moskva*, is being developed to coordinate the work of data processing sections in city agencies. For 1990, 87 agencywide subsystems are planned.[55] In Leningrad as well, a citywide system is being developed by *Lensystemotekhnika* and other departments of the city's executive committee. The system was initiated in 1970, has 1,500 employees, and provides training for the city's technical and managerial personnel in the use of computer systems.[56] The system is designed to automate a large array of management functions in construction, retail trade, planning, transportation, housing, labor resources, and other areas. A citizen inquiry system, which will provide for the processing of citizen complaints, is ranked as one of the six priority subsystems.[57]

Leningrad's system seems more attuned to considerations of cost efficiency. Here, citywide automation has been found to be "flagrantly wasteful" where there are networks of small providers in scattered service locations (for example, dining, tailoring, trade).[58] It has been suggested that Leningrad's less complex system and attention to cost efficiency is also a function of its having less equipment and personnel available than does Moscow.[59]

It is clear that priorities for computers and their support equipment favor the high-ranking, large cities. Edge-cut cards were still being used in manual systems by the party organization in the city of Serpukhov in the mid-1970s.[60] This outcome resembles the distribution of financial resources where relative advantage also depends on access to the bureaucratic center. In the case of Moscow, requests for hardware from city organizations are channeled through the city's Main Computer Center and then forwarded directly to the State Committee for Science and Technology and to *Gosplan* for funding approval.[61] Given a commitment to computerization, expansion is limited by the industry (available hardware, support equipment, programmers), by budget allocations, and by success in pressing the city's claims.

In this respect, U.S. experience suggests that some highly sophisticated urban applications actually may be cost inefficient outcomes of competition. In the U.S. competition for the cumulative $1-2 billion federal investment in state and local information systems, experimental and innovative projects were rewarded. Federal funds were made available to support highly visible products (like sophisticated applications and expanded facilities) rather than to develop fully existing capabilities. Thus, automated information systems in U.S. cities may be said to have developed "too far, too fast,"[62] Similarly, in the Soviet case, Moscow and Leningrad, and to a lesser extent, Kiev have relatively elaborate systems and facilities, while most other city governments have none whatsoever.

The role accorded the State Committee for Science and Technology and *Gosplan* in approving and funding automated urban information systems at the national level serves to further centralize their structure. The result has been a few select and massive systems. In the United States, by way of comparison, the federal government has also played an important role in the development of urban information systems. Support has been extended through a variety of mechanisms, including general program support, demonstration projects, and intergovernmental systems. But overall, the federal role appears "sporadic and piecemeal," especially by comparison with the USSR. It remains characterized by fluctuation and a lack of coordination as mission agencies concentrate on specific projects.[63]

In the Soviet Union, the thrust remains in the opposite direction. Centralized planning has led to a centralized organization of information systems. In Moscow, the basic goal is identified as the "creation of a unified complex of automated management systems for city services of Moscow" (the *Moskva* system).[64] In fact, the potential for integration goes well beyond the city's boundaries. Since 1972, a computer-based planning system has been under development in *Gosplan*'s Main Computer Center. It receives the finest available equipment and personnel to aid it in developing planning estimates for the national economic plan. It is to be connected through subsystems with national and republic agencies involved in economic planning.[65] This is illustrative of a systemic, holistic approach to computerization that stresses the creation of a network of central, regional, and departmental computer centers.[66] There has also been discussion of a project to develop a unified system of documentation (EDP) for the entire country.[67] In line with this, standards have been published for automated urban information systems.[68]

In technological adaptation, as in housing standards and other areas of city government operations, systemic and systematic approaches are all too easily transformed into systems of *uniform* standards. This overview underscores the outstanding advantage of the Soviet system—the opportunity for integrated development. On the other hand, it also pinpoints its greatest weakness: anything less than a clear contribution to an integrated system fares poorly in the hierarchically structured competition for resources.

CITIZEN ACCESS AND INFORMATION

There are other modes of enhancing the information dimension of urban management. Human factors can be relied upon to supplement and extend technological innovations. This information mode, as we noted earlier, may be of a participatory or elite nature, depending upon whether the data it provides are generated from without or are the products of new skills and training among urban bureaucrats themselves. Turning our attention to the human aspects of information, we will consider citizen access to administrative policy making and new methods of professional training for administrators as two variants of the "human mode."

Citizen access—institutionalized channels through which information is provided by urban residents—provides the first focus for our investigation of nontechnical means by which information can be gathered in Soviet cities. Considered as feedback, citizen access operates as a device to insure that administrative agencies effectively pursue the goals specified by the political process. It thereby confronts and interfaces the pressing problems of control, accountability, and responsiveness on the part of urban bureaucracies. These functions are rendered increasingly problematic by the same factors that place urban management on the agenda as a pressing concern in the modern city. Indeed, sociologists have long observed that the responsiveness of bureaucratic organizations to their clients diminishes as the size of the organization increases and as the distance between administrator and client grows as a function of complexity.[69] It is these issues of size, complexity, and fragmentation of roles and responsibilities that make access a particularly urgent requirement for the transition to complete urban management.

Soviet descriptions of urban political processes traditionally attach a great deal of importance to citizen access and administrative accountability as one of the chief strengths of a socialist urban system. Recent discussions of the 1977 constitution underline this formal commitment and the ways in which unimpaired access to decision makers at the local level either prevents or eliminates conflict between administrative decisions and "public opinion." These discussions point to the fact that every citizen is guaranteed the right to submit proposals to state agencies, which then must respond within the time allotted by law (article 49 of the constitution). They also note that in the USSR, opinion polling has achieved the status of a constitutionally protected right for the population (article 5). Article 8 continues by listing "constant responsiveness to public opinion" as one of the requisites of socialist democracy at the national as well as local level.[70]

Many Soviet specialists argue that the masses already participate in "the management of social processes" through such devices as letters to the press and government agencies, public discussions of drafts of major legislation, public initiative in suggesting legislative revisions, and public supervision of administrative implementation of policy.[71] Other discussions of citizen access stress the importance of institutional channels: scientific-technical councils that function as consultative bodies in the municipal arena; social councils (presumably drawn from the citizenry) attached to all administrative agencies; and the use of nonstaff administrators to supplement or substitute for paid, professional bureaucrats.[72] The various types of councils, however, are actually drawn from the ranks of specialists and not from among the population at large. In any case, they enjoy only a consultative status. And nonstaff administration, while formerly important, is presently on the wane as a later section of this chapter shows.[73]

This leaves five major institutional sources that, Soviet sources claim, function to provide the urban citizenry with the access to urban administration needed to ensure real control and real accountability. These include: the reports utilized in public accountings of the activities of administrative agencies (*otchyoty*); instructions to local soviet deputies from the citizenry regarding the impact of specific government outputs (*nakazy*); citizen complaints about administrative behavior (*zhaloby*); legislative inquiries aimed at administrative operations (*zaprosy*); and the social surveys developed to elicit the views of the population (*anketnyi opros*). In theory, each of these provides urban inhabitants with a systematic, politically acceptable way to evaluate the stewardship of public officials. In view of current U.S. concern for upgrading municipal reporting practices to reflect more completely the impact of agency programs on clienteles, Soviet practice in this area of citizen access and participation ought not to be dismissed lightly.[74]

The formal public report or *otchyot* has a long history in Soviet urban administration. According to the legislation, periodic *otchyoty* by departments or by the entire executive committee of a local soviet are designed to insure direct control by elected representatives (and, through them, by the citizenry) over the daily functioning of administrative departments.[75] As far back as 1957, however, a Central Committee resolution noted that most local bodies were not fulfilling their obligations along these lines. As of 1955, only 67.5 percent of all executive committees in the RSFSR regularly delivered reports to plenary sessions of the local soviets. By 1964, the situation registered a dramatic improvement, with 97 percent reporting once a year or more.[76] A detailed, time-series study of *otchyot* reporting in the Belorussian republic indicates that the number of executive committees reporting at least once a year rose from 90.3 percent in 1963 to 96.2 percent in 1965, 99.5 percent in 1967, and to 100 percent by 1968.[77] This increase occurred partly in response to a resolution of the Twenty-Third Party Congress in 1966 that exhorted both executive committees and administrative departments to take their *otchyot* responsibilities more seriously. In one city of the republic, Borisov, formal notices regarding an impending *otchyot* were being sent to all voters by the end of the 1960s. In Minsk, the republic capital, *otchyoty* were being televised in the early 1970s.[78]

Nevertheless, the current situation vis-a-vis the *otchyot* provides only the most diffuse sort of administrative accountability. Both the 1966 and the 1971 party congresses criticized the *otchyoty* for too frequently assuming an excessively formalistic air and for displaying "an inadequate sense of purpose."[79] While *otchyoty* contain general economic statistics and overall profiles of current conditions in a given territorial unit, they seldom relate these outcomes directly to the department or executive committee involved. More frequently, in the words of one Soviet source, such information serves "as a screen which hides from the eyes of the deputies and the population shortcomings, oversights, and mistakes in concrete operations."[80] The compendium of facts an *otchyot* provides is generated by the responsible agency itself, without any independent verification by any kind of watchdog commission. Nor is there any widespread opportunity for the population or deputies to criticize or query the interpretation provided. Most reports are delivered before closed sessions of the soviet's executive committee—a committee on which the head of the reporting agency frequently sits as a voting member.[81] At least in the larger cities, departments seldom report to plenary sessions of the city councils.

Our own research into the scheduling of *otchyot* reports confirms these Soviet findings.[82] A sample of work plans for municipal and urban district soviets covering the early 1970s reveals that reporting by both departments and by executive committees remains a matter of extremely low priority. The 1970 work plan for the city soviet of the town of Gorky failed to schedule a single departmental report for that year, and the same held true for the Ussurskii city soviet in Siberia in 1971. In Vilnius, the situation was only slightly improved; only a single departmental report (out of a possible 14) was scheduled for 1971. An analogous situation prevailed in the town of Podolya in the Ukraine in 1972. And in Moscow, the "model" for the future communist city, the track record appears little improved. A review of agenda scheduling for Moscow's Tushinskii district soviet between 1973 and 1975 shows only 4 of the district's 22 departments delivering a formal *otchyot*.[83] Similarly, the plan of Moscow's Gargarin district for 1975-76 scheduled only three departments for *otchyoty* during that period.[84] Reports also appear infrequently at the levels of the province and the region.

Interviews with Soviet specialists on local government, coupled with the results of an unusual public opinion survey in Kallinin province during 1971, provide further, more systematic corroboration of the initial data on *otchyoty*, which are otherwise quite idiosyncratic in their origins. The sample survey in Kallinin province revealed that when queried about the inadequacies of information pertaining to local agencies' activities, a sizable number of citizen respondents (47 percent) singled out the *otchyoty* as a prime culprit.[85] When, on rare occasion, departments and executive committees do report directly to the public in the form of a mass meeting, these "reports" usually amount to nothing more than informational communiques designed to publicize the work plans of departments. They have no legal standing and in no way evaluate the operations of departments after the fact.[86] At best, a department may report to a plenary session of a soviet only two or three times during the lifetime of that soviet.

According to interview data, reports before the executive committees, while today more frequent, are still given by no more than two-thirds of all local departments. In any case, the tenor of such sessions remains very much *mezhdu soboi*, "among ourselves." There is still little formal criticizing or questioning of the report. Further, given the fact that city soviets meet only four times a year and urban district soviets once a fortnight, it is doubtful whether the amount of departmental reporting could, in fact, be increased.[87] When this situation is joined to the practice of not providing either departmental report or corroborating information to the deputies before the report is actually delivered, it becomes clear that public accountability through the *otchyot* system remains as much facade as substance.[88]

The *nakazy*, or mandates from urban constituents to their deputies, provide inhabitants of the Soviet city with their second, indirect channel into urban administration and policy making. Usually the *nakazy* are generated during election campaigns. Soviet voters are encouraged to deposit, together with their ballots, statements of grievances, suggestions, and demands for remedial action by agencies. As the data provided below suggest, the majority of these probably deal with housing issues or road maintenance, followed by such topics as consumer services and urban transport, the retail trade network, and medical facilities.[89]

Subject Area of Nakazy	Lenin District, Moscow, June 1975 (N = 49) (percent)	Tushinskii District, Moscow, June 1975 (N = 55) (percent)
Housing	36.7	16.4
Trade and public dining establishments	18.4	16.4
Transport	26.5	16.4
Medical, consumer services, other	18.4	
Road repairs, lighting, and the like	0.0	50.9

The impact of *nakazy* on policy formulation varies. Most become part of a work plan that, in turn, forms part of the local soviet's yearly agenda. At the same time, deputies are called upon to explain to voters why certain *nakazy* will not be fulfilled, usually because resources are lacking or because certain preconditions, such as planned allocations, are not present.[90] Normally, members of the executive committee sift through the *nakazy* and send them on for comment to appropriate departments, the department of finance, and the local planning commission.[91]

The rate of acceptance, while high, is not universal. According to one report, the national average for rejections stands at 20 percent. Unacceptable *nakazy* are usually ones that touch on questions of construction or the retail trade network; these generally make demands on labor resources and materials that cannot be fit into the municipal economic plans or budgets.[92] In the case of the Lenin district described above, 28.6 percent of all *nakazy* submitted in 1975 were subsequently scheduled for short-term realization, 10.2 percent for long-term fulfillment, and 49 percent were totally rejected. In the Tushinskii district for the same year, 47.2 percent were set for immediate fulfillment, 34.5 percent were postponed until the next five-year plan, and 3.6 percent were deemed impossible to implement.[93] For the city of Moscow as a whole, however, the acceptance rate decreases. Between 1975 and 1977, 19.3 percent of all *nakazy* were scheduled for immediate implementation, 30.3 percent for intermediate-range realization (1976-80), 8.7 percent for long-range fulfillment (after 1980), and 41.7 percent were rejected outright.[94] On balance, therefore, the extent to which city government operations are, in any sense, actually directed by the urban citizenry is rather limited. Moreover, such *nakazy* are typically handled not by the entire soviet sitting in plenary session but by the executive committee.[95] Given that this unit is less inclined than the entire group of deputies to respond favorably to complaints of administrative inadequacies and shortcomings, the system of *nakazy* probably provides the Soviet city resident with little substantial opportunity to shape administrative decisions.

The legislative inquiry or *zapros* operates as another device whereby Soviet citizens potentially can call administrators to account through elected representatives. The inquiry can be directed either to a department head or to the executive committee as a whole, and it becomes part of a local soviet's agenda. In theory, deputies employ the *zapros* to gain information about administrative progress in implementing specific directives, to obtain a clarification of general departmental policies, or to analyze the origins of certain unfavorable outcomes.[96] The individual to be addressed is forewarned, and the inquiry is formally launched in either written or oral form. If a deputy is satisfied with the response, the matter is allowed to drop; if not, the soviet as a body can pass a resolution obligating the official and department to undertake remedial action.[97]

The frequency with which the legislative inquiry is invoked varies widely from soviet to soviet, although its use is increasing.[98] The national average for all soviets is still quite low, less than one inquiry per year.[99] When its use by city soviets is separated from this average, it appears that *zaprosy* are used less frequently than in rural soviets. Materials from the state archives in Minsk province, Belorussia, suggest that until 1967 only 16.7 percent of all city councils utilized the *zapros* even on an occasional basis. In rural soviets the proportion rose to 43.5 percent. All soviets in Minsk province, urban as well as rural, employed this mechanism from 1969 onward, and by 1972 they heard on the average 3.3 *zaprosy* during each session.

By 1972, the inquiry apparently had grown in popularity. There were 55 inquiries per deputy for city and urban districts in 1968, compared to 28 for each city soviet deputy and 50 for each urban district deputy in 1972.[100] Given that the number of deputies remained constant and the number of *zaprosy* rose, two interpretations are possible: either the same deputies introduced more inquiries or, as the source suggests, more deputies were actually involved. In any event, the legislative inquiry was still used far less frequently in city soviets than in rural ones.[101] This indicates relatively less access for city residents through this mechanism of feedback and control, owing to a lower level of deputy involvement in cities than villages.

In order to establish to what extent the *zaprosy* can, in fact, serve as a channel of citizen access to city administration, it is useful to look both at the social status of deputies who function as activist controllers and at the targets of their inquiries. Data drawn from the records of the 1971-73 sessions of urban and rural soviets in Minsk province reveal that by far the largest group of activist deputies, 67 percent, consisted of those who were employees of the local soviets, directors of collective farms or factories, administrative executives, and party workers.[102] Materials for the urban soviets for the same years indicate also that only 27.3 percent of all *zaprosy* were introduced by deputies drawn from among rank-and-file workers or peasants. For the rest of the cases, 31.8 percent of the inquiries originated with deputies who were organizational chiefs or factory directors. An additional 31.8 percent came from those who were members of the technical or professional intelligentsia.[103] For the province as a whole, male deputies employed the *zapros* twice as often as female deputies, a finding consistent with other studies showing the relatively lower levels of political activism among Soviet women.[104] These findings are also consistent with other studies relating to the political activism of Soviet citizens; as in the United States, it is those who are better educated, who hold white-collar jobs, and who enjoy higher social status who are the most likely to make their voices heard in local councils.[105]

The origins and frequency of the *zaprosy* also conceal another important fact, namely, that the targets of these inquiries are only infrequently the activities of the administrative agencies themselves. More often, the *zapros* is directed against local construction trusts or against the executives of the factories and collective farms for whose operations and outputs the local soviet bears the responsibility. Out of 184 *zaprosy* in the city and country soviets of Grodensk province, Belorussia, during 1972-73, 37 were aimed at construction activities, 28 at subordinate enterprises or farms, and only 4 at the operations of departments and agencies per se.[106] A larger sample drawn from the rural and city soviets of Minsk province during 1969-71 presents a similar picture: 83 percent of all inquires went to directors of enterprises and other production units under the direct control of the local councils; 8.5 percent to local departments and administrative agencies; and 5.7 percent to executive committees.[107] An examination of only the cities of Minsk province during 1971-73 shows that enterprises subordinate to the city government accounted for 33.3 percent of the *zaprosy*. An additional 26 percent were directed at enterprises located within the city but not under the city's jurisdiction.[108] Such data have led one Soviet analyst to conclude that "inquiries into the work of local administration are still few and far between."[109]

Do *zaprosy* have any impact on city operations or services? During the 1971-73 session of city soviets in Minsk province, the sample revealed that deputies judged the answers "satisfactory" in 49.2 percent of all cases.[110] When responses did not provide an adequate explanation, the local soviet then directed that particular remedies be applied. In the larger cities, such as Minsk itself, these are recorded on a control card that registers the subject of the *zapros*, the identity of the deputy making the inquiry, the data on which the *zapros* was reviewed, the decision of the soviet, the individuals responsible for developing remedies, and the period of time allotted for action.[111] Whether and in what kinds of cases actual results are forthcoming, however, cannot be determined from the data available. In any event, the absence of widespread information or publicity regarding the targets of *zaprosy* and the outcomes of such inquiries suggest that they probably do little to enhance citizen perceptions of participation and control. A study of 35 meetings of four urban soviets in Minsk province between 1971 and 1973 showed that information concerning the *zaprosy* was made available to the general public in only one-third of all cases.[112] When coupled with the infrequency of the *zaprosy* and the fact that in most instances they do not address directly the operations of city bureaucracies, the absence of publicity raises doubts about the effectiveness of *zaprosy* as a control mechanism over administrative operations.

From the perspective of every channel of citizen access that we have reviewed—legislative inquiries, public accountings, instructions from voters, and social surveys conducted by administrative agencies—Soviet city government is still a long way from ensuring citizen access.[113] But the most formidable barriers still lie not in the institutional obstacles but in the administrative culture itself. If the findings of the 1971 survey of administrative attitudes in Kallinin province, RSFSR, can be taken as representative of national tendencies (as the author of that study suggests), then Soviet administrators at the local level do not value citizen participation and involvement very highly. The survey of government personnel at various levels within the province revealed that only 10.1 percent of the respondents supported the use of social surveys as a way of tapping public opinion. An additional 39 percent favored the traditional forms embodied in the use of *nakazy* or oral and written petitions by individuals. An almost equal proportion (34.9 percent), however, stressed only random personal contacts with individuals or indirect involvement through such institutions as the many mass organizations or "peoples' control" watchdog commissions. This was all that was needed in their eyes. The remainder, 15.9 percent, felt that letters to the editor in local newspapers or publication of the proceedings of local soviets was a sufficient forum for public opinion and citizen input.[114] In short, from the perspective of local administrators' role orientations, the future for enhanced citizen participation does not look promising. Less than half of all administrative respondents registered approval even for the standard institutional channels that are most widespread among Soviet city governments today.[115] Further, it appears from the Kallinin study that even when information from such devices as social surveys is available, it is frequently ignored by the very administrative agencies at which it is directed.[116]

Soviet administrative culture may be hostile to enhanced citizen access and participation in other ways as well. When asked, "Who ought to participate in decisions taken by local departments or executive committees?" the Kallinin respondents came down squarely in favor of one composite group—"experts," such as the employees of the agencies themselves, specialists employed by local governments, and directors of industrial enterprises. Only 9.6 percent spoke out in favor of widespread citizen involvement, and only 14.6 percent favored an enhanced role for local soviet deputies.[117] Such orientations were reinforced by a second feature of Soviet administrative culture at the local level, that is, a limited recognition on the part of local bureaucrats (49.5 percent of the sample) that administrative decisions and public wants may not always correspond.[118] Additional questions designed to elicit administrators' views on the legitimate focus for public involvement in administrative decision making stressed only the remedial and control aspects of this information. The importance of participation as a source of policy initiatives received little support. The single largest bloc of opinion, 42.3 percent, stressed public participation as a device used only to point out shortcomings in administrative operations to the officials involved. Presumably, these respondents would still leave the choice of remedies and supervision of implementation in the hands of administrative professionals.[119]

Cognitive as well as effective barriers to increased citizen participation characterize Soviet administrative culture. Not only do local administrators not value increased citizen participation, they also claim that, measured "objectively," the mechanisms as presently constituted are more than adequate.[120] The citizenry itself, however, views the situation far less optimistically. In so doing, it reveals that the subjective sense of meaningful participation among the population is far less than the administrators believe.

Question: "In your opinion, to what extent do executive committees, departments, and administrative agencies actually take account of public opinion in reaching their decisions?"

| | Percent Response | |
	Administrator Sample	Citizen Sample
Fully consider	5.4	6.9
Partially consider	80.8	55.1
Don't consider	4.0	11.4
Difficult to say	7.6	22.3
No answer	2.2	4.3

Thus, while neither administrative personnel nor the population at large views local bureaucrats as *wholly* responsive, administrators are far more confident than their clients that public opinion is *partially* taken into account in decision making (80.8 percent versus 55.1 percent). Along the same lines, a larger segment of the citizen sample is convinced that administrators ignore public needs altogether (11.4 percent versus 4.0 percent). Or, alternately, this group sees no real evidence of administrative responsiveness (22.3 percent versus 7.6 percent).[121] It may be that administrators are unreceptive to arguments for new techniques to enhance citizen participation in large part because they believe that public opinion and client needs are already adequately represented.

The composite picture of citizen access to administration that the Soviet data provide suggests that, in many respects, the limits to citizen participation in urban government in the United States and the USSR are remarkably similar. As in the United States and Western Europe, Soviet citizens become involved in the public sector largely out of a concern for their private interests and pursuits.[122] Sixty years of socialist rule and exhortation to collectivism have yet to produce a radical turn toward public-mindedness among the Soviet population, at least so far as the political process itself is concerned.[123] The data reviewed in this chapter suggest that Soviet citizens commonly become involved in city government primarily out of a concern for their private interests and personal needs, such as a specific grievance regarding a particular service or amenity. In this respect, the engaged Soviet urban resident differs little, if at all, from his counterpart in other systems.

Along the same lines, it is likely that there also exists in the USSR a disjuncture between those who feel themselves efficacious in local politics and those who actually participate and get involved. As the study of "civic culture" by Almond and Verba some years ago revealed, there is frequently a gap between those who *believe* that they can affect policy outcomes at the local level and those who *actually try* to accomplish something in the local setting.[124] As a transnational phenomenon, this generalization might also apply to the Soviet urban resident; as Robert Dahl has repeatedly stressed (in other contexts), "interest" is always a cheap commodity, while activity appears far more costly.[125] This may describe a second important barrier to enhanced citizen access in the USSR.

The Soviet data also remind us that citizen participation ultimately must be evaluated in terms of the real power over decision making it confers.[126] Soviet methods and techniques can be viewed in terms of a continuum ranging from participation-as-manipulation to participation-as-control. It then becomes apparent that citizen access *with a significant effect on the content as well as form of administrative decision making* remains just as elusive a phenomenon in the Soviet as in the U.S. city.[127] Citizen access to administration in the Soviet Union still aims primarily to check, control, inform, or cure. As such, its impact may properly be judged manipulative and therapeutic rather than directive and preventative. It is kept strictly within the bounds of a set of feedback functions. To be sure, inviting public opinion through institutional channels—or emphasizing means for informing the public of administrative outputs and government operations—does constitute a step toward enhancing the information dimension of urban management. From a perspective of the political rather than managerial "good," Soviet urban residents, like those in the United States, may hear and be heard by their city officials. But they may also remain as powerless—and probably even more so—to ensure that their voices are heeded.[128]

ADMINISTRATIVE TRAINING AND NEW INFORMATION

Information also may be made available to urban management through the strengthening of professional training. However, there is widespread disagreement over the kinds of training to be preferred and the benefits each brings.[129] In the United States, the faith in perfecting the human component of information is reflected in the fact that almost one-half of the $54 million granted under the Intergovernmental Personnel Act of 1970 has gone toward better training of state and municipal employees.[130] Yet, the absence of proper evaluation techniques leaves the efficacy of a general managerial education for urban administrators open to serious question. Thus, the generalist-versus-specialist issue as a proper goal of professional training remains unresolved.[131] At best, some kind of professional training for urban management remains an attractive mode to be used to enhance indirectly information inputs into the administrative process.

In the United States, trends already point in the direction of increased importance for formal training as a vital aspect of urban management. To be sure, no single approach has received wholehearted acclaim. In 1971, surveys and workshops revealed that U.S. practitioners still regarded on-the-job experience as more valuable than professional, preentry training. In-service training was accorded the lowest priority.[132] The 1970 Personnel Act had only just begun to open up federal in-service training programs to state and local employees, and grants to local units for personnel development were only getting under way.[133] Pilot projects aimed at upgrading urban management education in the United States (there were 20 instituted in 1974) were still in the future.[134]

The status of urban management education in the United States, however, rose quickly within the space of a few short years. Between 1973 and 1975, surveys conducted by the National Association of Schools of Public Administration and Affairs (NASPAA) revealed that four dozen new preentry programs had been established in the interim.[135] Of the almost 4,000 graduates of the 138 programs reported in 1975, the largest single bloc (35 percent) gravitated to posts in local government.[136] Over half of the 138 programs represented separate professional schools likely to feature broad, cross-disciplinary curricula. The training provided in these schools covered the areas of public administration, political science, economics, business administration, sociology, planning, urban affairs, law, health sciences, and statistics.[137] Courses in organizational theory, personnel management, public policy analysis, budgeting, and intergovernmental relations were accompanied by others in planning (75 percent of programs), statistics (84 percent), and economics (60 percent). Furthermore, 70 percent of all programs had well-developed internship components.[138]

In contrast to a rather long tradition of education for public service in both the United States and in continental Europe, administrative training programs have never taken firm root in either tsarist Russia or the Soviet Union.[139] Indeed, Soviet policy has, until relatively recently, deliberately downplayed the significance of professional training—and professionalism in public administration more generally. This was reflected most dramatically in campaigns of the Khrushchev years and afterward (1957-66), which aimed to replace regular administrative personnel at the local level with nonstaff, unpaid "volunteers" who would perform the same duties.[140] Such a reliance on what can only be termed labor-extensive measures to improve administrative resources at minimal cost to the budget was conceived as part of a broader ideological drive to convert the "dictatorship of the proletariat" (the label affixed to the Soviet state since 1917) into an "all-people's state."[141] In concrete terms, measures of this sort promised important economies in administrative expenditures. These, as Chapter 3 shows, were probably considerably in excess of the nominal sums reported in official budget figures.

By the end of the 1960s, published figures detailing the spread of nonstaff administration at the local level looked impressive indeed. The city of Leningrad alone "employed" 3,684 nonstaff personnel, and the city's districts used an additional 15,300. At the lower level, 69 departments functioned on a totally nonstaff basis.[142] In Rostov province, RSFSR, the introduction of nonstaff administrative agencies increased throughout the decade. They accounted for 8.9 percent of all units in 1961, 21.4 percent in 1965, and 30.1 percent by the beginning of 1968.[143] In the RSFSR, the largest and most important republic of the Soviet Union, some 50,000 nonstaff personnel were at work, spread across a total of 5,307 departments and agencies by 1969. At the local level, most deputy chairmen of municipal executive committees worked as unpaid officials, as did some 500 chairmen.[144]

To what extent this attack on professionalism and bureaucracy actually succeeded in removing the professional administrator from the Soviet city remains unclear. By 1970, approximately half of all Soviet cities operated under the auspices of a chief executive who functioned on a nonstaff basis. Yet, of the 5,300 nonstaff departments in the RSFSR—and of the 10,000 listed for the entire nation—no more than 20 percent were attached to city governments.[145] Further, the proportion of nonpaid personnel to professional bureaucrats (excluding inspectors) never rose above 6.3 percent. And this figure probably includes instances in which "volunteers" supplemented rather than replaced existing bureaucrats.[146] Soviet evaluations of the outcome also incline us to caution in interpreting the results. These increasingly emphasized the "natural limits" of the process while underlining the specialist requirements of contemporary urban operations.[147]

In recent years, Soviet enthusiasm for the idea of nonstaff administrative personnel has abated considerably. The number of nonstaff departments in the country's urban districts shrank by some 500 between 1968 and 1970.[148] Similarly, scholarly advocacy of this tactic peaked during the years 1961-65. It became noticeably muted with the popularization of "scientific management" and with the rising importance attached to the "scientific-technical revolution in human affairs" by the party leadership.[149] Currently, nonstaff personnel at the local level are employed primarily to fill positions that would otherwise be left vacant—and that presumably are judged not to affect critically overall administrative capacity. Unless we include such organizations as watchdog commissions or "commissions for checking the implementation of decisions," volunteer administrative personnel today play an insignificant role numerically in the running of the country's great cities.[150]

On a national basis, there are two types of nonstaff administrators. The first includes those specialists and deputies to local soviets who "volunteer" for administrative duties in a department or agency as a way of fulfilling the "socialist obligation" they automatically carry as a condition of their party membership.[151] The second group is composed of retired specialists or bureaucrats who formerly worked as paid employees in a given functional area or agency.[152] Most nonstaff administrators in cities operate within departments devoted to personnel, trade, or consumer services.[153] Areas such as finance, public health, local industry, transport, construction, police, and justice have remained almost totally unaffected. Further, according to one interviewee, the utilization of nonstaff personnel by 1975-76 was concentrated mostly in rural units (*raion* administrations and village executive committees). Here the dispersion of population, coupled with the relative unimportance of many administrative functions, makes the use of unpaid volunteers an attractive alternative for local authorities.[154]

As a result of the long campaign against professionalism in administration, Soviet interest in and commitment to some form of preentry education for urban administrators appears a relatively recent and as yet weak phenomenon. As the examination of career profiles of departmental and agency executives in Chapter 3 demonstrated, preparation in engineering or economics remains typical for many top-level personnel in Soviet cities. Overall, special preparation of urban administrative staffs is still subordinated to the general manpower needs and manpower planning techniques in operation at the national level.[155] Staff needs are projected by individual agencies, passed on to the relevant republic and national ministries, and coordinated through the joint efforts of the State Planning Commission and the ministry of higher and specialized secondary education. The ministry draws up quotas of specialists to be trained by the various universities and technical institutes throughout the USSR; it also draws up lists of job openings for the graduates produced by these institutions.[156] In the absence of any widespread training programs in public administration or urban management, Soviet city administrative personnel have been and still are drawn almost exclusively from the general pool of functional specialists that the system of higher and specialized secondary education in the USSR is geared to produce. Specialized administrative training even today operates primarily for those already working in administrative positions.

Programs for in-service training, the principal type that operates in the USSR today, date from a series of Central Committee resolutions promulgated in the latter half of the 1960s.[157] More recently, as a result of a joint resolution of the Central Committee and the all-union Council of Ministers ("On Measures for the Further Improvement of Higher Education"), many higher education institutions (*vuzy*) have introduced special courses in managerial skills for the specialists they graduate.[158] These include courses in "scientific management" (organization theory), "the scientific organization of labor" (reflecting the influence of "Taylorism"), and "engineering psychology."

The retooling of administrative personnel for Soviet cities, however, is concentrated not in the regular educational establishments but in institutions under direct party supervision and control: the party schools, and soviet-party bodies. The ministry of higher education also runs a correspondence law faculty for individuals with administrative experience, enrolling about 600 students in a two-year law program. Individual ministries maintain their own "institutes for raising qualifications," designed to impart new techniques and areas of specialist knowledge to those already working in posts at the national or republic level.[159] Although Soviet experts on urban government have recently recommended the revival of separate training institutions for local administrators along the lines of the "institutes for Soviet state development" that flourished in the 1920s, some party officials oppose such a move. Apparently, they prefer the politically less risky strategy of training government personnel in party-controlled institutions with some modifications of the traditional curricula.[160]

Important incentives serve to induce the upwardly mobile administrator to enroll in some form of postentry training. In contrast to current practice throughout the United States, successful matriculation does not bring in its wake immediate material rewards in the form of salary increases, at least insofar as the data reveal. It does, however, provide a golden opportunity for job mobility. Like the regular educational institutions of the Soviet Union, these programs also operate according to plans that dictate job placement opportunities for their graduates. These usually include the more desirable posts. For example, in 1974 the city of Voronezh drew the majority of its new administrative recruitees from the reserve pool created by the higher party school and party schools operating in the area.[161]

All the same, it is important to recognize that this kind of training can only impart some generalist attitudes and skills to specialists already firmly ensconced in their respective areas of expertise. From this perspective, the ability of Soviet in-service training to inject a managerial orientation into the work milieu of urban administration still appears quite limited, especially by contrast with the U.S. trends described earlier. The management courses created in *vuzy* in the aftermath of the joint resolution of 1972 do not aim exclusively at state administrative personnel. Indeed, they were intended primarily to impart some management training to future directors of industrial enterprises.

Retraining for existing officials, as in the case of Voronezh, may amount to little more than a three-week course of lectures and seminars, offered biennially.[162] Moreover, administrative training still relies heavily on legal knowledge and familiarization with the various laws nominally governing the operation of different branches of the national economy.[163] Retraining programs instituted through the party schools generally run for about three months, with one or two meetings each week. The programs sponsored by local soviets are also of short duration, and since 1971, many municipal departments have included "raising staff qualifications" as part of their annual plans. There is no evidence that intensive kinds of specialist retooling, such as that offered to staff and executives in departments of finance through the Voznesenskii Financial-Economic Institute in Leningrad, extend as far down as the city within the territorial administrative hierarchy.[164]

Nor have the Soviet efforts kept pace with the turn toward management education and professional training that has occurred in some East European countries. Here there are already special schools and courses devoted primarily to government management. Examples cited would include the Higher School of Social Administration in Bulgaria and the Institute of Administration in Czechoslovakia.[165]

No assessment of current Soviet efforts to upgrade the quality of urban administrators would be complete without some attention to the kinds of curricula various programs provide. Examination of curriculum materials and course syllabi gathered on site reveals a preponderant concern with conceptual problems. By this we mean attention to such issues as the meaning of "social management" in a Marxist-Leninist framework or the kinds of administrative principles that are consistent with "scientific communism." The theoretic, political, and ideological components of the curriculum thus dramatically overshadow any concern with managerial skills, organizational dynamics, or client-administrator relationships.

The comprehensive study plan for in-service training programs drawn up by Moscow's higher party school in 1974 outlined various courses of study for a period of one and one-half months. The core of 20 lectures was to be supplemented by separate sessions devoted to each functional and branch department in local administration. In addition, there was to be a practicum lasting a day or two, student reports, and a "special theme" seminar. The political-theoretic component of this instructional guideline (aimed at programs run by local soviets themselves) occupied 36 percent of the instructional hours scheduled. Less than 20 percent of all class time was allotted to training in specific administrative skills. And, for the most part, this time segment was geared to an understanding of the structural complexities of Soviet local government. A separate cycle of lectures prepared specifically for department heads emphasized the different functions of local government units, familiarity with the basic legislation governing their operations, and the relevant party resolutions. General management skills, training in policy analysis, and a learning environment geared to participant involvement were absent, as were case studies and training in problem-solving or information-processing techniques.[166]

A review of other outlines for administrative training programs reinforces the impression that the Moscow guidelines are in no way atypical. In 1967 and 1973, the "peoples' universities" (which specialize in continuing education on a broad scale) prepared outlines and curriculum materials for in-service programs run by their faculties of Soviet state development.[167] The 1967 variant provided for a year-long program of 64 two-hour lectures, meeting weekly or slightly more often. The legal aspects of local administration provided the focus for 25 of the sessions while 14 were to be devoted to an analysis of actual administrative operations.[168] Like their predecessors, the 1973 materials also emphasized the formal rights and responsibilities of departments, plus their political-ideological goals. There was no mention of "administrative science" per se and no effort to utilize case studies or other modes of problem solving as part of the training.[169] Examination of one of the special textbooks prepared for these courses again reveals a preoccupation with conceptual clarification abstract theorizing and the personal traits of the "good administrator."[170] The picture is reproduced once again in a comprehensive compendium of 15 "model course outlines" for administrative education that were prepared by the interdepartmental Institute for Raising Officials' Qualifications, which operates under the auspices of the republic government in Latvia.[171] The principles of "scientific communism" and Lenin's pronouncements regarding personnel policy take precedence over that segment of the course entitled "Sociological, Social Psychological and Legal Methods in Staff Work."[172]

The actual impact of these limited efforts are difficult to assess. But apparently their acceptance has not been unimpeded or noticeably widespread. In 1970 the Leningrad city soviet candidly observed that its efforts to provide administrative training for its staff had not met with unqualified success.[173] Some personnel dropped out of the courses very quickly or else registered and never appeared. The courses themselves did not distinguish the varying kinds of educational qualifications administrators might already possess. Moreover, the program's limited capacity to process trainees rendered all projections of a five-year cycle for systematic retraining totally unrealistic. Department heads apparently saw little value in the courses from the perspective of improved staff performance. Hence, they frequently refused to grant release-time privileges or to alter work schedules to make attendance possible.[174]

On a national scale, it appears that retraining programs still exercise a very modest reach. The absence of any laudatory statistics in the literature on administrative education is itself indicative of the limited scale of such programs—and perhaps also demonstrates a lack of high-level support. Uncorroborated claims—such as those advanced for Latvia that "all city officials in the republic have undergone extensive retraining"—must be treated with extreme caution.[175] Of the total of 19,000 individuals who passed through the administration courses of Moscow's higher party school between 1966 and 1971, only a little over 2,000 were drawn from the ranks of government personnel.[176] As of 1969, this school enrolled only 280 state administrators as students, and most of these were drawn from the ranks of province- or region-level staffs.[177] The in-house "short courses" run by the local soviets themselves have undoubtedly affected the careers of a far larger number of city employees (15,000 in 1969). But serious questions about the substance of such courses and the validity of these statistics remain to be answered.[178] Soviet observers themselves have commented on the absence of planning, sequencing, and quality control in these programs, thus heightening our suspicion that professional training remains more a Potemkin village than a real effort to strengthen the information dimension of urban management in the USSR.[179]

Perhaps the explanation of the still primitive state of professional education for urban management in the USSR lies partly with time. The commitment to administrative professionalism is still relatively new in the Soviet Union and has barely been extended to sustained efforts to develop programs for generalist education in urban management. We have seen in the U.S. case, however, that large strides can be taken both quickly and effectively in a short period of time. In the Soviet case, much of the responsibility for the relatively retarded state of professional education must be laid at the door of Khrushchev's now-discredited efforts to replace a full-time, professionally qualified, paid administrative staff with a bureaucracy of cooks and chimney sweeps. This was an idea that Lenin briefly considered—and then quickly discarded in the halycon days of 1917.[180]

Thus, we return to our starting point. At least in the foreseeable future, the generation of information within urban bureaucracies and the skills brought to bear on urban problem solving will continue to depend on the kinds of personnel trained under a system already in place. Innovations—in the form of new analytic tools, the use of automated information systems, and the creation of new kinds of personnel—are instituted through highly centralized modes and then only in a few, select cities. Methods of citizen access provide only limited information of a participatory nature and are not a source of institutional innovation. Finally, urban administrators, trained much like their predecessors, bring unintegrated, specialist skills into urban bureaucracies even as they face a world beset by managerial rather than administrative problems.

NOTES

1. What constitutes "reliability" may vary. In one view, the first requirement for sociological information is that it be based on a "class approach." V. G. Afanasyev, *The Scientific and Technological Revolution—Its Impact on Management and Education* (Moscow: Progress, 1975), p. 184.

2. Erik P. Hoffmann, "Soviet Information Processing: Recent Theory and Experience," *Soviet Union* 2 (1975): 39.

3. Some of these alternatives are discussed in Afanasyev, op. cit., chap. 7; and Main Scientific Research Computer Center of the Moscow City Soviet Executive Committee, *Ex-*

perimental Development of Automated City Management Systems for the City of Leningrad, Preliminary report on scientific research performed in accordance with the Government Agreement of 1972 for Scientific and Technological Cooperation between the USSR and USA, Topic no. 3, Project no. 2 (New York: Columbia University, Graduate School of Business, Center for Government Studies, November 1975), p. 93.

4. On administrative accountability and links between bureaucracies and the rest of society, see E. Katz and B. Danet, "Introduction: Bureaucracy as a Problem for Sociology and Society," in *Bureaucracy and the Public: A Reader in Official-Client Relations,* ed. E. Katz and B. Danet (New York: Basic Books, 1973), pp. 3-4. See also Amitai Etzioni, *A Comparative Analysis of Complex Organizations* (New York: Free Press, 1961), pp. 3-10, 71-88. On rewarding citizen input with shifts in government outputs, see Frank S. Levy, Arnold J. Meltsner, and Aaron Wildavsky, *Urban Outcomes: Schools, Streets, and Libraries* (Berkeley: University of California Press, 1974), introduction and chap. 2.

5. For public opinion and public needs as components of self-regulating urban systems, see Kiev NIIP Gradostroitel'stva, *Sotsial'nye osnovy razvitiia gorodov (sotsial'nye problemy rasseleniia)* (Moscow: Stroizdat, 1975), p. 5. See also Katz and Danet, op. cit., pp. 8-9.

6. Anthony J. Catanese, *Scientific Methods of Urban Analysis* (Urbana: University of Illinois Press, 1972), p. 296.

7. *Automated Systems for Leningrad,* p. 19.

8. Robert J. Osborn, *Soviet Social Policies: Welfare, Equality, and Community* (Homewood, Ill.: Dorsey Press, 1970), p. 194.

9. Maurice Hookham, "Introduction," in *Town, Country and People,* ed. G. V. Osipov (London: Tavistock, 1969), p. 9.

10. Afanasyev, op. cit., p. 220.

11. Hoffmann, "Soviet Information Processing," p. 24.

12. Author's notes of interview at Central Scientific Research and Design Institute for City Construction (TsNIIP gradostroitel'stva), Moscow, June 1977 (hereafter cited as TsNIIP). On some special information needs of the city seen as a unique environment, see *Automated Systems for Leningrad,* pp. 5-6.

13. Kenneth Kraemer et al., *Integrated Municipal Information Systems: The Use of the Computer in Local Government* (New York: Praeger, 1974), p. 4. For similar problems in master planning in the United States, see Melville C. Branch, "Delusions and Diffusions of City Planning in the United States," *Management Science* 16 (August 1970): B717.

14. TsNIIP, June 1977. For applications of *Lenproekt's* transportation model, see *Automated Systems for Leningrad,* p. 56.

15. TsNIIP, June 1977.

16. Ibid.; and Catanese, op. cit., p. 18.

17. *Automated Systems for Leningrad,* p. 20. A potential problem stemming from reliance on mathematical modeling for urban management has been suggested: "excessive confidence." Furthermore, centralized planning could permit an erroneous algorithm to pervade the system. John A. Kaiser, "The Use of Computer Systems by Local Governments" (New York: Columbia University, Graduate School of Business, Center for Government Studies), p. 11. Reprint of paper presented at the Fourteenth Annual Conference of the Urban and Regional Information Systems Association, August-September 1976.

18. For denials of the impact of analytic tools, see E. G. Chistiakov and A. K. Semenov, *Balansovye modeli khoziaistva goroda* (Moscow: Ekonomika, 1977), p. 28; and author's notes of discussions at TsNIIP, Moscow, June 1977. For confirmation, see P. N. Tkachenko et al., *A Control System for the Implementation of Decisions of the Moscow City Soviet Executive Committee* (New York: Columbia University, Graduate School of Business, Center for Government Studies, March 1975), p. 4. This was originally published in

Gorodskoe khozaiistvo Moskvy (October 1974). See also Main Scientific Research Computer Center of the Moscow City Soviet Executive Committee, *Characteristics of Municipal Data Processing Systems in Moscow*, Research performed in accordance with the Government Agreement of 1972 for Scientific and Technological Cooperation between the USSR and USA, Topic no. 3, Project no. 2 (New York: Columbia University, Graduate School of Business, Center for Government Studies, June 1975), p. 5.

19. *Control System for Moscow*, p. 2.

20. Ibid., p. 4.

21. This effect has been associated with urban problem solving on a global scale. See Thomas L. Blair, *The International Urban Crisis* (St. Albans, Great Britain: Paladin, 1974), p. 141.

22. Hoffmann, "Soviet Information Processing," pp. 46-47; and idem, "The 'Scientific Management of Soviet Society,'" *Problems of Communism* 26 (May 1977): 60.

23. For a brief reference to the USSR Master Scheme of Residential Distribution, complete in 1975, see D. G. Tonsky et al., *Current Trends and National Policy in the Field of Housing, Building and Town Planning in the USSR* (Moscow: TsNIIP zhilishcha, 1976), p. 35. For a report of *Gosplan*'s computer-based planning system, see John E. Austin, "Computer-Aided Planning and Decision-Making in the U.S.S.R.," *Datamation* 23 (December 1977): 71-74.

24. Main Scientific Research Computer Center of the Moscow City Soviet Executive Committee, "Description of the Management System of the City of Moscow," Report on the scientific research performed according to the Government Agreement of 1972 for Scientific and Technological Cooperation between the USSR and USA, Topic no. 3, Project no. 1 (New York: Columbia University, Graduate School of Business, Center for Government Studies, ©1975), p. 97. Uncirculated draft report; Soviet source document unverified by independent research.

25. *Automated Systems for Leningrad*, p. 19.

26. Author's notes of discussions at Main Scientific Research Computer Center of the Moscow City Soviet Executive Committee, June 1977.

27. "Local Government Chief Executives Report Computers Essential," *EDP Weekly*, October 20, 1975, p. 11. For a more complete report, see National League of Cities Research Report, *Municipal Inventory of Business Machines, Computers and Communications Equipment* (Washington, D.C.: National League of Cities, 1974). See also "City Hall Has Mixed Reaction to Computers," *Infosystems* 25 (July 1978): 34. For an examination of the application of analytic tools, techniques, and technologies, see E. E. Cooper, *Management Science (Urban Issues)* 16 (August 1970).

28. The controversy over the quality of the Soviet computer industry (hardware and software) has appeared on the pages of *Datamation* over the last several years. For example, see Donald J. Reifer, "Snapshots of Soviet Computing," *Datamation* 24 (February 1978): 133-38. See also Bohdan O. Szuprowicz, "Riads Solidly Implanted in Comecon Nations," *Computerworld*, July 3, 1978, p. 41. For a critical view of Soviet computer applications and computer trade policies, see Umni Glaz, "The Silicon Curtain," *Computer Decisions* 9 (September 1977): 30-34.

29. Afanasyev, op. cit., p. 210.

30. Ibid., p. 123.

31. Kaiser, op. cit., p. 9.

32. *Automated Systems for Leningrad*, p. 5.

33. Some indications of this development are given in Tim Scannell, "Prestige Symbol No Longer, Russian CPU Gets the Boot," *Computerworld*, March 22, 1978, p. 2.

34. Ibid. It is interesting to note here that New York City's new integrated financial management system is aimed at improving both the audit function and financial decision

making. Steven R. Wrisman, "New York about to Get Integrated Management of City Fiscal Matters," New York *Times*, March 25, 1977, p. B1.

35. "City Hall Has Mixed Reaction to Computers." This source is a report on a national study of computers in cities directed by Kenneth L. Kraemer and undertaken by the Public Policy Research Organization, University of California, Irvine.

36. Cantanese, op. cit., p. 287; Kraemer, *Integrated Municipal Information Systems*, p. 91; and Afanasyev, op. cit., pp. 119-22.

37. *Automated Systems for Leningrad*, p. 44.

38. Ibid., pp. 2, 20.

39. Ibid., p. 60.

40. Kaiser, op. cit., p. 8.

41. *Automated Systems for Leningrad*, p. 54.

42. For an elaborate list of purposes and tasks to which these systems ideally are to be put in city services, see *Characteristics of Data Processing*, chap. 2. For operational automated information systems, see Kaiser, op. cit., p. 7; for a description of the automated housing system (entitled "Exchange") that went into experimental use in November 1975, see *Automated Systems for Leningrad*, pp. 62-63.

43. Ibid., p. 64; and *Management System of Moscow*, p. 97. For a detailed description of the Leningrad system, "Signal," see Tkachenko, op. cit.

44. Information on *AIS trudoustroistvo* is from unpublished documents of the Main Scientific Research Computer Center of the Moscow City Soviet Executive Committee and the publication under its authorship, *Avtomatizirovannaia informatsionnaia sistema "trudoustroistvo"* (Moscow: Pechatnik UIM, 1976), n.p.

45. For some advantages and disadvantages of relying on routine data processing applications in U.S. cities, see Kraemer, *Integrated Municipal Information Systems*, pp. 2-3.

46. National League of Cities Research Report, p. 30.

47. Cantanese, op. cit., p. 297.

48. Ibid., pp. 287, 297.

49. Ibid., p. 307.

50. Ibid., pp. 305-7.

51. National League of Cities Research Report, p. 31.

52. Ibid.

53. *Management System of Moscow*, figures 2, 3.

54. Kaiser, op. cit., p. 5.

55. Ibid., p. 7; *Management Systems of Moscow; Control System for Moscow; Characteristics of Data Processing*; and author's notes of discussions at Main Scientific Research Computer Center of the Moscow City Soviet Executive Committee, June 1977.

56. Kaiser, op. cit., p. 9; *Automated Systems for Leningrad* describes its components. On the need for an integrated citywide system and the unacceptability of overlap, see Main Scientific Research Computer Center of the Moscow City Soviet Executive Committee, *Description of the Standard Methods of Design, Development and Implementation of Large Automated Systems of Data Processing for the Needs of Municipal Managers*, Research performed according to the Government Agreement of 1972 for Scientific and Technological Cooperation between the USSR and USA, Topic no. 3, Project no. 5 (New York: Columbia University, Graduate School of Business, Center for Government Studies, June 1975), p. 97.

57. *Automated Systems for Leningrad*, pp. 40, 42.

58. Ibid., p. 43.

59. Kaiser, op. cit., p. 10.

60. Ibid., p. 40; and Hoffmann, "Soviet Information Processing," p. 43.

61. Kaiser, op. cit., p. 5.

62. Kenneth L. Kraemer and John Leslie King, "A Critique of Federal Involvement in City Information: Part 2," *Government Data Systems* 6 (July-August 1977): 12.

63. Kenneth L. Kraemer and John Leslie King, "In City Information: A Critique of Federal Involvement," *Government Data Systems* 6 (May-June 1977): 35, 38.

64. *Characteristics of Data Processing*, p. 14.

65. Austin, op. cit., p. 71.

66. Tonsky, op. cit., pp. 10-11.

67. Afanasyev, op. cit., p. 129.

68. *Description of Standard Methods.*

69. Amitai Etzioni, "Two Approaches to Organizational Effectiveness: A Critique and a Suggestion," *Administrative Science Quarterly* 5 (1960): 257-78. Talcott Parsons has suggested that the concept of civil service tenure developed in direct response to the extension of the franchise and opportunities for more groups to influence the operations of government. From this perspective, it represents a way for bureaucracies to insulate themselves from client demands. Talcott Parsons, "Components and Types of Formal Organization, in *Comparative Administrative Theory*, ed. Preston P. LeBaron (Seattle: University of Washington Press, 1968), pp. 3-22.

70. R. A. Safarov, "Obshchestvennoe mnenie pri usloviiakh razvitogo sotsializma," *Kommunist* 12 (August 1977): 30-31.

71. Ibid., pp. 34-35.

72. I. A. Azovkin, *Mestnye sovety v sisteme organov vlasti* (Moscow: Izd. Iuridicheskaia literatura, 1971), pp. 162, 163 (n. 1), 264. In 1969 in the RSFSR, there were some 6,000 social councils with approximately 9,000 members.

73. Ibid., p. 164; M. S. Zemlianskii, *Deiatel'nost' raionnogo gorodskogo soveta po rukovodstvu narodnogo obrazovaniia i kul'turno-prosvetitel'noi raboty* (Moscow: Izd. Iuridicheskaia literatura, 1973), pp. 50-52.

74. Arie Lewin and Robert W. Blanning, "The Urban Government Annual Report," in *Improving the Quality of Urban Management*, ed. Willis D. Hawley and David Rogers (Beverly Hills, Calif: Sage, 1976), pp. 67-71. A "sample" public account is presented on pp. 72-77.

75. I. Moskalav, *Sovershenstvovanie deiatel'nosti mestnykh sovetov* (Moscow: Mysl', 1975), p. 73.

76. Ibid., p. 80.

77. Computed on the basis of data from A. T. Leizerov, "Kontrol' izbiratelei," in *Pravovye voprosy upravleniia* (Perm: Permskii gosudarstvennyi universitet, 1973), pp. 41-42.

78. Ibid., pp. 42, 43.

79. Moskalev, op. cit., p. 80.

80. Ibid., p. 81; interviews, law faculty, Moscow State University, 1976.

81. Moskalev, op. cit., p. 82. According to this author, as of 1974 there were "still an insignificant number of executive committees who regularly inform the plenary sessions of the soviets as to whether and to what extent the critical proposals and comments of the deputies [regarding otchyoty] are executed." Ibid., p. 85.

82. *Pravila vnutrennogo trudovogo rasporiadka dlia rabotnikov apparata ispol'nitel'nogo komiteta Moskovskogo oblastnogo soveta*, rotoprint (Moscow: Mosobispolkoma, 1968); *Perspektivnyi plan zaniatii postoianno deistvuiushchego seminara dlia deputatov Tushinskogo raisoveta 15 sozyva no 1975-1977 goda*, rotoprint (Moscow: DOSAAF, 1975).

83. *Spravka a khode vypolneniia kriticheskikh zamechanii i predlozhenii vyskazannykh deputatami 10-13 sessii Mosgorispolkoma*, rotoprint (Moscow: Mosgorispolkoma, 1975); *Perspektivnyi plan raboty Gagarinskogo raionnogo Soveta deputatov trudiashchikhsia na 1976 g.*, rotoprint (Moscow, 1976); *Perspektivnyi plan raboty ispolkoma Oktiabr'skogo raisoveta na 1971*, rotoprint (Vilnius, 1972); *Perspektivnyi plan raboty ispolkoma Rostovskogo oblastnogo soveta na 1971-1972 goda*, rotoprint (Rostov, 1971); *Plan raboty ispolkoma Podol'skogo gorsoveta*, rotoprint (Podol'sk, 1972); *O perspektivnom plane ra-*

boty ispol'nitel'nogo komiteta Khabarovskogo kraevogo soveta na 1971 godu, rotoprint (Khabarovsk, 1971);*Perspektivnyi plan raboty Ussurskogo gorodskogo soveta na 1971 godu*, rotoprint (Ussursk, 1971); *Perspektivnyi plan raboty Sormovskogo raionnogo soveta goroda Gor'kogo*, rotoprint (Gorky, 1971).

84. *Perspektivnyi plan Gagarinskogo soveta.*

85. R. A. Safarov, *Obshchestvennoe mnenie i gosudarstvennoe upravlenie* (Moscow: Izd. Iuridicheskaia literatura, 1975), pp. 233, 297.

86. Interviews, Faculty of Law, Moscow State University, 1976.

87. Ibid. In Moscow, the city soviet meets for one six-hour session every three months, which lasts from 10:00 A.M. until 4:00 P.M. (with a break for lunch).

88. Ibid. Only materials related to departmental implementation of specific party directives are distributed prior to reporting sessions. The standing commissions of the soviet devote most of their time to supervising institutions and organizations subordinate to the city; they spend little time on direct supervision of the departments themselves.

89. *Reshenie o nakazakh izbiratelei: Tushinskii raionnyi sovet* (Moscow: Mosgorispolkom, 1975), pp. 3-4; *Reshenie o nakazakh izbiratelei: Leninskii raion*, rotoprint (Moscow: August 20, 1975), pp. 1-2.

90. *Reshenie Tushinskii*, p. 17; *Reshenie o nakazakh izbiratelei postupivshikh v periode podgotovki k vyboram v Verkhovnyi Sovet RSFSR v iiune 1975 g.* (Moscow: Mosgorispolkoma, 1975); *Meropriiatiia po vypolneniiu zamechanii i predlozhenii, postupivshikh v Mosgorsovet v iiune 1975*, rotoprint (Moscow, 1975).

91. Interview, Faculty of Law, Moscow State University, 1975.

92. Ibid.

93. *Reshenie Tushinskii*, pp. 10-14, 36; *Reshenie Leninskii*, pp. 15-18, 21-24.

94. Calculated on the basis of data in *Reshenie o nakazakh . . . Verkhovnyi Sovet* (N = 300).

95. Interview, Faculty of Law, Moscow State University, 1976.

96. O. K. Zastrozhnaia, "Nekotorye voprosy sovershenstvovaniia kontrolia," in *Problemy nauchnoi organizatsii truda v apparate mestnykh sovetov* (Voronezh: Izd. Voronezhskogo gosudarstvennogo universiteta, 1974), pp. 96-97.

97. *V pomosch' deputatu: zapros deputata mestnogo soveta*, rotoprint (Minsk, 1973), pp. 3, 9, 11.

98. See Leizerov, op. cit., pp. 35-36; and *V pomoshch' deputatu*, p. 16.

99. Zastrozhnaia, op. cit., p. 97.

100. Ibid., p. 1.

101. Ibid., p. 16.

102. Ibid., p. 6.

103. Ibid., p. 15 (table 1).

104. Ibid., p. 14.

105. V. M. Vinogradov, "Ob opyte organizatsii i metodike provedeniia sotsissledovaniia," *Voprosy teorii i praktiki Sovetskogo gosudarstvovedeniia: Trudy, Seriia iuridicheskaia* (Irkutsk) 77 (1970): 63-72 (tables 1-3). The data were collected in 1967 for the cities of Blagoveshchenskii, Chita, Irkutsk, Angarsk, and Krasnoyarsk. On the United States see, for example, Lester Milbraith, *Political Participation* (Chicago: Rand McNally, 1965); Norman H. Nie, G. Bingham Powell, Jr., and Kenneth Prewitt, "Social Structure and Political Participation II," *American Political Science Review* 63 (September 1969): 808-28.

106. *V pomoshch' deputatu*, p. 12.

107. Leizerov, op. cit., pp. 35-36.

108. *V pomoshch' deputatu*, p. 6.

109. Ibid., pp. 6-7. The Minsk province data for 1971-73 show 27 inquiries in all, less than one per urban soviet.

110. Ibid., p. 11.

111. Ibid., p. 17.

112. Ibid., p. 18.

113. On the use of social surveys and the problems encountered, see Safarov, *Obshchestvennoe mnenie*, p. 138. See also note 115, below.

114. Ibid., p. 100.

115. Ibid., p. 115. Safarov's own survey revealed that social surveys were the least favored mode of citizen feedback for administrator respondents. Improved legal guarantees and statutory guidelines were the most favored. See pp. 109-10.

116. Ibid., pp. 113 (n. 2), 126 (n. 2).

117. Ibid., p. 155.

118. Ibid., p. 159. In the survey, 32.1 percent of administrators felt that public needs and administrative perceptions of problems "always corresponded," and 12.4 percent had "no opinion." The rest replied "occasionally correspond."

119. Ibid., p. 133. Only 17.1 percent of the administrator respondents expressed unconditional support for citizen inputs (for example, "citizen advice and recommendations are necessary even in the absence of urgent problems").

120. Ibid., p. 121. Neither the size of the N nor the raw results are presented.

121. Ibid., p. 123.

122. "Citizen Participation and Local Government in Europe and the United States," *Studies in Comparative Local Government* 5 (Winter 1971): 45; John C. Bollens and Henry J. Schmandt, *The Metropolis: Its People, Politics and Economic Life*, 2d ed. (New York: Harper & Row, 1970), p. 46.

123. This is not to say, however, that Soviet political socialization techniques have not produced a genuine concern for an orientation toward the collective rather than the individual in daily life situations. See Yuri Bronfenbrenner, *Two Worlds of Childhood: USA and USSR* (New York: Russell Sage Foundation, 1970), pp. 15-91.

124. Bollens and Schmandt, op. cit., p. 85; G. Almond and S. Verba, *The Civic Culture: Political Attitudes and Democracy in Five Nations* (Boston: Little, Brown and Co., 1965).

125. Bollens and Schmandt, op. cit., p. 86; Robert Dahl, *After the Revolution: Authority in a Good Society* (New Haven, Conn.: Yale University Press, 1970), pp. 40-56.

126. For alternative interpretations of citizen participation in the Soviet Union, see Jerry F. Hough, "Political Participation in the Soviet Union," *Soviet Studies* 28 (January 1976): 3-20; and T. H. Rigby, "Hough on Political Participation in the Soviet Union," *Soviet Studies* 28 (April 1976): 257-61.

127. On the Western experience, see Tony Eddison, *Local Government Management and Corporate Planning* (New York: Barnes and Noble, 1973), pp. 126-39.

128. This point is made in a verbal exchange in 1977 between the head of the planning department of Los Angeles and the head of the planning commission and chief architect in Tallin, Estonia. In response to the first official's question regarding the role of Estonian citizens in the planning of the Blossom Hills housing complex outside the city, both the architect and the planning commission head admitted that there had been opposition from local residents regarding the erection of a new high-rise, high density complex. But while members of the Tallin city government attended meetings and listened to these complaints, the complex was built anyway according to the original plans.

129. James F. Guyot, "How Do We Know Which Training Is Good Medicine for Managers," *Public Administration Review* (hereafter *PAR*) 37 (November-December 1977): 698.

130. Ibid., pp. 698-99.

131. Ibid., pp. 702-4; Frederick C. Mosher, "End-Product Objectives of Pre-Entry Professional Education for Urban Administrators and Their Implications for Curriculum Focus,"

in *Education for Urban Administration*, ed. Frederic N. Cleaveland (Philadelphia: American Academy of Political and Social Science, 1973), pp. 151-52. See also *Strengthening Public Management in the Intergovernmental System: A Report for the OMB* (Washington, D.C.: U.S. Government Printing Office, 1975).

132. Robert F. Wilcox, "Commentaries on the Davy Paper," in Cleaveland, op. cit., p. 223. For a more recent evaluation drawing similar conclusions, see Frank Thompson, "Is University Training Practical? Perspectives of Public Personnel Officials," *PAR* 38 (January-February 1978): 82-83.

133. Nicolas Henry, *Public Administration and Public Affairs* (Englewood Cliffs, N.J.: Prentice-Hall, 1975), p. 202.

134. Lynn S. Miller and Laurence Rutter, "Strengthening the Quality of Urban Management Education: A Symposium," *PAR* 37 (September-October 1977): 568-69; Mel D. Powell, "Recommendations for Strengthening Urban Management Education and ICMA/ NASPAA Cooperation," *PAR* 37 (September-October 1977): 578 (table 1). See also Raymond A. Shapek, "Breaking Barriers: Urban Managers and Academics Working Together," *PAR* 37 (September-October 1977): 583-85.

135. A. Lee Fritschler and A. J. Mackleprang, "Graduate Education in Public Affairs/ Public Administration: Results of 1975 Survey," *PAR* 37 (September-October 1977): 494.

136. Ibid., p. 492. The number of degrees awarded rose 56 percent over 1973; state and local government absorbed 21 percent of the graduates of such programs.

137. Ibid., p. 489.

138. Ibid., p. 491. In core course requirements, 50 percent of the programs demanded organization theory, 48 percent courses in program management, 43 percent public policy training, 39 percent education in public finance, and 38 percent quantitative methods beyond elementary statistics.

139. Stephen Sternheimer, "Administration and Political Development: An Inquiry into the Tsarist and Soviet Experiences" (Ph.D. diss., University of Chicago, 1974), pp. 276-87, 291-99; Brian Chapman, *The Profession of Government: The Public Service in Europe* (London: George Allen and Unwin, 1959), pp. 28-29, 108-9, 183-84, 190-91; Carl Friedrich, "The Continental Tradition of Training Administrators in Law and Jurisprudence," *Journal of Modern History* 11 (March 1939): 130-32, 134-35, 138.

140. Robert F. Miller, "The Scientific-Technical Revolution and the Soviet Administrative Debate," in *The Dynamics of Soviet Politics*, ed. Paul Cocks et al. (Cambridge, Mass.: Harvard University Press, 1976), pp. 142-44.

141. George A. Brinkley, "Khrushchev Remembered: On the Theory of Soviet Statehood," *Soviet Studies* 24 (January 1973): 387-401.

142. E. V. Rudkovskaia, "Partiinoe rukovodstvo deiatel'nosti sovetov" (Master's thesis, Leningrad State University, 1975), p. 154.

143. A. S. Bezmat'ev, "Sovershenstvovanie partiinogo rukovodstva mestnym sovetam deputatov trudiashchikhsia na etape razvernutogo kommunisticheskogo stroi.'el'stva (1961-67); na materialakh Rostovskoi oblastnoi partiinoi organizatsii" (Master's thesis, Rostov State University, 1971), pp. 207, 210, 213.

144. M. I. Bannykh, *Uchastie obshchestvennosti v deiatel'nosti ispolkomov mestnykh sovetov* (Moscow: Izd. Iuridicheskaia literatura, 1972), p. 33.

145. Based on calculations from ibid., pp. 38-39, 53; and *RSFSR: Administrativnye-territorial'nye deleniia za 1974* (Moscow: Statistika, 1974), p. 7.

146. Bannykh, op. cit., p. 33.

147. Ibid., p. 32. Most of the enabling statutes pertaining to nonprofessional administrators were promulgated during 1963-64, and little new policy is evident after Khrushchev's fall in 1964. Ibid., p. 57 (n. 1).

148. Ibid., pp. 128-32.

149. On the impact of the "scientific-technical revolution," see Miller, op. cit., pp. 144-49, 152.

150. Interviews, Faculty of Law, Moscow State University, 1976; interviews, Institute of Philosophy, Academy of Sciences, USSR (Leningrad), 1976.

151. Bennykh, op. cit., p. 55.

152. Ibid., pp. 51, 59, 71, 72; interviews, Faculty of Law, Moscow State University, 1976. In Leningrad, the personnel department of the city soviet recruits its new inspectors from the ranks of those already serving as volunteers in many cases. Interview, Department of Personnel, Leningrad City Soviet, 1975.

153. Bannykh, op. cit., pp. 56-57.

154. Interview, Faculty of Law, Moscow State University, 1976.

155. On manpower planning, see *Planning of Manpower in the Soviet Union* (Moscow: Progress, 1975), pp. 37-38.

156. Interviews, Institute of State and Law, Academy of Sciences, USSR, 1976.

157. F. G. Apostol, "Partiinoe rukovodstvo mestnym sovetam v razvitom sotsialisticheskom obshchestve" (Master's thesis, Moscow State University, 1973), p. 67.

158. I. A. Rozenbaum, "O spetsial'noi podgotovke upravlensheskikh kadrov," *Sovetskoe gosudarstvo i pravo* 1 (1976): 55.

159. Ibid.; and interviews, Faculty of Law, Leningrad State University, 1975-76.

160. Interviews, Institute of State and Law, Academy of Sciences, USSR, 1976, and Faculty of Law, Moscow State University, 1976.

161. E. K. Tsiukina, "Problemy sovershenstvovaniia apparata," in *Problemy nauchnoi organizatsii truda v apparate*, ed. V. S. Osnovin (Voronezh: Izd. Voronezhskogo gosudarstvennogo universiteta, 1974), pp. 62-64.

162. Ibid.

163. Ibid., pp. 57-58.

164. Interviews, Voznesenskii Financial-Economics Institute, Leningrad. Conversations with the director revealed that the institute services only *Gosplan* employees and heads of departments of finance at the republic and provincial levels.

165. Rozenbaum, in *Sovetskoe gosudarstvo i pravo*, p. 59.

166. *Uchebnyi plan kursov perepodgotovki rukovodiashchikh partiinykh i sovetskikh kadrov* (Moscow: Vyshaia partiinaia shkola pri KPSS, 1974), inter alia. By contrast, recent discussions of urban management training in Western Europe stress the importance of individualized training programs, participant involvement, and extensive reliance on practitioners as instructors. Stig Askenborn, "Some Experience from Local Government Management Courses," *Studies in Comparative Local Government* 12 (Summer 1973): 34-37.

167. While the "peoples' universities" (or Evening Universities of Marxism-Leninism) do not confer a degree, they remain important as a major channel for disseminating political information and knowledge. See Ellen Mickiewicz, *Soviet Political Schools: The Communist Party Adult Instruction System* (New Haven, Conn.: Yale University Press, 1967), pp. 51-61.

168. *Primernyi uchebno-tematicheskii plan i programma fakul'tetov sovetskogo stroitel'stva narodnykh universitetov pravovykh znanii* (Moscow: Izd. Znanie, 1967).

169. *Programma po osnovam sovetskogo gosudarstvennogo stroitel'stva i prava (dlia rabotnikov ispolkomov gorodskikh, sel'skikh, i poselkovykh sovetov Latviiskoi SSR)* (Riga: Izd. Mezhotraslevogo instituta povysheniia kvalifikatsii, 1974). Of the 292 lecture hours scheduled, 10 were assigned to straight political indoctrination, 88 to legislation relating to various policy areas, 30 to a structural analysis of Soviet government, 24 to techniques of office management, and 68 to the history and operations of local soviets.

170. V. A. Dinevich, *Nauchnye osnovy upravleniia v gosudarstvennom apparate: uchebnoe posobie* (Riga: Izd. Mezhotraslevogo instituta povysheniia kvalifikatsii, 1971), pp. 3, 11-38, 58-62.

171. *Sbornik primernykh uchebnykh planov kafedr i fakul'tetov sovetskogo stroitel'-stva i prava*, rotoprint (Riga: Mezhotraslevogo instituta, 1970), pp. 132-39.

172. Ibid., pp. 9-10, 18, 31-36.

173. *Biulleten' ispolkoma Leningradskogo soveta deputatov trudiashchikhsia*, no. 12 (June 1970), pp. 1-13. At the end of 1968, Leningrad formally instituted training for some 5,000 city employees of all descriptions. Rudkovskaia, op. cit., p. 9.

174. Many of the programs have a distinct "POSDCORB" flavor reminiscent of training in the "principles of scientific management" in vogue in the United States during the 1920s and 1930s. See, for example, P. G. Ablakova, "Deiatel'nost' KPSS po dal'neishemu povysheniiu roli mestnykh sovetov" (Master's thesis, Kazakhstan State University, 1969), pp. 178-79.

175. Iu. Ruden, "Nauchnaia organizatsiia truda i apparat," in *Rabota sovetov na uroven' novykh zadach* (Moscow: *Izvestiia*, 1973), p. 233; P. Pigalev, "Zakonodatel'stvo o sovetakh," in ibid., pp. 264-81.

176. According to Rudkovskaia (op cit., pp. 18-19), 14,576 were party *apparatchiki*, 834 *Komsomol* officials, 1,084 middle-level executives concerned with mass media, and 223 trade union officials.

177. I. Azovkin, *Mestnye sovety v sisteme organov vlasti* (Moscow: Izd. Iuridicheskai literatura, 1971), p. 160 (n. 1). Given that there are 3,000 chairmen of *raion*-level executive committees alone, plus at least 1,000 province-level department heads, the Higher Party School at best instructed only 7 percent of the top strata of local officialdom.

178. Ibid. In Moldavia, preentry training apparently meant mostly one-day conferences and seminars. Apostol, op. cit., p. 71.

179. This is true despite the much-touted claim that all higher party schools combined enrolled a total of some 190,000 individuals in 1970 in "special courses for raising qualifications." Most of these individuals returned to careers in party or trade union work and did not enter state administrative ranks. Ibid., pp. 67, 71; interviews, Faculty of Law, Leningrad State University, 1975.

180. Stephen Sternheimer, "The Origins of Soviet Administrative Science" (Paper delivered at the Second Conference on Russian and Soviet Officialdom, Kennan Institute, Washington, D.C., 1976).

7

CONCLUSION

Like the study of cities more generally, our comparative study of urban management has taken as its starting point the assumption that various facets of the urban environment can be manipulated and reordered to make the urban habitat more desirable. Differences in ideology, social structure, and economic organization have not insulated the "socialist" city entirely from those pressures created by urban growth in other advanced industrial societies. Nor have some 60 years of "building socialism and communism" precluded such urban problems as increasing functional complexity, heightened interdependencies, and program ineffectiveness in Soviet cities. These pressures and problems underscore the importance both of urban management and its study cross-nationally. To put the matter somewhat differently, patterns of contemporary urban life in the USSR and United States accentuate the importance of policy implementation's organizational dimensions and the administrative factors that shape city government outputs and outcomes.

To understand how Soviet cities are governed, we have argued, it is not sufficient to describe the dynamics of Soviet city politics. A perspective on this problem, which is simultaneously analytic and projective, has led us to investigate in some detail such issues as resource management, program management, and policy management as they presently operate in Soviet and U.S. cities. We have sought to determine whether the Soviet urban picture, when viewed along the three dimensions just stated, is more managerial or more administrative in terms of a net assessment of the factors involved. These factors include culturally defined images that shape the thinking of decision makers, the human, technological, and financial resources at their disposal, and the organization of work roles and structures for coordination. Planning mechanisms plus the informational tools used in policy formulation and problem solving complete the catalog. The analysis has demonstrated that, in the contemporary urban world, how cities are to be governed depends in large part on how they are managed.

Against the backdrop these assumptions provide, our study of Soviet urban bureaucracies and their operations has pursued two main avenues of inquiry. The first is defined by a single, straightforward question: do current practices in Soviet city bureaucracies more closely approximate the "traditional" mode of urban administration, or do they signal a move in the direction of what in the Introduction is described as management transformation? More concretely, the study has explored to what extent—and why— administrative practices in Soviet cities are still characterized by fragmented resources, ill-coordinated chains of command, insufficient numbers of administrative professionals, and a sectoral approach to planning and problem solving. Alternately, it has examined the scope and methods whereby Soviet city officials apply sophisticated information gathering techniques, client analysis, and resource allocation according to need and equity considerations.

This line of inquiry immediately raised a second question, namely, what does the future hold? Given high levels of interdependency between local and national policies in the contemporary world, the answer to this question invariably takes on macro- as well as microanalytic significance. In particular, the study has probed ways in which current and emerging administrative practices might move Soviet urban life in the direction of either the "populist city" or "technocratic city." The answers provided by the previous chapters are summarized and integrated below.

The investigation of the cultural and value parameters that, we hypothesized, shape Soviet urban policy and city government operations demonstrated that Soviet conceptions of the city have deep roots in Russian traditions and Russian history. Although we started with the assumption that Marxist ideology and Marxist-Leninist prescriptions for the "socialist city" would play a dominant role in the creation of national urban policies after the Revolution, our analysis has shown something quite different. The investigation suggests that the values inherent in the "city of reason" of eighteenth century rationalism influenced approaches to urban development and administration under tsars and commissars alike. In the later era, these values were reinforced by the image of the industrial city as the "city of progress," which Marxism projects. After 1917, Russia's rulers inherited a generally positive view of the city and urban life, a view that was underscored by a newly found faith in their ability to shape and manipulate urban life according to specific social and economic goals. This legacy continues to inform contemporary Soviet thinking. Marxism, meanwhile, continues to provide a general framework for debate and discussion rather than a focused picture of a clearly delineated urban future for Soviet decision makers.

In the absence of direct evidence regarding mass perspectives on urban life or views of the "city" in the Soviet Union, our analysis relied on the picture provided by the demographic data. Here, we found that faith in the urban life as the "good life" is evidenced most dramatically by the way Soviet citizens vote with their feet. The fact that Soviet urbanization rates have consistently stood higher than the world average coupled with the pronounced preference for large cities suggests that in popular thinking as well as to the official mind urban life represents the most desirable future. At the same time, such increases in city size and spatial concentration, when combined with the newness of the urban environment for many residents, have meant that the pressures for urban management and service delivery have increased continually.

Our study of the structural and organizational arrangements that define the institutional limits within which Soviet city bureaucrats operate has revealed forces that both facilitate and oppose any movement toward increased urban management. The data suggest that coordination is both necessary and difficult, especially in a setting still dominated by fragmented resources and authority, rather rigid vertical lines of subordination, and inadequate mechanisms for horizontal accountability. But we also found that the Communist party works to counterbalance these tendencies. Its hold over city administration has, if anything, grown rather than diminished over the course of the past decade or so. It is the political script—rather than the bureaucratic stage or its props—that inclines Soviet administrative personnel to behave as managers rather than as classical bureaucrats. At the same time, the fact that many Soviet public officials find themselves operating simultaneously both as members of the orchestra in their administrative roles and as conductors in their political roles means that the managerial thrust of the party's operations always remains muted.

The capacity for urban management is a function not only of values and the management environment but also of the resources an urban bureaucracy commands. As a component of urban management, resource management demands, first, personnel who are managerially as well as technically proficient, who are adequate in number, properly rewarded, and distributed among cities according to the kinds of management problems they confront. Here, our investigation suggests, movement away from urban administration toward urban management is still quite limited.

Our study of recruitment procedures and subsequent career patterns among top administrative officials in Soviet "great cities," large, medium, and small cities, and within urban districts suggests that merit and politically ascriptive criteria are not always successfully combined. Indeed, the recruitment balance shifts decisively in favor of age, political tenure, and administrative seniority as one moves up the national ladder of cities. The largest cities—which, we hypothesized, were likely to experience the most pressing need for urban management—were not noted for managerial skills among their officials. Nor has the zigzag pattern of career development involving crossover among party, economic, and local government hierarchies really taken hold. Personnel turnover remains a problem even in the most important cities and among those most in need of management skills in urban administration. In Moscow, the "model Communist city" of the future, most of the city bureaucracy's "new blood" remains old blood, both physiologically and in terms of the political generation to which these urban bureaucrats belong.

In light of such facts, it seems probable that at the local level political conservatism will continue to march hand in hand with rising levels of technical proficiency. Few signs of change in the immediate future are evident. Moreover, there is some evidence, again based primarily on the data for Moscow city administration as a whole, that technically modernizing as well as politically conserving tendencies operate for the staff as well as for top-ranking officials and agency chiefs.

Just as there is little to suggest any uniform direction of change for personnel resources in Soviet cities, so there is little to support any claim that financial resources and practices contribute to the spread of urban management in the Soviet Union. Large cities may lack the types of personnel needed for managerial transformation, but they enjoy a relatively advantageous financial position. In fact, they command more than their share of budgetary expenditures calculated on a per capita basis. As a result, the rich are rewarded, while the poorer, smaller, non-Russian cities undergo a relative decline. This means a steadily widening gap in areas such as consumer services, housing, transportation networks, and other urban outputs. This gap makes the largest, oldest, and most populous cities the most attractive to rural migrants and economic planners alike; this situation promises to aggravate rather than alleviate the kinds of management problems cities in the RSFSR and large cities elsewhere already confront. One example is the cost changes that are largely beyond the control of city budgets and city officials. The continued importance of off-budget resources in areas such as housing, industrial construction, and wages for some personnel further impedes the development of integrated planning and contributes to the differential provision of development opportunities.

What, then, can we conclude about the impact of current Soviet budgetary practice on resource management? On the credit side of the ledger, we find that the generation and allocation of monies for cities remain in the hands of national policy makers, thereby creating the potential for the kinds of concentration, coordination, and planned allocations urban management requires. This same feature, however, has implications for the debit column as well. The allocation processes themselves and the high level at which resources are centralized diminish local autonomy. In this way, as we pointed out in the Introduction, one of the major pressures for urban management disappears. Insofar as routine bureaucratic allocation processes do not allow for or encourage coordination at the point of implementation—the city itself—the managerial thrust of allocations in the urban sector remains negligible. Further, Soviet experiences spotlight the fact that management transformation demands determination not only of what is required but also of how much. In sum, centralization is not an adequate substitute for concentration and coordination.

In the area of planning, we find that the movement to urban social planning, while much heralded by planning specialists and political leaders in the early 1970s, has promised more than it has delivered. Drawing upon a systems approach to urban problem solving, social planning was designed to operational-ize the canons of "good" resource management, "good" policy management, and "good" program management in a number of ways. First, resources were to be brought into balance with needs, both in terms of the city's labor force re-quirements and in terms of the demand for housing, consumer services, and pub-lic facilities. Second, the plans themselves were to deal with programs rather than policies, with measures addressed to problems from a social and economic rather than merely an agency perspective. Finally, the importance the planners attached to sociological investigations, interdependencies among social and eco-nomic factors, and information processing imparted a managerial thrust to the entire concept.

A closer inquiry, however, has revealed that many of these goals have been realized only on the drawing board—or on the pages of monographs and journals. There are still no "universal social indicators" that would permit the kinds of calculations across the many dimensions of Soviet urban life that operational plans demand. The way in which social plan balances are still "adjusted" to coor-dinate with interbranch balances of the city's economic plan testifies to the con-tinued subordination of social planning to sectoral planning. The fact remains that many of these "social plans" are merely the old economic plans relabeled. Others simply total the indicators of all enterprises located within the city while ignoring the urban elements. Here, as in housing and automated information sys-tems, the goals of national policy are transformed into uniform standards. Needs assessment and subcommunity analysis, despite much fanfare, seem to have won little real acceptance.

The impact of social planning also remains marginal in terms of its scope. Only 33 of the more than 2,000 jurisdictions officially designated as "cities" currently have social plans of any sort. When we remember that there are 13 "great cities" that, by definition, would require social planning as a vital com-ponent of urban management, and an additional 227 cities with 100,000 popula-tion or over, the contribution of Soviet urban social planning to the spread of ur-ban management appears all the more limited.

Urban management also requires improved techniques and methods in the area of policy management. Accordingly, management transformation in this area requires new kinds of information, new methods of information processing and feedback, the use of various analytic and technical tools, and a commitment to considerations of cost effectiveness and program effectiveness. In the area of new technology and automated urban information systems in particular, in-field developments are still weaker than formal assurances and emerging commitments. The retraining of bureaucrats with any eye to developing both a more manage-rial orientation toward problem solving as well as familiarity with these tools and technologies still leaves much undone. Existing mechanisms for citizen access and administrative accountability in city government operations remain more formal than operative and are quite limited in their scope. Moreover, the feedback mechanisms that do exist are used far too sporadically to make up for the lack of either impact evaluation (which is absent from Soviet budgetary procedures) or citizen needs assessment (which social planning ignores). Equally important, Soviet survey research indicates that local administrators have little sympathy with the idea of participatory planning and citizen involvement in administrative decision making. This remains an obstacle that "new" methods of training or information gathering have not squarely confronted.

When we view the question of policy management technology through the use of computers as an urban management tool, we find that computer application in Soviet cities is still quite restricted. Much like financial resources, computer systems are distributed unevenly among cities. Several automated control systems designed to monitor timely execution of the local city soviet's decisions (or, at least, *reports* of such execution) are in operation. Automated information systems also are applied to sectors such as urban transit, housing, and the monitoring of citizen complaints. In sum, developments in this area point in the direction of massive, centralized systems in a few preferred cities.

This brings us to our second avenue of inquiry: the examination of a set of general hypotheses linking the emergence of urban management to certain kinds of changes in urban life. Having decided on urban management as a dependent variable that is both interesting and susceptible to empirical investigation, we considered the kinds of independent variables that are closely associated with urban management transformation. Again, the site of our investigation was primarily the Soviet Union, with U.S. experiences balancing interpretations and suggesting avenues of inquiry.

While there is some evidence to suggest, as we hypothesized, that the amount of management transformation in any city will vary with the *unit autonomy* within a system, the Soviet data yield inconclusive results. Cities at the top—the most autonomous by virtue of their administrative rank—do have more financial resources and better educated and more politically committed administrative personnel. They are more likely to have or to receive in the near future automated information systems, and it is in these cities where we see a wider, more substantive use of social planning techniques. These preferred cities include the great cities of Leningrad and Moscow. By the same token, however, the bureaucracies in these cities are still far from being truly managerial in many respects: the content of members' education and training, their career patterns, their ability to effect program coordination, and their ability to transform budget resources into satisfactory government outputs and urban outcomes.

In many respects this conclusion confirms one of the suspicions voiced earlier in the study, namely, that in cross-national comparisons the fragmentation of resources within urban systems (which are otherwise dissimilar) will cancel the controlling influence of the other variables. The failure of Soviet cities to achieve managerial transformation appears a function of strong and persistent institutional habits and interests. These inhibit concentration despite a high level of centralization. There is no reason to suppose that members of existing departments, boards, and ministries have not taken up the political cudgels at their command in defense of more traditional kinds of urban administrative arrangements. Moreover, the aging process has undoubtedly affected Soviet administrative organizations, as it has their personnel. This has probably given rise to the familiar situation in which organizational survival has proved compatible with ongoing technical and technological adaptation in Soviet city administration.

Social planning has yet to find a way to overcome the fragmentation of resources and authority that continues to shape the Soviet urban environment. Indeed, getting information from "uncle" (another ministry, agency, or sector) in many cases proves as difficult for the urban social planner as does getting money or materials for the urban decision maker. These are longstanding problems in the urban environment, and social planning appears unable to eliminate them.

Thus, Soviet experience does provide strong support for the proposition that unit fragmentation and managerial transformation of city bureaucracies vary inversely. To the extent that urban bureaucracies in cities of various types in the USSR still resemble fractured mirrors—and our research indicates that this is very much the case—they remain strongly resistant to managerial transformation. From this perspective, the concentration of control over urban resources at the national level appears to exercise a negative effect in the local setting as much as it enhances coordination for national urban policy.

Our research has also revealed that increases in unit size and unit complexity have become increasingly dominant features of the Soviet urban landscape, creating real pressures for urban management transformation. The largest, oldest, and most economically diversified cities figure most prominently in this process. But here, as in the case of unit autonomy, the study suggests that size and complexity have made only a limited contribution to a decisive transformation from urban administration to urban management. For example, core cities of large metropolitan areas in the USSR command the largest per capita budget expenditures. However, their budgets remain those of the line-item type rather than a program management type; significant portions of these cities' financial resources remain largely uncoordinated with budget allocations. Similarly, while their personnel resources and technological resources are relatively impressive, they are not necessarily more oriented toward management than those of their smaller and poorer urban counterparts.

What of scenarios for the future, our final concern? As smaller cities fall behind in their relative development, it seems likely that they will continue to be characterized by vertical fragmentation in a highly centralized system. As such, they will continue as the "attenuated city" of today. For the preferred cities, the bulk of the evidence confirms our initial hypothesis: insofar as change is occurring in city government operations, the probable variant—the "technocratic city"—appears the only one likely to emerge. A growth orientation is still strong in Soviet urban planning. New developments, such as the introduction of social planning, have done little to curtail the operation of an economic planning system geared to continued expansion of productive capacity. By the same token, our examination of budgetary practices, career patterns among urban bureaucrats, patterns of resource allocation among cities, and the organizational framework of Soviet city administration reveals that the themes of national control and a national orientation for local administration are still quite strong. Mechanisms for citizen participation in such new areas as social planning are nonexistent, while those traditionally used to ensure administrative responsiveness and accountability are, at best, more at home in a bureaucratic than in a populist urban future. Along the same lines, we find that the stress is still on technicians, not managers.

From the standpoint of individual cities or national trends, the "populist city" seems unlikely to emerge. This impression is reinforced when another factor is added to the scale: the importance attached to technological development rather than to any slowdown or postponement of growth in the name of decentralization or citizen participation. The traditions of hierarchical control and sectoral implementation are far too strong to be discarded overnight or, perhaps, even over several generations.

For Soviet cities, large and small, the past then constitutes a prologue. The challenge of urban government in the USSR will be met in the future as it always has been: within the traditions of administrative centralization, fragmented authority and control, a heavy reliance on technological adaptation, and the multifaceted commitment to political control and direction that the Soviet city displays today.

SELECTED BIBLIOGRAPHY

Certain primary documents that are unpublished and are not generally accessible in either the USSR or the United States have been omitted from this bibliography. These have been cited in full in the Notes sections, especially in Chapter 6. Other sources used only in the most general way also have been excluded in order to keep the size of the bibliography manageable.

Ablakova, R. G. "Deiatel'nost KPSS po dal'neishemu povysheniiu roli mestnykh sovetov." Master's thesis, Kazakhstan State University, 1969.

Afanasyev, V. G. *The Scientific and Technical Revolution—Its Impact on Management and Education*. Moscow: Progress, 1975.

Agger, Robert E.; Goldrich, David; and Swanson, Bert E. *The Rulers and the Ruled: Political Power and Impotence in American Communities*. New York: John Wiley, 1964.

Aiken, Michael. "Urban Social Structure and Political Competition: A Comparative Study of Local Politics in Four European Nations." *Urban Affairs Quarterly* 1 (September 1975): 82-116.

————, and Castells, Manuel. "New Trends in Urban Studies—Introduction." *Comparative Urban Research* 4 (1977): 7-10.

Aitov, N. A. "Voprosy teorii i praktiki regional'nogo sotsial'nogo planirovaniia." In *Aktual' nye problemy sotsial'nogo planirovaniia: Sektsiia "Sotsial'nogo planirovaniia v regione,"* pp. 56-71. Moscow: Izd. Bashkirskogo obkoma KPSS, 1975.

Aldasheva, Sh. B. "Opyt raboty gorodskogo soveta po planirovaniiu." In *Planirovanie sotsial'nogo razvitiia*, edited by D. A. Kerimov, pp. 84-99. Moscow: Mysl', 1976.

Alford, Robert. "Explanatory Variables in the Study of Urban Politics." In *Comparative Urban Research*, edited by Robert Daland, pp. 272-32. Beverly Hills, Calif.: Sage, 1969.

————, and Scoble, Harry. *Bureaucracy and Participation in Four Wisconsin Cities*. Chicago: Rand McNally, 1969.

Aliev, G. A. "O zadachakh partiinoi organizatsii Azerbaidzhana po dal'neishemu uluchsheniiu podbora, rasstanovki, i vospitaniia kadrov." *Bakiinskii rabochii*, July 31, 1975, pp. 2-6.

Anton, Thomas J. *Governing Greater Stockholm: A Study of Policy Development and System Change*. Berkeley: University of California Press, 1975.

Apostol, F. G. "Partiinoe rukovodstvo mestnym sovetam v rasvitom sotsialisticheskom obshchestve." Master's thesis, Moscow State University, 1973.

Armstrong, John. *The European Administrative Elite*. Princeton, N.J.: Princeton University Press, 1973.

Askenborn, Stig. "Some Experience from Local Government Management Courses." *Studies in Comparative Local Government* 12 (Summer 1973): 31-38.

Auletta, Ken. "A Reporter at Large: More for Less." *The New Yorker*, August 1, 1977, pp. 28-48.

Austin, John E. "Computer-Aided Planning and Decision-Making in the USSR." *Datamation* 23 (December 1977): 71-74.

Azovkin, I. A. *Mestnye sovety v sisteme organov vlasti*. Moscow: Izd. Iuridicheskaia literatura, 1971.

Azrael, Jeremy R. *Managerial Power and Soviet Politics*. Cambridge, Mass.: Harvard University Press, 1966.

Bachrach, Peter, and Baratz, Morton S. "The Two Faces of Power." In *The Bias of Pluralism*, edited by William E. Connolly, pp. 51-61. New York: Atherton Press, 1969.

Baibakov, N. K. "Zakliuchitel'noe slovo." *Izvestiia*, December 21, 1974, p. 2.

Banfield, Edward, and Wilson, James Q. *City Politics*. New York: Vintage Books, 1973.

Bannykh, M. I. *Uchastie obshchestvennosti v deiatel'nosti ispolkomov mestnykh sovetov*. Moscow: Izd. Iuridicheskaia literatura, 1972.

Banovetz, James M. "Attracting and Stimulating a New Generation of Urban Administrators." In *Education for Urban Administration*, edited by Frederic N. Cleaveland, pp. 105-20. Philadelphia: American Academy of Political and Social Science, 1973.

————, ed. *Managing the Modern City*. Washington, D.C.: International City Management Association, 1971.

Baranov, V. "Problemy razvitiia malykh gorodov." *Ekonomicheskaia gazeta* 40 (October 1974): 9.

Barsik, V. L. "Opyt sotsial'nogo planirovaniia krupnogo industrial'nogo tsentra." In *Aktual'nye problemy sotsial'nogo planirovaniia: Sektsiia "Sotsial'nogo planirovaniia v regione,"* pp. 78-81. Moscow: Izd. Bashkirskogo obkoma KPSS, 1975.

Bater, James H. *St. Petersburg: Industrialization and Change*. London: Edward Arnold, 1976.

Beketov, V. "Zavod v raitsentre." *Pravda*, September 9, 1975, p. 2.

Bellush, Jewel, and Hausknecht, Murray. *Urban Renewal: People, Politics and Planning*. Garden City, N.Y.: Anchor Books, 1967.

Belyi, Andrei. *St. Petersburg*. New York: Grove Press, 1969.

Bem Daryl J. *Beliefs, Attitudes and Human Affairs*. Belmont, Calif.: Brooks-Cole, 1970.

Berry, Brian J. L. "The Counter-Urbanization Process in Urban America." In *Urbanization and Counter-Urbanization*, edited by Brian Berry, pp. 17-30. Beverly Hills, Calif.: Sage, 1976.

————. "On Urbanization and Counter-Urbanization. In *Urbanization and Counter-Urbanization*, edited by Brian Berry, pp. 7-14. Beverly Hills, Calif.: Sage, 1976.

Bezmat'ev, A. S. *Sovershenstvovanie partiinogo rukovodstva mestnymi sovetami na etape razvernutogo kommunizma*. Rostov-on-Don: Izd. Rostovskogo gosudarstvennogo univer-siteta, 1971.

————. "Sovershenstvovanie partiinogo rukovodstva mestnymi sovetami deputatov tru-diashchikhsia na etape razvernutogo kommunisticheskogo stroitel'stva (1961-67 gg): na materialakh Rostovskoi oblastnoi partiinoi organizatsii." Master's thesis, Rostov State University, 1971.

Biudzhet goroda Moskvy na 1976. Moscow: Mosgorispolkom, 1975.

Biulleten' ispolkoma Leningradskogo soveta deputatov trudiashchikhsia 12 (June 1970): 1-13; 17 (September 1973): 16; 24 (December 1973): 10.

Blackwell, William. "Modernization and Urbanization in Russia: A Comparative View." In *The City in Russian History*, edited by Michael Hamm, pp. 291-330. Lexington: Univer-sity of Kentucky Press, 1976.

Blinova, V. V. et al. *Metodicheskie rekomendatsii po kompleksnomu planirovaniiu sotsial'-nogo-ekonomicheskogo razvitiia gorodskogo-administrativnogo raiona*. Leningrad: Nauka, 1971.

Bliznakov, Milka. "Urban Planning in the USSR: Integrative Theories." In *The City in Rus-sian History*, edited by Michael Hamm, pp. 243-56. Lexington: University of Kentucky Press, 1976.

Blykhan, L., and Shkaratan, O. *Man at Work*. Moscow: Progress, 1977.

Boiko, V., and Buinova, S. F. "Problema rozhdaemosti kak sotsial'no-psihologicheskaia problema kompleksnogo planirovaniia." In *Aktual'nye problemy sotsial'nogo planiro-vaniia: Sektsiia "Sotsial'nogo planirovaniia v regione,"* pp. 170-72. Moscow: Izd. Bash-kirskogo obkoma KPSS, 1975.

Bollens, John C., and Ries, John C. *The City Manager Profession: Myths and Realities*. Chicago: Public Administration Service, 1969.

————, and Schmandt, Henry J. *The Metropolis: Its People, Politics and Economic Life*. 2d ed. New York: Harper & Row, 1970.

Borshchevskii, M. V. "Metodologicheskie problemy." In *Chelovek i obshchestvo*, no. 15, pp. 35-47. Leningrad: Izd. Leningradskogo gosudarstvennogo universiteta, 1976.

Bradley, Joseph C., Jr. "Muzhik and Muscovite: Peasants in Late Nineteenth Century Urban Russia." Ph.D. dissertation, Harvard University, 1977.

Branch, Melville C. "Delusions and Diffusions of City Planning in the United States." *Management Science* 16 (August 1970): B714-B732.

Breslauer, George "Khrushchev Revisited." *Problems of Communism* 25 (September-October 1976): 18-33.

Brezhnev, Leonid Il'ich. "Rech' tovarishcha L. I. Brezhneva." *Pravda*, April 14, 1970, pp. 1-2.

Brinkley, George A. "Khrushchev Remembered: On the Theory of Soviet Statehood." *Soviet Studies* 24 (January 1973): 387-401.

Broady, M. "The Social Aspects of Town Development." In *Taming Megalopolis*, 2 vols., edited by H. Wentworth Eldredge, 2: 929-53. Garden City, N.Y.: Anchor Books, 1967.

Bronfenbrenner, Yuri. *Two Worlds of Childhood: USA and USSR*. New York: Russell Sage Foundation, 1970.

Buck, J. Vincent. *Politics and Professionalism in Municipal Planning*. Administrative and Policy Studies Series, no. 3. Beverly Hills, Calif.: Sage Professional Papers, 1976.

Bykovskii, D. A. *Organizatsiia raboty ispolkomov mestnykh sovetov*. Moscow: Izd. Iuridicheskaia literatura, 1968.

Caiden, Gerald. *The Dynamics of Public Administration*. New York: Holt, Rinehart and Winston, 1971.

Carlisle, Donald S. "Uzbekistan and the Uzbeks." In *Handbook of Major Soviet Nationalities*, edited by Zev Katz, Rosemarie Rodgers, and Frederic Harned, pp. 283-314. New York: Free Press, 1975.

Catanese, Anthony J. *Scientific Methods of Urban Analysis*. Urbana: University of Illinois Press, 1972.

Cattell, David T. *Leningrad: A Case Study of Soviet Urban Government*. New York: Praeger, 1968.

Cayer, N. Joseph. *Public Personnel Administration*. New York: St. Martin's Press, 1975.

Central Committee, Communist Party of the Soviet Union. "O merakh po dal'neishemu uluchsheniiu raboty raionnykh i gorodskikh sovetov deputatov trudiashchikhsia." *Pravda*, March 14, 1971, pp. 1-2.

Chaplin, B. N., and Bokarev, N. N. "Sotsial'noe razvitie gorodskogo raiona." In *Planirovanie sotsial'nogo razvitiia*, edited by D. A. Kerimov, pp. 69-83. Moscow: Mysl', 1976.

Chapman, Brian. *The Profession of Government: The Public Service in Europe*. London: George Allen and Unwin, 1959.

Chin, Jeff. *Manipulating Soviet Population Resources*. London: Macmillan, 1977.

Chistiakov, E. G., and Semenov, A. K. *Balansovye modeli khoziaistva goroda*. Moscow: Ekonomika, 1977.

Churchward, L. G. "Soviet Local Government Today." *Soviet Studies* 14 (1966): 446-50.

"Citizen Participation and Local Government in Europe and the United States." *Studies in Comparative Local Government* 5 (Winter 1971): 9-96.

"City Hall Has Mixed Reaction to Computers." *Infosystems* 25 (July 1978): 34.

Clark, Terry N. "Community Structure, Decision-Making, Budget Expenditures and Urban Renewal in 51 American Communities." In *The Search for Community Power*, edited by Charles M. Bonjean, Terry N. Clark, and Robert L. Lineberry, pp. 291-308. Englewood Cliffs, N.J.: Prentice-Hall, 1974.

————, ed. *Comparative Community Politics*. New York: John Wiley, 1974.

Cocks, Paul M. "Retooling the Directed Society: Administrative Modernization and Developed Socialism." In *Political Development in Eastern Europe*, edited by Jan Triska and Paul M. Cocks, pp. 53-92. New York: Praeger, 1977.

Coleman, B. I., ed. *The Idea of the City in Nineteenth Century Britain*. London: Routledge and Kegan Paul, 1973.

Cousins, Albert H., and Bagpaul, Hans, eds. *Urban Man and Society: A Reader in Urban Sociology*. New York: Alfred A. Knopf, 1970.

Crecine, John P. *Governmental Problem Solving: A Computer Simulation of Municipal Budgeting*. Chicago: Rand McNally, 1969.

Crick, Bernard, and Green, G. "People and Planning." *New Society* 5 (September 1968): 334-35.

Current Digest of the Soviet Press 29 (August 3, 1977): 8.

Dahl, Robert. *After the Revolution: Authority in a Good Society*. New Haven, Conn.: Yale University Press, 1970.

Daland, Robert. "Comparative Perspectives on Urban Systems." In *Comparative Urban Research*, edited by Robert Daland, pp. 15-59. Beverly Hills, Calif.: Sage, 1969.

Darkov, G. V. "Mestnye biudzhety (statisticheskii obzor)." *Finansy SSSR* 43 (January 1969): 28-32.

————, and Maksimov, G. K. *Finansovaia statistika*. Moscow: Finansy, 1975.

Davidoff, Paul, and Thomas A. Reiner. "A Choice Theory of Planning." *Journal of the American Institute of Planners* 28 (May 1962): 103-15.

Davidovich, Vladimir G. *Planirovka gorodov i raionov*. Moscow: Stroizdat, 1964.

Davidow, Mike. *Cities without Crises*. New York: International, 1976.

Davy, Thomas J. "The University and Pre-Entry Professional Education for Urban Administrators." In *Education for Urban Administration*, edited by Frederic N. Cleaveland, pp. 191-208. Philadelphia: American Academy of Political and Social Science, 1973.

DeMaio, Alfred, Jr. *Soviet Urban Housing*. New York: Praeger, 1973.

Demchenkov, V. S., and Uzhvenko, M. F. *Regulirovanie mestnykh biudzhetov.*   Moscow: Finansy, 1975.

Demidov, P. "Poisk." *Izvestiia*, July 5, 1975, p. 3.

Dimancescu, Dan. "Managing High Density Living." In *Toward a National Urban Policy*. U.S., Congress, House. Subcommittee on the City, Committee on Banking, Finance and Urban Affairs, pp. 109-16. Washington, D.C.: Government Printing Office, April 1977.

Dmitriev, A. V. "Edinii plan goroda." *Izvestiia* (Moscow edition), October 19, 1977, p. 5.

————. "Rol' Leningradskoi partiinoi organizatsii v razvitii praktiki i teorii sotsial'nogo planirovaniia." In *Chelovek i obshchestvo*, no. 15, pp. 21-26. Leningrad: Izd. Leningradskogo gosudarstvennogo universiteta, 1976.

————, and Mezhevich, M. N. "Kompleksnoe planirovanie v gorodakh." *Sotsiologicheskoe issledovanie* 4 (1976): 53-57.

————, and Tiukaev, M. "Nekotorye voprosy kompleksnogo sotsial'nogo planirovaniia." In *Aktual'nye problemy sotsial'nogo planirovaniia: Sektsiia "Sotsial'nogo planirovaniia v regione,"* pp. 50-54. Moscow: Izd. Bashkirskogo obkoma KPSS, 1975.

Dornan, Paul B. "Whither Urban Policy Analysis? A Review Essay." *Polity* 14 (Summer 1977): 503-27.

Doxiadis, C. A. *Anthropopolis: City for Human Development*. New York: W. W. Norton, 1975.

Dye, Thomas R. "Executive Power and Public Policy in the States." *Western Political Quarterly* 22 (December 1969): 926-39.

————. *Politics, Economics and the Public: Policy Outcomes in American States*. Chicago: Rand McNally, 1966.

————. *Understanding Public Policy*. Englewood Cliffs, N.J.: Prentice-Hall, 1972.

Easton, David. *A Systems Analysis of Political Life*. New York: John Wiley, 1965.

Eddison, Tony. *Local Government Management and Corporate Planning*. New York: Barnes and Noble, 1973.

Etzioni, Amitai. *A Comparative Analysis of Complex Organizations.* New York: Free Press, 1961.

———. "Two Approaches to Organizational Effectiveness: A Critique and a Suggestion." *Administrative Science Quarterly* 5 (1960): 257-78.

Eyestone, Robert, and Eulau, Heinz. "City Councils and Policy Outcomes: Developmental Profiles." In *City Politics and Public Policy*, edited by James Q. Wilson, pp. 37-65. New York: John Wiley, 1968.

Fainberg, Z. I. "K voprosu o perspektivnykh tseliakh dolgosrochnogo regional'nogo-sotsial'nogo planirovaniia." In *Aktual'nye problemy sotsial'nogo planirovaniia: Sektsiia sotsial'nogo planirovaniia v regione,*" pp. 187-92. Moscow: Izd. Bashkirskogo obkoma KPSS, 1975.

Fedor, Thomas Stanley. *Patterns of Urban Growth in the Russian Empire during the Nineteenth Century.* Chicago: University of Chicago, Department of Geography, 1975.

Fischer, George. *Russian Liberalism.* Cambridge, Mass.: Harvard University Press, 1958.

Fisher, Jack. "Urban Planning in the Soviet Union and Eastern Europe." In *Taming Megalopolis*, edited by H. Wentworth Eldredge, 2 vols., 2: 1068-99. Garden City, N.Y.: Anchor Books, 1967.

Fleron, Frederic J., Jr. "Co-optation as a Mechanism of Adaptation to Change." In *The Behavioral Revolution and Communist Studies*, edited by Roger E. Kanet, pp. 125-50. New York: Free Press, 1971.

———. "System Attributes and Career Attributes." In *Comparative Communist Political Leadership*, edited by Carl Beck et al., pp. 43-79. New York: David McKay, 1973.

Frankel, Laurie S., and Pigeon, Carol A. "Municipal Managers and Chief Administrative Officers: A Statistical Profile." *Urban Data Service Reports*, vol. 7, no. 2. Washington, D.C.: International City Management Association, February 1975.

Frederickson, H. George. "Commentaries on the Banovetz Paper." In *Education for Urban Administration*, edited by Frederic N. Cleaveland, pp. 121-28. Philadelphia: American Academy of Political and Social Science, 1973.

Fried, Robert C. "Communism, Urban Budgets, and the Two Italies: A Case Study in Comparative Urban Government." *Journal of Politics* 33 (November 1971): 1008-51.

———. "Review: *International Community Power Structure* by Delbert C. Miller." *Midwest Journal of Political Science* 5 (1971): 630-31.

Frieden, Bernard J., and Kaplan, Marshall. *The Politics of Neglect.* Cambridge, Mass.: MIT Press, 1975.

Friedgut, T. H. "Community Structure, Political Participation, and Soviet Local Government." In *Soviet Politics and Society in the 1970s*, edited by Henry Morton and Rudolph Tokes, pp. 261-98. New York: Free Press, 1974.

Friedman, John. *Retracking America: A Theory of Transactive Planning*. Garden City, N.Y.: Anchor Books, 1973.

―――. "The Role of Cities in National Development." *American Behavioral Scientist* 12 (May-June 1969): 13-21.

Frisova, N.P., and Ertov, V. S. "Sovershenstvovanie systemy torgovli v plane." In *Chelovek i obshchestvo*, vyp. 15, pp. 89-93. Leningrad: Izd. Leningradskogo gosudarstvennogo universiteta, 1976.

Fritschler, A. Lee, and Mackelprang, A. J. "Graduate Education in Public Affairs/Public Administration: Results of 1975 Survey." *Public Administration Review* 37 (September-October 1977): 488-94.

Frolic, B. M. "Decision Making in Soviet Cities." *American Political Science Review* 66 (March 1972): 38-52.

―――. "Municipal Administration, Departments, Commissions and Organizations." *Soviet Studies* 22 (January 1971): 376-93.

―――. "Non-Comparative Communism: Chinese and Soviet Urbanization." In *Social Consequences of Modernization in Communist Societies*, edited by Mark Field, pp. 149-61. Baltimore: Johns Hopkins University Press, 1976.

―――. "Soviet Cities in Transition." Unpublished manuscript, 1977.

―――. "The Soviet City." *Town Planning Review* 34 (January 1964): 300-2.

Frolov, S. F. "Planirovanie sotsial'nogo razvitiia na razynykh urovniakh sotsial'noi organizatsii." In *Aktual'nye problemy sotsiologii truda*, edited by G. Vasil'ev, pp. 105-11. Moscow: Institut sotsiologii, Akademiia nauk SSSR, 1975.

Fromin, I., and Kliushnichenko, E. E. *Tekhniko-ekonomicheskie raschety v general'nykh planakh gorodov*. Vol. 1. Kiev: Gosstroi USSR, 1973.

Gabrichidze, B. N. *Gorodskie sovety deputatov trudiashchikhsia*. Moscow: Izd. Iuridicheskaia literatura, 1968.

Gans, Herbert J. "Planning for People, Not Building." In *Urban Administration: Management, Politics and Change*, edited by Alan Edward Bent and Ralph A. Rossum, pp. 152-71. Port Washington, N.Y.: Kennikat Press, 1976.

―――. "Social and Physical Planning for the Elimination of Urban Poverty." In *Urban Planning and Social Policy*, edited by Bernard J. Freiden and Robert Morris, pp. 319-54. New York: Basic Books, 1968.

German, I. M., and Mal'tsev, V. I. *Sotsial'noe planirovanie v gorodskom raione*. Saratov: Privolzhnoe knizhnoe izdatel'stvo, 1976.

Gilinskii, Ia. I. "Vremai kak faktor." In *Chelovek i Obshchestvo*, no. 15, pp. 68-72. Leningrad: Izd. Leningradskogo gosudarstvennogo universiteta, 1976.

Gillison, Jerome. "Soviet Elections as a Measure of Dissent: The Missing One Percent." *American Political Science Review* 62 (1968): 814-26.

Gimpel'son, E. G. *Sovety v gody innostrannoi interventsii i grazhdanskoi voiny.* Moscow: Nauka, 1968.

Gitelman, Zvi. "Soviet Political Culture: Insights from Jewish Emigres." *Soviet Studies* 29 (October 1977): 543-74.

Glaz, Umni. "The Silicon Curtain." *Computer Decisions* 9 (September 1977): 30-34.

Golembiewski, Robert, ed. *People in Public Service: A Reader in Public Personnel Administration.* Itasca, Ill.: F. E. Peacock, 1970.

Gordon, George J. *Public Administration in America.* New York: St. Martin's Press, 1978.

Gordon, L., and Klopov, E. *Man after Work.* Moscow: Progress, 1975.

Gortner, Harold. *Administration in the Public Sector.* New York: John Wiley, 1977.

Greer, Scott. *The Emerging City: Myth and Reality.* New York: Free Press of Glencoe, 1962.

Grove, J. T., and Procter, S. C. "Citizen Participation in Planning." *Journal of the Town Planning Institute* 55 (July-August 1969): 292-95.

Gruzinov, A. S., and Riumin, V. P. *Gorod: upravlenie, problemy.* Leningrad: Lenizdat, 1977.

Gutnov, Alexei et al. *The Ideal Communist City.* Translated by Renee Neu Watkins. New York: George Braziller, 1968.

Guyot, James F. "How Do We Know Which Training Is Good Medicine for Managers?" *Public Administration Review* 37 (November-December 1977): 698-705.

Haimson, Leopold. "The Problem of Social Stability in Urban Russia, 1905-1917 (Part One)." *Slavic Review* 23 (December 1964): 619-42.

————. "The Problem of Social Stability in Urban Russia, 1905-1917 (Part Two)." *Slavic Review* 24 (March 1965): 1-22.

Hamilton, F. R. Ian. *The Moscow City Region.* Problem Regions of Europe. London: Oxford University Press, 1976.

Hamm, Michael. "The Breakdown of Urban Modernization." In *The City in Russian History*, edited by Michael Hamm, pp. 182-200. Lexington: University of Kentucky Press, 1976.

Hanchett, Walter. "Tsarist Statutory Regulation of Municipal Government in the Nineteenth Century." In *The City in Russian History*, edited by Michael Hamm, pp. 91-114. Lexington: University of Kentucky Press, 1976.

Hardt, John P., and Holliday, George. "Technology Transfer and Change in the Soviet Economic System." In *Technology and Communist Culture*, edited by Frederic J. Fleron, Jr., pp. 211-18. New York: Praeger, 1977.

Hargrove, Erwin C. *The Missing Link: The Study of the Implementation of Social Policy.* Washington, D.C.: The Urban Institute, 1975.

Harvey, David. *Social Justice and the City*. London: Edward Arnold, 1973.

Hawley, Willis D., and Wirt, Frederick M., eds. *The Search for Community Power*. Englewood Cliffs, N.J.: Prentice-Hall, 1974.

Hayes, Frederick O. "Changes and Innovation in City Government." In *Improving the Quality of Urban Management*, edited by Willis D. Hawley and David Rogers, pp. 129-50. Beverly Hills, Calif.: Sage, 1976.

Heidenheimer, Arnold et al. *Comparative Public Policy: The Politics of Social Choice in Europe and America*. New York: St. Martin's Press, 1975.

Henrichs, Harley H., and Taylor, Graem M. *Program Budgeting and Benefit—Cost Analysis*. Pacific Palisades, Calif.: Goodyear, 1969.

Henry, Nicholas. *Public Administration and Public Affairs*. Englewood Cliffs, N.J.: Prentice-Hall, 1975.

Hill, Ronald J. *The Soviet Political Elite*. New York: St. Martin's Press, 1977.

Hittle, J. M. "The City in Muscovite and Early Imperial Russia." Ph.D. dissertation, Harvard University, 1969.

————. "The Service City in the Eighteenth Century." In *The City in Russian History*, edited by Michael Hamm, pp. 53-68. Lexington: University of Kentucky Press, 1976.

Hofferbert, Richard. "Socio-Economic Dimensions of the American States, 1860-1960." *Midwest Journal of Political Science* 12 (August 1968): 401-18.

Hoffmann, Erik P. "Role Conflict and Ambiguity in the Communist Party of the Soviet Union." In *The Behavioral Revolution and Communist Studies*, edited by Roger Kanet, pp. 233-58. New York: Free Press, 1971.

————. "Social Science and Soviet Administrative Behavior." *World Politics* 24 (April 1972): 444-71.

————. "Soviet Information Processing: Recent Theory and Experience." *Soviet Union* 2 (1975): 22-49.

————. "Technology, Values and Political Power." In *Technology and Communist Culture*, edited by Frederic J. Fleron, Jr., pp. 397-436. New York: Praeger, 1977.

Holden, Matthew, Jr. "Imperialism in Bureaucracy." In *Bureaucratic Power in National Politics*, edited by Francis E. Rourke, pp. 97-113. Boston: Little, Brown and Co., 1965.

Hough, Jerry F. "Political Participation in the Soviet Union." *Soviet Studies* 28 (January 1976): 3-20.

————. "The Soviet Concept of the Relationship between the Lower Party Organs and State Administration." *Slavic Review* 24 (June 1965): 215-40.

Hummel, Ralph P. *The Bureaucratic Experience.* New York: St. Martin's Press, 1977.

Huntington, Samuel P., and Nelson, Joan. *No Easy Choice: Political Participation in Developing Countries.* Cambridge, Mass.: Harvard University Press, 1976.

Iakovlev, G. V. *Apparat upravleniia.* Moscow: Izd. Iuridicheskaia literatura, 1974.

Inkeles, A., and Bauer, R. *The Soviet Citizen: Daily Life in a Totalitarian Society.* Cambridge, Mass.: Harvard University Press, 1961.

Interview in Department of Justice, Leningrad *gorispolkom*, 1976.

Interview in Institute of Philosophy, Leningrad Branch, Academy of Sciences, USSR, 1976.

Interview in Institute of State and Law, Academy of Sciences, USSR, 1976.

Interviews at housing projects, Leningrad, Tallin, Moscow, 1977.

Interviews in City Planning and Building Institute, Vilnius, June 1977.

Interviews in Faculty of Law, Leningrad State University, 1975.

Interviews in Faculty of Law, Moscow State University, 1976.

Interviews in Gosgrazhdanstroi, Moscow, 1977.

Interviews in Gosstroi, Moscow, 1977.

Interviews in Kiev NIIP Gradostroitel'stva, Kiev, 1977.

Interviews in Leningrad *gorispolkom*, Leningrad, 1976.

Interviews in Main Scientific Research Computer Center, Moscow City Soviet, 1977.

Interviews in NIIKSI, Leningrad State University, Leningrad, 1976.

Interviews in Tallin *gorispolkom*, Tallin, 1977.

Interviews in TsNIPP Gradostroitel'stva, Moscow, 1977.

Interviews in Vilnius *gorispolkom*, Vilnius, 1977.

Interview with G. V. Osipov, Deputy Director, Institute of Sociology, Academy of Sciences, USSR, 1977.

Itogi vyborov i sostav deputatov mestnykh sovetov deputatov trudiashchikhsia, 1969 g. Moscow: Izvestiia, 1969.

Itogi vyborov sostav deputatov mestnykh sovetov deputatov trudiashchikhsia, 1973 g. Moscow: Izvestiia, 1973.

Jacobs, Everett M. "Soviet Local Elections: What They Are, and What They Are Not." *Soviet Studies* 22 (1970): 61-76.

Jacobs, Jane. *The Death and Life of Great American Cities.* New York: Vintage Books, 1961.

————. *The Economy of Cities.* New York: Vintage Books, 1969.

Jensen, Robert G. "Urban Environments in the United States and the Soviet Union." In *Urbanization and Counterurbanization*, edited by Brian J. L. Berry, pp. 31-42. Beverly Hills, Calif.: Sage, 1976.

Joravsky, David. "Soviet Ideology." *Soviet Studies* 18 (July 1966): 2-18.

"KPSS v tsifrakh." *Partiinaia zhizn'* 14 (July 1973): 9-26.

Kaiser, John A. "The Use of Computer Systems by Local Government in the Soviet Union." New York: Columbia University, Graduate School of Business, Center for Government Studies. Reprint of paper presented at the Fourteenth Annual Conference of the Urban and Regional Information Systems Association, Atlanta, Ga., August-September 1976.

Kak organizovat' upravlencheskii trud. Moscow: For Izvestiia, 1971.

Kansky, Karl Joseph. *Urbanization under Socialism: The Case of Czechoslovakia.* New York: Praeger, 1976.

Katz, E., and Danet, B. "Introduction: Bureaucracy as a Problem for Sociology and Society." In *Bureaucracy and the Public: A Reader in Official-Client Relations*, edited by E. Katz and B. Danet, pp. 3-18. New York: Basic Books, 1973.

Kerimov, D. A., ed. *Problemy sotsial'nogo planirovaniia.* Moscow: Mysl', 1974.

Kesselman, Mark. *The Ambiguous Consensus: A Study of Local Government in France.* New York: Alfred A. Knopf, 1967.

————. "Political Parties and Local Government in France: Differentiation and Opposition." In *Comparative Community Politics*, edited by Terry N. Clark, pp. 111-38. New York: John Wiley, 1974.

————. "Research Perspectives on Comparative Local Politics: Pitfalls, Prospects, and Notes on the French Case." In *Comparative Community Politics*, edited by Terry N. Clark, pp. 352-81. New York: John Wiley, 1974.

Khorev, B. S. *Problemy gorodov.* Moscow: Nauka, 1971.

Kiev NIIP Gradostroitel'stva. *Sotsial'nye osnovy razvitiia gorodov (sotsial'nye problemy rasseleniia)*. Moscow: Stroizdat, 1975.

Kilpatrick, Franklin P. et al. *The Image of the Federal Civil Service*. Washington, D. C.: Brookings Institution, 1964.

Kirsch, Leonard. *Soviet Wages: Changes in Structure and Administration since 1956*. Cambridge, Mass.: MIT Press, 1972.

Koteen, Jack. "Key Problems in Development Administration." In *Administrative Issues in Developing Economies*, edited by Kenneth Rothwell, pp. 47-68. Lexington, Mass.: Lexington Books, 1972.

Kraemer, Kenneth L. et al. *Integrated Municipal Information Systems: The Use of the Computer in Local Government*. New York: Praeger, 1974.

————, and King, John Leslie. "A Critique of Federal Involvement in City Information: Part 2." *Government Data Systems* 6 (July-August 1977): 12, 16-17.

————. "In City Information: A Critique of Federal Involvement." *Government Data Systems* 6 (May-June 1977): 35-38.

Kramer, Fred A. *Dynamics of Public Bureaucracy*. Cambridge, Mass.: Winthrop, 1977.

Krueckerberg, Donald A., and Silbers, Arthur L. *Urban Planning Analysis: Methods and Models*. New York: John Wiley, 1974.

Kutafin, O. E. *Mestnye sovety i narodno-khoziaistvennoe planirovanie*. Moscow: Izd. Moskovskogo gosudarstvennogo universiteta, 1976.

Kuznetsov, Iu. M. "Povyshenie roli i otvetstvennosti mestnykh sovetov." In *Kommunisty i ekonomicheskaia reforma*, pp. 323-56. Moscow: Mysl', 1972.

Kvalifikatsionnyi spravochnik dolzhnostei sliuzhashchikh. Moscow: NII Truda, 1970 and 1972.

Langer, Lawrence. "The Medieval Russian Town." In *The City in Russian History*, edited by Michael Hamm, pp. 11-31. Lexington: University of Kentucky Press, 1976.

Lapin, N. I. et al. *Teoriia i praktika sotsial'nogo planirovaniia*. Moscow: Izd. politicheskaia literatura, 1976.

Lasswell, Harold. *Politics: Who Gets What, When, How*. New York: P. Smith, 1950.

Lees, Andrews, and Lynn, Lees, eds. *The Urbanization of European Society in the Nineteenth Century*. Lexington, Mass.: D. C. Heath, 1976.

Leizerov, A. T. "Kontrol' izbiratelei." In *Pravovye voprosy upravleniia*, pp. 31-49. Perm: Permskii gosudarstvennyi universiteta, 1973.

Leningrad i Leningradskaia oblast' v tsifrakh. Leningrad: Lenizdat, 1964.

Lewin, Arie, and Blanning, Robert W. "The Urban Government Annual Report." In *Improving the Quality of Urban Management*, edited by Willis D. Hawley and David Rogers, pp. 65-92. Beverly Hills, Calif.: Sage, 1976.

Lewis, Carol W. "The Beggar Bureaucrat: Linking National and City Politics in the Soviet Union." Paper delivered at the annual conference of the American Society for Public Administration, Washington, D.C., April 1976.

————, *The Budgetary Process in Soviet Cities.* New York: Columbia University, Graduate School of Business, Center for Government Studies, 1976.

————. "Comparing City Budgets: The Soviet Case." *Comparative Urban Research* 5 (November 1977): 46-57.

————. "The CPSU and Urban Management." Paper delivered at the Northeastern Political Science Association Conference, South Egremont, Mass., 1976.

————. "The Harvard Conference on Soviet Urban Research." *Comparative Urban Research* 5 (November 1977): 72-76.

————. "Managing Soviet Cities." In *Municipal Year Book 1977*, pp. 84-91. Washington, D.C.: International City Management Association, 1978.

————. "Politics and the Budget in Soviet Cities." Ph.D. dissertation, Princeton University, 1975.

Levy, Frank S.; Meltsner, Arnold J.; and Wildavsky, Aaron. *Urban Outcomes: Schools, Streets, and Libraries.* Berkeley: University of California Press, 1974.

Liaporov, N. "Vperedi god boevoi napriazhennoi raboty (s plenuma Moskovskogo gorkoma KPSS." *Pravda*, December 24, 1974, p. 2.

Limarenko, A. I. "Problemy sovershenstvovaniia organizatsionno-instruktorskogo apparata mestnykh sovetov (na materialakh Ukrainskoi SSR)." Master's thesis, Lvov State University, 1972.

Lindenmeyr, Adele. "Raskolnikov's City and the Napoleonic Plan." *Slavic Review* 35 (March 1976): 37-47.

Lineberry, Robert L. *Equality and Urban Policy: Distribution of Municipal Services.* Beverly Hills, Calif.: Sage, 1977.

————, and Fowler, Edmond P. "Reformism and Public Policies in American Cities." In *Community Politics: A Behavioral Approach*, edited by Charles M. Bonjean, Terry N. Clark, and Robert L. Lineberry, pp. 277-92. New York: Free Press, 1971.

————, and Sharkansky, Ira. *Urban Politics and Public Policy.* New York: Harper & Row, 1971.

Liubovny, V. Ia., and Savalev, V. K. "Russia's Small and Large Cities." *Current Digest of the Soviet Press* 24 (September 28, 1977): 7-8.

"Local Government Chief Executives Report Computer Essential." *EDP Weekly*, October 20, 1975, p. 11.

Loveday, Peter. "Citizen Participation in Urban Planning." In *The Politics of Urban Growth* edited by R. S. Parker and P. N. Troy, pp. 129-48. Canberra: Australian National University Press, 1972.

Lowi, Theodore. *The End of Liberalism*. New York: W. W. Norton, 1969.

Main Scientific Research Computer Center of the Moscow City Soviet Executive Committee. *Characteristics of Municipal Data Processing Systems in Moscow*. New York: Columbia University, Graduate School of Business, Center for Government Studies, June 1975.

————. "Description of the Management System of the City of Moscow." New York: Columbia University, Graduate School of Business, Center for Government Studies. Uncirculated draft report; Soviet source document unverified by independent research.

————. *Description of the Standard Methods of Design, Development and Implementation of Large Automated Systems of Data Processing for the Needs of Municipal Managers*. New York: Columbia University, Graduate School of Business, Center for Government Studies, June 1975.

————. *Experimental Development of Automated City Management Systems for the City of Leningrad*. New York: Columbia University, Graduate School of Business, Center for Government Studies, November 1975.

Management Science (Urban Issues) 16 (August 1970).

Masotti, Louis, and Walton, John. "Comparative Urban Research: The Logic of Comparisons." In *The City in Comparative Perspective*, edited by John Walton and Louis Masotti, pp. 1-16. Beverly Hills, Calif.: Sage, 1976.

Mazyrin, V. P. "Planirovanie razvitiia uchrezhdenii kul'tury v Sverdlovskoi oblasti." *Sotsiologicheskoe issledovanie* 3 (1976): 113-18.

Meadows, Paul, and Mizruchi, Ephriam H., eds. *Urbanism, Urbanization and Change*. 2d ed. Reading, Mass.: Addison-Wesley, 1969.

Mendel, Arthur. *Dilemmas of Progress in Tsarist Russia*. Cambridge, Mass.: Harvard University Press, 1961.

Merewitz, Leonard, and Sosnick, Stephen H. *The Budget's New Clothes*. Chicago: Rand McNally, 1971.

Metodicheskie rekomendatsii po sostavleniiu kompleksnogo plana sotsial'no-ekonomicheskogo razvitiia. Minsk: Izd. Raikoma KPB, 1975.

Meyer, Alfred E. "The Functions of Ideology in the Soviet Political System." *Soviet Studies* 17 (January 1966): 273-85.

Mezhevich, M. N. "Sovershenstvovanie upravleniia v gorodakh." In *Chelovek i obshchestvo*, no. 15, pp. 47-67. Leningrad: Izd. Leningradskogo gosudarstvennogo universiteta, 1976.

Miasnikov, A. "There Should Be One Master." *Current Digest of the Soviet Press* 24 (September 28, 1977): 8-9.

Miller, David. "State and Society in Seventeenth Century Muscovy." In *The City in Russian History*, edited by Michael Hamm, pp. 34-52. Lexington: University of Kentucky Press, 1976.

Miller, Lynn S., and Rutter, Laurence. "Strengthening the Quality of Urban Management Education: A Symposium." *Public Administration Review* 37 (September-October 1977): 567-70.

Miller, Robert F. "The Scientific-Technical Revolution and the Soviet Administrative Debate." In *The Dynamics of Soviet Politics*, edited by Paul Cocks et al., pp. 137-55. Cambridge, Mass.: Harvard University Press, 1976.

Mingione, Enzo. "Sociological Approaches to Regional and Urban Development: Some Methodological and Theoretical Issues." *Comparative Urban Research* 4 (1977): 21-38.

Miromenko, I. "Kogda odin khozian." *Pravda*, June 10, 1975, p. 3.

Mohr, Lawrence B. "Determinants of Innovation." In *Organizational and Managerial Innovation*, edited by Lloyd A. Rowe and William Boise, pp. 31-48. Pacific Palisades, Calif.: Goodyear, 1973.

Moore, Barrington, Jr. *Soviet Politics: The Dilemmas of Power*. New York: Harper & Row, 1965.

Morton, Henry. "The Leningrad District: An Inside Look," *Soviet Studies* 20 (October 1968): 206-18.

—————. "The Soviet Urban Scene." *Problems of Communism* 26 (January-February 1977): 73-75.

—————. "What Have Soviet Leaders Done about the Housing Crisis." In *Soviet Politics and Society in the 1970s*, edited by Henry Morton and Rudolph Tokes, pp. 163-99. New York: Free Press, 1974.

Mosher, Frederick C. "End-Product Objectives of Pre-Entry Professional Education for Urban Administrators and Their Implication for Curriculum Focus." In *Education for Urban Administration*, edited by Frederic N. Cleaveland, pp. 146-62. Philadelphia: American Academy of Political and Social Science, 1973.

—————. "Professions in Public Service." *Public Administration Review* 2 (March-April 1978): 144-51.

—————, and Stillman, Richard J., Jr. "Introduction: The Professions in Government." *Public Administration Review* 37 (November-December 1977): 631-33.

Moskalev, I. *Sovershenstvovanie deiatel'nosti mestnykh sovetov*. Moscow: Mysl', 1975.

Moskva v tsifrakh. Moscow: Statistika, 1976.

Moskva v tsifrakh, 1966-1970: kratikii statisticheskii spravochnik. Moscow: Statistika, 1972.

Moskva v tsifrakh za gody Sovetskoi vlasti. Moscow: Statistika, 1967.

Mosolov, Iu. P. et al. "Dukhovnye potrebnosti." In *Chelovek i obshchestvo*, no. 15, pp. 116-20. Leningrad: Izd. Leningradskogo gosudarstvennogo universiteta, 1976.

Mote, Max. *Soviet Local and Republic Elections.* Stanford, Calif.: Hoover Institution, 1965.

Muller, Thomas. *Growing and Declining Urban Areas: A Fiscal Comparison.* Washington, D.C.: The Urban Institute, 1975.

Mumford, Lewis. *The City in History.* New York: Harcourt, Brace and World, 1961.

———. *The Culture of Cities.* New York: Harcourt, Brace & Co., 1938.

Muraviev, E. P., and Uspenskii, S. V. *Metodologicheskie problemy planirovaniia gorodoskogo rasseleniia.* Leningrad: Izd. Leningradskogo gosudarstvennogo universiteta, 1974.

Narodnoe khoziaistvo Rostovskoi oblasti: statisticheskii sbornik. Rostov: Statistika, 1971.

Narodnoe khoziaistvo SSSR v 1970 godu. Moscow: Statistika, 1971.

National League of Cities Research Report. *Municipal Inventory of Business Machines, Computers and Communications Equipment.* Washington, D.C.: National League of Cities, 1974.

Nechemias, Carol. "Soviet Housing Policy." Paper delivered at the Southeastern Social Sciences Association Convention, Houston, Texas, 1978.

Newton, Kenneth. "Community Decision-Makers and Community Decision-Making in England and the U.S." In *Comparative Community Politics*, edited by Terry N. Clark, pp. 55-86. New York: John Wiley, 1974.

O gosudarstvennom biudzhete RSFSR na 1975 god i ob ispolnenii gosudarstvennogo biudzheta RSFSR za 1973 god. Moscow: Finansy, 1975.

"O rabote obkoma Volgogradskoi oblasti (TsK, KPSS, sentiabr', 1968 g.)" In *KPSS v resoliutsiiakh i resheniiakh (1966-1968)*, 10 vols., 9:468-73. Moscow: Politizdat, 1972.

Orlov, I. M. *Deiatel'nost' KPSS po povysheniiu roli sovetov v stroitel'stve kommunizma.* Moscow: Vyshaia shkola, 1970.

Osborn, Robert J. *Soviet Social Policies: Welfare, Equality, and Community.* Homewood, Ill.: Dorsey Press, 1970.

Palen, J. J. *The Urban World.* New York: McGraw-Hill, 1975.

Parsons, Talcott. "Components and Types of Formal Organization." In *Comparative Administrative Theory*, edited by Preston LeBaron, pp. 3-22. Seattle: University of Washington Press, 1968.

Pashkov, A. S. "Metodologicheskie i metodicheskie voprosy sotsial'nogo planirovaniia." In *Kompleksnoe sotsial'noe planirovanie*, edited by A. S. Pashkov, pp. 112-32. Leningrad: Izd. Leningradskogo gosudarstvennogo universiteta, 1976.

————, and Mezhevich, M. N. "Sotsial'noe planirovanie." In *Chelovek i obshchestvo*, no. 15, pp. 9-20. Leningrad: Izd. Leningradskogo gosudarstvennogo universiteta, 1976.

Perevedentsev, Viktor. "The Concentration of Urban Population and the Criteria of Optimality of a City." *International Journal of Sociology* 5 (Summer-Fall 1975): 18-36.

————. "Zhilishcha." *Zhurnalist* 10 (October 1974): 76-77.

Perloff, Harvey S. "New Directions in Social Planning." In *Taming the Megalopolis*, edited by H. Wentworth Eldredge, 2 vols., 2: 877-96. Garden City, N.Y.: Anchor Books, 1967.

Pertsik, V. A., and Kazaniuk, A. I. "O povyshenii effektivnosti." In *Voprosy Sovetskogo gosudarstvovedeniia: trudy*, 71 vols., 71: 14-22. Irkutsk: Izd. Irkutskogo universiteta, 1970.

Peters, B. Guy. *The Politics of Bureaucracy: A Comparative Perspective*. New York: Longman, 1978.

Pigalev, P. "Zakonodatel'stvo o sovetakh." In *Rabota sovetov na uroven' novykh zadach*, pp. 264-81. Moscow: Izvestiia, 1973.

Pirenne, Henri. *Medieval Cities: Their Origins and the Revival of Medieval Trade*. Princeton, N.J.: Princeton University Press, 1969.

Plax, Martin. "The Use and Abuse of Political Ethos for the Study of Urban Politics." *Urban Affairs Quarterly* 11 (March 1976): 375-86.

Pokrovskii, M. "Vneklassovaia teoriia razvitiia russkogo samoderzhaviia." *Vestnik sotsialisticheskoi akademii* 1 (November 1922): 56-63.

Poliak, G. B., and Sofronova, E. V. *General'nyi plan i biudzhet Moskvy*. Moscow: Finansy, 1973.

Poliakov, I. "Vliiat', a ne podmeniat'." *Izvestiia*, February 29, 1968, p. 3.

Polozov, V. P. "Napravleniia i ob"ekty sotsial'nogo planirovaniia." In *Chelovek i obshchestvo*, no. 15, pp. 26-34. Leningrad: Izd. Leningradskogo gosudarstvennogo universiteta, 1976.

Polozov, Ye. "Sotsial'noe planirovanie: tseli, zadachi, ob"ekt." In *Kompleksnoe sotsial'noe issledovanie*, edited by A. S. Pashkov, pp. 56-66. Leningrad: Izd. Leningradskogo gosudarstvennogo universiteta, 1976.

Poltaranin, M., and Sevastianov, V. "On the Banks of the Irtysh." *Current Digest of the Soviet Press* 24 (August 3, 1977): 7.

Popov, V. D. "K voprosu o planirovanii razvitiia sistema obrazovaniia." In *Aktual'nye problemy sotsial'nogo planirovaniia: Sektsiia "Sotsial'nogo planirovaniia v regione,"* pp. 45-49. Moscow: Izd. Bashkirskogo obkoma, 1975.

Posokhin, Mikhail Vasil'evich. *Cities to Live in.* Moscow: Novosti Press, 1974.

Powell, David E. "Labor Turnover in the Soviet Union." *Slavic Review* 36 (June 1977): 268-84.

Powell, Mel D. "Recommendations for Strengthening Urban Management Education and ICMA/NASPAA Cooperation." *Public Administration Review* 37 (September-October 1977): 575-79.

Powers, Stanley et al. *Developing the Municipal Organization.* Washington, D.C.: International City Management Association, 1974.

Pravovye voprosy raboty mestnykh sovetov. Moscow: Izd. Iuridicheskaia literatura, 1974.

Pressman, Jeffrey L., and Wildavsky, Aaron B. *Implementation: How Great Expectations in Washington Were Dashed in Oakland.* Berkeley: University of California Press, 1973.

Price, Don. *The Scientific Estate.* Cambridge, Mass.: Harvard University Press, 1965.

Price, Richard. *Society and Bureaucracy in Ghana.* Berkeley: University of California Press, 1974.

Problemy Sovetskogo stroitel'stva gosudarstvennogo upravleniia i pravovogo vospitaniia na sovremennom etape. Ufa: Izd. Upravleniia delami soveta ministrov, BASSR, 1975.

Przeworski, Adam, and Teune, Henry. *The Logic of Comparative Social Inquiry.* New York: John Wiley, 1970.

Pugh, D. S. et al. *Writers on Organizations.* Hammondsworth, England: Penguin Books, 1971.

Rabinovitz, Francine F. "Urban Development and Political Development in Latin America." In *Comparative Urban Research: The Administration and Politics of Cities,* edited by Robert T. Daland, pp. 88-123. Beverly Hills, Calif.: Sage, 1969.

————, and Trueblood, Felicity M., eds. *Latin American Urban Research.* Beverly Hills, Calif.: Sage, 1973.

Reddaway, Peter. "Aspects of Ideological Belief in the Soviet Union." *Soviet Studies* 17 (April 1966): 473-83.

Rehfuss, John. *Public Administration as Political Process.* New York: Scribners, 1973.

Reifer, Donald J. "Snapshots of Soviet Computing." *Datamation* 24 (February 1978): 133-38.

Rein, Martin. "Social Planning: The Search for Legitimacy." *Journal of the American Institute of Planners* 35 (July 1969): 233-44.

Reinhold, Robert. "Cities in North Face Reduced Federal Aid under Block Grants." New York *Times*, February 13, 1977, p. 1.

Reissman, Leonard. *The Urban Process: Cities in Industrial Societies.* New York: Free Press, 1970.

Remnev, V. I. *Problemy NOTa v apparate upravleniia.* Moscow: Nauka, 1973.

Riasnovsky, Nicolas. *Russia and the West in the Teachings of the Slavophiles.* Cambridge, Mass.: Harvard University Press, 1952.

Rigby, T. H. "Hough on Political Participation in the Soviet Union." *Soviet Studies* 28 (April 1976): 257-61.

Riggs, Fred. *Administration in Developing Countries.* Boston: Houghton Mifflin and Co., 1964.

Rogers, David, and Hawley, Willis D. "The Mismanagement of Cities." In *Improving the Quality of Urban Management*, edited by Willis D. Hawley and David Rogers, pp. 11-31. Beverly Hills, Calif.: Sage, 1976.

Rostovskaia oblast' za 50 let. Rostov: Statistika, 1967.

Rowland, Richard H. "Urban In-Migration." In *The City in Russian History*, edited by Michael Hamm, pp. 115-25. Lexington: University of Kentucky Press, 1976.

Rozenbaum, I. A. "O spetsial'noi podgotovke upravlencheskikh kadrov." *Sovetskoe gosudarstvo i pravo* 1 (1976): 55-59.

Rozman, Gilbert. *Urban Networks in Russia, 1750-1800, and Premodern Periodicization.* Princeton, N.J.: Princeton University Press, 1976.

Ruden, Iu. "Nauchnaia organizatsiia truda i apparat." In *Rabota sovetov na uroven' novykh zadach*, pp. 229-35. Moscow: Izvestiia, 1973.

Rudkovskaia, E. V. "Partiinoe rukovodstvo deiatel'nosti sovetov." Master's thesis, Leningrad State University, 1975.

Russell, John R. *Cases in Urban Management.* Cambridge, Mass.: MIT Press, 1974.

Rutkevich, M. N. "Nekotorye problemy." In *Planirovaniia sotsial'nogo razvitiia*, edited by D. Kerimov, pp. 23-30. Moscow: Mysl', 1976.

Rzhanitsyna, Ludmila. *Soviet Family Budgets.* Moscow: Progress, 1977.

Sabaneev, S., and Konovalov, G. "Ruka ob ruku." *Izvestiia*, May 17, 1967, p. 3.

Safarov, R. A. *Obshchestvennoe mnenie i gosudarstvennoe upravlenie.* Moscow: Izd. Iuridicheskaia literatura, 1975.

———. "Obshchestvennoe mnenie pri usloviiakh razvitogo sotsializma." *Kommunist* 12 (August 1977): 29-40.

Salisbury, Robert. "The Analysis of Public Policy: A Search for Theories and Roles." In *Political Science and Public Policy*, edited by Austin Ranney, pp. 151-78. Chicago: Markham, 1968.

Savas, E. S., and Ginsburg, S. G. "The Civil Service: A Meritless System." In *Current Issues in Public Administration*, edited by Frederick S. Lane, pp. 257-68. New York: St. Martin's Press, 1978.

Savio, Charles J. "Revenue-Sharing in Practice: National-State-Local Subventions in Venezuela." In *Latin American Urban Research*, edited by Francine F. Rabinovitz and Felicity M. Trueblood, pp. 79-96. Beverly Hills, Calif.: Sage, 1973.

Scannell, Tim. "Prestige Symbol No Longer, Russian CPU Gets the Boot." *Computerworld*, March 22, 1978, p. 2.

Schoenberg, Sandra P. "A Typology of Leadership Styles." In *Organizational and Managerial Innovation*, edited by Lloyd A. Rowe and William Boise, pp. 177-85. Pacific Palisades, Calif.: Goodyear, 1973.

Schott, Richard L. "Public Administration as a Profession." In *Current Issues in Public Administration*, edited by Frederick S. Lane, pp. 273-80. New York: St. Martin's Press, 1978.

Schroeder, Gertrude E. "A Critique of Official Statistics on Public Administration in the USSR." *Association for Comparative Economic Studies Bulletin* 18 (Spring 1976): 23-44.

Schwartz, Donald V. "Information and Administration in the Soviet Union." *Canadian Journal of Political Science* 7 (June 1974): 228-47.

———. "Recent Soviet Adaptations of Systems Theory to Administrative Theory." *Journal of Comparative Administration* 5 (August 1973): 233-64.

Schwartz, Joel J. "The Elusive 'New Soviet Man.'" *Problems of Communism* 22 (September-October 1973): 39-50.

Selivanov, T. A., and Gel'perin, M. A. *Planirovanie gorodskogo khoziaistva (na primera Moskvy).* Moscow: Ekonomika, 1970.

Semeniuk, N. S. "Voprosy planirovaniia migratsionnykh potokov molodezhi." In *Aktual'nye problemy sotsial'nogo planirovaniia: Sektsiia "Sotsial'nogo planirovaniia v regione,"* pp. 123-25. Moscow: Izd. Bashkirskogo obkoma, 1975.

Semenov, N. N. *Samoderzhavie kak gosudarstvennyi stroi.* St. Petersburg: n.p., 1905.

Shannon, John, and Gabler, L. Richard. "Tax Lids and Expenditure Mandates: The Case for Fiscal Fair Play." *Intergovernmental Perspective* 3 (Summer 1977): 7-12.

Shapek, Raymond A. "Breaking Barriers: Urban Managers and Academics Working Together." *Public Administration Review* 37 (September-October 1977): 581-85.

Sharkansky, Ira. "Government Expenditures and Public Services in the American States." *American Political Science Review* 61 (December 1967): 1066-77.

Shevardnadze, E. A. "Sovershenstvovat' sistemu kontrolia i proverki ispolneniia v svete reshenii XXIV s"ezda KPSS." *Zaria vostoka*, November 15, 1974, pp. 1-5.

Shirkevich, Nina Aleksandrovna. "Arifmetika biudzheta." *Sovety deputatov trudiashchikhsia*, June 1968, pp. 29-31.

————. *Mestnye biudzhety SSSR*. Moscow: Finansy, 1965.

Shishkina, L. I. "Voprosy proforientatsii." In *Chelovek i obshchestvo*, no. 15, pp. 93-97. Leningrad: Izd.Leningradskogo gosudarstvennogo universiteta, 1976.

Significant Features of Fiscal Federalism. 1976-77 ed., vols. 1-3. Washington, D.C.: Advisory Commission on Intergovernmental Relations, 1976-77.

Sjoberg, Gideon. *The Preindustrial City: Past and Present*. New York: Free Press of Glencoe, 1960.

Skinner, Frederick W. "Trends in Building Practices: The Building of Odessa, 1794-1917." In *The City in Russian History*, edited by Michael Hamm, pp. 139-59. Lexington: University of Kentucky Press, 1976.

Slozberg, G. B. *Dorevoliutsionnyi stroi Rossii*. Paris: Imprimateur Pascal, 1933.

Stanley, David T. *The Higher Civil Service*. Washington, D.C.: Brookings Institution, 1964.

————. "What's Happening to the Civil Service." In *Current Issues in Public Administration*, edited by Frederick S. Lane, pp. 251-56. New York: St. Martin's Press, 1978.

Starling, Grover. *Managing the Public Sector*. Homewood, Ill.: Dorsey Press, 1977.

Starovoitov, N. G. *Nakazy izbiratelei*. Moscow: Izd. Iuridicheskaia literatura, 1975.

Starr, S. Frederick. "The Revival and Schism of Urban Planning in Twentieth Century Russia." In *The City in Russian History*, edited by Michael Hamm, pp. 222-42. Lexington: University of Kentucky Press, 1976.

Sternheimer, Stephen. "Administration and Political Development: An Inquiry into the Tsarist and Soviet Experiences." Ph.D. dissertation, University of Chicago, 1974.

————. "Administration for Development: The Transformation of the Soviet Bureaucracy, 1920-1930." In *Russian Officialdom from the Ninth through the Twentieth Centuries: The Bureaucratization of Russian Society*, edited by Walter Pintner and Don K. Rowney. Chapel Hill: University of North Carolina Press, forthcoming, 1979.

————. "Modernizing Administrative Elites: The Making of Managers for Soviet Cities." *Comparative Politics*, forthcoming, 1979.

————. "The Origins of Soviet Administrative Science." Paper delivered at the Second Conference on Russian and Soviet Officialdom, Kennan Institute, Smithsonian Institution, Washington, D.C., 1976.

————. "Social Planning in the Soviet Factory." In *Industrial Labor in the Soviet Union*, edited by A. Kahan and B. Ruble. Forthcoming.

Stil', metody i kul'tura raboty gosudarstvennogo apparata: materialy nauchno-prakticheskoi konferentsii rabotnikov Primorskogo kraia. Vladivostok: Dal'nevostochnoe knizhnoe izdatel'stvo, 1974.

Stillman, Richard J., Jr. "The City Manager: Professional Helping Hand or Political Hired Hand?" *Public Administration Review* 37 (November-December 1977): 659-71.

Strengthening Public Management in the Intergovernmental System: A Report for the OMB. Washington, D.C.: U.S. Government Printing Office, 1975.

Strogina, M. L. "Problemy razvitiia bol'shikh gorodov i agglomeratsii." *Sotsial'noe issledovanie* 4 (1970): 49-60.

Susskind, Lawrence. "Revenue Sharing and the Lessons of the New Federalism." *Urban Law Annual* 8 (1974): 33-37.

Svetlichnii, B. E. "Planirovanie gradoobrazuiushchikh protsessov i problemy rasseleniia." *Planovoe khoziaistvo*, September 1974, pp. 140-44.

Swearer, Howard R. "The Function of Soviet Local Elections." *Midwest Journal of Political Science* 5 (1961): 126-49.

Szelenyi, Ivan. "Urban Sociology and Community Studies in Eastern Europe: Reflections and Comparisons with American Approaches." *Comparative Urban Research* 4 (1977): 11-20.

Taubman, William. *Governing Soviet Cities: Bureaucratic Politics and Urban Development in the USSR.* New York: Praeger, 1973.

Thiede, Roger L. "Industry and Urbanization in New Russia from 1860 to 1910." In *The City in Russian History*, edited by Michael Hamm, pp. 125-38. Lexington: University of Kentucky Press, 1976.

Thompson, Frank. "Is University Training Practical? Perspectives of Public Personnel Officials." *Public Administration Review* 38 (January-February 1978): 82-84.

Thornley, N. R., and McLoughlin, J. B. *Aspects of Urban Management.* Izmir: Organization for Economic Cooperation and Development, 1976.

Tiebout, Charles M. "A Pure Theory of Local Expenditures." *Journal of Political Economy* 64 (October 1956): 416-24.

Tilly, Charles. "The Chaos of the Living City." In *Comparative Community Politics*, edited by Terry N. Clark, pp. 203-27. New York: John Wiley, 1974.

Tkachenko, P. N. et al. *A Control System for the Implementation of Decisions of the Moscow City Soviet Executive Committee.* New York: Columbia University, Graduate School of Business, Center for Government Studies, March 1975.

Toffler, Alvin. "Organizations." In *Organizational and Managerial Innovation,* edited by Lloyd A. Rowe and William Boise, pp. 333-49. Pacific Palisades, Calif.: Goodyear, 1973.

Tokes, Rudolph. *Dissent in the USSR.* Baltimore: Johns Hopkins University Press, 1975.

Tonsky, D. G. et al. *Current Trends and National Policy in the Field of Housing, Building and Town Planning in the USSR.* Moscow: Gosgrazhdanstroi, 1976.

Trufanov, Ivan. *Problems of Soviet Urban Life.* Translated by James Riordan. Newtonville, Mass.: Oriental Research Partners, 1977.

Tsentr nauchno-tekhnicheskoi informatsii po grazhdanskomu stroitel'stvu i arkhitekture. *Gradostroitel'stvo SSSR.* Moscow: Gosgrazhdanstroi SSSR, 1976.

Tsiukina, E. K. "Problemy sovershenstvovaniia apparata." In *Problemy nauchnoi organizatsii truda v apparate,* edited by V. S. Osnovin, pp. 61-70. Voronezh: Izd. Voronezhskogo gosudarstvennogo universiteta, 1974.

U.S., Congress, House, Subcommittee on the City, Committee on Banking, Finance, and Urban Affairs. *Success Abroad: What Foreign Cities Can Teach American Cities.* Washington, D.C.: Government Printing Office, April 1977.

USSR Gosstroi, Centre of Scientific and Technical Information in Civil Construction and Architecture. *Urban Development in the Ukrainian SSR.* Report prepared for UN Conference on Human Settlements, Vancouver, Canada, June 1976.

USSR: Some Implications of Demographic Trends for Economic Policies. ER71-10012. Washington, D.C.: Central Intelligence Agency, January 1977.

V pomoshch' deputatu: zapros deputata mestnogo soveta. Minsk: 1973. Rotoprint.

Vasilev, B. S., and Stolbov, A. G. "Ways of Building up the Urban Infrastructure." *Current Digest of the Soviet Press* 24 (September 18, 1977): 9.

Vasil'eva, Evelina Karlovna. *The Young People of Leningrad: School and Work Options and Attitudes.* Translated by Arlo Schultz and Andrew J. Smith. White Plains, N.Y.: International Arts and Sciences Press, 1976.

Vasil'evich, N. "Vozmozhnost' primeneniia programno-tselovogo podkhoda dlia kompleksnogo planirovaniia." In *Chelovek i obshchestvo,* no. 15, pp. 83-88. Leningrad: Izd. Leningradskogo gosudarstvennogo universiteta, 1976.

Vinogradov, V. M. "Ob opyte organizatsii i metodiki provedeniia sotsissledovaniia." *Voprosy teorii i praktiki Sovetskogo gosudarstvovedeniia: Trudy, Seriia iuridicheskaia* (Irkustk) 17 (1970): 55-78.

Voroninskii, S. "Den'gi liubiat khoziaina." *Izvestiia,* February 9, 1968, p. 3.

"Vvedenie." In *Chelovek i obshchestvo*, no. 15, pp. 5-6. Leningrad: Izd. Leningradskogo gosudarstvennogo universiteta, 1976.

Waldo, Dwight, ed. *Temporal Dimensions of Development Administration*. Durham, N.C.: Duke University Press, 1970.

Walicki, Andrezej. *The Slavophile Controversy: A History of Conservative Utopia in Nineteenth Century Russian Thought*. Oxford: Clarendon Press, 1975.

Walsh, Annemarie. *The Urban Challenge to Government*. New York: Praeger, 1969.

Walton, John. "Problems of Method and Theory in Comparative Urban Studies." *Urban Affairs Quarterly* 11 (September 1975): 3-12.

————. "Structures of Power in Latin American Cities: Toward a Summary and Interpretation." In *Urban Latin America: The Political Condition from Above and from Below*, edited by A. Portes and John Walton, pp. 136-68. Austin: University of Texas Press, 1976.

————. "The Vertical Axis of Community Organization and the Structure of Power." In *Community Politics: A Behavioral Approach*, edited by Charles M. Bonjean et al., pp. 188-97. New York: Free Press, 1971.

Ward, Barbara. *The Home of Man*. New York: W. W. Norton, 1976.

Weber, M. M. "Comprehensive Planning and Social Responsibility." In *Urban Planning and Social Policy*, edited by Bernard J. Frieden and Robert Morris, pp. 9-22. New York: Basic Books, 1968.

Weinberg, Elizabeth Ann. *The Development of Sociology in the Soviet Union*. London: Routledge and Kegan Paul, 1974.

Weisman, Steven R. "New York about to Get Integrated Management of City Fiscal Matters." New York *Times*, March 25, 1977, p. B1.

Weiss, Carol H. *Evaluation Research*. Englewood Cliffs, N.J.: Prentice-Hall, 1972.

Weitz, Raan, ed. *Urbanization and the Developing Countries: Report of the Sixth Rehovot Conference*. New York: Praeger, 1973.

Welsh, William. "Introduction: The Comparative Study of Political Leadership in Communist Systems." In *Comparative Communist Political Leadership*, edited by Carl Beck et al., pp. 1-42. New York: David McKay, 1973.

Westcott, Jay. "Governmental Organization and Methods in Developing Countries." In *Development Administration: Concepts and Problems*, edited by Irving Swerdlow, pp. 45-67. Syracuse, N.Y.: Syracuse University Press, 1963.

Whyte, William H., Jr. *The Organization Man*. Garden City, N.Y.: Anchor Books, 1956.

Wildavsky, Aaron. *Budgeting: A Comparative Theory of Budgetary Processes*. Boston: Little, Brown and Company, 1975.

Wilensky, H. "The Professionalization of Everyone." *American Journal of Sociology* 70 (September 1964): 137-57.

Wilson, James Q. "Innovation in Organization." In *Organizational and Managerial Innovation*, edited by Lloyd A. Rowe and William Boise, pp. 31-48. Pacific Palisades, Calif.: Goodyear, 1973.

Wirth, Louis. "Urbanism as a Way of Life." *American Journal of Sociology* 44 (July 1938): 1-24.

Wolfinger, Raymond, and Field, John Osgood. "Political Ethos and the Structure of City Government." *American Political Science Review* 60 (June 1966): 306-26.

Wolfson, Stanley M. "Salaries of Municipal Officials for 1976." *Urban Data Service Reports*. Vol. 8, no. 4. Washington, D.C.: International City Management Association, 1976.

Wu, Chi-Yuen. "Public Administration in the 1970s." In *Administrative Issues in Developing Economies*, edited by Kenneth Rothwell, pp. 205-28. Lexington, Mass.: Lexington Books, 1972.

Yanowitch, Murray. *Social and Economic Inequality: Soviet Union.* New York: M. E. Sharpe, 1977.

Yates, Douglas. *The Ungovernable City: The Politics of Urban Problems and Policy Making.* Cambridge, Mass.: MIT Press, 1977.

Zaltman, Gerald et al. *Innovation and Organizations.* New York: John Wiley, 1973.

Zastrozhnaia, O. K. "Nekotorye voprosy sovershenstvovaniia kontroliia." In *Problemy nauchnoi organizatsii truda v apparate mestnykh sovetov*, pp. 96-102. Voronezh: Izd. Voronezhskogo gosudarstvennogo universiteta, 1974.

Zemlianskii, M. S. *Deiatel'nost' raionnogo gorodskogo soveta po rukovodstvu narodnogo obrazovaniia i kul'turno-prosvetitel'noi raboty.* Moscow: Izd Iuridicheskai literatura, 1973.

"Zhiloi fond—narodnoe dostoianie." *Pravda*, February 1, 1975, p. 1.

Zwick, Peter. "Socioeconomic Policy and National Integration in the USSR." Paper delivered at the Southwestern Social Science Association Conference, Houston, Texas, April 1978.

INDEX

Academy of Sciences, 129, 133, 134
Academy of Social Sciences, 133
accountability: citizen access and, 38, 43, 151-59, 180-81; and instructions to soviet deputies by citizenry (*nakazy*), 151-52, 153-55; and legislative inquiries aimed at administrative operations (*zaprosy*), 152, 155-57; and reports by agencies (*otchyoty*), 151-53; and subordination, 26, 30, 31
administration, urban, 178; organizational milieu, 24-35 (*see also* bureaucracy; personnel, administrative); political dimension, 35-44 (*see also* Communist party; politics); (*see also* subjects)
administrative city, 3-4, 8, 10, 11
agencies, administrative (*see* departments and agencies; subjects)
Alma Ata, 43, 92, 100
Almond, G., 159
autonomy: and centralization, 2-4, 129; and management transformation, 84, 181-82; (*see also* subordination)
Azerbaidzhan, 38

Bashkior Autonomous Republic, 115
Beard, Charles, 83
Belinsky, V. G., 6
Belorussian republic, 29, 152, 155, 156; (*see also* place names)
Belyi, Andrei, 5
Bolsheviks, 7-8, 9
Borisov, 152
Bratsk, 87
Brezhnev, Leonid, 35, 61, 116
"Bronze Horse, The" (Pushkin), 6
Brookings Institution, 52-53
budgets (*see* finances, resources and management)
Bulgaria, 164
bureaucracy, 177; accountability and citizen access, 38, 43, 151-59, 180-81; compensation, 72-73, 175; conservatism and traditionalism, 5-6, 50, 181-82; education and training, 63, 68, 69, 133, 143, 160-66, 180; feminization, 63; future, 178; growth, 61; hierarchy, administrative, 26-29, 177;

institutionalization, 181-82; and management transformation, 181-82; and non-staff administrators, 151, 161-62; organizational milieu, 24-35; political dimension and, 35-44, 178-79 (*see also* Communist party; politics); response to citizen involvement, 154-58; status and power, 26; subordination, dual and, 26-28; tenure, 60-61, 63; (*see also* personnel, administrative)

Catherine II, 4
centralization: and autonomy, 2-4, 179; of computer information facilities, 148-50; departmental, 30-31; and social planning, 113
Chernyshevsky, N., 6
citizen access to administration, 5, 150-51, 181; and accountability, 38, 43, 151, 180-81; and agency activity reports (*otchyoty*), 151-53; and complaint mechanisms, 38, 43, 152; councils, consultative, and, 151; and information, 150-59, 181; institutional channels for, 151-52; instructions to soviet deputies (*nakazy*), 151-52, 153-55; and legislative inquiries (*zaprosy*), 153, 155-57; limits to, 159; newspapers, letters to, and, 157; opinion polls, 151, 153; political activism of, and social planning, 120, 124-25; response of bureaucracy to, 154-58; U.S. comparison, 159
city, conceptions of, 1; agglomerations, 10-11; administrative city, 3-4, 8, 10, 11; communist model, 29-30, 57, 90-91; and culture, 1-2, 4, 8, 176; Enlightenment and rationalism, 4-5, 177; and history, Russian, 2-12; holistic, 10; Marxist and Soviet, 6, 7-12; Westernizers versus Slavophiles (populists), 4, 5-6; (*see also* urbanization; subjects)
city councils, 25-26; activist deputies, social status of, 155-56; administrator selection, 55-56; and changes in administrative structure, 29; executive committee (*see* executive committee); functions, 26; instruc-

ABOUT THE AUTHORS

Carol W. Lewis is currently an assistant professor at the University of Connecticut and an associate of the Russian Research Center, Harvard University. She received her Ph.D. from Princeton University. She has participated on the U.S. Project Team on New Towns of the U.S.-USSR Agreement on Housing and Other Construction and is on the advisory panel of the U.S. Project Team of the Joint U.S.-USSR Study of Computer Applications to Large City Management. She has published articles in *Comparative Urban Research, Polity,* and *Municipal Year Book* and is the author of *The Budgetary Process in Soviet Cities.*

Stephen Sternheimer is currently an assistant professor of political science at Boston University and an associate of the Russian Research Center, Harvard University. He received his Ph.D. from the University of Chicago. He has done field research in the Soviet Union under the auspices of the Inter-University Committee on Travel Grants, 1968-69, and the International Research and Exchanges Board, 1975-76. His publications include articles in *Comparative Politics, Canadian-American Slavic Review,* and other journals. He is the author of forthcoming essays on the Soviet administrative elite and industrial social planning.

RELATED TITLES
Published by
Praeger Special Studies

Citizen Inspectors in the Soviet Union: The People's Control Committee

Jan S. Adams
foreword by
Jerry Hough

Social Scientists and Policy Making in the the USSR
edited by
Richard B. Remnek

Soviet Sociology, 1964-75: A Bibliography
Mervyn Matthews
in collaboration with
T. Anthony Jones

The Soviet Threat: Myths and Realities
edited by
Grayson Kirk
Nils Wessell

Technology and Communist Culture: The Socio-Cultural Impact of Technology Transfer under Socialism
edited by
Frederic J. Fleron, Jr.